VOLUME ONE

ADVANCES IN TRANSPORT POLICY AND PLANNING

Preparing for the New Era of Transport Policies: Learning from Experience

VOLUME ONE

ADVANCES IN TRANSPORT POLICY AND PLANNING

Preparing for the New Era of Transport Policies: Learning from Experience

Edited by

YORAM SHIFTAN
Civil and Environmental Engineering,
Technion, Israel Institute of Technology,
Haifa, Israel

MARIA KAMARGIANNI
MaaSLab, Energy Institute,
University College London,
London, United Kingdom

ELSEVIER

ACADEMIC PRESS
An imprint of Elsevier

Academic Press is an imprint of Elsevier
50 Hampshire Street, 5th Floor, Cambridge, MA 02139, United States
525 B Street, Suite 1650, San Diego, CA 92101, United States
The Boulevard, Langford Lane, Kidlington, Oxford OX5 1GB, United Kingdom
125 London Wall, London, EC2Y 5AS, United Kingdom

First edition 2018

ISBN: 978-0-12-815294-2
ISSN: 2543-0009

Publisher: Zoe Kruze
Acquisition Editor: Sam Mahfoudh
Editorial Project Manager: Shellie Bryant
Production Project Manager: James Selvam
Cover Designer: Alan Studholme

Typeset by SPi Global, India

CONTENTS

CONTRIBUTORS

Paulus T. Aditjandra
Newcastle University Business School, Newcastle upon Tyne, United Kingdom

Emine Zehra Akgün
Transport Research Institute, Edinburgh Napier University, Edinburgh, United Kingdom

Farzad Alemi
Institute of Transportation Studies, University of California, Davis, CA, United States

Ali Arian
Department of Civil Engineering and Engineering Mechanics, The University of Arizona, Tucson, AZ, United States

Roby Carmel
Transportation Research Institute, Technion City, Haifa, Israel

Federico Cavallaro
Department of Architecture and Arts, IUAV University of Venice, Venice; Eurac Research, Institute for Regional Development, Bolzano, Italy

Yi-Chang Chiu
Department of Civil Engineering and Engineering Mechanics, The University of Arizona, Tucson, AZ, United States

Giovanni Circella
Institute of Transportation Studies, University of California, Davis, CA; School of Civil and Environmental Engineering, Georgia Institute of Technology, Atlanta, GA, United States

Alberto Dianin
Eurac Research, Institute for Regional Development, Bolzano, Italy

Alireza Ermagun
Mississippi State University, Department of Civil and Environmental Engineering, Starkville, MS, United States

Victoria Gitelman
Transportation Research Institute, Technion City, Haifa, Israel

Anna Korchatov
Transportation Research Institute, Technion City, Haifa, Israel

Tao Liu
Department of Rapid Road Transport, TUMCREATE Ltd., Singapore, Singapore

Jason Monios
Kedge Business School, Marseille, France

Minh Hieu Nguyen
Department of Economics and Sociology of Transport (DEST), The French Institute of Science and Technology for Transport, Development and Networks (IFSTTAR), Champs-sur-Marne, France; Faculty of Transport Economics, University of Transport and Communications (UTC), Hanoi, Vietnam

Silvio Nocera
Department of Architecture and Arts, IUAV University of Venice, Venice, Italy

Dorina Pojani
School of Earth and Environmental Sciences, The University of Queensland, Brisbane, QLD, Australia

Dominic Stead
Faculty of Architecture and the Built Environment, Delft University of Technology, Delft, Netherlands

Meng Xu
State Key Laboratory of Rail Traffic Control and Safety, Beijing Jiaotong University, Beijing, China

Xiaoyu Zhu
Metropia Inc., Tucson, AZ, United States

PREFACE

Hyper urbanization, climate change, and demographic and societal changes are some of the megatrends that have imposed pressure on the transport networks and set obstacles to sustainable mobility. For most of its history, the transport sector has remained largely unchanged, characterized by slow incremental innovations due to the costly infrastructure. Technological advancement, the availability of big data, and the new information and communication technologies increasingly foster the development of new mobility concepts for more efficient and safe use of vehicles, better infrastructure utilization, smarter travel choices, and seamless trips. At the same time, all these also increase the uncertainty of what will be the shape of our future transportation system.

Against this background, several policies have been imposed in passenger and freight transport to accelerate innovation adoption and contribute to the vision of smart and sustainable mobility. In this volume, we bring together and assess several successful but also unsuccessful practices and policies from around the world, with the objective to learn from these experiences, and help prepare the ground for the new era in transport sector for passengers and freight.

Public transit systems are an important component of any large urban area, and considerable efforts have been done to foster their usage. In Chapter 1, Liu and Xu provide a systematical examination, analysis, and evaluation of the combinatorial effects of multilevel policy measures in Beijing to identify the transformation process of Beijing to a transit metropolis. The authors provide a background on the fast travel demand growth of Beijing and its public transport systems followed by a comprehensive retrospective of the integrated multilevel policy measures developed for transportation systems management in Beijing from three different levels, i.e., national, municipal, and local levels. The authors conduct a quantitative evaluation using various performance indicators to understand the implementation effects of the integrated multilevel transportation policy measures and evaluate the sustainability of these integrated multilevel transportation policy measures. The findings indicate that Beijing has successfully transformed its transportation system into a transit-oriented one after implementing a package of integrated multilevel policy measures. However, there are some unsuccessful practices and still more effective, efficient, and equitable policy measures are required to develop a sustainable urban mobility system.

While it is important to look at successful examples like Beijing, it is also important to learn from practices that were unsuccessful mainly due to the policy side. One of the most appealing mass transit systems is Bus Rapid Transit (BRT), aiming at providing high level of service at much lower cost than rail-based systems. In Chapter 2, Nguyen examines the reasons for failures of some BRT systems analyzing five case studies: Bangkok, Delhi, Hanoi, Lagos, and Lima. The criteria used for assessing the concept of the BRT are: (1) institutional and legislative context; (2) political leadership and commitment; (3) management of competing modes; (4) public participation; (5) funding and coordination; (6) physical design; and (7) image promotion. The authors indicate that the BRT systems in these areas were curtailed due to a combination of reasons. The institutional setup was too complex to coordinate and implement this concept. Local transportation agencies were cast in past roles and purposes which they were unable and/or unwilling to change. In some cases, the selection of the first corridor was ineffective. While most projects had the support and commitment of a high-level politician or party, they did not amass the necessary political pull and popular goodwill to push the concept forward within a short time before the novelty effect wore off. Partly this owes to feeble promotional and communication efforts targeting potential users and stakeholders, but also to opposition based on political affiliation rather than concern for the city.

A major concern with BRT operating with various levels of separation from the general traffic and pedestrian is safety. In Chapter 3, Gitelman, Carmel, and Korchatov explore safety impacts of a BRT system that was introduced in the Haifa metropolitan area, Israel, in August 2013. The study examines accident changes on roads with the BRT routes, related to comparison sites, and safety performance of streets with various BRT configurations, during the first 2 years of the BRT operation. In spite of concerns related to the complexity of BRT settings and high traffic volumes, the BRT operation did not lead to a worsening in road safety, while decreasing trends were not observed in some accident types and high shares of severe or pedestrian accidents. Such results were judged as successful and supporting the appropriateness of the design solutions adopted in the BRT system. The findings did not indicate significant differences in safety performance of streets with various BRT configurations, thus leaving space for continued use of various forms. The major safety problem is seen in pedestrian accidents at BRT junctions for which new engineering solutions are needed.

The effectiveness of public transit systems and any transit-oriented development (TOD) also depends on spatial planning. In Chapter 4, Stead and

Pojani examine the development of spatial planning in the Netherlands, Sweden, and Austria since World War II, highlighting policies that have had an influence on TOD, and discuss the implications of these policies in terms of TOD planning and practice in three capital city-regions: Amsterdam, Stockholm, and Vienna. The authors summarize the development of spatial planning in these three areas, highlighting policies that have had an influence on TOD, and discuss the implications of these policies in terms of past, present, and future TOD planning and practice in the respective three capital city regions. It is identified that TOD has been an intrinsic principle of planning in Austria, the Netherlands, and Sweden and in their respective capitals since. The discourses contained in various policy documents in these countries express support for sustainable and resilient urban and regional development and include reference to various TOD principles. Notwithstanding the intensity of interactions and the internationalization of planning ideas, efforts to transfer policy and practice from Austria, the Netherlands, and Sweden have rarely resulted in specific actions or hard outcomes.

Recently, ridehailing became a new major mode of travel in various cities and raises a major concern whether it competes with public transit systems or complements it. In Chapter 5, Circella and Alemi analyze the use of ridehailing services in California, USA. The data used for the analysis originate from the California Millennials Dataset. It is found that users of ridehailing are predominantly well-educated independent millennials or young Gen Xers, who do not have children and live in urban neighborhoods. These travelers also tend to use ridehailing more frequently. Suburban residents who live with their families are less likely to use ridehailing frequently, though their likelihood of using ridehailing increases if they make long-distance trips by plane. It is also found that single-user ridehailing replaces the use of public transit, walking and bicycling, and, to some extent, the use of a private vehicle. Only a minority of travelers increase the public transportation use, e.g., through using ridehailing for first-/last-mile access to public transportation terminals. Based on the results from this research, the authors conclude that planners and policy makers should regulate these services to maximize societal benefits through a combination of pricing and other policies that lead to the integration of ridehailing with other transportation options, expand travel options for those that do not own a car, increase shared used of vehicles, and support the use of public transportation and active travel modes.

Innovative approaches to improve the efficiency of the transport system are also being introduced by the private sector. In Chapter 6, Ermagun,

Arian, Zhu, and Chiu discuss the impact of using apps to provide incentives to travelers to shift trips departure time. It analyzes departure time for seven main trip purposes to further provide a personalized incentive scheme to achieve an optimal manner at the system wide level. It compares two consecutive incentive schemes, each lasting for over a 1-year period, to understand how effectively these incentive scenarios influence the departure time of different trip purposes. The data used for the analysis have been collected by the Metropia app, one of the first reward-based travels demand management smartphone applications. The authors develop four accelerated failure time models to explain the time to observe a departure event and the acceleration factors. The results suggest that peak-hour travelers may be open to behavioral incentive that promotes nonpeak-hour departure time. The incentives, however, may need to be tailored based on time of the day and the purpose of the trip. The findings highlight that traveling for recreation, errands, and work are the most sensitive trip purposes to the incentives in the morning peak hour. However, in the evening peak hour, traveling for other purposes, errands, and school become the most sensitive trip purposes. These results can facilitate the design of incentives tailored to a specific individual and trip, to incentivize lasting and meaningful behavioral changes.

Freight and good movement are important elements of any transportation system. Urban freight transport (UFT) provides the last mile delivery of goods, return of unwanted or recyclable goods, and the removal of waste. Despite such benefits, freight vehicles often cause adverse impacts on the economy, environment, and society such as air pollution, reduced mobility, congestion, and road casualties. Today, local authorities implement various regulations and initiatives to mitigate the problems caused by freight vehicles and to decrease contradictions between various road users. In Chapter 7, Monios and Akgün investigate how institutional influences on local authorities determine urban freight transport policy, paying particular attention to three pressure factors (coercive, normative, and mimetic) that cause institutional isomorphism. The authors compare three countries (Scotland, England, and Sweden) based on data collected from 11 cities, each exhibiting different levels of intervention in terms of UFT policy. The results show that the impact of normative and mimetic factors on local authorities is more intense than the impact of coercive factors, with social pressure generally being stronger than national government mandate. The case cities in England and particularly Scotland demonstrated a limited vision when incorporating urban freight in their local transport planning, being reluctant to enforce restrictions on users to meet urban freight goals. By contrast, evidence from Sweden suggests that a better relationship between public and private stakeholders makes it easier to implement freight policies in partnership.

In Chapter 8, Aditjandra maps the changing nature of European Union (EU) surface freight transport policy since 2000. Over this period the policy, based on the liberalization of the Single European Market in the 10 years before 2000, changed from purely national to supranational, on a pan-European scale. The review shows that, by 2011, intervention, modal shift, and intermodality have been replaced by "smart," "green," and "integrated" themes, alongside economic competitiveness and growth. The key change is that policy now looks to separate mobility from its negative effects; for example, behavioral change orientation programs, such as road pricing for freight, have declined in importance. Innovative technology, by contrast, is the chosen tool of the current EU freight policy to meet ambitious emission reduction targets, led by the decarbonization of road haulage. The tension between technocracy and explicit political intent is evident in the development and is discussed. Successful and unsuccessful freight policies are also drawn, discussed, and concluded.

Finally, reducing carbon emissions is a relevant aspect that helps achieving sustainability in transport planning. However, most of the mobility plans have not yet adopted a shared methodology to internalize these emissions and to make them one of the parameters able to influence the final choices on the policies and measures to be taken. In Chapter 9, Nocera, Dianin, and Cavallaro present the methodologies currently in use to quantify and to assign a unitary economic value to GHG emissions and the vast degree of scientific and economic uncertainty that characterizes them. Through an extensive review of the plans and the urban strategies adopted (mostly in Europe), the authors analyze the current stand of transport policy for carbon emissions, draw conclusions, and provide possible future perspectives to control the effects of this issue in the long run.

This volume provides policy makers, planners, and researchers the documentation and lessons learned from various experiences around the world to help them design a more sustainable transportation system for the future taking into account societal and technological changes.

Yoram Shiftan and Maria Kamargianni

CHAPTER ONE

Integrated Multilevel Measures for the Transformation to a Transit Metropolis: The Successful and Unsuccessful Practices in Beijing

Tao Liu*,[1], Meng Xu†
*Department of Rapid Road Transport, TUMCREATE Ltd., Singapore, Singapore
†State Key Laboratory of Rail Traffic Control and Safety, Beijing Jiaotong University, Beijing, China
[1]Corresponding author: e-mail address: tliu773@aucklanduni.ac.nz

Contents

Abstract

The concept of transit metropolis provides a paradigm for sustainable regional development. Faced with the ever-increasingly serious traffic-related problems, such as traffic congestion, traffic fatalities and injuries, emissions, noises and increased energy consumption, Beijing, one of the largest cities in the world, has decided to transform itself into a transit metropolis. Over a period of 20 years, a series of transport policy measures have been implemented in Beijing. This work tries to develop a methodological framework for conducting an initial investigation, review, analysis and evaluation of both these successful and

Advances in Transport Policy and Planning, Volume 1
ISSN 2543-0009
https://doi.org/10.1016/bs.atpp.2018.07.007

unsuccessful practices resulted from the implementation of integrated multilevel transport policy measures in Beijing. This framework integrates components of implementation effects analysis and sustainability evaluation, and it is threefold. First, a three-dimensional decomposition scheme is established to decompose the integrated multilevel policy documents implemented in Beijing; second, a set of quantitative performance indicators are proposed to analyze the implementation effects; third, a multi-dimensional qualitative evaluation framework is established to conduct sustainability evaluation. The case study demonstrates the effectiveness of the proposed methodological framework, and shows that Beijing has successfully transformed its transportation system into a transit-oriented one after implementing a package of integrated multilevel policy measures. However, there are some unsuccessful practices. More effective, efficient and equitable policy measures are required to develop a sustainable urban mobility system.

Keywords: Transport policy, Transit metropolis, Policy measures, Transformation, Sustainable development, Beijing

ABBREVIATIONS

BMBS-NBSSOB	Beijing Municipal Bureau of Statistics and NBS Survey Office in Beijing
BMCEIT	Beijing Municipal Commission of Economy and Information Technology
BMCT	Beijing Municipal Commission of Transport
BMDRC	Beijing Municipal Development and Reform Commission
BPTC	Beijing Public Transport Corporation
BRT	Bus Rapid Transit
BTDRI	Beijing Transportation Development & Research Institute
BTMB	Beijing Traffic Management Bureau
GAQS	General Administration of Quality Supervision
GDP	Gross Domestic Product
GOMoTPRC	General Office of the Ministry of Transport of the People's Republic of China
IE	Individual Equilibrium
IQCAC	Inspection and Quarantine, and the Cyberspace Administration of China
ITS	Intelligent Transportation System
MoC	Ministry of Commerce
MoIIT	Ministry of Industry and Information Technology
MoPS	Ministry of Public Security
MoTPRC	Ministry of Transport of the People's Republic of China
PC	Private Car
PD	Policy Document
PGBM	The People's Government of Beijing Municipality
PT	Public Transit
SAIC	State Administration for Industry and Commerce
SCPRC	State Council of the People's Republic of China
SO	System Optimum
TOC	Transit-Oriented Corridor
TOD	Transit-Oriented Development
TOM	Transit-Oriented Metropolis
UE	User Equilibrium

1. INTRODUCTION

The combination of rapid urbanization and motorization has been placing an ever-increasing amount of pressure on the current transportation infrastructure throughout the world, resulting in such widespread problems as traffic congestion, traffic fatalities and injuries, emissions, noises and increased energy consumption. Because land and road resources are finite and subject to competing uses, government resources are constrained and traditional private cars (PCs) cannot meet ever-increasing, diversified, urban mobility needs. Public transit (PT) as a safe, sustainable, and cost-effective travel mode contributes to improving urban mobility, reducing road traffic accidents, decreasing overall green gas emissions, and fostering more livable cities. PT is now looked upon by transportation policy decision-makers as one of the best choices to solve these traffic-related problems so as to achieve sustainable mobility (Ceder, 2016; Vuchic, 1999). The design and implementation of more effective, efficient and equitable policy measures for successful PT management so as to achieve sustainable urban mobility thus has become one of the most challenging tasks for transportation policy decision-makers.

Beijing is currently the capital and major political, cultural and educational center of China. As a city, it has a history of more than 3000 years and as a capital, it has a history of more than 800 years. Beijing is located in the north of China and surrounded by Hebei province and close to Tianjin municipality, another important city in China. These three places are now together known as the Jingjinji Metropolitan Region, which is the national capital region of China. An effective transportation system plays an important role in supporting the rapid development and growth of economy and society in this region. Similar to other Asian cities, such as Hong Kong, Singapore and Tokyo, Beijing has a high population density, rapidly developing transportation infrastructure and increasing travel demand. The PT systems in Beijing, including bus, subway/metro, bus rapid transit (BRT), etc., have been significantly improved since the Beijing 2008 Olympic and Paralympic Games. However, the PT systems are still sometimes criticized as inefficient, inconvenient and inaccessible. The design and implementation of more effective, efficient and equitable policy measures for developing better PT systems have become a key priority for this highly populated megacity (Guo et al., 2015; Liu, 2009a; Song, 2013; Xu et al., 2010; Zhao et al., 2000).

In the past two decades, a package of integrated multilevel policy measures has been developed and implemented in Beijing for managing its transportation systems with the key aim of transforming Beijing to a transit metropolitan. These policy measures can be categorized into three groups, namely (i) national level policy measures; (ii) municipal level policy measures; and (iii) local level policy measures. It is known that the implementation of policy packages (combinations and integrations of policy measures) can help minimize possible unintended effects and increase the chance of a policy intervention's success (Bruun and Givoni, 2015). An in-depth analysis of the integrated multilevel policy measures implemented in Beijing is thus urgently needed to help both transportation policy decision-makers and the public to understand the implementation effects so as to further develop and improve more sustainable transportation policies for the megacity.

The objective of this work is to provide a systematical examination, analysis and evaluation of the combinatorial effects of multilevel policy measures in Beijing so as to identify the transformation process of Beijing to a transit metropolis. To achieve this objective, a background on the fast travel demand growth of Beijing and its PT systems is first provided. Then, a comprehensive retrospective of the integrated multilevel policy measures developed for transportation systems management in Beijing is conducted from three different levels, i.e., national, municipal and local levels. Third, a quantitative evaluation using various performance indicators is provided to understand the implementation effects of the integrated multilevel transportation policy measures. Fourth, a sustainability evaluation of these integrated multilevel transportation policy measures is conducted.

2. BACKGROUND AND LITERATURE REVIEW

2.1 Fast Travel Demand Growth of Beijing

In an early study by Liu and Guan (2005), the urban transportation development process in China was divided into three eras, namely the first era—from 1949 to the early 1980s, the second era—from the early 1980s to the early 1990s, and the third era—from the early 1990s to 2005. During the first era, Beijing, like other cities in China, was governed by a special planned economic system, which results in a slow urban transportation development process and a very low travel demand growth. Walking and bicycling are the two dominant travel modes with a mode share of more than 70%. At this period, Beijing is known to be the "kingdom of bicycles". Following the implementation of economic reform and open-door policy in 1978, the economy of China experienced remarkable growth, which led, among others, to rapid social changes, urban transportation development and travel behavior changes. Therefore, in this work we mainly focus on investigating the travel demand growth in Beijing during the second and third eras and a new fourth era—from 2005 to present.

There are some important indicators for the fast travel demand growth in Beijing. Among them, population growth is one of the most important indicators. Over the past 40 years, the population in Beijing has increased remarkably. Fig. 1A shows the rapid increase of population in Beijing from 1978 to 2015. The total population increased from 8.715 million in 1978 to 21.705 million in 2015. The total population mainly includes two categories, namely residing population and floating population. The floating

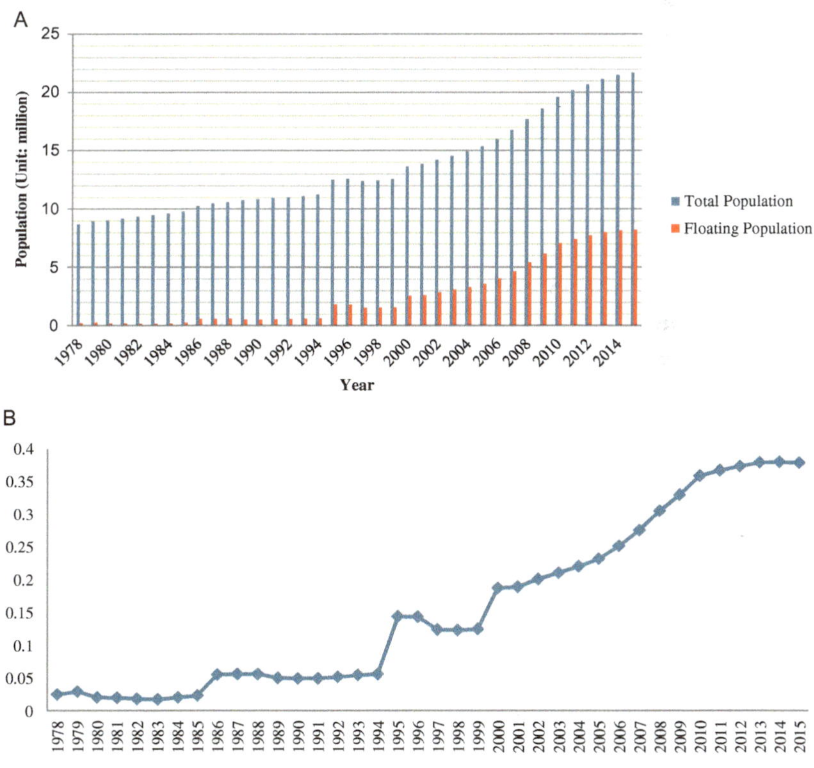

Fig. 1 Population statistics of Beijing municipality (1978–2015): (A) total population and floating population; (B) the ratio of floating population to total population. Data source: *Beijing Municipal Bureau of Statistics and NBS Survey Office in Beijing, 2016, http://www.bjstats.gov.cn/English/.*

population is defined as a group of people who are absorbed into a city due to urbanization process or other reasons, such as employment and education opportunities, but do not live there permanently. As shown in Fig. 1A, there is also a considerable increase of the floating population in Beijing. The number of floating population was only 0.218 million in 1978 and dramatically increased to 8.226 million in 2015. Fig. 1B shows the change of the ratio of the floating population to the total population in Beijing. From it we can see that the proportion of the floating population in the total population in Beijing has significantly increased from 2.5% in 1978 to 37.9% in 2015. As pointed out by Xu et al. (2015), the fast-growing floating population has a significant impact on the existing transportation systems and provides new challenge to the operation and management of the existing transportation systems, especially PT systems, in Beijing. Furthermore, the distribution of population in Beijing is uneven. Most of the population is distributed within the city's central area, which mainly includes six districts, namely Dongcheng, Xicheng, Chaoyang, Fengtai, Shijingshan, Haidian. The total area of these six districts is 1368.32 km^2, which accounts for only 8.3% of the total area of Beijing municipality. However, by the end of 2015, the total population of these six districts is 12.828 million, which accounts for 59.1% of the total population. It clearly shows that there is a very high population density in the city's central area where travel demand increased a lot in the past years.

Another important indicator of the fast travel demand growth in Beijing is its gross domestic product (GDP). After implementing the economic reform and open-door policy, marketing principles are introduced and a series of economic reform policies have been implemented. The economic system has gradually changed from the traditional planned economy to the socialist market economy. The success of economic reforms leads to rapid growth of economic activities of Beijing municipality. Fig. 2A shows the rapid GDP increase of Beijing municipality from 1978 to 2015. The GDP per capita is shown in Fig. 2B. It shows the GDP per capita in Beijing considerably increased from 1257 RMB in 1978 to 106,497 RMB in 2015, an almost 85-fold increase. The fast economy development and rising income definitely lead to increased travel demand in Beijing. According to the fifth comprehensive transportation survey report of Beijing municipality (BMCT, 2016), the average number of trips increased from 1.61 trips per person per day in 1986 to 2.75 trips per person per day in 2014.

The fast travel demand growth in Beijing can also be derived from the total number of motor vehicles. The motorization process in Beijing is much faster than that in other cities. Fig. 3 shows the rapid growth trend of the number of motor vehicles in Beijing. From 1978 to 2015, the number of

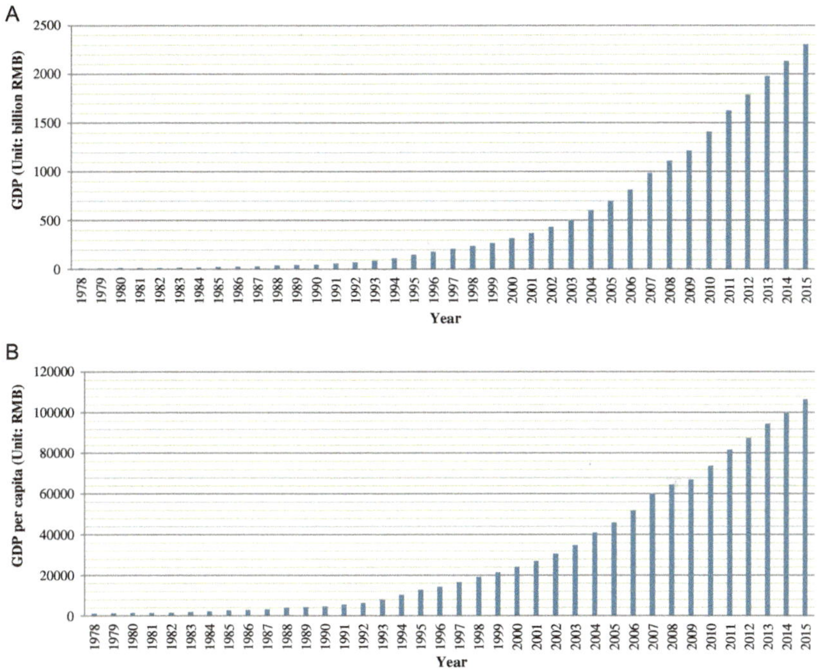

Fig. 2 GDP trend of Beijing municipality from 1978 to 2015: (A) total GDP; (B) GDP per capita. Data source: *Beijing Municipal Bureau of Statistics and NBS Survey Office in Beijing, 2016, http://www.bjstats.gov.cn/English/.*

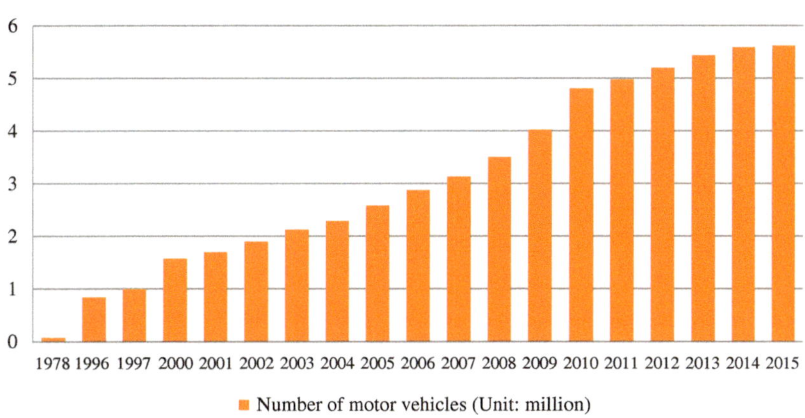

Fig. 3 Growth of motor vehicles in Beijing municipality. Data source: *Beijing Traffic Management Bureau, 2017, http://www.bjjtgl.gov.cn/english/.*

vehicles increased from 0.077 million to 5.619 million. It reached the first million vehicles in 1997. Then, it takes 6.5, 3.9, 2.5, and 2 years to reach the second, third, fourth and fifth million vehicles, respectively. We can see the growth of motor vehicles in Beijing is very fast. Among these motor vehicles, PCs contribute a lot to the total growth. By the end of 2015, the total number of private cars in Beijing is 4.403 million.

The rapid population growth, rising personal income, urbanization and motorization processes are the main forces behind the fast travel demand growth in Beijing. By the end of 2016, the average total number of trips made in the city's central area per day increased to 27.29 million (BTDRI, 2017). The fast travel demand growth in Beijing is placing an ever increasing amount of pressure on the existing transportation systems, generating various negative externalities (e.g., traffic congestion, air pollution and noise), and significantly reducing the livability and sustainability of the city. PT systems are therefore regarded as a potential feasible approach to solving traffic-related problems and catering for the ever-increasing travel demand in Beijing.

2.2 Public Transit Systems in Beijing

Over the past several decades, Beijing has developed a hierarchical and integrated multi-modal PT system, which includes subway, BRT, tram, bus, taxi and some on-demand transit systems. Fig. 4 provides a categorization

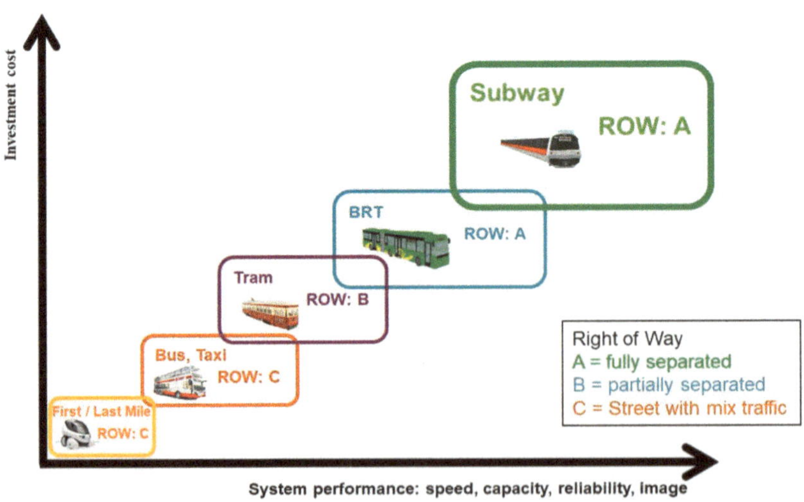

Fig. 4 Categorization of the multi-modal PT system in Beijing municipality. *Adapted from Vuchic, V.R., 2005. Urban Transit: Operations, Planning and Economics. John Wiley & Sons, Hoboken, NJ.*

of these PT modes according to their investment cost and system performance. From this figure we can see there is a continued growth of system performance, and no significantly big gaps with respect to supply and efficiency between these multi-modal PT modes.

The tram service is the earliest PT service in Beijing. The first tram line with a length of 7.5 km was introduced in 1899 and operated between Majiapu and Yongdingmen. Today the tram service is mainly provided to tourists at Qianmen Avenue. The first bus line in Beijing was opened for full operation in January 1935. Nowadays, there are more than 800 bus lines are in daily operation in Beijing. Generally speaking, subway systems, also known as metros and rapid rail transit, have the highest system performance of all PT modes in terms of speed, capacity, reliability, and image. However, they also require very high investment cost (Vuchic, 2005). Beijing started to construct subway in 1965. The first subway system in Beijing, Line 1, which is also the oldest subway line in mainland China, was opened for trial operation on January 15, 1971. Initially, the subway system was constructed for military use, and was not open to the public until in 1981. After 2002, boosted by hosting the 29th summer Olympic Games, the subway system in Beijing has a rapid expansion. Taxi service, which is another kind of flexible PT service, was offered in Beijing in the late 1980s. After more than three decades' development, the taxi service in Beijing is much better, more convenient and comfortable now. BRT is another high-quality bus-based PT system with a relatively low capital and operating cost, but much less costly than subway systems. Initially, BRT was introduced to Beijing to bridge the capacity gap between conventional bus systems and subway systems. The first BRT line, Beijing Southern Axis BRT Line 1, was opened for full operation in December 2015 (Deng and Nelson, 2013). It has a length of 16 km with 17 stations. Currently, there are four BRT lines in operation in Beijing. In recent years, with the wide use of smartphone apps, some flexible paratransit and on-demand transit services, e.g., customized bus (Liu and Ceder, 2015), on-demand ride-sharing services, e.g., DiDi Chuxing, and bike-sharing services, e.g., ofo, oBike and Mobike, are appeared in Beijing. These innovative and emerging forms of PT services support the ever-increasing diversified mobility needs.

2.3 Transformation to a Transit Metropolis

In an early study by Zhao et al. (2000), the period from 2000 to 2015 was identified as the golden time for developing PT systems, especially subway systems, in China. In the past two decades, Beijing has implemented a package of transportation policies to manage its transportation systems and speed up its PT systems development with the aim of transformation to a transit metropolis. Generally speaking, the concept of transit metropolis was formally proposed and defined by Cervero (1998). In this book, a transit metropolis is defined as a region where a workable fit exists between transit services and urban form. The key point is that transit and the city can co-exist together in harmony. In this book, 4 classes of transit metropolises, namely adaptive cities, adaptive transit, the hybrids, and strong core cities, are identified, and 12 transit metropolises around the world are used as case studies. Cervero (1998) highlighted that the concept of transit metropolis can be used as a paradigm for future sustainable regional development. This book was later translated into Chinese and published with the same title by China Architecture & Building Press in 2007. It is generally regarded that this book provides the theoretical origin of developing transit metropolises in China (Liu, 2013).

In April 2005, the Beijing Municipal Commission of Transport released a policy document (PD), named Outline of Beijing Transportation Development (2004–2020). This PD points out the importance of transit priority development in developing a comprehensive transportation system for Beijing. It also proposed a series of transit-related policy measures, which include transit land use priority, increasing transit investment, reducing transit company's tax and increasing transit subsidy, to transform Beijing into a transit city. In an earlier research conducted by Mao et al. (2008), the transportation development process in Beijing is divided into five phases. The fifth phase, which is after 2006, is a rail transit-oriented development phase that is good for developing an adaptive transit-based transit metropolis. Liu (2009a,b) proposed some ideas and practical policy measures for transforming Beijing into a transit city. Later in November 2011, the Ministry of Transport of the People's Republic of China (MoTPRC) released another document that formally initiated the national transit metropolis program in China. The main objectives of launching the transit metropolis program in China are to implement national PT priority development strategy, improve the level-of-service of existing PT systems, cope with ever-increasing and diversified travel demands, alleviate urban traffic congestion, and reverse environmental degradation and energy crisis (MoTPRC, 2011). In October 2012, a group of 15 cities, including Beijing, was selected by the MoTPRC as the demonstration cities for implementing the transit metropolis construction program. Using both subjective comparisons and objective comparisons, Zhou (2016) systematically analyzed the similarities and differences of Cervero's transit metropolis concept and MoTPRC's transit metropolis concept. The analysis results show that there are some similarities between these two concept regarding the purpose and motivations of developing transit metropolises. However, these two concepts are actually different. Cervero (1998) and MoTPRC (2011) have different understanding of the transit metropolis concept and also have different performance indicators for the concept (Zhou, 2016). Velasquez et al. (2016) analyzed the strengths and drawbacks of the transit metropolis demonstration project implemented in some selected Chinese cities by MoTPRC. It identified some local measures that can be used to increase the demonstration effects of the transit metropolis program.

The transit metropolis concept proposed by Cervero (1998) mainly discussed the relationship of transit and urbanization at regional scale. Another similar concept, named transit-oriented development (TOD), however, measures the relationship at the neighborhood and community levels, which is from local micro-scale (Cervero, 1998). TOD is defined as a compact, mixed-use, pedestrian-friendly transit development pattern that is mainly organized around a transit station. By locating amenities, employment, retail shops, and housing around transit hubs, TOD can help promote transit usage and non-motorized travel (Cervero and Day, 2008; Suzuki et al., 2013). Chen (2010) pointed out that due to the substantial differences existed between the United States and China in population density, land use intensity, personal income level, urban spatial structure, and propensity to use PT, it is improper to directly apply the US TOD-related planning parameters to Chinese cities. It suggests that there should be an intermediate process, named transit-oriented corridor (TOC), when making a transition from TOD to transit-oriented metropolis (TOM).

The above background information and literature review clearly indicate the importance of transforming Beijing into a transit metropolis. However, there is very little research conducted to understand the implementation effects of various policy measures and the transformation process of Beijing to a transit metropolis. To bridge this gap, we propose a methodology that can be utilized for analyzing and evaluating the related policy measures implemented in Beijing in next section.

3. METHODOLOGY

The overall research methodology for transportation policy analysis and evaluation is graphically illustrated in Fig. 5. This methodological

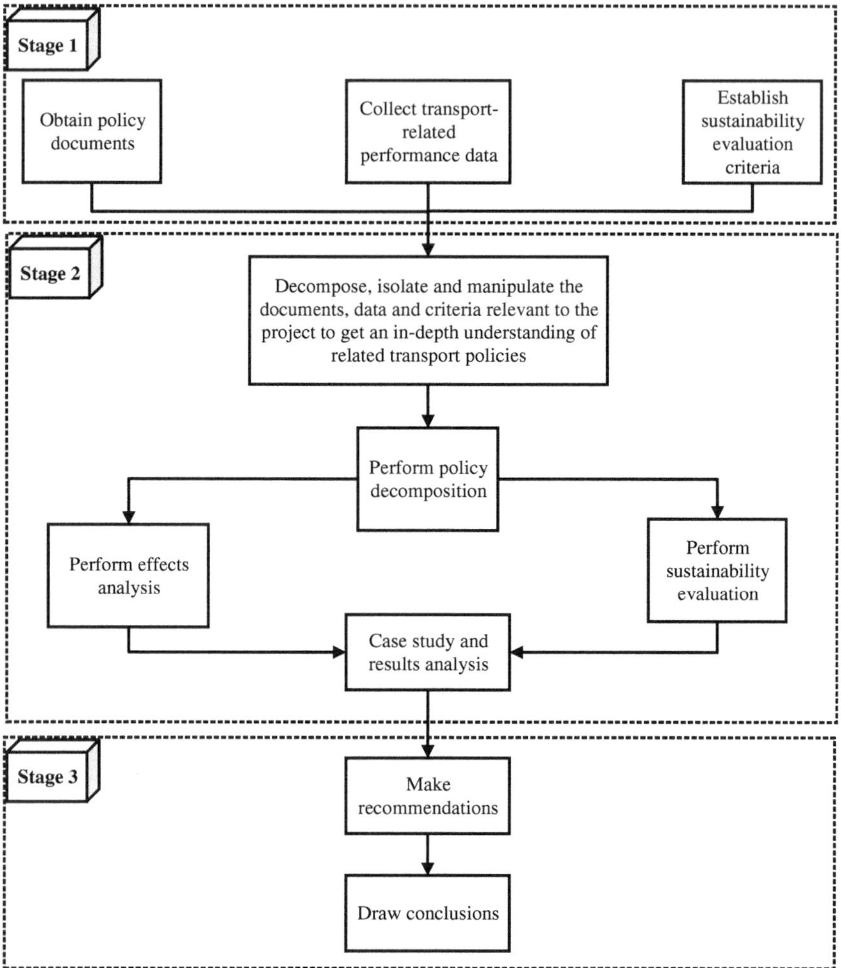

Fig. 5 Methodological framework.

framework is constructed in a flowchart format with input and output elements, elaborating the systematic decision sequence and process of the analysis and evaluation.

This first stage of this methodology involves obtaining transportation PDs, transportation-related performance data collection, and sustainability evaluation criteria establishment. In the case of this work, the transportation PDs and transportation-related performance data are mainly collected from the government and transportation agencies. The second stage decomposes the obtained PDs, isolates and manipulates the performance data and evaluation criteria, which is relevant to the study, so as to get an in-depth understanding of the implementation effects of related transportation polices. This stage mainly includes three components, namely (i) transportation policy decomposition; (ii) implementation effects analysis; and (iii) sustainability evaluation. In the last stage, based on the case study results, policy recommendations are made and conclusions are drawn.

Overall, the proposed methodological framework can help us to better understand the transportation policy formulation process, the implementation effects, and the sustainability aspects. It can also help in planning and design for future transportation policy improvements. In below, we provide detailed explanations of the three components appeared in stage 2.

3.1 Transportation Policy Decomposition

According to their characteristics, transportation polices implemented in China can be decomposed from three different dimensions, namely time dimension, level dimension, and content dimension. First, at the time dimension, transportation policies can be decomposed in the light of their implementation date. Second, according to the different policy makers, transportation policies can be decomposed into different levels, i.e., national level, municipal level, and local level. Third, based on the different contents of transportation policies, they can also be classified into different categories, such as urban planning and land use-related transportation polices, PT-related transportation polices, energy saving-related polices, intelligent transportation system (ITS) technology-related transportation polices, etc.

PC and PT are usually the two dominated travel modes in most cities around the world. Transportation policies can also be decomposed into two groups; that is, PT incentive polices and PC disincentive policies. These PC and PT related transportation polices can be analyzed by using the well-known PC–PT intermodal balance diagram, as shown in Fig. 6. In this diagram, curves *C* and *T* represent the average travel cost functions for PC and PT, respectively. This average travel cost function includes many components, which reflects travel time, cost of travel, comfort, safety, and others. It can be described as a disutility function of different travel modes. Note that we revise the *T* curve, which is now a little different from Vuchic's version. That is, with the increase of PT travel volume, the value of *T* will not keep decreasing. On the contrary, it will increase after reaching a lowest point. Because excessive increase of PT volume will cause passengers' discomfort due to congestion in PT vehicles and also increased travel time

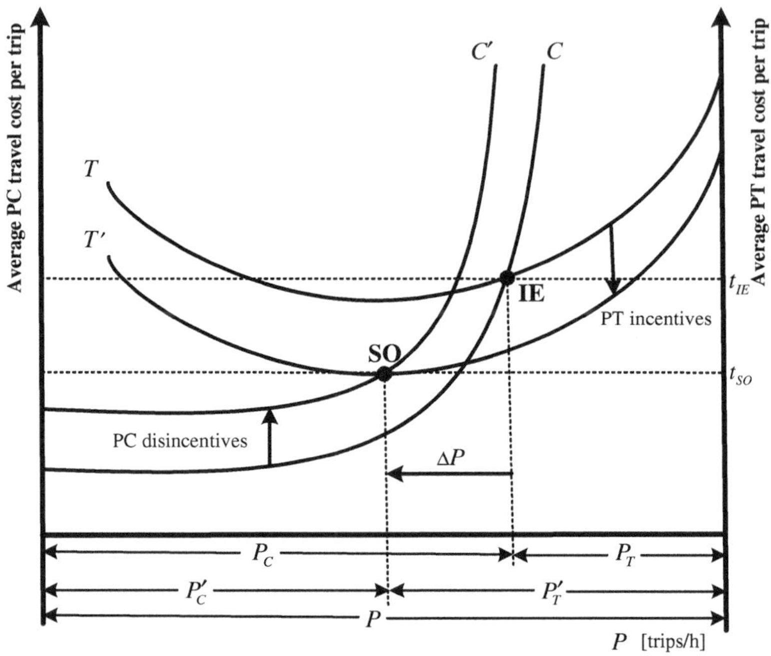

Fig. 6 PC–PT intermodal balance diagram. *Revised and adapted from Vuchic, V.R., 1999. Transportation for livable cities. Center for Urban Policy Research, New Brunswick, NJ.*

due to passengers failing to board the first vehicle and have to wait for next vehicles. Without implementing any policy intervention, the total travel volume P intends to distribute among PC and PT in an individual equilibrium (IE) manner, which is similar to Wardrop's first principle, a.k.a., user equilibrium (Wardrop, 1952). That is,

$$t_C = t_T = t_{\mathrm{IE}} \tag{1}$$

$$P_C + P_T = P \tag{2}$$

where t_C and t_T are the average travel cost for PC and PT, respectively; t_{IE} is the average travel cost at IE condition; P_C and P_T are the travel volumes for PC and PT, respectively.

After implementing appropriate PT incentive measures and PC disincentive measures, the travel cost curves for PC and PT change to C' and T', respectively. Accordingly, the distribution of the total travel volume P change to a social optimum (SO) condition, which is similar to Wardrop's second principle, a.k.a., SO (Wardrop, 1952). The travel volumes for PC and PT thus change to P'_C and P'_T, respectively. As can be seen from

Fig. 6, after shifting ΔP travel volumes from PC to PT, the system changes from IE condition to SO condition, and the total benefit obtained can be measured by

$$P \cdot (t_{\mathrm{IE}} - t_{\mathrm{SO}}) \tag{3}$$

where t_{SO} is the average travel cost at SO condition.

By conducting policy decomposition, we can have an in-depth understanding of various kinds of transportation PDs and policy measures. This can further help us to understand the implementation effects of different policy measures.

3.2 Implementation Effects Analysis

The examination of the policy measures calls for criteria in evaluating their implementation effects and also in selection of the best combination of policy measures for actual implementation. With respect to the impacts on travel behavior, Litman (2013) proposed eight indicators, namely vehicle ownership, vehicle type, route change, time change, mode shift, destination change, trip generation, and land use changes. Based on these eight indicators, Xu et al. (2017) conducted an initial qualitative investigation of the impacts of implementation five PT and PC related policy measures implemented in Beijing. In this study, we focused on investigating the quantitative impacts of transportation policy measures, especially those on the transformation of Beijing into a transit metropolis. Considering the availability of data, performance indicators concerned with the transportation infrastructure investment, the growth of transportation infrastructure, the changes of PT volume, the number of motor vehicles, travel mode shares, and the average travel distance are used in this study.

- Transportation infrastructure investment

  Transportation infrastructure investment covers the spending of government and transportation agencies on constructing new transportation infrastructure and the improvement of the existing transportation infrastructure. Increased transportation infrastructure investment can have direct impacts on enhancing the supply of transportation services. Therefore, transportation infrastructure investment data can provide important information on the implementation effects of transportation policy measures.

- Growth of transportation infrastructure

  The growth of transportation infrastructure is a direct result from the increased transportation infrastructure investment. The growth of PT infrastructure can definitely provide us some "large picture" information on the development of PT systems. Therefore, the growth of transportation infrastructure is an important performance indicator for measuring the implementation effects of transportation policy measures.

- Changes of PT volume

  Rapid transportation infrastructure growth is usually accompanied by the increased travel demand. For example, newly opened urban roads are usually quickly filled with vehicles by induced traffic demand and become congested soon after opening. Therefore, the changes of PT volume can serve as a good measure of the changes of PT systems.

- Number of motor vehicles

  The number of motor vehicles is a good indicator of the implementation effects of PC-related policy measures. A reduced growth trend of motor vehicles can serve as a good measure of the effectiveness of PC-related policy measures. It can also shed some insights on the effectiveness of PT-related policy measures.

- Travel mode share

  Travel mode share is the percentage of travelers using a particular travel mode, which is an important component in developing a sustainable transportation system in a city or region. The travel mode share information can provide a direct measure of the implementation effects of transportation policy measures in distributing travelers into different travel modes.

- Average travel distance

  The average travel distance of travelers can be used as another general measure of the implementation effects of transportation policies. However, it may also result from other factors, such as urban development, housing price and job-housing relationship.

3.3 Sustainability Evaluation

Sustainability is a very important aspect of an urban transportation system. Unsustainable transportation systems will accelerate environment degradations, increase non-renewable resource consumptions, and produce various adverse externalities. An evaluation of the sustainability impacts of various transportation policy measures can help us to better understand the long-term impacts of transportation policy measures on our society, economy and environment. More importantly, how combinatorial effects of transportation policy measures can help develop sustainable transit metropolises.

The concept of sustainable development was first formally proposed in the document of World's Natural Resources Protection Strategy jointly issued by the International Union for Conservation of Nature, the United Nations Environment Programme, and World Wildlife Fund in 1980 (Lu et al., 2008). As for the definition of sustainable transportation development, there are several different versions, such as the version by the Canadian Transport sustainable development report, the version by the Centre for Sustainable Transport (CST) at the University Winnipeg, and the version by Tsinghua University. However, all these different versions have similar goals, i.e., to change the existing modes of transportation development and reduce traffic-related pollutions and hazards to human health. In this study, the CST version was used for its simplicity and authenticity. It defines a sustainable transportation system as one that "allows the basic access needs of individuals and societies to be met safely and in a manner consistent with human and ecosystem health, considers equity within and between generations; is affordable, operates efficiently, offers choice of transportation mode, and supports a vibrant economy; and limits emissions and waste within the planet's ability to absorb them, minimizes consumption of non-renewable resources, limits consumption of renewable resources to the sustainable yield level, reuses and recycles its components, and minimizes the use of land and the production of noise." This CST definition therefore recognizes the social, economic and environmental aspects of transportation sustainability.

The CTS definition was also used in a recent study by Xu et al. (2017) to evaluate the implementation effects of transportation management measures that were introduced following the Beijing 2008 Olympic and Paralympic Games. It shows the CTS definition can provide a practical qualitative evaluation framework for transportation policy evaluation. For this reason, we adopt the CTS definition-based qualitative evaluation framework, but with revised evaluation criteria from social, economic and environmental aspects that are list below.

With respect to society, transportation systems should:

- (So1) Meet basic human needs for health, comfort, and convenience in ways that do not stress the social fabric
- (So2) Allow and support development at a human scale, and provide for a reasonable choice of transportation modes, types of housing and community, and living styles
- (So3) Produce no more noise than is acceptable by communities
- (So4) Be safe for people and their property

With respect to the economy, transportation systems should:
- (Ec1) Provide cost-effective service and capacity
- (Ec2) Be financially affordable in each generation
- (Ec3) Provide viable service without serious fiscal deficits or heavy subsidies from government agencies
- (Ec4) Support vibrant, sustainable economic activity

With respect to the environment, transportation systems should:
- (En1) Make use of land in a way that has little or no impact on the integrity of ecosystems
- (En2) Use sparingly energy sources that are essentially not renewable or inexhaustible
- (En3) Use other resources that are renewable or inexhaustible, achieved in part through the reuse of items and the recycling of materials used in vehicles and infrastructure
- (En4) Produce no more emissions and waste than can be accommodated by the planet's restorative ability

These 12 criteria together naturally form a multi-dimensional evaluation framework that can be used for qualitatively evaluating the sustainability impacts of transportation policy measures.

4. CASE STUDY AND RESULTS ANALYSIS

The proposed methodology was applied to analyze and evaluate the key transportation polices implemented in Beijing municipality. Following the classifications of the transportation development process in Beijing municipality by Liu and Guan (2005), Liu (2009a), Mao et al. (2008), and Xu et al. (2010), we selected the period from 2005 to 2017 as the case study period. Actually, this period is pointed out by some previous studies, such as Liu (2009a), Mao et al. (2008), and Xu et al. (2010), as the main phase for PT developments, and various kinds of transportation polices are released during this period.

4.1 Transport Policy Decomposition Results Analysis

In this study, 24 relevant PDs released during the study period are collected from government and transportation agencies. Detailed descriptions of these PDs can be found in Table 1. Using the transportation policy decomposition method introduced in Section 3.1, these 24 PDs can be decomposed into three different dimensions, which is graphically shown in Fig. 7. The horizontal axis represents the time dimension; the vertical axis represents the level

Table 1 Summary of the Main Policy Documents Released for Managing the Transportation Systems in Beijing Municipality

Policy Document	Release Date	Released by	Title
PD1	2005-09-23	SCPRC	• Notice of the General Office of the State Council of the People's Republic of China on Forwarding the Proposal from the Ministry of Construction and Other Departments on <Advice on the Priority Development of Public Transport>
PD2	2011-11-09	MoTPRC	• Notice of the Ministry of Transport of the People's Republic of China on the Implementation of National Transit Metropolis Pilot Project
PD3	2012-06-28	SCPRC	• Energy Saving and New Energy Automobile Industry Development Planning
PD4	2012-12-29	SCPRC	• Guidance of the State Council of the People's Republic of China on the Priority Development of Public Transport in Cities
PD5	2013-06-14	MoTPRC	• Advice of Ministry of Transport of the People's Republic of China on the Implementation of <Guidance of the State Council on the Priority Development of Public Transport in Cities>
PD6	2013-07-15	MoTPRC	• Notice of the Ministry of Transport of the People's Republic of China on Promoting the Development of Transit Metropolis

Continued

Table 1 Summary of the Main Policy Documents Released for Managing the Transportation Systems in Beijing Municipality—cont'd

Policy Document	Release Date	Released by	Title
PD7	2014-03-16	SCPRC	• National New Urbanization Plan of China(2014–2020)
PD8	2014-11-19	MoTPRC	• Guideline on Urban Public Transportation Plan Compilation
PD9	2016-03-17	SCPRC	• Outline of the 13th Five-Year Plan for Economic and Social Development of the People's Republic of China (2016–2020)
PD10	2016-07-20	MoTPRC	• Outline of the 13th 5-Year Plan for Urban Public Transportation
PD11	2016-11-1	MoTPRC, MoIIT, MoPS, MoC, SAIC, GAQS, IQCAC	• Interim Measures for the Administration of Online Taxi Booking Business Operations and Services
PD12	2016-11-30	GOMoTPRC	• Notice of General Office of the Ministry of Transport of the People's Republic of China on Fully Promoting the Development of Transit Metropolis
PD13	2005-04	BMCT	• Outline of Beijing Transportation Development (2004–2020)
PD14	2006-12-08	PGBM	• Advice on the Priority Development of Public Transport
PD15	2007-03-26	BMCT	• Work Arrangement of the Priority Development of Public Transport in Beijing in 2007

Table 1 Summary of the Main Policy Documents Released for Managing the Transportation Systems in Beijing Municipality—cont'd

Policy Document	Release Date	Released by	Title
PD16	2009-07-03	PGBM	• Action Plan (2009–2015) of Beijing Municipality for the Development of Humanistic, High-Tech and Green Transportation
PD17	2010-12-23	PGBM	• Interim Regulation of the Quantity of Small Passenger Vehicles in Beijing
PD18	2012-07	BMCT, BMCDR	• The 12th Five-Year Plan for Transportation Development in Beijing Municipality
PD19	2013-09-11	PGBM	• Beijing Municipal Clean Air Action Plan (2013–2017)
PD20	2014-11-27	BMDRC	• Beijing Public Transport Pricing Adjustment Plan
PD21	2016-06	BMCT	• The 13th Five-Year Plan for Transportation Development in Beijing Municipality
PD22	2017-12-15	BMCT, BTMB, BMCEIT	• Road Test Management Regulations of Automated Vehicles in Beijing (Trial Version)
PD23	2015-09-14	BMDRC	• Beijing Urban Rail Transit Phase II Construction Plan (2015–2021)
PD24	2016-09-28	BPTC	• Outline of the 13th Five-Year Plan for the Beijing Public Transport Corporation

dimension; and the shape, together with the corresponding color, of each PD represents the content dimension. Fig. 7 provides a lot of important and useful information. First, it shows 50% PDs are released by the national-level government agencies. The PDs released by the municipal-level government agencies and the local-level transportation agencies account for 41.67% and 8.33%, respectively. This phenomenon may be explained by

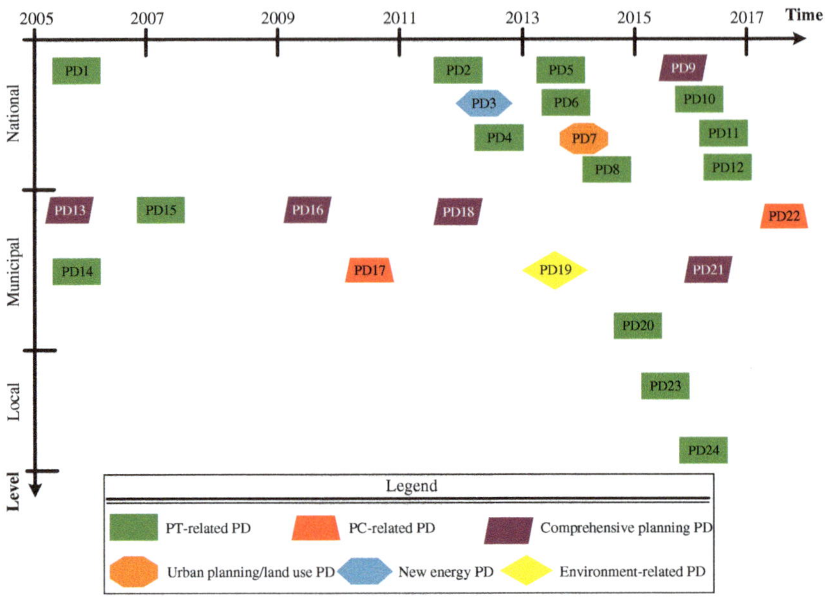

Fig. 7 Three-dimensional decomposition of the integrated multilevel policy documents implemented in Beijing Municipality (2005–2017).

the special political ideology in China. That is, the PDs released by the lower-level government agencies should follow the content of the PDs released by the upper-level government agencies. Second, 75% PDs are released after 2011. This indicates the transportation-related problems in Beijing attract more and more attentions in recent years. Third, 58.33% PDs are related to PT. This clearly shows that all the national government agencies, municipal government agencies, and local transportation agencies are increasingly paying attention on PT development in Beijing municipality.

After a careful study and classification of their contents, the integrated multilevel PDs that have been implemented in Beijing municipality can be further decomposed into the following eight main policy measures:

- (M1) Increasing investments for transportation infrastructure expansion and system update;
- (M2) Improving PT and land use integration for sustainable urban development;
- (M3) Improving PT service planning and design;
- (M4) Enhancing PT operations management;
- (M5) Promoting new and innovative PT systems to meet the ever-increasing and diversified mobility needs;

- (M6) Increasing the development and implementation of ITS and new energy technologies;
- (M7) Managing PC ownership;
- (M8) Managing PC usage.

Policy measures M2, M3, M4, and M5 are directly related to PT; policy measures M7 and M8 are directly related to PC; and policy measures M1 and M6 are related to both PT and PC. Generally speaking, these PT-related policy measures can be regarded as "carrot" policy measures, and PC-related policy measures are "stick" policy measures. Detailed descriptions of these policy measures proposed for Beijing municipality can be found in these 24 PDs and also previous studies, such as Liu (2009a,b), Liu et al. (2014, 2017) and Xu et al. (2010, 2015, 2017). It is expected that a virtuous cycle can be created with respect to shifting an appropriate proportion of PC users to PT, after implementing these combined PT and PC related policy measures, so as to achieve a SO transportation system for Beijing municipality.

4.2 Implementation Effects Analysis

The implementation effects of the eight transportation policy measures in Beijing Municipality are evaluated by using the six performance indicators proposed in Section 3.2. Data used in this evaluation are mainly collected from the Beijing Statistical Yearbook 2016 released by the Beijing Municipal Bureau of Statistics and NBS Survey Office in Beijing, and the comprehensive transportation survey reports released by the Beijing Municipal Commission of Transportation and the Beijing Transportation Development & Research Institute.

- Transportation infrastructure investment

  The distribution of infrastructure investment in Beijing municipality from 2005 to 2015 is summarized in Table 2. From it we can draw an immediate conclusion that the investment in transportation is the biggest among others, such as energy, posts and telecommunications, and public services. The investment for transportation is mainly used for constructing new transportation systems or renovating existing transportation systems, which include railway, highway, aviation and PT. Among them, PT received the most investments. This clearly indicates that in the past decade the Beijing municipality provided very strong financial support for developing PT systems. The increasing and stable funding sources can definitely support the long-term sustainable development of PT systems in offering better PT services in Beijing

Table 2 Infrastructure Investment in Beijing Municipality (2005–2015) (Unit: Billion RMB)

	Transportation									
Year	Railway	Highway	Public Transit	Aviation	Sub Total	Percentage	Energy	Posts and Tele.	Public Services	Total Infrastructure Investment
2005	0.39	4.07	11.32	6.62	22.42	36.71%	10.23	6.99	16.03	61.07
2006	2.51	14.06	20.10	7.22	43.96	47.00%	11.34	7.23	26.53	93.53
2007	6.57	18.96	20.24	8.75	54.80	46.61%	20.02	8.48	28.95	117.58
2008	7.59	17.05	21.58	14.18	60.42	52.05%	14.41	8.67	29.16	116.07
2009	11.49	13.48	42.67	2.19	69.86	47.78%	16.54	12.49	43.45	146.20
2010	7.71	9.73	41.08	13.43	72.05	51.34%	15.72	9.42	35.91	140.35
2011	4.36	10.77	35.13	17.66	68.07	48.61%	17.11	8.23	37.94	140.02
2012	4.30	9.82	39.10	17.81	71.20	39.79%	23.19	12.20	50.81	178.92
2013	3.69	12.75	31.09	16.25	66.45	37.21%	27.02	13.29	45.13	178.57
2014	0.90	8.46	49.16	16.60	75.65	37.49%	35.27	12.73	50.25	201.81
2015	5.93	8.88	37.41	30.47	82.70	38.03%	29.73	17.23	49.44	217.45

Data Source: BMBS-NBSSOB.

municipality. The increase of transportation infrastructure investment mainly results from the implementation of transportation policy measure of M1.

- Growth of transportation infrastructure

  The growth of transportation infrastructure in Beijing municipality from 2005 to 2015 is summarized in Table 3. The second column shows the rapid increase of the length of roads. The construction of ring roads, including the second, third, fourth, and fifth ring roads, is mainly finished before 2005. The sixth ring road was opened in 2009. This increase of road length mainly results from the construction of urban roads and expressways. Table 3 also clearly shows the implementation of PT-related policy measures lead to a rapid growth of the number of PT lines, the length of PT lines, and the number of PT vehicles. For example, the rail transit lines have a remarkable increase before and after the Beijing 2008 Olympic and Paralympic Games. The growth trend of PT infrastructures continues in recent years. Another interesting finding is that the number of taxis keeps the same as 66,646 vehicles from 2006 to 2012, and has a slight increase after 2012. This may result from the taxi regulation policies that restrict the number of taxi vehicles in Beijing municipality.

- Changes of PT volume

  The changes of PT volume are graphically illustrated in Fig. 8. From it we can see that there is a stable increase of PT volume for all PT modes. The total PT volume has increased from 5827.69 million in 2005 to 7971.34 million in 2015. Among all the PT modes, the rail transit systems, which mainly includes the subway systems, have the most increase of PT volume, an remarkable increase from 679.76 million in 2005 to 3323.81 million in 2015, an almost fivefold increase. This may result from the policy measure of M1 that leads to the rapid expansion of the subway network in Beijing municipality.

- Number of motor vehicles

  The annual variations of the number of vehicles in Beijing municipality are shown in Fig. 9A and B. Fig. 9A shows there is a continued growth of both the total number of motor vehicles and the number of private vehicles. However, as shown in Fig. 9B, the increased numbers of motor vehicles and private vehicles per yeas are both reduced significantly after 2010. This significant reduction mainly comes from the implementation of policy measures of M7 and M8, which are stated in the PD17 on the Interim Regulation of the Quantity of Small Passenger

Table 3 Transportation Infrastructure in Beijing Municipality (2005–2015)

		No. of PT Lines (veh)			Length of PT Lines (km)			No. of PT Vehicles (veh)			
Year	Total Length of Roads (km)	Buses and Trolley Buses	Rail Transit	Total	Buses and Trolley Buses	Rail Transit	Total	Buses and Trolley Buses	Rail Transit	Taxis	Total
2005	19,015	622	4	626	18,214	114	18,328	18,503	968	66,000	85,471
2006	25,377	620	4	624	18,468	114	18,582	19,522	967	66,646	87,135
2007	25,765	644	5	649	17,353	142	17,495	19,395	1130	66,646	87,171
2008	26,921	671	8	679	17,857	200	18,057	21,507	1714	66,646	89,867
2009	27,436	692	9	701	18,270	228	18,498	21,716	2014	66,646	90,376
2010	27,907	713	14	727	18,743	336	19,079	21,548	2463	66,646	90,657
2011	28,446	749	15	764	19,460	372	19,832	21,628	2850	66,646	91,124
2012	28,585	779	16	795	19,547	442	19,989	22,146	3685	66,646	92,477
2013	28,808	813	17	830	19,688	465	20,153	23,592	3998	67,046	94,636
2014	29,209	877	18	895	20,249	527	20,776	23,667	4664	67,546	95,877
2015	29,069	876	18	894	20,186	554	20,740	23,287	5024	68,284	96,595

Data Source: BMBS-NBSSOB.

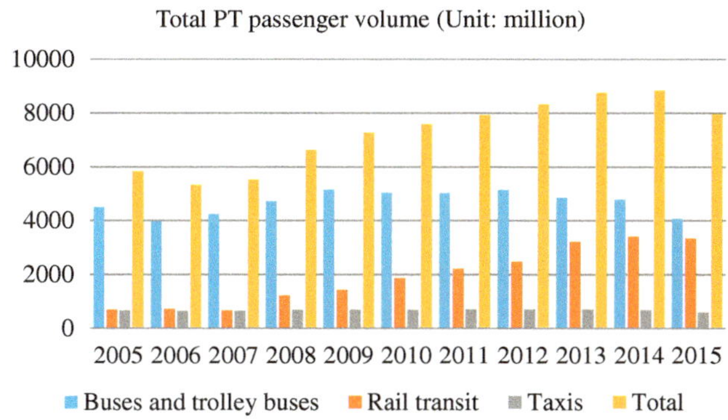

Fig. 8 Total PT passenger volume in Beijing Municipality (2005–2017).

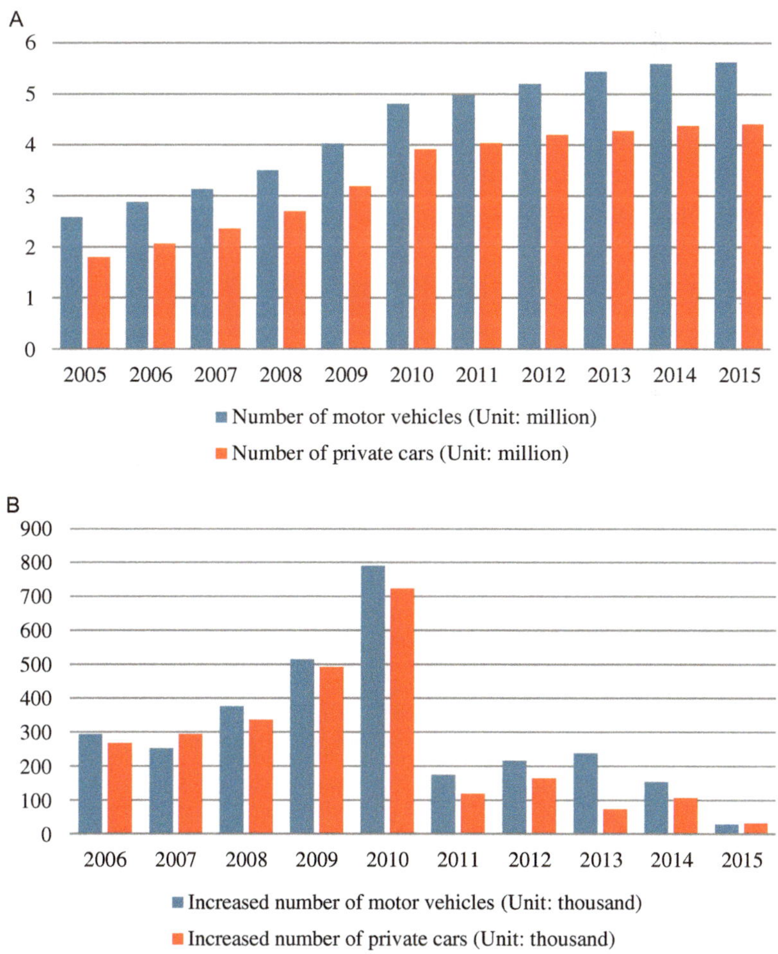

Fig. 9 Annual variations of the number of vehicles in Beijing municipality (2005–2015): (A) number of vehicles per year; (B) increased number of vehicles per year.

Vehicles in Beijing (see Table 1 for details.). After 2013, there is a stable decrease of the increased number of motor vehicles in Beijing municipality. The decrease of motor growth may suggest the increase of PT users, which have some positive effects on the current transportation system in Beijing municipality.

- Travel mode share

  The evolution of mode split in Beijing municipality from 1986 to 2015 is graphically shown in Fig. 10. From it we can see that there is a stable increase of subway mode share and a slight decrease car mode share after 2010, which mainly results from the implementation of policy measures of M7 and M8. This indicates a slight shifting of PC users to PT, which is good for changing the current transportation system from IE condition to SO condition as suggested by the PC–PT intermodal balance diagram. The total PT mode share reached 66% in 2015. Among them, bus mode accounts for 25.00% and the same to subway mode. Another surprising result is the significant reduction of bike mode share. In 1986, the mode share of bike is 62.70%. However, it reduced to 12.40% in 2015. This indicates the reduced use of non-motor vehicles in Beijing municipality.

	1986	2000	2005	2006	2007	2008	2009	2010	2011	2012	2013	2014	2015
Others	3.80%	3.00%	2.50%	2.40%	2.20%	1.90%	1.90%	3.00%	4.20%	2.90%	2.70%	1.70%	2.10%
Bike	62.70%	38.50%	30.30%	27.70%	23.00%	20.30%	18.10%	16.40%	16.40%	13.90%	12.10%	12.60%	12.40%
Taxi	0.30%	8.80%	7.60%	8.10%	7.70%	7.40%	7.10%	6.70%	6.70%	6.60%	6.50%	6.20%	3.60%
Subway	1.70%	3.60%	5.70%	5.80%	7.00%	8.00%	10.00%	11.50%	11.50%	16.80%	20.60%	19.40%	25.00%
Bus	26.50%	22.90%	24.10%	24.40%	27.50%	28.80%	28.90%	28.20%	28.20%	27.20%	25.40%	28.60%	25.00%
Car	5.00%	23.20%	29.80%	31.60%	32.60%	33.60%	34.00%	34.20%	33.00%	32.60%	32.70%	31.50%	31.90%

Fig. 10 Evolution of mode split in Beijing municipality, from 1986 to 2015. Data source: *Guo, J., Sun, M., Wang, T., Lu, L., 2015. Transportation development and congestion mitigation measures of Beijing, China. Mitig. Adapt. Strat. Glob. Chang. 20 (5), 651–663 and Beijing Transportation Development & Research Institute (BTDRI). 2017. 2015–2016 Beijing Transport Annual Report, [Online]. Available from: http://www.bjtrc.org.cn/JGJS.aspx?id=5.2&Menu=GZCG.*

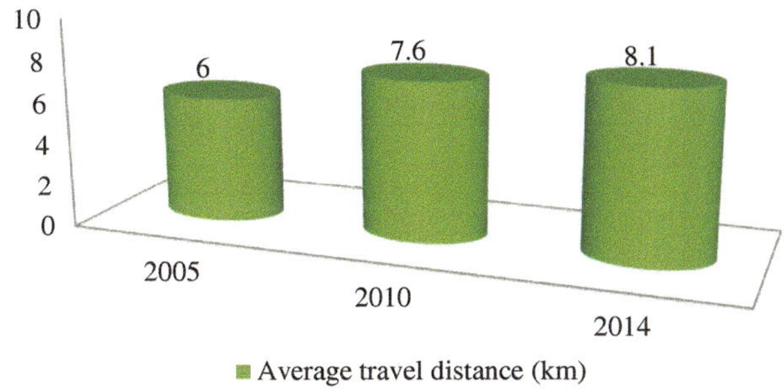

Fig. 11 Average travel distance in Beijing municipality. Data source: *BMCT*.

- Average travel distance

  The average travel distance of citizens within the sixth ring road area of Beijing municipality is shown in Fig. 11. From it we can see that the average travel distance has increased from 6 km in 2005 to 8.1 km in 2014. This may result from the increased rapid urban sprawl, rising housing price in the city central area, and job-housing imbalance. This, on the other side, suggests the implementation of policy measures can help support longer travel distances. The increased average travel distance in Beijing municipality may speed up the development of high-capacity and high-speed PT systems, such as regional rapid rail transit and maglev train. This can bring more diversified PT modes in Beijing and help transform it into a well-integrated multi-modal PT based transit metropolis.

4.3 Sustainability Evaluation Results Analysis

This section discusses the results of sustainability evaluation of the decomposed eight groups of transportation policy measures by using the multi-dimensional qualitative evaluation framework proposed in Section 3.3. The evaluation process can be carried out by an expert panel. The evaluation results are systematically shown in Table 4. The notation of "$\surd$" represents "principle/target satisfied"; the notation of "×" represents "principle/target not satisfied"; and the notation of "–" represents "not applicable" for the evaluation. For example, the notation of "$\surd$" in the cell crossing M1 and So1 indicates that the policy measure of increasing investments for transportation infrastructure expansion and system update can satisfy the principle of So1. From Table 4, it can be clearly seen that policy measures M2, M3, M4, M5, and M6 can satisfy almost all the suitability principles of social, economic

Table 4 Sustainability Evaluation of the Eight Transportation Policies Implemented in Beijing Municipality

Sustainability Aspects	Sustainability Components	M1	M2	M3	M4	M5	M6	M7	M8
Society	So1	√	√	√	√	√	√	×	×
	So2	√	√	√	√	√	√	–	–
	So3	–	–	√	√	–	√	–	×
	So4	–	–	√	√	√	√	√	√
Economy	Ec1	√	–	√	√	√	√	×	×
	Ec2	×	√	√	√	√	√	–	–
	Ec3	×	√	√	√	√	√	–	–
	Ec4	√	√	√	√	√	√	×	×
Environment	En1	×	√	√	–	–	–	–	–
	En2	–	–	√	√	√	√	–	–
	En3	–	–	–	–	√	√	–	–
	En4	–	–	√	√	√	√	√	√

Note: "√" means yes; "×" means no; "–" means not applicable.

and environmental aspects. This indicates that measures of improving PT and land use integration, enhancing PT service planning and operations, application of ITS technologies, and implementation of new and innovative PT modes are sustainable policy measures for future urban transportation system development. Table 4 also shows M7 and M8 cannot satisfy most of suitability principles. This indicates, from the long-term point of view, policy measures of managing PC ownership and usage are not very sustainable. Their implementation must be accompanied by sustainable PT policy measures so as to minimize their adverse effects on the sustainability of transportation systems. What's more, as seen in Table 4, the policy measure of increasing investments for transportation infrastructure expansion and system update can only satisfy principles related to social and economic aspects, and cannot satisfy or applicable to environmental aspects. This also indicates the short-term effects of building more road infrastructures.

5. DISCUSSIONS

The above case study has demonstrated the effectiveness of the proposed methodological framework in decomposing policy documents, analyzing the implementation effects and evaluating the sustainability of transportation policy measures. This methodological framework can help us to understand the implementation effects of a package of transportation polices that are aimed at transforming a city into a transit metropolis. However, the case study results presented in this study by using the proposed methodological framework are very general initial results. That is, before applying this methodological framework to analyze and evaluate real-life transportation polices, and further formulate future sustainable transportation polices, the following extensions should be carefully considered.

First, it is better to establish the quantitative relationships between transportation policy measures and implementation performance indicators, especially those related to PT and PC. These quantitative relationships can help us to better understand the implementation effects of various transportation policy measures, and also can be used to conduct sensitivity analysis. Second, it is better to provide formal mathematical definitions and formulations of the IE and SO conditions in the intermodal balance diagram so that transportation policymakers can conduct strict mathematical analysis and computational experiments on the implementation effects analysis and also evaluation of various possible combinations of transportation polices. Third, except the six performance indicators proposed in this study, other relevant performance indicators can also be incorporated into the methodological framework based on the availability of data. Fourth, except the sustainability dimension, there are also some other possible dimensions, such as equity and efficiency dimensions, which can be further incorporated into the current evaluation framework. By doing so, we can establish a comprehensive multi-dimensional qualitative evaluation framework for conducting integrated evaluation of transportation polices.

6. SUMMARY AND CONCLUSIONS

Travel behavior has already changed considerably as lifestyles change during the past two decades, and it will continue to change in the future. To cope with this change, the current urban transportation systems need to be reshaped so as to better support future urban mobility as well as the sustainable development of our society, economy and environment. Faced with the ever-increasingly serious traffic-related problems, Beijing, one of the largest cities in the world, has decided to develop a transit metropolis. Over a period of 20 years, a series of transportation policy measures have been implemented in Beijing in transforming this city into a transit metropolis. This work proposed a methodological framework for the initial investigation, analysis and evaluation of both the successful and unsuccessful practices resulted from the implementation of integrated multilevel policy measures for transportation management in Beijing. This framework integrates components of implementation effects analysis and sustainability evaluation, and it is threefold. First, a three-dimensional decomposition scheme is established to decompose the integrated multilevel policy documents implemented in Beijing. Second, a set of quantitative performance indicators are established to analyze the implementation effects. Third, a multi-dimensional qualitative evaluation framework is established to conduct sustainability evaluation.

The results of the case study in Beijing municipality show some successful and unsuccessful practices while implementing a package of policy measures. The successful practices include: (1) policy measures of increasing investment for transportation infrastructure improvement and system update helped increase road network coverage as well as PT line length; (2) policy measures of improving PT service planning and operations, implementation of ITS technologies, and application of new and innovative PT modes helped increase PT patronage and PT mode share; (3) policy measures of managing PC ownership and usage helped reduce the growth trend of motor vehicle numbers and also reduce its mode share. The unsuccessful practices include: (1) the combinatorial effects of policy measures lead to a reduced mode share of non-motorized travel modes; (2) the average travel distance of travelers has been increased. The sustainability evaluation results show that from long-term perspective policy measures of restricting PC ownership and usage are not sustainable, and policy measures of promoting PT development are mostly sustainable. It should be noted that these initial findings are mainly based on the data collected and methodological framework used in this study. More concrete work can be done to understand the successful and unsuccessful practices in Beijing so as to further support the conclusions. It is anticipated that the empirical results presented in this study will first shed light on the implementation effects of integrated multilevel policy measures implemented in Beijing from different dimensions, and second support transportation policymakers to conduct effective and efficient design of future PT policy measures for Beijing and other cities with similar contexts in both China and the world.

ACKNOWLEDGMENTS

The work described in this paper was jointly supported by the National Natural Science Foundation of China (71771015 and 71422010).

REFERENCES

Beijing Municipal Commission of Transportation (BMCT), 2016. The Fifth Comprehensive Transportation Survey Report of Beijing Municipality. Beijing, China.

Beijing Transportation Development & Research Institute (BTDRI), 2017. 2015–2016 Beijing Transport Annual Report. [Online]. Available from: http://www.bjtrc.org.cn/JGJS.aspx?id=5.2&Menu=GZCG.

Bruun, E., Givoni, M., 2015. Six research routes to steer transport policy. Nature 523, 29–31.

Ceder, A., 2016. Public Transit Planning and Operation: Modeling, Practice and Behavior, second ed. CRC Press, Boca Raton, FL.

Cervero, R., 1998. The Transit Metropolis: A Global Inquiry. Island Press.

Cervero, R., Day, J., 2008. Suburbanization and transit-oriented development in China. Transp. Policy 15 (5), 315–323.

Chen, X.M., 2010. Prospect of the transit-oriented development in China. Manag. Res. Pract. 2 (1), 83–93.

Deng, T., Nelson, J.D., 2013. Bus rapid transit implementation in Beijing: an evaluation of performance and impacts. Res. Transp. Econ. 39 (1), 108–113.

Guo, J., Sun, M., Wang, T., Lu, L., 2015. Transportation development and congestion mitigation measures of Beijing, China. Mitig. Adapt. Strat. Glob. Chang. 20 (5), 651–663.

Litman, T., 2013. Transport Elasticities: Impacts on Travel Behavior. Available from: www.vtpi.org.

Liu, X.M., 2009a. Advancing a scientific development of transportation to construct a transit-oriented Beijing. Urban Trans. China 7 (6), 1–7.

Liu, X.M., 2009b. Promote green travel and develop transit cities. Construction Technol. 17, 21–23.

Liu, L., 2013. Theoretical source of public bus cities and advices on multiple construction. Urban Management 45, 44–48.

Liu, T., Ceder, A., 2015. Analysis of a new public-transport-service concept: customized bus in China. Transp. Policy 39, 63–76.

Liu, R., Guan, C.Q., 2005. Mode biases of urban transportation policies in China and their implications. J. Urban Plann. Dev. 131 (2), 58–70.

Liu, T., Ceder, A., Ma, J., Guan, W., 2014. Synchronizing public transport transfers by using intervehicle communication scheme: case study. J. Transp. Res. Board 2417, 78–91.

Liu, T., Ceder, A., Ma, J., Guan, W., Zhou, L., 2017. Graphical human-machine interactive approach for integrated bus transit scheduling: lessons gained from a large bus company. IEEE Trans. Intell. Transp. Syst. 18 (4), 1023–1028.

Lu, H.P., Mao, Q.Z., Li, Z., He, K.B., Shuai, S.J., Zhang, X.L., 2008. Sustainable Urban Mobility in Rapid Urbanization: Theory and Practice in China. China Railway Publishing House, Beijing, China.

Mao, B.H., Guo, J.F., Chen, J.C., Jia, S.P., 2008. Some historical comments on urban transportation development of Beijing. J. Transp. Syst. Eng. Inf. Technol. 8 (3), 6–13.

Ministry of Transport of the People's Republic of China (MoTPRC), 2011. Notice of the Ministry of Transport of the People's Republic of China on the Implementation of National Transit Metropolis Pilot Project. Beijing, China.
Song, Z., 2013. Transition to a transit city: case of Beijing. J. Transp. Res. Board 2394, 38–44.
Suzuki, H., Cervero, R., Iuchi, K., 2013. Transforming Cities with Transit: Transit and Land-Use Integration for Sustainable Urban Development. World Bank Publications, Washington DC.
Velasquez, J.M., Li, W., Xue, L., Hidalgo, D., 2016. In: Challenges and Opportunities of China's "National Transit Metropolis Demonstration Program". Proceedings of the Transportation Research Board 95th Annual Meeting, January 10–14, 2016, Washington DC, USA.
Vuchic, V.R., 1999. Transportation for Livable Cities. Center for Urban Policy Research, New Brunswick, NJ.
Vuchic, V.R., 2005. Urban Transit: Operations, Planning and Economics. John Wiley & Sons, Hoboken, NJ.
Wardrop, J.G., 1952. Some theoretical aspects of road traffic research. Proc. Inst. Civ. Eng. 1 (3), 325–362.
Xu, M., Ceder, A., Gao, Z., Guan, W., 2010. Mass transit systems of Beijing: governance evolution and analysis. Transportation 37 (5), 709–729.
Xu, M., Grant-Muller, S., Huang, H.J., Gao, Z., 2015. Transport management measures in the post-Olympic games period: supporting sustainable urban mobility for Beijing? Int. J. Sust. Dev. World. 22 (1), 50–63.
Xu, M., Grant-Muller, S., Gao, Z., 2017. Implementation effects and integration evaluation of a selection of transport management measures in Beijing. Case Stud. Transp. Policy 5 (4), 604–614.
Zhao, B., Zhao, J., Wang, J., 2000. In: Prospects and characteristics of urban public transport in China. Proceedings of the First International Conference on Urban Public Transportation Systems, Pages 58–67, March 21–25, 1999, Miami, Florida, USA.
Zhou, J., 2016. The transit metropolis of Chinese characteristics? Literature review, interviews, surveys and case studies. Transp. Policy 51, 115–125.

FURTHER READING

People's Government of Beijing Municipality, 2009. Action Plan on Building Humanistic, Scientific and Technological, and Green Transportation Systems for Beijing (2009–2015). [Online] Available from:http://www.gov.cn/zwgk/2009-07/20/content_1369638.htm.
State Council of the People's Republic of China (SCPRC), 2012. Guidance of the State Council on the Prior Development of Public Transport in Cities. [Online]. Available from:http://www.gov.cn/zwgk/2013-01/05/content_2304962.htm.

CHAPTER TWO

Why Do Some BRT Systems in the Global South Fail to Perform or Expand?

Minh Hieu Nguyen[*,†,1], **Dorina Pojani**[‡]
*Department of Economics and Sociology of Transport (DEST), The French Institute of Science and Technology for Transport, Development and Networks (IFSTTAR), Champs-sur-Marne, France
†Faculty of Transport Economics, University of Transport and Communications (UTC), Hanoi, Vietnam
‡School of Earth and Environmental Sciences, The University of Queensland, Brisbane, QLD, Australia
[1]Corresponding author: e-mail address: minh-hieu.nguyen@ifsttar.fr

Contents

Abstract

More than 165 cities on 6 continents have implemented BRT systems. While most have been successful, some have failed—either to perform at a high level or to expand further. This chapter examines the reasons for failures, which can be as illuminating as the reasons for successes. Five case studies are included: Bangkok, Delhi, Hanoi, Lagos, and Lima. The analysis is structured according to an existing theoretical framework, which considers: (1) *institutional and legislative context*; (2) *political leadership and commitment*; (3) *management of competing modes*; (4) *public participation*; (5) *funding and coordination*; (6) *physical design*; and (7) *image promotion*.

Keywords: Bus rapid transit (BRT), Bangkok, Hanoi, Delhi, Lima, Lagos, Barriers

ISSN 2543-0009
https://doi.org/10.1016/bs.atpp.2018.07.005

1. INTRODUCTION

Bus rapid transit (BRT) is a bus-based public transit system, which emulates the performance and amenities of modern light and heavy rail systems, including segregated rights of way, closed stations, and pre-board ticketing. However, it has major advantages over rail-based transit, including much lower construction costs, short implementation periods, accommodation of many route permutations, and flexibility to adapt to a range of urban conditions (Pojani, 2014).

BRT originated in Latin America, with Bogotá's TransMilenio being the most famous system worldwide. Currently, TransMilenio encompasses 113 km, distributed among 117 trunk corridors, and 107 feeder routes. It moves more than 2.2 million passengers daily. The Latin American experience has been successfully transferred to many Asian and African cities. Also BRT has been introduced in cities in Europe, North America, and Australia. More than 165 cities on 6 continents have implemented BRT systems (Global BRT Data, 2017). Innovative technologies, such as "trackless trains"—i.e., electric self-driving buses that follow markings painted on the road, instead of conventional rail tracks—promise to fully blur the difference between BRT and rail.

Notwithstanding its advantages, BRT is not a panacea. While BRT has scored outstanding successes around the world, it has also suffered substantial failures. Its introduction require complex planning taking into account not only technical, financial, and design aspects but also local institutional, legislative, and political contexts. Some systems consist of a single corridor, which serves a limited portion of the city. A few systems have already been dismantled. This chapter examines the reasons for failures—to perform at high level or to expand a successful corridor. While transportation policy reviews most often showcase "best practice," an analysis of problematic cases can also help decision-makers to avoid newcomer costs and learn from the mistakes of others (Marsden and Stead, 2011).

Five case studies are considered in this chapter: Bangkok, Delhi, Hanoi, Lagos, and Lima. Bangkok and Hanoi have implemented systems limited in size, which have fallen below expectations in terms of ridership, and are struggling to survive. Lima's BRT corridor is of high quality but the city has failed to extend it. The BRT system in Lagos is only "lite"—although superior to the paratransit services that it replaced. After major controversy, Delhi has already removed its BRT line.

A focus on the problems experienced by BRT systems in the Global South is crucial because, as Chandran Nair puts it: "The west isn't going to sort [the climate crisis] out. Its democracies face huge difficulties when confronted by the need for unpopular decisions that dramatically shift lifestyles and mean people must give up privileges such as car and air travel that they have taken for granted. Perhaps inevitably, western politicians prefer to seek solutions through market mechanisms and technological "innovations". When it comes to the future of the planet, decisions in Beijing, New Delhi, Jakarta and Lagos will be more important than those taken in Washington or Brussels" (Nair, 2017).

The information for this chapter on the difficulties and failings of individual BRT systems comes from academic papers, industry reports, and newspaper articles on the respective BRT systems, as well as the field observations of the authors. BRT issues are placed in the broader context of public transport politics in the Global South, which helps explain why BRT projects may fail.

2. BACKGROUND: OBSTACLES TO PUBLIC TRANSPORT IN THE GLOBAL SOUTH

Neoliberalism has made a clear imprint on the cities of the Global South, which has not been viewed as positive (Harvey, 2007). It has led to socio-spatial polarization and segregation. Where they existed, welfare states have been mostly dismantled. Elsewhere they have been prevented from forming, in favor of policies that encourage family, neighborhood, informal, or market-based and market-sustaining solutions (e.g., public–private partnerships or PPPs) to social problems. The emphasis has been on not allowing citizens to burden the state or demand entitlements (Jessop, 2002).

In urban transport, neoliberalism has produced a vicious circle. In unequal and stratified societies, car ownership has become an important a status signifier, and a tool to avoid contact with lower income groups (Ashmore et al., 2017, 2018; Pojani et al., 2018). A focus on cars and driving has led to lower investments in public transport. Declining public transport quality has driven away passengers, while the utilitarian need for cars (or for private car-sharing services) has become stronger, especially among the financial elites. Governments have rushed to accommodate the travel needs and desires of these elites, ignoring the rest of the population. This loop stems from a core issue: the withdrawal of the state as an active agent in equalizing access to the city and in providing public services and infrastructure systems. At the same time, many neoliberal Global South governments are also authoritarian and hierarchical. Corruption and generally dysfunctional (post)colonial legacies have exacerbated the effects of neoliberalism and authoritarianism (Fig. 1).

Consequently, public transport governance is very inefficient. In many Global South cities, a combination of weak administrative arrangements, limited planning capacity, and a lack of coordination between land use and transport policy-making prevails, which inhibits the development of more innovative, integrated, sustainable policies. Most often, transport tasks are spread across a myriad of agencies, especially in large metropolitan areas which contain several local governments. Disciplinary "silos" are also common where different departments make decisions without interdepartmental

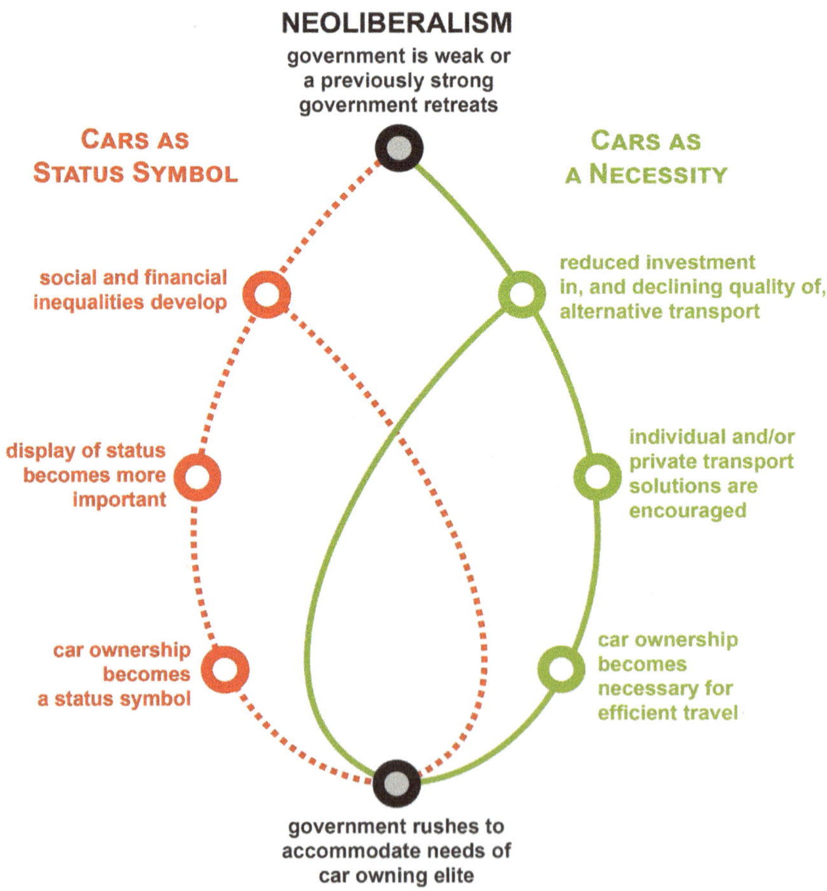

Fig. 1 Conceptual diagram.

dialog. Regional transportation bodies exist in some cases but these often lack technical and financial capacity. Where local and regional institutions share real decision-making power, they often have differing ideologies and areas of focus. Comprehensive and integrated long-term visions for sustainable transport are rare. In many cases, municipalities lack the budget to fulfill their transport-related responsibilities. As a result, they rely on financial help from higher levels of governments, especially for large capital investments, which then leads to political and "turf" struggles. Even public–private partnerships (PPPs), rather than easing the financial burden of cities, have often led to legal and financial disputes to the detriment of transport operations and management (Stead and Pojani, 2017). However, policies to promote public transport, including BRT, cannot materialize without adequate government management of the economy.

3. CASE STUDY CONTEXTS: BANGKOK, DELHI, HANOI, LAGOS, AND LIMA

Table 1 provides information on population, density, and travel modes in the case study cities, as well as the basic indicators of the respective BRT systems. Bogotá's TransMilenio—arguably the most successful BRT system worldwide is used as a benchmark. Of course, systems do not have to be as highly performing and as extensive as TransMilenio in order to be considered a success. Also, "success" and "failure" are somewhat ambiguous terms, and depend on context and perceptions. As Fjellstrom (2017b) notes: "Just because a project is labelled 'BRT' does not mean that the project is good, or that it provides a superior service to regular buses, or that it provides any net benefit to road users or the city."

The Institute for Transportation & Development Policy (ITDP) has made a substantive effort to quantify BRT "success" and "failure," rank systems, and come up with a standard, which employs a wide range of metrics, including BRT basic features, service planning, quality of infrastructure/stations, communications, and access and integration. ITDP's standard recognizes particularly high-quality corridors with either Bronze, Silver, or Gold rankings (ITDP, 2016). However, the authors argue that in megacities such as the case studies in this chapters, a single BRT corridor, however highly performing can hardly be considered as a solution to transport problems. Cities cannot be regarded as successful in their efforts to create BRT until an extensive network has been established which covers most of the city.

Table 1 Basic Overview of the Five Case Study Cities and Their BRT Systems

	Bangkok	**Delhi**	**Hanoi**	**Lagos**	**Lima**	**Bogotá (Benchmark)**
City indicator						
Population (city) (*persons*)	8,305,218				7,605,742	7,760,500
Population (metropolitan region) (*persons*)	14,565,547	14,400,000[a]	7,328,400[b]	22,583,305	8,482,619	9,155,100
Population density (*persons/km*^{2})	1876	9710[a]	2182[b]	11,009	3009	3347
GDP per capita	5816 US$	950 $[a]	2186 US$	2640 US$	6122 US$	5806 US$
Available travel modes	(1) Elevated train/ Skytrain; (2) Metro; (3) Regular bus; (4) Taxi; (5) Paratransit; (6) Car; (7) Motorcycle; (8) Bicycle and walking; (9) BRT	(1) Metro; (2) Regular bus; (3) Taxi; (4) Paratransit; (5) Car; (6) Motorcycle; (7) Bicycle and walking	(1) Regular bus; (2) Taxi; (3) Paratransit; (4) Car; (5) Motorcycle; (6) Bicycle and walking; (7) BRT	(1) Regular bus; (2) Taxi; (3) Paratransit; (4) Car; (5) Motorcycle; (6) Bicycle and walking; (7) BRT	(1) Metro; (2) Regular bus; (3) Taxi; (4) Paratransit; (5) Car; (6) Motorcycle; (7) Bicycle and walking; (8) BRT	(1) Regular bus; (2) Taxi; (3) Paratransit; (4) Car; (5) Motorcycle; (6) Bicycle and walking; (7) BRT
Modal split (%)						
Private transport	60	22[a]	88	15	12	26
Public transport	30	38[a]	11	72	62	59
Non-motorized transport	10	40[a]	1	13	26	15
BRT indicator						
Number and type of corridor(s)	1 (closed)	1 (open)[c]	1 (closed)	1 (closed)	1 (closed)	11 (closed)

Years of operation	2010[d]	2008[c]	2007	2008	2010[e]	2000
Total corridor length (*km*)	15.3[d]	5.8[c]	14.5	22.0	26.78[e]	113
Length of dedicated lane (*km*)	6.6[d]	5.8[c]	14.0	14.3	26.78[e]	113
Number of stations	12[d]	9[c]	23	28	36	139
Average speed (*km/h*)	26[d]	18[c]	19.6	30	25.5	26.2
Bus frequency per peak hour	7[d]	120[c]	14	—	117	320
Passenger per peak hour per direction	1100	5.500[f]	520	10,000[g]	22,800	48,000
Daily ridership *(thousand passengers)*	15	53.5[f]	8	195[g]	350	2213
Capital cost (*10^9 US$*)	75[h]	17.4[c]	53	36[i]	—	—
Standard one-way ticket fare (*US$*)	0.57	0.1[c]	0.31[j]	0.97	0.74	0.67
Quality standard	Bronze[d]	Basic[k]	—	Lite[g]	Gold[k]	Among 11 corridors: 3 Gold, 5 Silver, 3 Basic

Sources: (a) (Thynell et al., 2010); (b) (General Statistics Office, 2017); (c) (Hidalgo and Pai, 2010); (d) (Far East BRT Data, 2017) (http://data.fareastbrt.com); (e) all other data are from Global BRT Data (2017) (https://brtdata.org/) and the authors' field observations; (f) (Kathuria et al., 2016); (g) (Kaenzig et al., 2010); (h) (Wu and Pojani, 2016); (i) (Independent Evaluation Group, 2016); (j) Estimated by the authors with the price of 7000 VND and an exchange rate of US$ to VND at 22,641; (k) (ITDP, 2017).

Note: An open BRT corridor allows all operators whereas a closed one allows only one licensed operator.

4. FINDINGS: BARRIERS TO THE CREATION OR EXPANSION OF SUCCESSFUL BUS RAPID TRANSIT (BRT)

This chapter employs a seven-point theoretical framework adapted from Mallqui and Pojani (2017), which is presented in Table 2. This framework was selected because, among the several reviews of BRT that exist, it is the only one specifically structured around potential reasons for failure. A similar framework has been used by Wu and Pojani (2016) and Lindau et al. (2014). The categories covered in the framework are: (1) *institutional and legislative context*; (2) *political leadership and commitment*; (3) *management of competing modes*; (4) *public participation*; (5) *funding and coordination*; (6) *physical design*; and (7) *image promotion*. Table 2 sets forth the issues associated with each category.

4.1 Institutional and Legislative Context

Institutional gaps and overlaps, along with a lack of coordination among public agencies are evident in all of the case study cities. In Lima, the Ministry of Transport and Communications, two agencies in the Metropolitan Municipality of Lima, and 43 boroughs are involved in planning and managing urban transport system (Mallqui and Pojani, 2017). In Bangkok and Hanoi, public transit provision and oversight responsibilities are similarly fragmented among a range of agencies. In line with the Southeast Asian culture, transport staff members tend not to propose innovations and make any decisions unless specifically instructed to do so by their superiors (Huynh and Gomez-Ibañez, 2017; World Bank, 2007).

In Delhi too, interagency conflicts are standard, in particular between the National Government and the Government of National Capital Territory of Delhi. For example, the Delhi police operates under the National Government umbrella, and because it had serious misgiving about the BRT approved by local authorities, it enforced traffic rules pertaining to BRT only cursorily (Kumar et al., 2012; Rizvi and Sclar, 2014). The BRT system was initiated by the Central Pollution Control Board and the Environmental Pollution Control Authority rather than a transport agency. These agencies emphasized the environmental aspects of the BRT planning process, such as requiring a longwinded environmental impact assessment, and highlighting the air pollution advantages of BRT. Other crucial aspects, such as convenience or time-savings, were disregarded (Kathuria et al., 2016).

Table 2 Theoretical Framework

	Key Barriers or Risks
1. Institutional and Legislative Context	Unaligned interests of involved city officials and stakeholders Uncoordinated, decentralized municipal transport departments (as opposed to regionally-based transport organizations) Limited in-house technical capacity Foreign consultancy services unfamiliar with the local culture, legislation, and political system Higher market demand for BRT consultancy services than experienced consultants can quickly provide Lack of bureaucratic sophistication and oversight to coordinate a variety of consultants (no single company can provide all elements from planning to implementation) Inexperienced local road building companies tasked with implementation Lack of specialized BRT agencies with coordinating and ruling capacity
2. Political Leadership and Commitment	Lack of commitment of city leaders (mayors, governors) as BRT champions Risk of discontinuation in case of electoral changes Top-down processes (conflicts with stakeholders)
3. Management of Competing Modes	Competition and opposition to BRT from private motorized vehicles (cars and motorcycles), especially in countries with domestic car industries Lack of complementary policies to reduce car traffic Opposition to BRT from existing transit operators (bus and rail) Lower image than rail-based urban transport Competition and opposition from myriad small enterprises (paratransit) Cycling lobbies might view BRT as their contestant for scarce road space Opposition from retail shop owners (over loss of on-street parking) Lack of intermodal facilities (BRT, rail, paratransit, cycling)

Continued

Table 2 Theoretical Framework—cont'd

	Key Barriers or Risks
4. Public Participation	Lack of communication, transparency, and media or community engagement Lack of public education activities (e.g., focus groups, workshops) on the advantages of BRT (e.g., over rail), on what to realistically expect, and on how to use the system once it is built Lack of negotiation and/or compromise with the car lobby (e.g., widening of some roads, provision of park-and-ride lots at suburban BRT stations, and construction of car flyovers)
5. Funding and Coordination	Large upfront public investment—directly (building infrastructure) or indirectly (providing road space/stations/bus depots/terminals) No novel funding sources (e.g., PPPs, transfers from regional/national government, taxes, value capture from TOD) Poor network planning Excessively large operators (declining economies of scale) Poor incentives for operators (e.g., guaranteed income, no periodic review of contracts) Poorly run user information offices or headway control system Fare enforcement/evasion Inadequate funding or very tight financial planning (to avoid operational subsidies) Low levels of service (i.e., crowded vehicles with 6–7 standees per sq.m) Downgrades (e.g., pavement quality, station design, problems with pickpockets) Maintenance provisions (e.g., for road surface) sometimes not built into the financial plan High land acquisition/compensation costs (not covered by development banks) Incumbent operators affected by the BRT might request compensation Strained negotiations with land and building owners Lengthy and litigious planning process (risk of external donors/loaners freezing funding) Low BRT fares are unlikely to cover high purchase costs of land while high fares lead to decreases in ridership

6. Physical Design	Poorly designed BRT system (no lane segregation, no special vehicles, no use of technology for information displays and fare payment, no raised platforms, poorly trained staff, etc.) Neglect of related issues (parking, non-motorized transport, TOD) Poor physical integration with other modes (e.g., intermodal stations, integration with backbone rail transit, bicycle parking facilities, bikesharing docks) Lack of access from low-income neighborhoods (e.g., though feeder services) Neglect of existing bus routes Development of isolated corridors with integration deferred to a later stage No scheduled reviews and revisions of BRT once in operation (e.g., to adjust routes, construct new connections between corridors, reduce parallel routes, expand bus fleet)
7. Image Promotion	No distinctive image, confusing maps and wayfinding, little information on/off-line Disruptive project implementation (e.g., lengthy construction process) No validation of transit users' concerns in promotional messages (e.g., about travel time/cost) Lack of awareness raising among users on the benefits of BRT over rail Negative publicity on part of the media Failing to capitalize on the support of stakeholders that stand to benefit from BRT (e.g., real estate owners/developers along a proposed route)

Additional sources: Carrigan et al. (2013), Deng and Nelson (2011), Flores-Dewey (2012), Flores-Dewey and Zegras (2012), Gilbert (2008), Hensher and Golob (2008), Hidalgo and Graftieaux (2008), Hidalgo and Gutiérrez (2013), ITDP (2016), Kühn (2002), Levinson et al. (2003), Lindau et al. (2014), Mallqui and Pojani (2017), Muñoz and Gschwender (2008), Muñoz and Hidalgo (2013), Muñoz and Paget-Seekins (2016), Nielsen et al. (2005), Pojani (2014), Rizvi and Sclar (2014), Wirasinghe et al. (2013), Wright and Hook (2007), and Wu and Pojani (2016).

In Delhi and Lagos, the creation of special purpose agencies—Delhi Integrated Multi-Modal Transit System (DIMTS) and Lagos Metropolitan Area Authority (LAMATA)—was instrumental in overcoming the barriers posed by institutional fragmentation and bringing the BRT projects to completion. While LAMATA soon gained substantial power, DIMTS did not have enough power to resolve conflicts between other agencies (Gorham, 2017; Kaenzig et al., 2010; Kathuria et al., 2016; Mason-Jones and Cohen, 2012). In Lagos, the National Union of Road Transport Workers—another powerful organization—was a key stakeholder during the planning and implementation of BRT. While initially its presence helped smooth the transition of some conventional bus operators to BRT operators, recently, its BRT franchise was terminated due to its non-compliance with operational requirements (Mason-Jones and Cohen, 2012). In Hanoi, the BRT service is overseen by a preexisting public agency (TRAMOC) and delivered by a state-owned enterprise (TRANSERCO). The institutional administration is similar for BRT and conventional buses. This is acceptable in the short term, while the BRT system is limited in size and conventional buses continue to have a leading role in public transport provision (Nguyen, 2016). However, a full BRT system would require a more sophisticated and specialized structure.

The involvement of foreign consultancy and advisory services has had different effects in the case study cities. Delhi benefited from technical support from the Institute for Transportation and Development Policy (ITDP) on an as-needed basis (Fjellstrom et al., 2004). Domestic staff was invited to participate in study tours, international conferences, and workshops. This helped locals to gain technical expertise, thoroughly research and comprehend the BRT concept (Thynell et al., 2010). However, it was insufficient to save the project. Bangkok did not benefit from foreign technical experience. The local staff was too focused on infrastructural components, neglecting other aspects such as promotion and public participation. Hanoi received very intensive input from the World Bank. But this has not been viewed as entirely positive. The implemented BRT system was considered as a product of negotiation and World Bank fiat rather than technical considerations. The World Bank was accused of railroading the BRT planning process and imposing its own pet design ideas (Hanoi Urban Transport Project Management Unit, n.d.; Fjellstrom, 2017a, b). In Lima and Lagos, the combination of local and foreign experts involved in the process was more balanced. Spanish and Colombian professionals supported Lima's BRT. Lagos' BRT received support from the World Bank (Independent Evaluation Group, 2016; Mallqui and Pojani, 2017), which sponsored the participation of local staff in training courses, in addition to providing technical assistance. Consequently, the systems were better suited for the specific regional conditions (Hidalgo, 2017).

The effect of the local legislative framework also varies among the case study cities. Lagos engaged in a radical legislative reform to accommodate its BRT. It adopted a new law for the LAMATA establishment, as well as a series of regulations regarding passenger road traffic and transport to shape a controlled-competition regime (Kaenzig et al., 2010). In Lima and Bangkok, new laws on segregated transit lanes were adopted. In contrast, the BRTs of Hanoi and Delhi were handicapped by legislative obstacles. The lack of specific legislation has been identified as a major cause for the excessive delays in BRT planning and implementation in Hanoi (Khanh Nguyen, 2016). Because BRT was a novel concept in Vietnam, time-consuming checks were undertaken to ensure that the system complied with local rules. In the Indian legal system, the jurisdictional boundaries are so broad that Delhi's High Judicial Court is entitled to govern controversial transport policies (such as banning cycle rickshaws or allowing private cars to use BRT lanes), which can and do result in major disruption and corruption (ITDP, 2006; Pucher et al., 2005). The High Court's position on BRT was inconsistent, which lowered public confidence in the system and contributed to its removal (Joshi, 2012; Velmurugan et al., 2012).

4.2 Political Leadership and Commitment

In all cases except for Hanoi, the BRT projects were championed by local politicians: Governor Amed Tinubu and his successor in Lagos, Mayors Alberto Andrade Carmona and Luis Castañeda Lossio in Lima, Governor Apirak Kosayaodhin in Bangkok, and Chairman of the Transport Corporation Rakesh Mehta in Delhi. In Lima, BRT systems in neighboring countries served as inspiration. Importantly, the knowledge that BRT had propelled the political careers of their proponents in places like Bogotá and Curitiba motivated politicians in Lima. Bangkok's governor made BRT the core of his political campaign in 2004. Similarly, BRT was a centerpiece of India's National Congress Party platform in 2001.

In Hanoi, by contrast, enthusiastic political support was not immediately forthcoming. Consecutive municipal leaders viewed BRT as a project "inherited" from their predecessors rather than as their own pet project. While the initial project approval was issued in 2007, the leadership of the People's Committee did not deliver instructions to prioritize BRT until late

2012 (Hanoi Urban Transport Project Management Unit, n.d.). At inauguration, People's Committee Chairman Nguyen Duc Chung was supportive but later, in view of poor BRT's performance and negative media publicity, he withdrew his support and even offered to allow conventional buses to share segregated BRT lanes (Xuân Hinh, 2017). While this proposal was ultimately rejected (Hung, 2018), it was viewed as a victory by BRT opponents.

However, political support was not firm nor continuous in the other cities either. Inconsistent political leadership hindered the BRT projects in all cities. For example, in Lima the political focus eventually shifted from BRT to metro construction (Independent Evaluation Group, 2015; Mallqui and Pojani, 2017). In Thailand, the Prime Minister during the inception period of the BRT belonged to a political party with strong ties to the automobile industry, and therefore opposed BRT (Wu and Pojani, 2016). Subtle tactics were used to delay the project (Sengers, 2016). The BRT corridor was finally completed after the Prime Minister had been deposed in a military coup.

4.3 Management of Competing Modes

In all of the case study cities, major clashes with private vehicle owners (cars and/or motorcycle) had to be overcome (Fig. 2). Preventing the incursion of private vehicles into the BRT lanes has been a big challenge—though in

Fig. 2 Hanoi's BRT lane is besieged by motorbikes. *Photo by Tran Thi My Linh.*

some cities, such as Hanoi, traffic cameras installed at intersections are helping identify and fine violators.

While car users comprise only a minority in these cities, they belong to the wealthy and powerful elites—and therefore feel entitled to all road space (Rizvi and Sclar, 2014). In Delhi, they waged a legal war against the BRT system in order to wrest more driving space (Joshi, 2012). Because the BRT frequency was not high, this gave the impression that numerous cars and motorbikes had to squeeze in a dense space while the dedicated lanes sat unoccupied (Pucher et al., 2005). The recent boom in car-sharing services (i.e., Grab and Uber) has generated more traffic on already hyper-congested urban roads—and therefore drivers feel that their cities do not have the "luxury" to set aside entire corridors for exclusive BRT use.

Even in the cities that still retain their BRTs, local governments have been reluctant to adopt strong policies that curtail private vehicle use. In Hanoi, policies such as capping motorcycle ownership or increasing registration fees were proposed but eventually set aside in view of public uproar about an invasion of citizens' rights and freedoms (Nguyen, 2013). In Bangkok, the government implicitly subsidizes car drivers by heavily investing in road construction, reducing car import duties, and keeping fuel prices artificially low (Wu and Pojani, 2016).

In Lagos, Lima, and Delhi, paratransit operators constituted a major competitor to BRT as well (Mallqui and Pojani, 2017; Mobereola, 2009; Velmurugan et al., 2012). *Molue/danfo* and *micro/combi* operators are particularly powerful in Lagos and Lima, respectively. While they provide a much needed public service, they are also responsible for producing much pollution, congestion, and road danger (Gorham, 2017; Mallqui and Pojani, 2017). Small operators feared that BRT would take away their customers along the most profitable routes; therefore, it was not easy to persuade them to give up operation rights along the proposed BRT lanes (Mobereola, 2009). As a compromise to appease opposition in Lagos, paratransit routes were reorganized but not superseded outright by BRT. Strict restriction of illegal stops by paratransit vehicles was enforced so that traffic could proceed at higher speeds in the lanes running alongside BRT. The advent of BRT acted as a motivator for paratransit operators to improve the quality of their service, in order to remain competitive (Kaenzig et al., 2010).

In Delhi, existing bus operators were opposed to BRT. A compromise had to be reached where conventional buses were allowed to use BRT lanes. With hindsight, this choice was disastrous: the frequent breakdowns of conventional buses obstructed the lanes and produced bunching and long queues

(Hidalgo and Pai, 2010). In Bangkok, conventional buses, which provide low-quality services, continue to be a favorite mode for the impoverished portions of the population that cannot afford BRT fares. While the domestic automotive manufacturers tend to mount an opposition to BRT, in Hanoi they have been supportive because production of virtually the entire BRT fleet (as of the conventional bus fleets) is locally sourced (Nguyen, 2016).

4.4 Public Participation

In Lima and Lagos, the BRT teams were able to garner public support for the projects. Lagos, in particular, conducted an aggressive and sophisticated public relations campaign aimed at instilling a sense of pride and active ownership among riders and appeasing the opposition of taxi drivers and haulage operators (Kaenzig et al., 2010).

The other three case study cities struggled with strong opposition. In Bangkok and Hanoi this was due to meek efforts to obtain public input. One-way communication prevailed here. In Hanoi, much information was treated as confidential, and workshop participation was restricted to experts and public officials while excluding the public. This is consistent with the generally low public participation in planning in Vietnam (Huynh and Gomez-Ibañez, 2017). On the face of it, limited communication with the media and the public helped avoid complaints and criticism. However, it led to stakeholder disengagement and disinformation over the advantages of BRT over rail and conventional buses (PV, 2017). In Bangkok, because the project was not owned by all stakeholders, after implementation the traffic police were uncooperative, turning a blind eye when BRT lanes were encroached by drivers (Sengers, 2016).

Delhi, at first, had a well thought-out awareness-raising scheme—including workshops, blogs, vlogs, and seminars with residents living along the proposed corridor, and even with local pupils. Initially, the media was optimistic and supportive (Kumar et al., 2012). But due to a very protracted planning and implementation process (10 years in total), these taxing participation activities eventually fizzled out.

4.5 Funding and Coordination

Financial barriers have been detrimental in all cases in different ways. The BRT systems of Lima and Hanoi received substantial sums from international agencies, including the Word Bank, whereas Lagos, Bangkok, and Delhi contributed a much larger portion of their own capital funding. Among the case studies, the Lagos BRT-Lite had the lowest delivery cost (Independent Evaluation Group, 2016; Mason-Jones and Cohen, 2012).

Projects that were less dependent on foreign loans, experienced fewer delays during planning and implementation. For example, the World Bank was heavily involved in Hanoi. While its financial assistance was welcome, its strict procedures became a liability. The BRT project was split into packages. The providers of packages were selected via a series of internationally competitive tenders. These were lengthy and drawn out processes, which also resulted in the deterioration of the infrastructure even before inauguration. Part of the "terminal and station package" was completed prematurely, but this infrastructure could not be used (or even maintained) until the "BRT vehicle procurement package" was complete. Notably, in Delhi, due to a shortage of funding, the analysis of car travel demand along the corridor was limited. This component turned out to be crucial as protest over congestion in the car traffic lanes running alongside the BRT lanes undermined the project (The Institute for Transportation and Development Policy [ITDP], 2017). By contrast, Lagos, which relied entirely on its domestic budget, was able to establish its BRT-Lite within 15 months (Kaenzig et al., 2010).

All of the case study cities struggled for compensation funds for landowners along the proposed corridors. The Delhi BRT corridor alignment was largely driven by a need to minimize compensation (Rizvi and Sclar, 2014). In Lima, eminent domain powers were so weak that the public sector ended up paying extortionate land prices to secure space for several stations. Here, the initially proposed BRT corridor was partly realigned so as to run on publicly-owned—but less convenient—land (Mallqui and Pojani, 2017). In Hanoi, to avoid high compensation costs, road medians were used as much as possible, which were on publicly owned land. Also, a former (public) inter-regional coach station was converted to a BRT terminal (World Bank, 2013).

In terms of operations, Hanoi is the only subsidized case study. The local government has concluded that an affordable price is key to attracting and retaining travelers; therefore the fare is set at the same level for BRT and conventional buses (Nguyen et al., 2017; Vu and Ha, 2016). However, this strains the local budget (Nguyen, 2015); consequently, the BRT service cannot be provided at higher frequency although passengers expect this during peak hours. In contrast, Lagos has been able to reduce its BRT fares since inception owing to a high passenger load factor (Mason-Jones and Cohen, 2012).

4.6 Physical Design

As noted, the physical design of the Lima BRT has the highest quality among the case studies. The system is classified as Gold BRT (ITDP, 2017). Lagos' system is classified as BRT-Lite, whereas Delhi's system was a "basic BRT" (ITDP, 2017)—although generally viewed as below accepted standards for BRT (Fjellstrom et al., 2004; Kumar et al., 2012). In Bangkok and Hanoi, the physical designs are of mixed quality and the system sizes are limited.

Critically, in all five cases, buses are air conditioned. Bangkok, Hanoi, and Lima feature platform level boarding and electronic passenger information systems. The BRT fleet in Lima is superior to the others with articulated vehicles using natural gas and complying with the EURO IV standard. Lagos' BRT fleet is less "green" than the other four's.

An inadequate selection of the initial corridor(s) was a common (and major) mistake in Bangkok, Hanoi, and Delhi. To avoid frictions with car drivers, the former two cities routed BRT along low travel-demand corridors. These crossed thinly populated areas and, in Hanoi's case, even expanses of agricultural land. Bangkok's BRT does not reach the main activity hub (Sukhumvit) in the center (Fig. 3). Moreover, it has not taken advantage of the abundant paratransit in the city as feeder services are not well-integrated (ITDP, 2017; Wu and Pojani, 2016). In contrast, Delhi chose to thread its first

Fig. 3 BRT lane on elevated road outside the Bangkok center. *Photo by Dorina Pojani.*

short corridor (less than 6 km) through one of the busiest intersections (Chirang) dominated by cars, which led to major resentment without demonstrating any BRT advantages (Rizvi and Sclar, 2014).

Overall, Lima and Lagos selected much more effective corridors. Throughout its length, Lima's BRT crosses high-density districts. The Lagos BRT connects the CBD on Lagos Island to the mainland, following the main direction of traffic flow. Apart from Lima and Delhi, BRT lanes are not exclusive along the entire the corridor. At narrow bottlenecks along the corridors, BRT lanes convert to mixed traffic. Unfortunately, rail lines in Hanoi and Lima have been planned which will operate in parallel with the BRT routes, thus risking to duplicate services.

A proper trunk-feeder structure, which integrates BRT lines (trunks) with conventional bus lines and paratransit (feeders), exists in Hanoi and Lima, but it is far better designed in the latter (ITDP, 2017; Nguyen, 2016). The Bangkok BRT connects with rail lines at two terminal stations whereas in the now defunct Delhi BRT, the connectivity between the BRT and the metro was rather poor. While in all five systems an effort was made to provide some bicycle parking, cycling levels are low in the respective cities and therefore bicycles do not play a major role as feeder (Hidalgo and Pai, 2010; Velmurugan et al., 2012).

The Hanoi, Delhi, and Bangkok BRTs did not incorporate passing lanes at stations. The BRTs of Lima and Lagos have passing lanes, which allow for regular and express services to be provided thus increasing ridership. However, both systems become overcrowded at peak hours. The Lagos BRT regularly experiences bus bunching and long passenger queues (more than 200 people) at some stops (Kaenzig et al., 2010). In Lima, passenger numbers significantly drop outside the peak resulting in a unsatisfactory overall daily ridership (Independent Evaluation Group, 2015). In terms of fare collection, Lima and Bangkok feature electronic cards and automatic turnstiles. In Hanoi and Lagos, tickets can be purchased before boarding but ticket control is manual (by a conductor), which causes queues during rush hours (Kaenzig et al., 2010).

Most stations are covered in all five case studies. In Bangkok, Hanoi, and Lima they are fully enclosed, consistent with international BRT best practice, whereas Lagos and Delhi only provide shelters—which are not very well maintained in Lagos (Fig. 4). Because all cities but Lima experience very hot weather and torrential rains, sheltered walkways, and stations are important. These are usually not provided, thus discouraging area residents from walking to a BRT station (Wu and Pojani, 2016). In Hanoi and Bangkok,

Fig. 4 Sheltered but unenclosed BRT stop in Lagos. *Photo by Dorina Pojani.*

access to BRT stations is challenging for the elderly and the handicapped. They must climb steep stairs up pedestrian bridges and overpasses or walk long distances from bus stops inconveniently located near signalized intersections to facilitate traffic flow (by taking advantage of the pedestrian phase). In Lima, traffic markers and ramps for the disabled are provided at stations but the gap between the edge of station platforms and bus floors is too wide in some places (Independent Evaluation Group, 2015). The capacity of Hanoi's BRT stations is too low. Because stations are designed to only be compatible with special BRT buses, conventional buses cannot dock at a BRT station. If they run on BRT lanes, conventional buses' constant lane switching to board and alight at curbside stops exacerbates traffic congestion (Fjellstrom, 2017b).

As for fare integration, in Lima, Hanoi, tickets are integrated with the conventional (feeder) buses but not with the rest of the public transport network. Overall, physical, operational, and fare integration with other modes is weak in Lagos, Delhi, and Bangkok. In no case are fares integrated with the (informal) paratransit extensive systems that operate in all cities.

4.7 Image Promotion

Brand identity has been strong in all cities. BRT buses have a distinctive appearance and recognizable logos. Stations are better designed in comparison to conventional bus stations. However, in Delhi's case, BRT lanes were open to other operators as well; an open system weakened brand recognition on part of users (Hook, 2005).

In Bangkok, Delhi, and Hanoi, sluggish and intermittent planning and implementation processes hurt the image of the BRT systems. Aiming for sensation, the media bombarded the projects with negative publicity, which was poorly managed by the local BRT teams. For example, when the system began operation in Delhi, it was referred to in the press as "Big Road Trauma"—a figure of speech that stuck in the public consciousness (Thynell et al., 2010).

In Bangkok, the failed example of an exclusive bus lane in the past was used to plant doubt about the potential of the new BRT corridor. The system was launched in tandem with the beginning of the school year—which is the peak of traffic jams in the city. On inauguration day, some bunching and a few minor accidents caused by poorly trained drivers were also used to undermine the project. The environmental merits of BRT were highlighted in promotional messages but these were not very convincing in a highly polluted city with just a single corridor. Most importantly, the announcement that additional BRT lines which had been planned for years would be canceled led to a complete loss of confidence among the public (Wu and Pojani, 2016).

In Hanoi, poorly executed implementation caused endless inconvenience to city dwellers but also placed them in danger. Moreover, suspicions arouse that BRT costs had been inflated by corrupt officials (VNS, 2017). In combination, these events drew negative media attention and resulted in mounting public protest against BRT. Hostility in conventional and social media tarnished the project image in a major way. The local Department of Transport sought to counter the criticism by highlighting trip reduction times (5–10 min per full trip) afforded by BRT (Vo Hai, 2016). But such a modest reduction was insufficient to appease detractors (Fjellstrom, 2017b). The presence of Miss Vietnam at inauguration and free service during the first month of operation helped build some enthusiasm, but this was short-lived.

BRT promotion was more successful in Lima and Lagos. These two systems appear to be well accepted by the public (Mallqui and Pojani, 2017; Mason-Jones and Cohen, 2012). Lima was in a more advantageous position, being able to capitalize on the positive BRT image in other Latin American cities, such as Bogotá, Curitiba, and Quito. However, the initial momentum was eventually lost. In contrast, the Lagos BRT which is of much lower quality continues to promote its BRT image. A weekly TV program dedicated to BRT provides a public discussion forum (Mobereola, 2009).

5. CONCLUSION

The BRT systems in the case study cities were curtailed due to a combination of reasons. The institutional setup was too complex to coordinate and implement this type of project. Local transportation agencies were cast in past roles and purposes which they were unable and/or unwilling to change. In some cases, the selection of the first corridor was ineffective. While most projects had the support and commitment of a high-level politician or party (at least part of the way), they did not amass the necessary political pull and popular goodwill to push the project forward within a short time before the novelty effect wore off. Partly this owes to feeble promotional and communication efforts targeting potential users and stakeholders, but also to opposition based on political affiliation rather than concern for the city. These outcomes confirm the findings of prior studies on BRT planning and implementation worldwide (Boncompte and Galilea, 2013; Hidalgo and Graftieaux, 2008; Lindau et al., 2014; Mallqui and Pojani, 2017; Wu and Pojani, 2016).

However, the key barriers to BRT are not the same in all cases. Because the BRT concept is multifaceted, the balance of issues varies from place to place depending on context. In a qualitative review such as this, it is impossible to quantify the weight of each factor for comparison purposes. With this qualification in mind, the following set of recommendations is provided which may help BRT planning and implementation to succeed.

- It is crucial that all parties come to own the project and work together toward a common goal. This includes government planners, private transport companies, and traffic enforcement agencies. To avoid "turf wars," a specialized BRT agency could be created, which oversees the planning/implementation process as well as BRT operations later on. In the case of megacities, their size certainly justifies this step. This agency needs to operate based on a long-term vision rather than short term action plans that fit within single political mandates. But even a specialized agency would benefit from political championship. Politicians need to be educated in BRT processes and outcomes and made to understand that a successful project can propel their career.
- The legal framework surrounding public transport and road space use needs to be updated ahead of the planning process so as not to constitute an impediment once BRT planning is under way.

- Specialized skills and approaches to BRT design, planning, and implementation are paramount. If these are lacking in-house, consultants—including international consultants—must be invited to join the team. Funding must be set aside for this purpose but funding bodies must not be allowed to control the process and impose their own agendas.
- BRT planning must move away from single corridors and embrace a network approach. The selection of routes must strike a balance between extending service coverage to areas underserved by public transport and minimizing compensation for landowners. In many cases, it may be cheaper to convert existing (public) road space into BRT corridors than to design new corridors running through privately owned land.
- The BRT network needs to integrate existing public transport, including paratransit. In cities with a substantial amount of informal transit, this is key in reducing opposition to BRT. Other modes, such as cycling, which provide "last mile connectivity" must be integrated, at least at BRT stations by providing secure parking.
- The BRT implementation steps need to be very carefully thought out so as not to prolong the timeline and to minimize any disruptions to urban space. Securing support from the traffic police and the media is crucial, especially in the aftermath of a BRT launch.
- Aggressive PR campaigns must be organized in conjunction with the BRT implementation process, which curate the image of BRT and highlight the similarities between BRT and rail. Purchasing distinctive vehicles which look like trams and unlike existing buses can persuade the public (including the middle-classes) to view BRT as an exciting innovation and a high-status mode rather than just another bus system. Air conditioned stations and vehicles are crucial for attracting passengers in warmer climates.

REFERENCES

Ashmore, D.P., Christie, N., Tyler, N.A., 2017. Symbolic transport choice across national cultures: theoretical considerations for research design. Transp. Plan. Technol. 40, 875–900. https://doi.org/10.1080/03081060.2017.1355882.

Ashmore, D.P., Pojani, D., Thoreau, R., Christie, N., Tyler, N.A., 2018. The symbolism of 'eco cars' across national cultures: potential implications for policy formulation and transfer. Transp. Res. Part D: Transp. Environ. 63, 560–575. https://doi.org/10.1016/j.trd.2018.06.024.

Boncompte, J., Galilea, P., 2013. Identification of key factors in the design and implementation of BRT systems in developing countries. In: Presented at the 13th World Conference on Transport Research, Rio de Janeiro, Brazil.

Carrigan, A., King, R., Velasquez, J.M., Raifman, M., Duduta, N., 2013. Social, Environmental and Economic Impacts of BRT Systems: Bus Rapid Transit Case Studies From Around the World. EMBARQ.

Deng, T., Nelson, J.D., 2011. Recent developments in bus rapid transit: a review of the literature. Transp. Rev. 31, 69–96. https://doi.org/10.1080/01441647.2010.492455.

Far East BRT Data, 2017. http://data.fareastbrt.com.

Fjellstrom, K., 2017a. BRT project risks. In: What Could Go Wrong? Far East BRT. https://www.fareastbrt.com/en/brt/risks.

Fjellstrom, K., 2017b. World Bank's First BRT in Asia Is Designed to Fail. Far East BRT. http://www.fareastbrt.com/en/feature/hnbrtjan17.

Fjellstrom, K., Diaz, O.E., Gauthier, A., 2004. BRT's great leap forward. Inst. Transp. Dev. Policy ITDP, Sustain. Transport. 24–28.

Flores-Dewey, O., 2012. Expanding Transportation Planning Capacity in Cities of the Global South: Public–Private Collaboration and Conflict in Chile and Mexico. Massachusetts Institute of Technology, Dept. of Urban Studies and Planning, Boston, MA, USA.

Flores-Dewey, O., Zegras, C., 2012. The costs of inclusion: incorporating existing bus operators into Mexico city's emerging bus rapid transit system. In: Presented at the 12th Conference on Advanced Systems for Public Transport, Santiago, Chile.

General Statistics Office, 2017. Statistical Yearbook of Vietnam. Statistical Publishing House, Vietnam.

Gilbert, A., 2008. Bus rapid transit: is Transmilenio a miracle cure? Transp. Rev. 28, 439–467. https://doi.org/10.1080/01441640701785733.

Global BRT Data, 2017. https://brtdata.org/.

Gorham, R., 2017. Nigeria. In: Pojani, D., Stead, D. (Eds.), The Urban Transport Crisis in Emerging Economies. Springer International Publishing, Cham, pp. 173–195. https://doi.org/10.1007/978-3-319-43851-1_9.

Vo Hai, 2016. Sở Giao thông Hà Nội: "Xe buýt nhanh hơn buýt thường 5-10 phút" [Department of Hanoi Transport: "BRT is from 5 to 10 minutes faster than conventional buses"]. vnexpress.net. https://vnexpress.net/tin-tuc/thoi-su/giao-thong/so-giao-thong-ha-noi-xe-buy-t-nhanh-hon-buyt-thuong-5-10-phut-3515921.html

Hanoi Urban Transport Project Management Unit, n.d. Vietnam—Hanoi Urban Transport Development Project: P083581—Implementation Status Results Report (From 2010 to 2016) (Implementation Status and Results Report no. from 4 to 16). World Bank, Hanoi, Vietnam.

Harvey, D., 2007. Neoliberalism as creative destruction. Ann. Am. Acad. Pol. Soc. Sci. 610, 21–44. https://doi.org/10.1177/0002716206296780.

Hensher, D.A., Golob, T.F., 2008. Bus rapid transit systems: a comparative assessment. Transportation 35, 501–518. https://doi.org/10.1007/s11116-008-9163-y.

Hidalgo, D., 2017. Bus rapid transit: end of a love affair in Latin America and South Asia? No, moving to a serious and long lasting relationship. In: Presented at the International Conference Series on Competition and Ownership in Land Passenger Transport—Thredbo 15, Stockholm, Sweden.

Hidalgo, D., Graftieaux, P., 2008. Bus rapid transit systems in Latin America and Asia: results and difficulties in 11 cities. Transp. Res. Rec. J. Transp. Res. Board 2072, 77–88. https://doi.org/10.3141/2072-09.

Hidalgo, D., Gutiérrez, L., 2013. BRT and BHLS around the world: explosive growth, large positive impacts and many issues outstanding. Res. Transp. Econ. 39, 8–13. THREDBO 12: recent developments in the reform of land passenger transport. https://doi.org/10.1016/j.retrec.2012.05.018.

Hidalgo, D., Pai, M., 2010. Evaluation of the Delhi bus corridor: lessons learnt and recommendations for improvement. In: Presented at the 12th World Conference on Transport Research, Lisbon, Portugal.

Xuân Hinh, 2017. Thí điểm cho xe buýt thường đi vào làn buýt nhanh [proposing a pilot test of sharing the bus rapid transit lanes with conventional buses]. Petrotimes.Vn. http://petrotimes.vn/thi-diem-cho-xe-buyt-thuong-di-vao-lan-buyt-nhanh-494496.html.

Hook, W., 2005. Institutional and regulatory options for bus rapid transit in developing countries: lessons from international experience. Transp. Res. Rec. J. Transp. Res. Board 1939, 184–191. https://doi.org/10.3141/1939-21.

D. Hung, 2018. Hà Nội khẳng định không cho xe buýt thường đi vào làn BRT [Hanoi confirms conventional buses are not allowed to run on the BRT lanes]. vov.vn. https://vov.vn/xa-hoi/ha-noi-khang-dinh-khong-cho-xe-buyt-thuong-di-vao-lan-brt-736594.vov.

Huynh, D.T., Gomez-Ibañez, J., 2017. Vietnam. In: Pojani, D., Stead, D. (Eds.), The Urban Transport Crisis in Emerging Economies. Springer International Publishing, Cham, pp. 267–282. https://doi.org/10.1007/978-3-319-43851-1_13.

Independent Evaluation Group, 2015. Republic of Peru: Lima Transport Project (Project Performance Assessment Report no. 102352). World Bank, Washington, DC.

Independent Evaluation Group, 2016. Nigeria: Lagos Urban Transport Project (Project Performance Assessment Report no. 103068). World Bank, Washington, DC.

Jessop, B., 2002. Liberalism, neoliberalism, and urban governance: a state-theoretical perspective. Antipode 34, 452–472. https://doi.org/10.1111/1467-8330.00250.

Joshi, R., 2012. Delhi Row Over Bus Lane Reveals Class Divide. (BBC News).

Kaenzig, R., Mobereola, D., Brader, C., 2010. Africa's first bus rapid transit system. Transp. Res. Rec. J. Transp. Res. Board 2193, 1–8. https://doi.org/10.3141/2193-01.

Kathuria, A., Parida, M., Sekhar, C.R., Sharma, A., 2016. A review of bus rapid transit implementation in India. Cogent Eng. 3, 1241168. https://doi.org/10.1080/23311916.2016.1241168.

Khanh Nguyen, 2016. Vì sao dự án bus nhanh Hà Nội chậm tiến độ [Why have the bus rapid transit project in Hanoi been behind schedule]. vtv.vn. http://vtv.vn/trong-nuoc/vi-sao-du-an-bus-nhanh-ha-noi-cham-tien-do-20161220155343838.htm.

Kühn, F., 2002. Bus rapid or light rail transit for intermediate cities? In: Urban Mobility For All: La Mobilité Urbaine pour TousFrance.

Kumar, A., Zimmerman, S., Agarwal, O.P., 2012. International Experience in Bus Rapid Transit Implementation: Synthesis of Lessons Learned from Lagos, Johannesburg, Jakarta, Delhi, and Ahmedabad. World Bank.

Levinson, H., Zimmerman, S., Clinger, J., Rutherford, S., Smith, R., Cracknell, J., Soberman, R., 2003. TCRP Report 90: Bus Rapid Transit, Volume 1: Case Studies in Bus Rapid Transit. Transportation Research Board, Washington, DC. https://doi.org/10.17226/24726.

Lindau, L.A., Hidalgo, D., de Almeida Lobo, A., 2014. Barriers to planning and implementing bus rapid transit systems. Res. Transp. Econ. 48, 9–15. competition and ownership in land passenger transport (selected papers from the Thredbo 13 conference). https://doi.org/10.1016/j.retrec.2014.09.026.

Mallqui, Y.Y.C., Pojani, D., 2017. Barriers to successful bus rapid transit expansion: developed cities versus developing megacities. Case Stud. Transp. Policy. https://doi.org/10.1016/j.cstp.2017.01.004

Marsden, G., Stead, D., 2011. Policy transfer and learning in the field of transport: a review of concepts and evidence. Transp. Policy 18, 492–500. https://doi.org/10.1016/j.tranpol.2010.10.007.

Mason-Jones, K., Cohen, B., 2012. Low Carbon Frameworks: Transport—Lagos BRT-Lite.

Mobereola, D., 2009. Africa's first bus rapid transit scheme: the Lagos BRT-lite system (no. discussion paper no. 9), urban transport series. Sub-Saharan Africa transport policy program (SSATP), Lagos.

Muñoz, J.C., Gschwender, A., 2008. Transantiago: a tale of two cities. Res. Transp. Econ. 22, 45–53. https://doi.org/10.1016/j.retrec.2008.05.010.

Muñoz, J.C., Hidalgo, D., 2013. Workshop 2: bus rapid transit as part of enhanced service provision. Res. Transp. Econ. 39, 104–107. https://doi.org/10.1016/j.retrec.2012.06.001.

Muñoz, J.C., Paget-Seekins, L. (Eds.), 2016. Restructuring Public Transport through Bus Rapid Transit: An International and Interdisciplinary Perspective. Policy Press, Bristol Chicago, IL.

Nair, C., 2017. The West can't Fix the Climate Crisis. Asia will have to do it. Theguardian. com.

Nguyen, M.H., 2013. Research on the servqual model for the analysis and evaluation of the taxi service of taxi group. Sci. J. Transp. Univ. Transp. Commun. Special volume 10/2013.

Nguyen, T.C., 2015. Revenue management solution for Hanoi public transport firms. J. Transp. Minist. Transp. 07/2015, 76–78.

Nguyen, T.C., 2016. Quality improvement and bus system development in Hanoi vision to 2025.

Nguyen, M.H., Ha, T.T., Le, T.L., Nguyen, T.C., 2017. In: Challenges to development of bus system evidence from a comparative analysis of surveys in Hanoi. Transportation for a Better Life: Mobility and Road Safety Managements. Presented at the Atrans Annual Conference, Bangkok, Thailand, pp. 1–10.

Nielsen, G., Nelson, J.D., Mulley, C., Tegnér, G., Lind, G., Lange, T., 2005. HiTrans Best Practice Guide: Public Transport—Planning the Networks (Civitas).

Pojani, D., 2014. Bus rapid transit, design and engineering of, in: Encyclopedia of Transportation: Social Science and Policy. SAGE Publications, Inc., 2455 teller road, Thousand Oaks, CA, USA. https://doi.org/10.4135/9781483346526.n119.

Pojani, E., Van Acker, V., Pojani, D., 2018. Cars as a status symbol: youth attitudes toward sustainable transport in a post-socialist city. Transport. Res. Part F: Traffic Psychol. Behav. 58, 210–227. https://doi.org/10.1016/j.trf.2018.06.003.

Pucher, J., Korattyswaropam, N., Mittal, N., Ittyerah, N., 2005. Urban transport crisis in India. Transp. Policy 12, 185–198. https://doi.org/10.1016/j.tranpol.2005.02.008.

PV, 2017. Xe buýt nhanh BRT: Đầu tư nghìn tỉ không hiệu quả, ai chịu trách nhiệm? [BRT: Huge Investment Is Not Effective, Who Is Responsible for the Waste?]. laodong.vn. https://laodong.vn/thoi-su/xe-buyt-nhanh-brt-dau-tu-nghin-ti-khong-hieu-qua-ai-chiu-trach-nhiem-661441.bld.

Rizvi, A., Sclar, E., 2014. Implementing bus rapid transit: a tale of two Indian cities. Res. Transp. Econ. 48, 194–204. Competition and Ownership in Land Passenger Transport (Selected Papers From the Thredbo 13 Conference). https://doi.org/10.1016/j.retrec.2014.09.043.

Sengers, F.-H., 2016. Transforming Transport in Thailand: Experimenting for Transitions in Sustainable Urban Mobility. Technische Universiteit Eindhoven, Eindhoven.

Stead, D., Pojani, D., 2017. The urban transport crisis in emerging economies: a comparative overview. In: Pojani, D., Stead, D. (Eds.), The Urban Transport Crisis in Emerging Economies. Springer International Publishing, Cham, pp. 283–295. https://doi.org/10.1007/978-3-319-43851-1_14.

The Institute for Transportation and Development Policy [ITDP], 2006. Position Paper on the Delhi High Court Decision to Ban Cycle Rickshaws on Old Delhi Roads. https://www.itdp.org/position-paper-on-the-delhi-high-court-decision-to-ban-cycle-rickshaws-on-old-delhi-roads/.

The Institute for Transportation and Development Policy [ITDP], 2016. Bus Rapid Transit Standard. ITDP, New York, NY, USA.

The Institute for Transportation and Development Policy [ITDP], 2017. BRT Planning Guide—4th Edition. ITDP. https://brtguide.itdp.org/.

Thynell, M., Mohan, D., Tiwari, G., 2010. Sustainable transport and the modernisation of urban transport in Delhi and Stockholm. Cities 27, 421–429. https://doi.org/10.1016/j.cities.2010.04.002.

Velmurugan, S., Ravinder, K., Madhu, E., Nataraju, J., Sekhar, C.R., Kumar, P.V.P., Kumar, R., Umat, S.K., 2012. Evaluating Bus Rapid Transit (BRT) Corridor Performance from Ambedkar Nagar to Moolchand, Delhi (no. Final Report). Delhi, Central Road Research Institute.

VNS, 2017. Hanoi's BRT Bus Prices Reported Wrongly. english.vietnamnet.vn. http://english.vietnamnet.vn/fms/society/174359/hanoi-s-brt-bus-prices-reported-wrongly.html.

Vu, H.T., Ha, T.T., 2016. Developing public transport systems—experience from practical activities of Hanoi bus system. J. Transp. Minist. Transp. 11/2016, 80–83.

Wirasinghe, S.C., Kattan, L., Rahman, M.M., Hubbell, J., Thilakaratne, R., Anowar, S., 2013. Bus rapid transit—a review. Int. J. Urban Sci. 17, 1–31. https://doi.org/10.1080/12265934.2013.777514.

World Bank, 2007. Strategic Urban Transport Policy Directions for Bangkok (the Urban Transport Development Partnership). World Bank.

World Bank, 2013. Integrated Safeguards Datasheet Appraisal Stage (Updated for Restructuring Project).

Wright, L., Hook, W., 2007. Bus Rapid Transit Planning Guide. Institute for Transportation and Development Policy, New York.

Wu, I., Pojani, D., 2016. Obstacles to the creation of successful bus rapid transit systems: the case of Bangkok. Res. Transp. Econ. Transport. Land Dev. A Global View 60, 44–53. https://doi.org/10.1016/j.retrec.2016.05.001.

CHAPTER THREE

Assessing Safety Implications of Bus Priority Systems: A Case-Study of a New BRT System in the Haifa Metropolitan Area

Victoria Gitelman[1], Roby Carmel, Anna Korchatov
Transportation Research Institute, Technion City, Haifa, Israel
[1]Corresponding author: e-mail address: trivica@technion.ac.il

Contents

Abstract

Bus priority systems promote public transport use in urban areas whereas knowledge on their safety implications is as yet insufficient. This study explored safety impacts of a new bus rapid transit (BRT) system that was introduced in the Haifa metropolitan area, Israel, in August 2013. The study examined accident changes on roads with the BRT routes, relative to comparison sites, and safety performance of streets with various BRT configurations, during the first 2 years of the BRT operation. In spite of concerns related to the complexity of BRT settings and high traffic volumes, the BRT operation did not lead to a

Advances in Transport Policy and Planning, Volume 1
ISSN 2543-0009
https://doi.org/10.1016/bs.atpp.2018.07.008

worsening in road safety, while decreasing trends were observed in some accident types and high shares of severe or pedestrian accidents did not appear. Such results were judged as successful and supporting the appropriateness of the design solutions adopted in the BRT system. The findings did not indicate significant differences in safety performance of streets with various BRT configurations, thus, leaving space for continued use of various forms. The major safety problem is seen in pedestrian accidents at BRT junctions, for which new engineering solutions are needed. More safety evaluation studies are required to support evidence-based decisions in planning BRT routes.

Keywords: Bus rapid transit, Safety performance, Monitoring, Bus route configurations, Planning, Design solutions, Pedestrian accidents

1. INTRODUCTION

Recent trends in urban mobility indicate a growing use of public transport as a mobility mode. A study conducted by the International Association of Public Transport collected data for 60 metropolitan areas worldwide and found an evolution in urban mobility patterns over the last decade, indicating a growth in the modal share of public transport (together with other sustainable modes, walking and cycling) (UITP, 2015). Urban mobility choices are strongly linked to density, while in more densely populated areas there is a higher propensity to travel by public transport. The UITP report showed that the rate of motorization (the number of cars per 1000 inhabitants) has slowed down in developed cities, from an annual average increase of 2.3% before 2001 to 0.5% in the period between 2001 and 2012. In parallel, the total number of journeys by public transport has steadily increased: at a rate of 1.5% per year before 2001 and 1.6% afterwards, in developed cities, and at a rate of 2.7%, in developing cities.

Public transport priority systems are becoming an attractive solution to improve mobility and promote public transport use in big cities, throughout the world (Hidalgo and Carrigan, 2010; ITDP, 2007; Panera et al., 2012). The idea of such systems appeared with the development of bus rapid transit (BRT), originally in South-American countries. Among the most famous BRT systems can be mentioned, for example, the bus system in the city of Curitiba in Brazil, which was introduced more than 40 years ago, and the Transmilenio system operating in Bogota, Columbia, that serves about 40,000 passengers per hour. Currently, various forms of public transport priority systems, including BRT, can also be seen in India, Mexico, Turkey, Australia, USA and European countries such as Finland, France, the

Netherlands, Spain, Sweden, United Kingdom (Duduta et al., 2012a; ITDP, 2007; Levinson, 2003; Panera et al., 2012).

The forms of bus priority systems include bus priority lanes, bus routes (or corridors) and BRT. A bus route is a special facility designed for public transport only, separated, usually physically, from the general traffic lanes, so that it is maintained exclusively for public transport vehicles enabling them to run at undisturbed travel speeds (ITDP, 2007). The bus priority lane is a more general notion as such lanes may have various locations across the road layout, e.g., curbside, median-side, counter-flow, etc., and apply various traffic management strategies, e.g., full-time or part-time. They do not have a strong physical separation from other traffic but, nevertheless, are intended for exclusive running of buses (in the dedicated hours) and may include signal priority settings at intersections. A BRT system is considered as an integrated system, which combines infrastructure facilities of exclusive bus running ways with elements of an intelligent management system and services (Levinson et al., 2003). Beside a physical segregation of bus lanes and stops, a BRT system typically includes additional features such as centralized operation control, off-board fare collection, level boarding and others, which are aimed at increasing operating speeds and service reliability (Duduta et al., 2015).

Regardless of their form, there has been extensive evidence that bus priority systems bring about improved passenger travel time, reliability and attractiveness of public transport (Duduta et al., 2014; Goh et al., 2014; Tse et al., 2014) and, thus, provide obvious transportation and environmental benefits. As these systems have gained in popularity, various studies and planning guides have appeared, documenting best practices (Gardner et al., 2009; ITDP, 2007; Levinson et al., 2003) and illustrating different design options and their impacts on the operational performance of the systems (Hidalgo and Carrigan, 2010; Panera et al., 2012). At the same time, less research has been dedicated to the study of road safety implications of bus priority systems (Duduta et al., 2012b; Goh et al., 2014; Vecino-Ortiz and Hyder, 2015), while available evidence on the safety impacts of such systems, in general, and of specific design solutions, in particular, is sparse and, sometimes, contradictory.

International findings show that the safety level of bus routes depends on the system's characteristics and on the characteristics of the streets where they are implemented. Evaluation examples, mostly, from South-American countries and Australia, demonstrated a positive impact of BRT implementation on the safety level of urban roads involved (Duduta et al., 2014, 2015).

However, in some cases, such as Belo Horizonte in Brazil and Delhi in India, the BRT operation was associated with an increase in the number of road accidents, whereas, in general, pedestrian injury is reported as one of major safety problems in BRT operation (Bocarejo et al., 2012; Duduta et al., 2012b, 2014).

In this paper, we present a case-study which examined safety implications of a new BRT system that was recently introduced in the Haifa metropolitan area, Israel. The study purposes were to two-fold. First, the study intended to examine accident changes associated with the introduction of the BRT routes on urban roads and, hence, to conclude on the BRT safety implications, in general. Second, the study aimed to compare the safety performance of streets with different BRT settings and, thus, if possible, to contribute to the knowledge on safety impacts of various design solutions. In the local context, the examination of the BRT safety impacts was essential for its maintenance and further extension. In addition, safety lessons learnt from the Haifa BRT system might be useful for selecting engineering solutions while planning other bus priority systems, in the country and, possibly, abroad.

The paper is structured as follows. Section 2 provides a summary of the current knowledge on safety impacts of bus priority systems based on a literature review. Section 3 describes the local context of the case-study: bus priority systems' policy related developments in Israel and the new BRT system that was established in Haifa. Section 4 describes the case-study methods and data. Section 5 shows the evaluation results. Section 6 provides a general discussion on the study findings and their practical implications as well as on future research needs to enhance the knowledge on safer design of bus priority systems.

2. CURRENT KNOWLEDGE ON SAFETY IMPACTS OF BUS PRIORITY SYSTEMS

As mentioned previously, empirical findings on safety impacts of bus priority lanes and BRT are not yet frequent (Goh et al., 2014; Vecino-Ortiz and Hyder, 2015). The majority of available evidence, with respective design recommendations, was summarized in the report prepared by EMBARQ, World Resources Institute—Duduta et al. (2014).

Goh et al. (2014) developed models for predicting bus accidents on road segments with bus service routes, in Metropolitan Melbourne, Australia—the "Smart-Bus" BRT system introduced in 2006. The study explored the incident database of a large bus company, with 1099 accidents over a 3-year period which occurred on 297 road segments of bus service routes; some of the segments had bus priority lanes and others not. Goh et al. found that accident numbers increase with higher vehicle traffic, bus service frequency and bus stop density, whereas segments with bus priority lanes were associated with a lower accident frequency relative to those without dedicated bus lanes. This result was consistent with a previous study (Goh et al., 2013), which examined police-reported accidents and found that the implementation of bus priority lanes in Melbourne resulted in a 14% reduction in accidents on streets where the BRT operated.

Tse et al. (2014) examined the safety impacts of bus-lane operation in Hong Kong, using before–after comparisons. The study considered seven sections of exclusive curbside bus lanes, which operated during selected hours. On road sections equipped with bus lanes, Tse et al. found decreasing trends in public bus accidents, of various severity levels (a mean change of 17–21%), but increasing trends in other vehicle accidents (a mean change of 5–20%). Most results were not statistically significant but indicated that only buses had benefited in terms of road safety from the bus-lane operation.

Bocarejo et al. (2012) examined road safety implications of implementation of the Transmilenio BRT system in Bogota, Colombia, between 1998 and 2008. They found that the BRT implementation was associated with an overall reduction in injury accidents along the BRT corridors: 60% reduction at the Caracas corridor and 48% reduction at the Norte-Quito-Sur corridor, compared with an average reduction in the city of Bogota (39%), yet, an increase in accidents was observed around some areas of the second corridor. In addition, an increase in accidents in the vicinity of stations was reported, apparently related to the higher flow of pedestrians around the stations.

Duduta et al. (2014, 2015) re-examined the experience of the introduction of BRT systems in Guadalajara (Mexico), Bogota (Columbia), and Ahmedabad (India), and reported substantial reductions in fatal, injury and all accidents, in the ranges of 48–55%, 21–69%, and 32–38%, respectively. The positive safety effects of the BRT remained in place when simultaneous accident reduction trends in the rest of the city were controlled for. In all cases, a median BRT configuration was operated, with one or two bus lanes per a direction. It should be noted that in the developing countries a BRT system typically replaced an old bus system introducing better separation between bus traffic and other road users, and providing a better bus operation. The implementation of a new transit system was typically accompanied by an overall improvement in the infrastructure, with better traffic control and road settings, all of which might also contribute to the improved safety records (Duduta et al., 2015). The difference in the magnitude of impacts evaluated in various cities can be attributed to differences in traffic conditions, the overall street layouts and intersection geometry across the various systems.

The accident data from BRT systems in South-American countries and India showed (Duduta et al., 2012b) that over 90% of accidents occurred outside the dedicated bus lanes and did not involve buses. Hence, the overall safety of bus systems is a matter of infrastructure design solutions and interaction with general vehicle traffic. Pedestrians represented only 7% of the total accidents but over half of the fatalities in the bus corridors (Duduta et al., 2012b, 2014). Among typical risky behaviors leading to accidents were: illegal mid-block crossings by pedestrians, walking in bus lanes, making a shortcut through traffic lanes from/to a bus stop on the median, and running a red light. Preventing pedestrian injury is stated as a primary issue in designing bus priority systems (Duduta et al., 2014, 2015).

Additional findings in the literature concern the impacts of BRT design features. The main forms of the bus system configurations, as opposed to conventional mixed traffic, are: center-lane (or median) bus-way, curbside bus lane and counter-flow bus lane. Duduta et al. (2012b) adjusted explanatory models for vehicle collisions and pedestrian accidents in the BRT systems in Mexico City, Porto Alegre (Brazil) and Guadalajara, to evaluate the impacts of various design characteristics. The results showed consistently that center-lane configurations had safety benefits compared to curbside systems, while counter-flow bus lanes were associated with the highest accident rates for both vehicles and pedestrians. Additional model findings showed that a higher number of legs at the intersection, a higher number of lanes for general traffic and presence of left turns for general traffic at junctions were correlated with higher accident numbers on the bus corridors. Thus, removing traffic lanes, converting four-way junctions into T-junctions and prohibiting left turns are suggested for improving safety in the BRT systems (Duduta et al., 2014). Similarly, based on the evaluation results, introducing a central median in the bus corridor and shortening pedestrian crosswalks are suggested for reducing crashes in bus priority systems (Duduta et al., 2014).

Nevertheless, knowledge of the safety impacts of particular design solutions is not sufficient. For example, in Israel, the common configuration of a bus route is a bus corridor situated in the center of an urban arterial, which is physically separated from other vehicle lanes and, typically, fenced, and includes signalized intersections only. All these features are in line with the international recommendations. However, evaluations showed that signalized intersections with bus corridors are characterized by higher numbers of total, severe and pedestrian accidents, relative to comparison sites without bus corridors, when controlling for other road characteristics (Gitelman et al., 2018). In other words, the presence of bus priority routes is associated with higher accident risks at urban intersections and does not improve safety. Another local study indicated that intersections with physically separated bus corridors (the form mostly advocated in the literature) are associated with higher accident rates compared to intersections with other bus route configurations: center and curbside bus lanes (Gitelman et al., 2015). The higher accident frequency can be explained by the higher complexity of traffic arrangements on streets with bus routes as opposed to regular urban arterials. Clearly, further research is needed to provide a better understanding of the relationships between the design characteristics of bus routes and accident occurrences. In this context, monitoring safety implications of a new BRT system can provide new insights into such relationships.

3. THE LOCAL CONTEXT OF THE STUDY

3.1 Bus Priority Policy Related Developments in Israel

In Israel, the development of public transport routes for buses is one of the main policies promoted today by the Ministry of Transport. The planning and implementation of bus priority lanes and routes in Israel began in the 1980s of the last century. Currently, certain bus priority systems are available in the metropolitan areas of major cities, i.e., Tel-Aviv, Jerusalem and Haifa. In the coming years, a rapid development of public transportation is expected in many cities of the country, including the planning and construction of hundreds of bus route kilometers. Hence, great importance is assigned today to the examination of planning and safety issues of such systems.

Summaries of international experience provide recommendations for integrating safety into the design and operation of bus routes (Duduta et al., 2014; Guide, 2016; Panera et al., 2012; TCRP, 2007). The guidelines typically emphasize the need for a physical separation of the bus lanes, highlighting them through a different aggregate color, fencing BRT street segments when applicable, and providing signalized intersections only, in order to reduce the interactions between buses and other vehicles and to prevent uncontrolled pedestrian crossings along the bus routes. Over the last 2 decades, in Israel, substantial efforts were undertaken in adopting the international recommendations for infrastructure design solutions applied on the new bus routes.

For example, a preferable bus route configuration on an urban road in Israel was a bus lane or corridor situated in the median of a dual-carriageway urban arterial, where on both sides of the bus route there are lanes of other motor vehicles. The bus route is physically separated from other vehicle lanes and, typically, fenced, thus reducing the interactions between buses and other vehicles and, also, preventing uncontrolled pedestrians crossings on the road segments. The bus stops are always adjacent to junctions, while mid-block pedestrian crossings along the bus corridors are typically avoided. In addition, all intersections and pedestrian crossings along the route are signalized, to prevent dangerous situations by means of time separation between different movements. Fig. 1 presents an example of pedestrian crossings at a signalized junction on a median bus corridor of an urban arterial in Israel. Such infrastructure design solutions are in line with the best practice safety-related recommendations of recent guidelines (Duduta et al., 2012a, 2014; ITDP, 2007; TCRP, 2007). However, despite the above efforts to prevent risky situations, the introduction of bus routes, in some cases, was associated with an increase in accidents, especially those involving pedestrians.

In particular, in 2013, a Ministerial commission was assigned to investigate the reasons for severe pedestrian accidents that occurred on a bus route situated on an arterial road (Jabotinsky road) of the city of Petah Tiqwa (MOT, 2013). The majority of pedestrian accidents, on this route, were concentrated at signalized intersections. Two phenomena were reported as contributing to creating high-risk situations at such sites: pedestrians

Fig. 1 Pedestrian crossings at a signalized intersection on a median bus corridor of an urban arterial in Israel. Location: Jabotinsky road, in Petah Tiqwa.

who cross on red lights and a higher-than-usual number of carriageways to be crossed by pedestrians. The latter implies a so-called "three-route effect," when pedestrians are expected to change the traditional rules of checking the direction of approaching traffic, i.e., they have to look left on the first route of general traffic and then to look left again while crossing the bus route, instead of looking right as in a regular crossing (see Fig. 1). However, a design solution to prevent pedestrian accident occurrences was not found.

3.2 The New BRT System in Haifa

Being aware of local and international developments, safety issues were of primary importance while a new BRT system was established in the Haifa metropolitan area, in Israel. The BRT system, called "Matronit," was built during 2006–13 and began its operation in August 2013. This system includes lanes and routes with priority and exclusive running for articulated buses (Fig. 2). In addition to segregated bus lanes and stops, the Haifa BRT system also includes centralized operation control, off-board fare collection and level boarding, which typify BRT (Duduta et al., 2015) and enable higher operating speeds and service reliability. Currently, the BRT system serves 90,000 passengers daily.

The BRT network includes three bus lines that connect the city of Haifa (with a population of over 250,000) and five satellite cities (over 200,000 inhabitants in total) (Fig. 3). It is over 40 km long, more than half of which belong to the city of Haifa. The infrastructure design solutions applied in the

Fig. 2 The BRT bus in Haifa.

Cities: 1 – Haifa, 2 – Qiryat Haim, 3 – Qiryat Yam, 4 – Qiryat Motzkin, 5 – Qiryat Bialik, 6 – Qiryat Atta.

Fig. 3 An overview of BRT routes in Haifa metropolitan area.

Haifa BRT system generally followed the recommendations of recent international guidelines, such as: bus lanes segregated by curbs and marked by a red aggregate color; median separation between travel directions on heavily-traveled road sections; fencing street segments when applicable; use of signalized intersections and pedestrian crossings. Examples of such arrangements are given in Fig. 4. At the same time, various configurations of the bus routes were set stemming from the hierarchy of streets in the existing urban network.

4. THE STUDY'S DATA AND METHODS

This study monitored the first 2-years of safety performance of the new BRT system based on road accident data collected for the city of Haifa. The main purposes of the study were to examine accident changes associated with the introduction of BRT routes on the urban roads and to compare the safety performance of streets with various BRT arrangements.

An example of a bus stop area: red aggregate color of bus lanes, median separation between travel direction, pedestrian fencing

An example of a road segment: a bus lane segregated by a curb, with red aggregate color; raised median between travel directions

An example of pedestrian crossings adjacent to a bus stop: signal control only; pedestrian fencing; raised medians between travel routes

Fig. 4 Examples of infrastructure design solutions applied in Haifa BRT system.

4.1 The Haifa BRT Configurations

The Haifa BRT system includes a variety of bus route configurations. For the study examinations, the BRT road sections were subdivided into homogeneous groups, accounting for the road layout, traffic and urban surrounding characteristics, such as:

– the placement of bus lanes in the road layout (a right or left lane in the carriageway, or a separate center bus corridor);

- the number of lanes for general vehicle traffic, in addition to BRT lanes;
- travel directions (one- or two-way directions for BRT and other traffic);
- type of urban area (built environment, non-built area, industrial zone, city center).

In addition, we considered the level of pedestrian activity (none, low, high), junction density (the average distance between junctions below or over 400 m), and exclusive versus combined use of BRT lanes by BRT and other buses. Five groups of bus route configurations were defined, of which four are homogeneous groups and the fifth ("others") includes the rest of the segments that did not fit the previous groups. The Haifa BRT configurations are:

(1) *Center-lane bus-way near two lanes for general traffic*—two-way BRT traffic on both sides of a built median, on a dual-carriageway arterial or collector road. The bus lane on segments is a left lane in each carriageway, for an exclusive running of BRT buses (yet, on some segments, the use by regular buses is permitted), segregated by a low curb and having a red aggregate color, where in the areas of bus stops (near junctions) it becomes a wall-separated bus route. About two-third of the length of this configuration has high junction density and runs through a built environment.

(2) *Center-lane bus-way near one lane for general traffic*—similar to the previous but situated on collector roads, with one lane for vehicle traffic per direction. Most segments of this configuration have high junction density and are situated in a built environment.

(3) *Curbside bus lane*—two-way BRT traffic on right-side lanes, on a dual-carriageway arterial or collector road, with two left lanes for general traffic, in each travel direction. The bus lane is indicated by yellow marking and a red aggregate color and is intended for running of BRT and other buses. Most segments have high junction density and are situated in non-built areas.

(4) *Counter-flow bus lane*—one-way BRT traffic running against one lane of opposite-direction vehicle traffic. The bus lane is separated by a marked median, has a red aggregate color and is intended for running of BRT and other buses. All the segments belong to the city center, with high pedestrian activity and high junction density. To prevent severe pedestrian injury, on such streets, the BRT bus speeds were limited to 30 km/h. On other roads, the speed limits of 50 and 70 km/h remained in place for the BRT, similar to the general traffic.

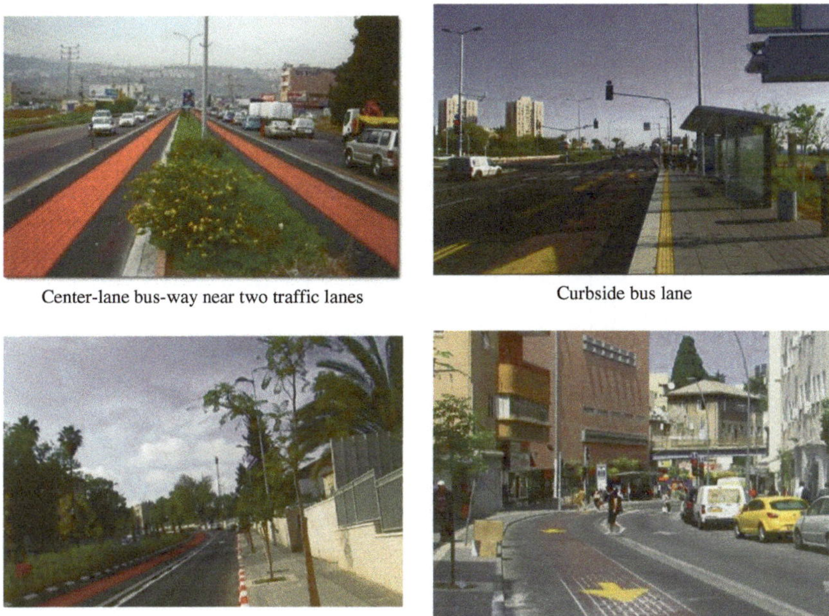

Center-lane bus-way near two traffic lanes

Curbside bus lane

Center-lane bus-way near one traffic lane

Counter-flow bus lane

Fig. 5 Main bus lane configurations in Haifa BRT system.

(5) *Others*—includes, mostly, one-way road segments, with left or right bus lanes near 1–2 lanes of general traffic, and physically separated bus routes. These segments belong mostly to an industrial zone and non-built areas, about half of them with low junction density.

Fig. 5 shows examples of bus lane settings in the Haifa BRT system. Table 1 summarizes the numbers and lengths of the BRT road sections according to the groups, with an indication of those belonging to the city of Haifa.

4.2 Accident Data

For each BRT site, detailed information on the period of construction (between 2006 and 2013) was collected, and then "before" and "after" periods were defined. The "after" period of 24 months, from August 2013 till July 2015, was considered for all BRT sites, whereas the "before" period moved depending on actual roadworks but typically comprised 3 years. The accident data were extracted from the Haifa municipality accident database, which is a refined data source compared to the national accident files, due to additional verifications versus the

Table 1 BRT Road Sections by Bus-Lane Configuration Groups, With the Total Number of Accidents Observed, During 24 Months of BRT Operation and in the Before Periods, in Haifa City

				Accidents on Road Sections, in Haifa				Accidents at Junctions, in Haifa			
Group by Bus Route Configuration	**No. of Road Sections (of Which in Haifa)**	**Total Length (km) (of Which in Haifa)**	**Period[a]**	**Total Injury**	**Severe**	**With Pedestrians**	**With Buses**	**Total Injury**	**Severe**	**With Pedestrians**	**With Buses**
G1 Center-lane bus-way near 2 lanes	13 (9)	17.4 (6.6)	b	167	32	41	4	254	26	35	3
			a	23	5	4	2	95	6	18	7
G2 Center-lane bus-way near one lane	4 (3)	2.2 (1.2)	b	22	6	11	0	27	2	11	1
			a	3	1	0	1	5	0	3	0
G3 Curbside bus lane	2 (2)	6.9 (6.9)	b	13	5	2	1	60	10	10	0
			a	15	2	3	0	38	5	7	1
G4 Counter-flow bus lane	4 (4)	2.3 (2.3)	b	11	2	6	0	48	4	13	1
			a	7	2	6	1	28	6	10	8
G5 Others	18 (18)	7.4 (7.4)	b	47	7	10	2	105	16	41	1
			a	13	1	8	3	46	5	11	7

[a]b—before, a—after.
Source: The study dataset.

original police files that are imposed on the data. (Such improved data are unavailable for other towns in the Haifa metropolitan area and, thus, only Haifa city BRT sites were included in the analyses.) The analyses referred separately to road sections and intersections and included total injury accidents and the subtotals of severe (fatal and serious), pedestrian and bus accidents. Table 1 provides the total number of accidents observed, during the BRT operation and in the before periods, on the BRT sites in Haifa city.

4.3 Accident Analyses

The safety evaluations in the study dealt with three main issues: (1) an examination of changes in accidents at BRT sites, during the BRT operation versus before periods; (2) monitoring trends in monthly accident series on the BRT routes; (3) a comparative analysis of safety levels of streets with various BRT configurations.

For the first analysis, odds-ratio estimates with a comparison-group and weighted mean effect were applied as is common in before–after road safety evaluations (Elvik et al., 2009; Gitelman et al., 2014). As a comparison-group for the BRT sites served the number of accidents in the whole city, similarly to previous studies on the topic (Duduta et al., 2015). To estimate the safety impact of BRT operation, the number of accidents observed in the "after" period (with BRT in place) at the BRT (or treatment) sites was compared with the number of accidents that would have occurred in the absence of treatment. The latter is estimated accounting for the accident changes observed, in the after versus before period, at the comparison sites.

The evaluation included two steps. First, the safety effect was estimated for each BRT site, where the before and after periods of the comparison-group were matched to the periods of the site examined. The evaluation was conducted by means of the odds-ratio of accident numbers observed at a BRT and comparison-group sites, in the before and after periods, as follows:

$$\theta_i = \left[X^i{}_a / X^i{}_b\right] / \left[C^i{}_a / C^i{}_b\right] \quad (1)$$

where θ_i is the estimate of the safety effect observed at a BRT site i; $X^i{}_a$ and $X^i{}_b$—the numbers of accidents at a BRT site i, in the "after" and "before" periods; $C^i{}_a$ and $C^i{}_b$—the numbers of accidents in comparison-group (for site i), in the "after" and "before" periods. (Unequal before and after periods of the BRT site are normalized in the odds-ratio by using the same time periods for the comparison sites.)

Second, a weighted safety effect was estimated for the group of sites with a similar BRT configuration. The weighted mean effect (WME) has the form:

$$\text{WME} = \exp\left(\frac{\sum_i w_i \ln(\theta_i)}{\sum_i w_i}\right) \tag{2}$$

$$w_i = \frac{1}{VAR(\ln(\theta_i))} = \frac{1}{\frac{1}{X^i{}_a} + \frac{1}{X^i{}_b} + \frac{1}{C^i{}_a} + \frac{1}{C^i{}_b}}$$

The confidence interval of WME is given by:

$$\left(\text{WME} \times \exp\left(\frac{z\frac{\alpha}{2}}{\sqrt{\sum_i w_i}}\right), \text{WME} \times \exp\left(\frac{z_{1-\frac{\alpha}{2}}}{\sqrt{\sum_i w_i}}\right)\right) \tag{3}$$

The accident reduction is significant when the whole WME confidence interval is below one. When it includes one, the result is not significant but a decreasing or increasing accident trend can be indicated depending on the WME-value. The safety effect is reported in percent and is calculated as (1 − WME) × 100.

For the second analysis, Poisson regression models with time as a linear explanatory variable were fitted to the monthly time-series of accident numbers on the BRT sites and comparison sites, in the 24 months of BRT operation. The models had the form of:

$$\lambda = e^{\alpha + \beta \cdot \text{time}} \tag{4}$$

where λ is the monthly accident expectancy; *time*—months; α, β—model coefficients. The models were fitted using the GLM function of *R*. To satisfy a Poisson distribution, data transformations were applied. As comparison sites at this step road sections from Haifa city were selected, with road layouts and traffic levels similar to the BRT road sections but without dedicated bus lanes. In total, 135 road sections and 269 junctions composed the comparison-groups, where dual-carriageway streets with two lanes per direction served as comparison sites for BRT groups *G1*, *G3* (see Table 1); dual-carriageway streets with one lane per direction served as comparison sites for BRT group *G2*; single-carriageway streets—for BRT group *G4*, and all comparison sites together—for BRT group *G5* and for all BRT sites together. When β (the slope) in Eq. (4) is significant, an over-time trend is found in the series examined. The slopes of the trend lines, during the period of the BRT operation, were compared between the BRT and comparison sites, using a *T-test* statistic.

For the third analysis, explanatory models were fitted to the number of accidents at the BRT sites. The analysis focused on the BRT sites of groups *G1–G4* (with homogeneous settings) and accidents observed during the BRT operation period. To ascertain the impact on accident occurrences of a certain design feature (a BRT configuration, in our case), other traffic and infrastructure characteristics should be accounted for (Elvik et al., 2009). Among those, traffic exposure is the most essential for understanding road accident occurrences (Elvik et al., 2009). Various exposure measures reflecting total vehicle traffic, pedestrian volumes and/or bus services, were applied by previous studies on BRT safety impacts, depending on data availability (Duduta et al., 2012b, 2015; Goh et al., 2014). In this study, the BRT sites of groups *G1–G4* were characterized in terms of traffic volumes of general vehicle traffic, BRT buses, all buses together and the level of crossing pedestrian activity. The numbers were extracted from available traffic counts at the BRT junctions and then classified into five categories, from low to high, for each type of traffic.

Concerning other features in the explanatory models, some previous studies considered road or junction layout characteristics, bus system design and, sometimes, other features (presence of certain land use, for example, a market area; presence of certain design feature, for example, pedestrian overpasses, etc.) (see Duduta et al. 2012b, 2015). In other cases, more information on the location of bus facilities (Goh et al., 2014) or on pedestrian crossings (Gitelman et al., 2018) was included in the analysis to satisfy specific purposes. In the current study, the type of bus route configuration reflected the road layout (number of lanes, presence of median), as explained in Section 4.1. Similarly, for most sites, the BRT group actually indicated a prominent type of urban area (built environment, non-built area or city center). Along the BRT routes in Haifa, all intersections with crossing traffic were signalized. However, a number of right-turn junctions, without crossing traffic on the main road, remained in place as un-signalized junctions. Thus, in addition to exposure measures and the type of bus route configuration, the type of junction (signalized or not) was added to the data. Other infrastructure features were not included in the model due to their unavailability in the study dataset.

To examine the impact on accident occurrences of BRT configurations, given other features, explanatory models were fitted to the number of accidents at the BRT sites, using MANOVA (multivariate analysis of variance) models (Tabachnik and Fidell, 2006). This model type presents an extension of the univariate analysis of variance (ANOVA), where it tests the hypothesis that one or more independent variables have an effect on a set of two or more dependent variables (various accidents types, in our case). MANOVA enables the simultaneous modeling of several accident types and its use is possible when dependent variables are correlated. In addition, an advantage of the MANOVA model against different ANOVA models is that in multiple comparisons the error rate accumulates and may lead to erroneous conclusions. Furthermore, the ANOVA model does not pay attention to correlations between dependent variables. It may lead to a situation when there is no significant difference for one specific variable, but there is a significant difference for a few dependent variables together. Therefore, the multivariate analysis is more powerful than for one variable.

The model satisfactorily predicts the dependent variable when the *F-test* of the whole model is significant ($P < 0.05$). In addition, the *adjusted R-squared* parameter is estimated to reflect the variance explained, where a higher value indicates a better model fit. The explanatory variables with a significant impact ($P < 0.05$) in the model are counted for the interpretation of results. The models were estimated using SPSS v.22 software.

5. EVALUATION RESULTS

In the first 2-years of the BRT operation, in total, 61 injury accidents occurred on the BRT road sections and 212 injury accidents—on the BRT junctions, in Haifa city (see Table 1). The total numbers of severe accidents were 11 and 22, respectively, the numbers of pedestrian accidents—21 and 49. The overall shares of severe and pedestrian accidents on the BRT streets (12% and 21%) were not exceptional but similar to the average shares of such accidents on urban roads in Israel. In total, seven accidents involving buses occurred on the BRT road sections and 23—at the BRT junctions, half of them were with the BRT buses. Accounting for both high traffic volumes and high frequency of bus services on the BRT lanes, the numbers of accidents observed in the BRT system were not considered high.

5.1 After–Before Comparisons

Table 2 shows a summary of accident changes observed at the BRT sites, during the BRT operation versus "before" periods and related to changes that occurred in the comparison-group sites. (Accident types with insufficient data—below 10, in before and after periods together, were not estimated.) The results indicate that the new BRT operation was associated with mixed accident trends. On streets with a center-lane bus-way (*G1–G2*) and *others* configurations (*G5*) decreasing accident trends were observed in total accidents on road sections, while on sections with curbside bus lane an increasing

Table 2 Accident Changes Observed at the BRT Sites, During 24 Months of BRT Operation

Accident Type	Weighted Mean Effect	95% Confidence Interval		Meaning
		G1 Center-lane bus-way near 2 lanes		
Severe accidents, on sections	0%	−67%	199%	No change
Total injury accidents, on sections	−37%	−62%	2%	Decreasing trend
Pedestrian accidents, on sections	−28%	−80%	163%	Decreasing trend
Severe accidents, at junctions	23%	−63%	308%	Increasing trend
Total injury accidents, at junctions	43%	10%	86%	Increase
Pedestrian accidents, at junctions	141%	14%	407%	Increase
		G2 Center-lane bus-way near one lane		
Total injury accidents, on sections	−70%	−95%	94%	Decreasing trend
Pedestrian accidents, on sections	−94%	−100%	234%	Decreasing trend
Total injury accidents, at junctions	−31%	−74%	83%	Decreasing trend
Pedestrian accidents, at junctions	54%	−66%	608%	Increasing trend

Continued

Table 2 Accident Changes Observed at the BRT Sites, During 24 Months of BRT Operation—cont'd

Accident Type	Weighted Mean Effect	95% Confidence Interval		Meaning
		G3 Curbside bus lane		
Total injury accidents, on sections	52%	−29%	223%	Increasing trend
Severe accidents, at junctions	−6%	−71%	201%	Decreasing trend
Total injury accidents, at junctions	26%	−18%	92%	Increasing trend
Pedestrian accidents, at junctions	30%	−52%	251%	Increasing trend
		G4 Counter-flow bus lane		
Total injury accidents, on sections	−3%	−64%	162%	No change
Pedestrian accidents, on sections	21%	−69%	363%	Increasing trend
Severe accidents, at junctions	215%	−23%	1192%	Increasing trend
Total injury accidents, at junctions	39%	−16%	130%	Increasing trend
Pedestrian accidents, at junctions	45%	−42%	259%	Increasing trend
		G5 Others		
Total injury accidents, on sections	−31%	−65%	37%	Decreasing trend
Pedestrian accidents, on sections	9%	−64%	226%	Increasing trend
Severe accidents, at junctions	−29%	−79%	147%	Decreasing trend
Total injury accidents, at junctions	10%	−24%	60%	Increasing trend
Pedestrian accidents, at junctions	−21%	−62%	66%	Decreasing trend

Source: The study analyses.

trend was found and no change—on sections with counter-flow bus lanes. It seems that a center-lane configuration reduces the interaction of BRT with other vehicle traffic, on road sections, thus diminishing the risk of accidents. In contrast, a curbside configuration does not prevent vehicles to enter the bus lane, e.g., of those who need to stop near a sidewalk or preparing to turn, and therefore, a higher frequency of bus services following the BRT introduction, may increase the accident occurrences.

On most BRT configurations (except for total accidents in *G2* and severe and pedestrian accidents in *G5*), increasing accident trends were observed at junctions. A possible reason for that can be the higher complexity of traffic arrangements at junctions including BRT lanes compared to regular urban intersections.

Pedestrian accidents showed decreasing trends on sections with center-lane bus-way that can be related to the presence of raised medians with obstacles and fences preventing uncontrolled pedestrian crossings. An increasing trend in pedestrian accidents was observed on streets with counter-flow bus lanes that can be expected due to high pedestrian activity on these streets, which were reconstructed for the BRT operation, belong to city center and incorporate plenty of commerce and business uses.

In all BRT groups, except for *G5* (with a lower pedestrian presence), increasing trends were found in pedestrian accidents at junctions. Such a result is expected due to a higher complexity of crosswalk arrangements at junctions with BRT lanes and longer waiting time for pedestrians, particularly on dual-carriageway roads with high traffic volumes. This problem was also raised by previous studies of BRT safety in Israel (Gitelman et al., 2015, 2018). However, most accident changes during the BRT operation were not significant and the amount of severe accidents was not high, indicating that the Haifa BRT introduction did not cause a substantial worsening in road safety as did happen in local experience with some previous projects of introducing bus priority lanes (MOT, 2013).

5.2 Monthly Accident Trends During BRT Operation

Table 3 presents a summary of slopes of the trend lines in monthly accident series at the BRT and comparison sites. (The models were fitted to cases where the number of months with accidents, during the BRT operation, was over eight.) The findings show that monthly series of total injury accidents on the BRT routes mostly indicated a decreasing trend over the BRT operation period, where some of them were significant, yet, no differences (in slopes) related to the comparison streets were ascertained. A close to

Table 3 Slopes of the Trend Lines in Monthly Accident Series at the BRT and Comparison Sites

Accident Type	Group of BRT Sections	On BRT Streets	On Comparison Streets
Total injury accidents, on sections	*G1*	0.0344	0.0041
	G3	−0.0146	−0.0073
	G5	−0.0137	−0.0239*
	All	−0.0016	−0.0239*
Total injury accidents, at junctions	*G1*#	−0.0391**	−0.0059
	G3	−0.0299	−0.0064
	G4	−0.0037	0.0089
	G5	0.0009	−0.0049
	All	−0.0235**	−0.0049
Pedestrian accidents, on sections	All	0.0425	0.0163
Pedestrian accidents, at junctions	*G1*	0.0035	−0.0087
	All	0.0021	0.0026

Significant with *$P<0.1$, **$P<0.05$. #Significant difference in slopes, with $P<0.1$, between BRT and comparison sites.
Source: The study analyses.

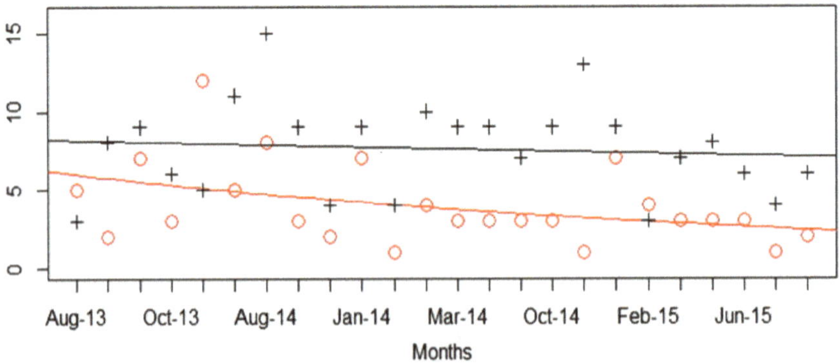

Fig. 6 Monthly numbers and trend lines of total injury accidents, at BRT junctions (in *red*) and comparison sites (in *black*), for *G1* configuration of bus lanes.

significant difference, with $P<0.1$, was found in one case—in total injury accidents at junctions, where a decreasing trend on BRT streets with center-lane bus-way near two lanes (*G1* group) was stronger than on comparison streets. This case is presented in Fig. 6. In the numbers of pedestrian accidents at the BRT sites increasing trends were observed over the BRT operation period but not significant, while at the comparison sites mixed trends were indicated (also, not significant). In general, accident trends at the BRT sites, during the first 2-years of its operation, were positive, indicating a slight over-time decrease in accident occurrences. However, further attention is required to pedestrian accidents, which demonstrated signs of increasing trends.

5.3 Factors Associated With Accident Occurrences at the BRT Sites

At this stage, we explored the impact of traffic and road layout characteristics on accident occurrences at the BRT sites. Group *G5* was excluded from this analysis due to the heterogeneous layouts of the bus lanes. The remaining sites included 18 road sections and 64 intersections (with BRT settings in the city of Haifa), thus, a reasonable analysis could refer to BRT junctions only.

Table 4 presents the mean values of characteristics of the BRT junctions, in four groups according to bus route configurations. The values in Table 4 indicate that higher frequencies of both total and pedestrian accidents refer to *G1* junctions, with a center-lane bus-way near two lanes of general traffic, similar to findings of another local study (Gitelman et al., 2015). Higher numbers of total and severe accidents were also observed at junctions with curbside bus lanes (*G3*). Both groups are characterized by higher levels of traffic volumes and *G1*—by higher frequency of BRT service, which may lead to higher accident numbers.

Table 5 presents the explanatory models adjusted to the numbers of total and pedestrian accidents that occurred at the BRT junctions, during the BRT operation period. (Severe accidents were excluded from the modeling due to low frequencies.) In a Spearman correlation analysis there were found significant weak and medium (up to $r=0.7$ by absolute value) correlations between dependent variables and a correlation in accident occurrence at the BRT sites ($r=0.41$, $P<0.001$). Table 5 shows that the models' predictability performance was satisfactory according to *F-tests*, with a significant value for total injury accidents ($P<0.01$) and close to significant value for pedestrian accidents ($P<0.06$). The variance explained by the models was 22.5% and 11.8%, respectively; such values can be seen as acceptable, accounting for the limited number of sites and accidents examined. (Alternative models with a reduced number of explanatory variables were tried, as well, but demonstrated a lower quality of fit.)

Table 4 Characteristics of BRT Junctions, in Groups of Bus Route Configuration (Mean Values per Junction)

Group	No. of Junctions (of Which Un-Signalized)	Total Injury Accidents per Junction[a]	Severe Accidents per Junction[a]	Pedestrian Accidents per Junction[a]	Total Vehicle Traffic[b]	BRT Traffic[c]	BRT and Bus Traffic Together[d]	Crossing Pedestrian Activity[e]
G1	26 (3)	3.65	0.23	0.69	3.8	3.7	2.2	2.3
G2	6 (0)	0.83	0	0.5	1.5	3.3	3.2	3.3
G3	13 (4)	2.92	0.38	0.54	3.8	3	3.2	1.7
G4	19 (0)	1.47	0.32	0.53	1	1	1	4.5

[a]In 2 years of BRT operation.
[b]According to five categories: (1) up to 10; (2) 10–20; (3) 20–30; (4) 30–40; (5) over 40 (thousands of vehicles).
[c]According to five categories: (1) 104; (2) 208; (3) 328; (4) 518; (5) 726 (BRT buses).
[d]According to five categories: (1) up to 0.75; (2) 0.75–1; (3) 1–1.25; (4) 1.25–1.5; (5) over 1.5 (thousands of buses). All traffic counts in 14 h, between hours 6 and 20, in both travel directions of the main road.
[e]According to six categories: (0) no crosswalks; (1) very low; (2) low; (3) medium; (4) high; (5) very high.
Notes to Table 4: The un-signalized junctions are right-turn junctions, without crossing traffic on the main road.
Source: The study dataset.

Table 5 Explanatory Models to Total and Pedestrian Accident Numbers, at the BRT Junctions

(A) Dependent Variable: Total Injury Accidents

Parameter	*B*	Std. Error	*t*	Sig.
Intercept	−4.45	1.95	−2.28	0.027
Total vehicle traffic	2.64	0.93	2.84	0.006
BRT traffic	−2.23	0.80	−2.79	0.007
BRT and bus traffic together	1.00	0.45	2.22	0.031
Crossing pedestrian activity	0.93	0.45	2.06	0.045
Signalized junction	0.30	1.63	0.18	0.855
G1	1.69	1.75	0.96	0.339
G2	2.18	1.84	1.18	0.242
G3	−1.03	2.03	−0.51	0.614
G4	0[a]			

(B) Dependent Variable: Pedestrian Accidents

Parameter	*B*	Std. Error	*t*	Sig.
Intercept	−1.86	0.77	−2.42	0.019
Total vehicle traffic	0.76	0.37	2.09	0.041
BRT traffic	−0.60	0.31	−1.90	0.063
BRT and bus traffic together	0.31	0.18	1.72	0.090
Crossing pedestrian activity	0.60	0.18	3.35	0.001
Signalized junction	−0.79	0.64	−1.23	0.223
G1	0.48	0.69	0.70	0.487
G2	1.03	0.73	1.42	0.161
G3	−0.18	0.80	−0.23	0.823
G4	0[b]			

[a]A reference group. Model statistics: $F_{(8,\ 55)}=3.29$, $P=0.004$; adjusted R-squared $=0.225$.
[b]A reference group. Model statistics: $F_{(8,\ 55)}=2.06$, $P=0.056$; adjusted R-squared $=0.118$.
Source: The study analyses.

The models in Table 5 show that bus route configurations did not have a significant impact on accident occurrence at the BRT junctions; for this variable both multivariate tests and *F-tests* of between-subject effects were insignificant. Similarly, the impact of the type of junction was insignificant in both models. At the same time, significant (with $P < 0.05$) or close to significant (with $P < 0.1$) impacts, in both models, were found for various exposure measures. The models indicate that more accidents of both types are expected at junctions with higher levels of general vehicle traffic, bus and BRT traffic together and crossing pedestrians, while a higher level of BRT traffic (only) has a moderating effect on accidents.

6. DISCUSSION AND FUTURE NEEDS

6.1 Safety Impacts of the New BRT System and Practical Implications

International research provided examples of accident reductions associated with BRT implementation on urban roads but also reported cases of an increase in accidents indicating a particular risk of pedestrian injury related to BRT operation (Duduta et al., 2014, 2015). Previous local experience showed that urban streets with bus priority routes frequently had worse safety records compared to other streets, due to the higher complexity of traffic arrangements on such streets (Gitelman et al., 2015, 2018; MOT, 2013). Hence, an increase in accidents during the initial BRT operation could be expected. However, during the first 2-year operation of the new BRT system in Haifa a substantial worsening in road safety was not found but mixed accident changes were observed. In after–before comparisons, the BRT sections with center-lane bus-ways showed decreasing trends, while for curbside and counter-flow bus lanes increasing trends were observed. On most BRT configurations, increasing accident trends were observed at junctions, particularly in pedestrian accidents. At the same time, most after–before accident changes were not significant. The monthly time-series of accidents during the BRT operation indicated a slight over-time decrease in total accidents (significant at junctions) but an increasing trend in pedestrian accidents (insignificant). Overall, the BRT operation was not associated with high accident numbers or unusual proportions of severe or pedestrian accidents, compared to other urban streets. Such results can be judged as successful and supporting the appropriateness of the design solutions adopted in the new BRT system. Hence, the safety performance of the Haifa BRT actually supports the policy of adopting best practice international recommendations while selecting design solutions for a new system.

The models fitted to accident occurrences at the BRT junctions in Haifa did not indicate significant differences in safety performance of streets with various BRT configurations, thus, leaving space for continued use of various forms. In general, sections with center-lane bus-ways and, particularly those having one traffic lane, demonstrated lower risk of accidents, which is in line with international experience (Duduta et al., 2012b, 2014). In spite of concerns in the literature, streets with counter-flow bus lanes did not experience high accident frequencies, apparently, due to lower speed limits (30 km/h) imposed on the BRT buses on such streets in Haifa. For most BRT configurations, the major safety problem should be seen in pedestrian accidents at signalized BRT junctions for which new engineering solutions are needed.

6.2 Future Needs

Bus priority systems stimulate a shift from private cars to the use of public transport in urban and metropolitan areas and, therefore, improve urban mobility and the quality of life. In light of increasing population density in urban areas and rising congestion on the transportation network, the popularity of bus priority systems is expected to be growing in the future. Simultaneously, the need for understanding of the whole range of implications of such systems, including safety impacts, will grow as well. However, as became evident from the literature review presented in this paper, assessing safety impacts of BRT and bus priority systems is still a challenge and much more empirical research is required concerning both the general effects of these systems on urban traffic safety and the implications of specific design solutions, in particular.

The extent of the safety impacts associated with the BRT systems introduced in various countries was wide and sometimes mixed, apparently reflecting differences in the background conditions, traffic volumes and road layouts across the various systems. A common observation is that in developing cities, following the implementation of a new transit system, accident reductions were typically observed, which may be attributed also to an overall improvement in the urban infrastructure associated with the BRT settings. At the same time, when bus priority lanes are introduced on urban streets with proper existing traffic arrangements, an increase in accidents may occur. Moreover, there is consistent evidence, in Israeli practice and in other countries, that urban sites with bus route features are characterized by higher accident frequencies compared to similar sites but without bus priorities. A reason for that may lie in the higher complexity of traffic arrangements, particularly at BRT intersections, which prolong the time of crossing (by both vehicles and pedestrians) and increase the probability of faulty or unsafe behaviors by road users. Thus, a possible direction of improving planning policies of bus priority systems in the future can be in seeking ways for simplification of road design solutions implemented in such systems. An alternative approach would be in stronger segregation of BRT traffic from other road users and, hence, reducing the areas of conflicts. This approach is already adopted, for example, on road segments with center-lane bus corridors, which are physically segregated from other traffic, thus, excluding the possibility of interaction and accidents with other traffic participants. However, for intersections with such bus route configurations safer design solutions still need to be developed.

Bus priority systems create more pedestrian traffic, particularly, at sites adjacent to bus stops. Not surprisingly, many evaluation studies reported higher pedestrian injury rates on streets with bus priority lanes than on other urban streets. In this context, current research and practice discuss pros and cons of various engineering solutions that may affect unsafe pedestrian behaviors (e.g., Duduta et al., 2014, 2015), while more radical solutions to eliminate pedestrian injury on BRT streets are still lacking.

In general, more safety evaluation studies based on observational data are required to support evidence-based decisions in planning BRT routes. In addition, in such evaluations, methodological issues of data collection and treatment of various confounding factors should be referred to, enabling better estimates of safety effects accounting for heterogeneity of urban environment and structural diversity of BRT systems (Vecino-Ortiz and Hyder, 2015).

ACKNOWLEDGMENTS

This study was commissioned by the Yefe Nof Company (Israel), which supervised the design and construction of the BRT system in the Haifa metropolitan area. Appreciation is extended to the engineers and managers from the Yefe Nof Company and Haifa municipality for providing data and information for the study analyses and multiple useful discussions of its findings.

REFERENCES

Bocarejo, J.P., Velasquez, J.M., Diaz, C.A., Tafur, L.E., 2012. Impact of BRT systems on road safety: lessons from Bogota. Transp. Res. Rec. 2317, 1–7.

Duduta, N., Adrizola, C., Wass, C., Hidalgo, D., Lindau, L.A., 2012a. Traffic Safety on Bus Corridors. Guidelines for Integrating Pedestrian Safety Into the Planning, Design, and Operation of BRT, Busways and Bus Lanes. Pilot Version—Road Test. EMBARQ, World Resources Institute, Washington, DC.

Duduta, N., Adrizola, C., Hidalgo, D., Lindau, L.A., Jaffe, R., 2012b. Understanding road safety impact of high-performance bus rapid transit and busway design features. Transp. Res. Rec. 2317, 8–14.

Duduta, N., Adriazola-Steli, K., Wass, C., Hidlago, D., Lindau, L.-A., John, V.-S., 2014. Traffic Safety on Bus Priority Systems. Recommendations for Integrating Safety into the Planning, Design and Operation of Major Bus Routes. World Resources Institute, Washington, DC.

Duduta, N., Adriazola, C., Hidalgo, D., Lindau, L.A., Jaffe, R., 2015. Traffic safety in surface public transport systems: a synthesis of research. Public Trans. 7 (2), 121–137.

Elvik, R., Hoya, A., Vaa, T., Sorensen, M., 2009. The Handbook of Road Safety Measures, second ed. Emerald.

Gardner, K., D'souza, C., Hounsell, N.B., Shrestha, B.P., Bretherton, D., 2009. In: Review of bus priority at traffic signals around the world. Final Report to UITP Working Group: Interaction of Buses and Signals at Road Crossings.

Gitelman, V., Carmel, R., Pesahov, F., 2014. The evaluation of safety efficiency of non-urban infrastructure improvements; a case-study. Eur. Transp. Res. Rev. 6, 477–491.

Gitelman, V., Carmel, R., Hakkert, S., 2015. An Examination of Road Accidents at Junctions and Sections With Center Bus Routes Versus Other Configurations of Dedicated Bus-Lanes. The Ministry of Transport, Jerusalem.

Gitelman, V., Carmel, R., Doveh, E., Hakkert, S., 2018. Exploring safety impacts of pedestrian-crossing configurations at signalized junctions on urban roads with public transport routes. Int. J. Inj. Contr. Saf. Promot. 25 (1), 31–40. https://doi.org/10.1080/17457300.2017.1310740.

Goh, K., Currie, G., Sarvi, M., Logan, D., 2013. Road safety benefits from bus priority. Transp. Res. Rec.: J. Transp. Res. Board 2352, 41–49.

Goh, K.C.K., Currie, G., Sarvi, M., Logan, D., 2014. Bus accident analysis of routes with/without bus priority. Accid. Anal. Prev. 65, 18–27.

Guide, 2016. Transit Street Design Guide. National Association of City Transportation Officials. Island Press, New York.

Hidalgo, D., Carrigan, A., 2010. Modernizing Public Transportation: Lessons Learned from Major Bus Improvements in Latin America and Asia. World Resources Institute, Washington, DC.

ITDP, 2007. Bus Rapid Transit Planning Guide. Institute for Transportation & Development Policy (ITDP), New York, USA.

Levinson, H.S., 2003. Bus rapid transit in city streets: how does it work. 2nd Urban Street Symposium, Anaheim, California.

Levinson, H., Zimmerman, S., Clinger, J., Rutherford, S., Smith, R.L., Cracknell, J., Soberman, R., 2003. Bus Rapid Transit: Case Studies in Bus Rapid Transit. TCRP Report 90, Volume I. Transportation Research Board of the National Academies, Washington, DC.

MOT, 2013. Safety of bus routes. In: Recommendations of a Ministerial Commission. Ministry of Transport (MOT), Jerusalem.

Panera, M., Shin, H., Zerkin, A., Zimmerman, S., 2012. Peer-To-Peer Information Exchange on Bus Rapid Transit and Bus Priority Practices. FTA Report 009. Federal Transit Administration, US Department of Transportation.

Tabachnik, B., Fidell, L., 2006. Using Multivariate Statistics, fifth ed. Allyn & Bacon.

TCRP, 2007. Bus Rapid Transit Practitioner's Guide. TCRP Report 118. Transit Cooperative Research Program (TCRP), Washington, DC.

Tse, L.Y., Hung, W.T., Sumalee, A., 2014. Bus lane safety implications: a case study in Hong Kong. Trans. A: Trans. Sci. 10 (2), 140–159.

UITP, 2015. Mobility in Cities Database. Synthesis Report, The International Association of Public Transport (UITP).

Vecino-Ortiz, A.I., Hyder, A.A., 2015. Road safety effects of bus rapid transit (BRT) systems: a call for evidence. J. Urban Health 92 (5), 940–946.

CHAPTER FOUR

Past, Present and Future of Transit-Oriented Development in Three European Capital City-Regions

Dorina Pojani*, Dominic Stead†,1
*School of Earth and Environmental Sciences, The University of Queensland, Brisbane, QLD, Australia
†Faculty of Architecture and the Built Environment, Delft University of Technology, Delft, Netherlands
1Corresponding author: e-mail address: d.stead@tudelft.nl

Contents

Abstract

The concept of Transit-Oriented Development—development near, and/or oriented to, mass transit facilities—has generated much interest in Europe over the last decade. Coined in the United States in the 1990s, the term "TOD" is frequently assumed to be a recent American import and a reaction to the consequences of mass motorization and sprawl. However, TOD is based on much older ideas of rail-based urban development that took place in many European cities during the 19th and 20th centuries. Arguably, the modern reincarnation of TOD is more focused on urban aesthetics. Other tenets, such as accessibility, density, and mixed-use, have remained more or less unchanged.

This article examines how planning policies in three European capital city-regions—Amsterdam, Stockholm, and Vienna—have been shaped by the ideas and principles underlying TOD. The three case studies were selected because all are located in European countries with mature systems of spatial planning: the Netherlands (Western Europe), Sweden (Northern Europe), and Austria (Central Europe). The article examines the extent to which planning policies from the mid-20th century to the present have

Advances in Transport Policy and Planning, Volume 1
ISSN 2543-0009
https://doi.org/10.1016/bs.atpp.2018.07.003

reflected TOD principles. The analysis is based on secondary sources (articles, books, and planning reports), and the focus of the study is on policy rather than measurements and metrics. The last three decades are explored more in depth as material is more readily available.

The first part of the analysis summarizes the development of spatial planning in the Netherlands, Sweden, and Austria since WWII, with an eye to highlighting policies that could be considered to be, or might affect, TOD. The second part deals with the implications of these policies in terms of past, present, and future TOD planning and practice in the respective capital city-regions: Amsterdam, Stockholm, and Vienna.

Keywords: Transit-Oriented Development, Planning, Netherlands, Sweden, Austria, City-regions

1. INTRODUCTION

The concept of Transit-Oriented Development—development near, and/or oriented to, mass transit facilities—has generated much interest in Europe over the last decade (Bertolini et al., 2012). Coined in the United States in the 1990s (Calthorpe, 1993), the term "TOD" is frequently assumed to be a recent American import and a reaction to the consequences of mass motorization and sprawl. However, TOD is based on much older ideas of rail-based urban development that took place in many European cities during the 19th and 20th centuries. Arguably, the modern reincarnation of TOD is more focused on urban aesthetics (Pojani and Stead, 2015a). Other characteristics, such as accessibility, density, and mixed-use, have remained more or less unchanged.

This chapter examines how planning policies in three European capital city-regions—Amsterdam, Stockholm, and Vienna—have been shaped by the various ideas and principles underlying TOD in its different forms (Fig. 1). The three city-regions studied are all located in European countries with mature systems of spatial planning: the Netherlands (Western Europe), Sweden (Northern Europe), and Austria (Central Europe), respectively. The chapter does not provide an analysis of direct references to TOD in planning policies in these city-regions, because the term is relatively recent and not necessarily used in local languages. Instead, it examines the extent to which planning policies from the mid-20th century to the present have reflected TOD principles. The analysis is based on secondary sources (articles, books, and planning reports), and the focus of the study is on policy rather than measurements and metrics. The last three decades are explored more in depth as material is more readily available.

Type	Key characteristics	Example of design
Single-node TOD	• Single neighborhood based around heavy rail stations • Development in circular pattern around a train station • Urban or suburban location • Optimal radius of 0.5 km (walkable distance to station)	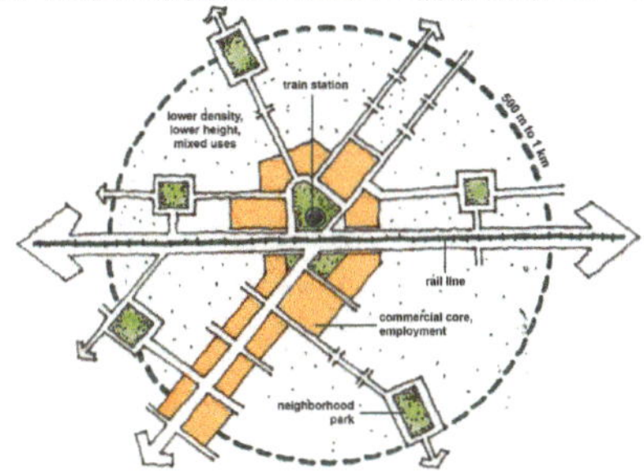
Multi-node TOD	• Regional network of nodes around heavy rail stations • Urban or suburban location • Circular or semi-circular nodes • Typical 'beads-in-a-string' pattern • Complementary rather than competing nodes • Work specialization at nodes (e.g., higher education node, health care node, etc.)	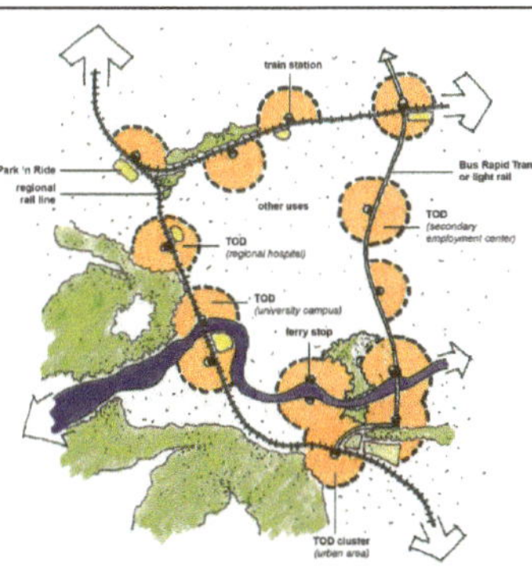
Corridor TOD	• Based around Light Rail Transit or Bus Rapid Transit stops • Urban location • Linear or ribbon-like development pattern along transit line(s) • Applicable to existing urban areas or planned urban extensions (i.e., along fingers or lobes)	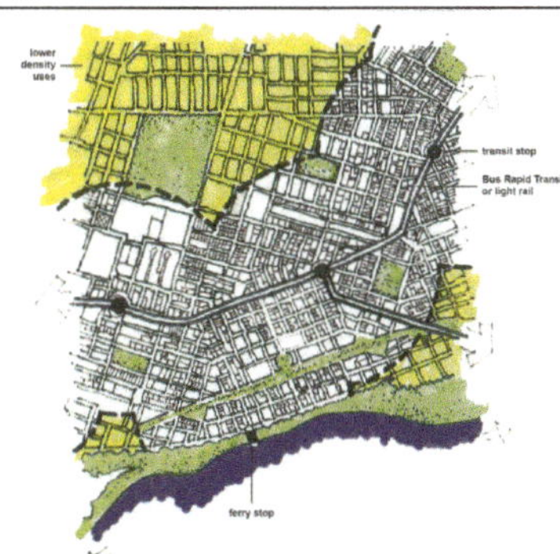

Source: authors' own work.

Fig. 1 Main types, characteristics and design of TOD. *Source: Authors' own work.*

The major contribution of this chapter is in cataloging how approaches to TOD have evolved over the long term in three European cities. The chapter is divided into three main parts. The first part summarizes the development of spatial planning in the Netherlands, Sweden, and Austria since WWII, with an eye to highlighting policies that have had an influence on TOD. The second part deals with the implications of these policies in terms of past, present, and future TOD planning and practice in the respective capital city-regions: Amsterdam, Stockholm, and Vienna. Third, the chapter identifies conclusions for the transfer of policy and practice.

2. SPATIAL PLANNING POLICY IN AUSTRIA, THE NETHERLANDS, AND SWEDEN

2.1 Austria

Austria is unique among the three countries in this study in that it has a federal system of government (comprising nine *Länder*). Austrian planning proceeds according to a top-down hierarchy, which is set out in the constitution. In terms of institutional arrangements for planning, the federal government seldom deals with physical planning (Dangschat, 2015). It is responsible for transport, infrastructure, and mobility programs of national importance.

Austria's *Länder* are responsible for preparing planning laws and state-level plans. Coordination and cooperation with the federal government and neighboring states, although voluntary, is customary. State-level plans are binding for the lower administrative levels but have no direct influence on citizens and businesses. There is a regional government as well, but historically it has been irrelevant in planning. However, with the advent of EU structural funds, which are delivered at regional level, the regions have strengthened their position. Municipalities are the key players in spatial planning issues. They are granted planning autonomy provided that they comply with the rules set by higher levels of government. As a result, mayors are seen as "local emperors" (Burtenshaw et al., 1981; Dangschat, 2015).

Since the signing of the Austrian State Treaty in 1955, a major objective underlying urban and regional planning was to equalize growth between the regions. The Netherlands and Sweden also followed a similar policy of promoting regional balance in postwar decades (see below). More recently, the dominant planning discourse concerns promoting regional "identity," rather than speaking of "regional disparity"—a term that carries negative connotations.

With the fall of the Iron Curtain, Austria's geopolitical situation changed dramatically. Proximity to Eastern Europe shifted from being a problem for regional development in the east to a major economic growth opportunity. Seeking to respond to EU enlargement, Austria was instrumental in establishing a new cross-border body (Centrope) encompassing the regions around Vienna, Brno, Bratislava, and Györ. The 60 km corridor between the twin capitals Vienna and Bratislava gained considerable importance in terms of development potential (Schremmer, 2014).

With much of the country being mountainous, urban structure in Austria is largely dictated by topography. Urban settlements are concentrated at relatively high densities in river valleys. Recent suburbanization trends have been substantial: between 1991 and 2001, suburban areas grew by 9% on average as compared to urban areas, which grew only 3% on average. Suburbanization has led to increasing car dependence and pollution but urban environment and traffic issues have only very recently been seen as tasks for spatial planners (Rubitzki and Schrenk, 2008).

At present, both objectives of economic growth and sustainability are centerpieces of planning discourse. Sustainability is articulated in terms of active and public transport promotion, pollution reduction, and quality of life enhancement. However, planning practice still strongly relies on quantitative evidence and scientific, technical, and expert-driven approaches. Meanwhile, NIMBYism is on the increase. Economic growth has led to population pressures and segregation, especially in the attractive Vienna region, which in turn has resulted in popular dissatisfaction and resistance (Dangschat, 2015).

2.2 The Netherlands

The Dutch government structure is a three-tiered, decentralized unitary model, based on the self-government of provinces and municipalities. Cogovernment between tiers is an underlying principle. Compared to many other European countries, the subnational levels of government have considerable responsibility and independence. Cooperation between Dutch municipalities is very common. Planning is a key institution in Dutch society and culture (Shetter, 1988). Unlike the Austrian technical approach, planning in the Netherlands has traditionally been based on doctrines or norms to guide politicians and practitioners (Roodbol-Mekkes et al., 2012).

The underlying philosophy of the Dutch planning doctrine has been "rule and order." This is the product of environmental conditions (e.g., flood risk due to low elevation and land reclamation from the sea), past economic hardships (i.e., famines during and after WWII), land scarcity, the Calvinist tradition of community orientation and cultural submission to governing authorities, and, in the postwar period, the presence of a strong and prosperous welfare state, somewhat similar to Sweden's. A selected number of interest groups are incorporated into the state system and are consulted at an early stage of planning procedures. In this system, planners are shielded from direct political interference. The "rule and order" doctrine primarily concerns urban growth control (and thus TOD) through policies that affect the location, intensity, and timing of development (Alexander, 2002; Faludi and van der Valk, 1994). Decision-making follows the so-called "polder model," a collaborative but time-consuming process aimed at reaching nearly universal consensus on any issue (Alpkokin, 2012). The dominant Dutch planning doctrine has been articulated in several different ways since WWII. The main stages, all of which are very relevant to TOD, are summarized below.

In the immediate postwar period, a "concentric growth" policy was in place, which aimed at preserving open spaces and minimizing the costs of servicing land. The First (postwar) Planning Memorandum was produced in 1960. The concept of the Randstad (a ring of cities including Amsterdam, Rotterdam, The Hague, and Utrecht, with a "green heart" in the middle) complemented the concentric growth policy (Burtenshaw et al., 1981).

In the 1960s and 1970s, a policy of "concentrated deconcentration" was followed which allowed for suburban development but only in designated growth centers and new towns outside existing cities. Through the Second and Third Planning Memorandum (1966 and 1974, respectively), the national government sought to take a powerful stand against sprawl, which reflected the middle-class desire to suburbanize. While successful in terms of concentrating suburban growth in designated areas, these policies also led to declines in urban population, public services, and employment. By the 1980s, "concentrated deconcentration" was terminated (Alpkokin, 2012).

In addition to spatial concepts, extensive regulations were developed around this time, which not only provided certainties for property owners but also helped to maintain an urban–rural divide and to distribute growth equally and equitably throughout the Netherlands. The latter policy was followed in Austria and Sweden as well. In the 1970s, national legislation was enacted to prohibit the construction of out-of-town shopping malls which were seen as a threat to the vitality of city centers. However, by the 1990s, legal restrictions on the location of big-box stores began to take the blame for decreasing retail competitiveness and creating barriers to the market entry of new firms. Meanwhile, car ownership continued to grow.

The 1980s and 1990s witnessed a revival of the "compact city" policy, which aimed at reconcentrating development in major urban centers and increasing density in existing suburbs. This policy was delineated in the

Fourth Planning Memorandum (1988) and its supplement, known locally as *Vinex* (1991). In conjunction with *Vinex*, the densification of station areas, especially in key *knooppunten* ("urban nodes"), was advocated as the logical corollary of the compact city policy. The dominant rail operator, Dutch Railways (NS), was strongly in favor of this redevelopment strategy which would increase its profits (Bertolini and Spit, 1998; Cavallo, 2007). In combination, the "compact city" and the "urban nodes" policies sought to stir development toward brownfield and wasteland sites in existing cities and greenfield sites adjacent to built-up areas (so-called *Vinex* locations). However, *Vinex* locations often comprised homogeneous housing. Public transport provision lagged behind; therefore, residents were dependent on private automobiles to reach necessary destinations. In parallel with *Vinex*, substantial urban renewal funds were made available to upgrade the quality of the housing stock in the urban cores of larger cities. Infill growth reduced open space and rising real estate prices in the central areas of expanding cities led to social segregation. Meanwhile, rural communities and small towns were left in limbo. These multiple shortcomings produced mounting criticism (Schwanen et al., 2004).

In addition to residential location policies, the Fourth Planning Memorandum produced a well-known business location policy called "ABC." Locations were labeled A, B, and C, according to the level of accessibility by public transport and automobile (i.e., city centers were A locations, first-ring suburbs were B locations, and exurban sites were C locations). Lack of parking and limited car access at premier A and B locations led businesses to relocate to toward cheaper, car-oriented C locations in the urban outskirts. Due to reasons of impracticality, the ABC policy was quietly shelved at the end of the 1990s (Gerrits et al., 2012; Spaans, 2006). Sweden also adopted an ABC policy but of a different form (see below).

In the new millennium, a decentralization and deregulation agenda strongly influenced planning in the Netherlands. The interventionist role of Dutch planners transitioned toward a facilitating and supporting role. The concepts of horizontal cooperation, "communicative planning," and "governance" (as opposed to "government") were introduced and became widespread.

The Fifth Planning Memorandum (2001) sought to introduce urban growth boundaries and no-growth zones whereas its successor, the National Planning Strategy (2006), marked a departure from earlier restrictive planning discourses. It also made a radical break with the centralist tradition in which the national government determined what would get built and where. This document also signaled a shift in emphasis from comprehensive planning to piecemeal development. The Strategy sought to fall in line with social trends rather than combat them. Unlike earlier policies that had striven for balanced growth throughout the country, now the focus was on the "mainports" of Amsterdam and Rotterdam (Van Duinen, 2013).

In terms of physical planning, the Strategy proposed that urban growth be accommodated along major transport corridors in order to reduce congestion and thus enhance economic performance. The Strategy also introduced the concept of "urban networks" and the Delta Metropolis (*Deltametropool*). *Deltametropool* was meant to conceptually replace the Randstad, the "green heart" of which had gradually filled with development. In the housing arena, large-scale residential projects were abandoned in favor of small-scale housing developments led by local and regional authorities. In conjunction with the National Planning Strategy, a new Spatial Planning Act was adopted in 2008, paving the way for a more decentralized and flexible planning milieu but also creating scope for competition and tension among cities. While developers still had to submit to stringent procedures, more freedom was allowed to the market and private initiatives than ever before (Anderton and Goedman, 2008; Waterhout et al., 2012).

The 2012 National Structural Vision took a more laissez-faire approach to development and renounced some physical planning duties at the national level. A key priority was to strengthen the country's economic growth poles (i.e., larger cities), by allocating priority funding, based on the "trickle-down theory." Concerns have been raised by environmental and poverty advocacy groups that this policy orientation will exacerbate spatial and economic inequalities in the country: the Randstad will absorb a disproportionate amount of people and jobs, peripheral regions will shrink and their resources would deplete, and most new urbanites will choose to live in ever-expanding suburban areas thus consuming green spaces and contributing to traffic congestion (Gerrits et al., 2012). Overall, this reorientation has somewhat eroded the Dutch planning tradition and quality (Ache, 2015).

2.3 Sweden

Local self-government and a communitarian spirit are central foundations of Swedish society. These notions are underpinned by the traditional right ("all men's right") of the public to enter and enjoy private property as long as no direct harm results. Compared to the Netherlands and Austria, Swedish municipalities are even stronger and more independent. In planning, a basic notion is the "local planning monopoly." For several decades (since 1987), municipalities have been in charge of comprehensive physical planning—which is seen as the heart of the profession, although efforts have been made to integrate other aspects (Khakee, 1996; Persson, 2013; Rydén et al., 2008; Strong, 1971). The solid municipal position is supported by a system of direct income tax, which constitutes more than 60% of the local budget.

In terms of the institutional structure of planning, two other levels of government (the county and state levels) are involved planning as well, but their policy instruments are only adopted on a voluntary basis. Proper "regional plans" are only prepared if municipalities agree to it, and at any rate, they are not binding. So far, Stockholm is the only county with a clear and sustained regional vision (see below). On planning matters, the national government is comparatively weak too. In relation to planning, its guidelines are advisory—not mandatory. Overall, the links between different levels of the planning system are either loose or entirely absent (Newman and Thornley, 1996; Schmitt, 2015).

Less emphasis on plan hierarchy makes Swedish planning very different from planning in Austria and the Netherlands. It creates controversy at the regional level in cases when sectorial interests must be balanced or when the impacts of large projects (such as shopping centers or transport infrastructure) must be assessed. This was particularly problematic in the 1990s, an era when large investments in roads and rail dominated the scene (Schulman and Böhme, 2000). Another difference with the Netherlands is the Swedish hands-on planning approach. Unlike the Dutch focus on planning doctrines and guiding principles, Swedish planning often has a more problem-based approach and a technical and pragmatic bias in which policies to address specific societal challenges are developed. This is also reflected in academic planning research, most of which focuses on physical rather than governance issues. However, the Dutch and Swedish planning systems are similar in other respects. As in the Netherlands, a tenet of Swedish society is consensus building, sometimes termed "corporate pluralism." The Swedish consensus orientation is closely linked to the concept of welfare society, which has been widely accepted in the postwar period and integrated into planning processes. Sweden's development of a welfare state has been guided by a so-called pragmatic "middle way" (Bourne, 1975; Khakee, 1996).

One similarity between Sweden, the Netherlands, and Austria is the tradition of public land ownership. In Sweden, a national land purchase grant was only introduced in 1968, which allowed municipalities to purchase land for future expansion decades in advance of need. However, the City of Stockholm (like Amsterdam and Vienna) has a much longer history of land purchase, dating from 1904. In 1980, the city owned 70% of land within its boundaries and nearly 600 km^2 outside the city limits. In some cases, Stockholm's aggressiveness in land purchase was seen as an encroachment on the rights of surrounding municipalities and created scope for conflict (Gullberg and Kaijser, 2004). However, other Swedish municipalities followed a similar practice of land consolidation, until the land purchase grant was abolished in 1981 (Khakee, 1996).

The Netherlands, Sweden, and Austria are also similar in their historical policy objective to maintain a regional balance in terms of resource and service distribution (Bourne, 1975). However, in the last few decades, all three countries have moved away from this approach toward a neoliberal one favoring larger urban agglomerations (Khakee, 1996). In Sweden, the parity principle has been particularly difficult to implement in practice because the country's urban network is largely dictated by climate. While its land area is large by European standards (450,000 km^2), most of the population is concentrated in the south where winter temperatures are more temperate.

Three main periods are discernable in postwar planning in Sweden. In the first period, starting with the enactment of the 1947 Building Act, planning was geared toward the production of mass housing and various forms of physical and social infrastructure. The public sector expanded considerably during this period but this expansion took place mostly at the local level. Municipalities were allocated legal and economic powers to prepare comprehensive plans. However, the most ambitious planning program of the 1960s—the construction of 1 million housing units to shelter new urbanites—was launched and managed by the Social Democratic national government. It aimed to overcome the general housing shortage while at the same time preventing speculators from making excessive profits (Burtenshaw et al., 1981; Rydén et al., 2008). The program resulted in high-rise, high-density new suburban towns, which followed TOD principles in the sense that they were served by transit. In terms of aesthetics, however, they were sterile and monotonous (Cervero, 1995; Khakee, 1996). The construction of new towns was complemented by informal controls on the siting and expansion of specific uses, relying primarily on negotiation and persuasion (Bourne, 1975).

The second period in postwar Swedish planning followed the economic downturn of the mid-1970s. This was primarily a time of crisis management. Large-scale housing construction came to a halt (Höjer et al., 2007).

However, national planning guidelines were introduced in this period. Environmental protection became a serious planning issue in response to a dramatic increase in car ownership. The economic recession, the energy crisis, as well as an influx of non-European migrants forced planners to move away from the assumption of a unitary public interest and introduce more flexibility into formerly rigid comprehensive plans. From the 1980s onward, Swedish planning switched focus from grand plans to individual projects. This turn was justified by a growing economic and political uncertainty and an intensified competition among municipalities for increasingly scarce resources (Khakee, 1996; Rydén et al., 2008).

In the contemporary era, starting around the departure of the Social Democratic Party in 1991, Swedish planning is primary concerned with environmental protection and economic development. As such, it has become more piecemeal, incremental, and reactive rather than proactive. Parts of the welfare state are being dismantled, competition among municipalities is growing, land in public ownership is being privatized, and many services, including public transport, are being contracted out. The national railway company (SJ) was privatized in 1988, ahead of most others in Europe. However, despite the growing market orientation of the public sector, sustainability is a dominant theme in urban development. While acknowledging a longing for cultural heritage and local character, local planners also view Sweden as a pioneer of new urban models including "eco-friendly planning," "carbon neutral cities," and "green urbanism," which are sometimes (but not always) coupled with TOD. As in Austria and the Netherlands, Swedish planning is increasingly driven by process than outcome (Cervero and Sullivan, 2011; Persson, 2013; Qviström and Bengtsson, 2015; Schmitt, 2015).

3. TOD POLICY AND PRACTICE IN VIENNA, AMSTERDAM, AND STOCKHOLM

3.1 Vienna

Vienna is a primate city whose region encompasses more than one-fourth of Austria's population of 8 million, while Graz, the second largest city, has only 300,000 inhabitants (Schremmer, 2014). As well as being a municipality, Vienna is one of Austria's nine *Länder*. This special independent status enables the capital to be in control of many spatial and economic development matters (Lichtenberger, 1993) and is an important dimension of the institutional structure of planning. From the end of WWI until the

1930s, providing affordable social housing and strictly controlling rents were cornerstones of urban policy in Vienna. Its municipal socialism ethos continued for decades afterward and influenced the general types of planning policy measures that were pursued in the city (Novy et al., 2001).

Vienna suffered greatly during WWII when a substantial proportion of the housing stock was destroyed. From 1945 and through the 1960s, urban planning was heavily preoccupied with reconstruction. At the time, Vienna was an exemplar of a top-down, corporatist form of social democratic urban governance. State and corporatist clientelism, based on party membership, played an important role in providing housing. Given that rent controls applied, urban location was of little monetary consequence. Planning was mainly seen as a technical exercise to be carried out by experts. The main instrument was the masterplan, which did not provide any procedural mechanism for public participation or conflict resolution. As a consequence, conflict avoidance became the leitmotif of social partnership at the top echelons of society, while antagonism persisted at the bottom (Novy et al., 2001). Dutch and Swedish planning processes were also historically guided by similar cultural preferences for consensus but unaccompanied by clientelism.

Due in part to the aid received through the Marshall Plan, Vienna embarked on an economic recovery process soon after the war. New housing projects were built throughout the 1950s and 1960s. Large housing estates were developed on vacant land south and east of the city, the dimensions of which were reminiscent of Eastern European socialist estates. During this time the capital no longer used its own funding for housing provision as it had done during the interwar years: the main source of funding was from the national government (Novy et al., 2001). Housing projects did not overwhelm the city, and a large amount of parkland was retained: more than half of Vienna's surface area is still green. The inner city was reluctant to adapt to the car: most streets remained narrow, the main exception being the monumental *Ringstrasse*, a 19th century boulevard, which replaced the historic city walls (Buehler et al., 2017).

In the 1960s, planning activities concentrated largely on the extension of the public transport network, in particular the underground railway (*U-Bahn*) under the leadership of Mayor Bruno Marek, although car ownership grew too in this period. These interventions were relatively easy to perform as a large portion of the city's area was in public ownership through the 1990s (Lichtenberger, 1993). By the 1970s, new construction in the inner city declined sharply in favor or urban expansion areas. Unlike Amsterdam and Stockholm, which opted for urban expansion patterns in fingers or lobes (see below), Vienna expanded in a circular fashion along the historical radial structure of the city. A crescent-shaped outer city formed beyond the *Ringstrasse*. This expansion pushed out into the agricultural zone immediately adjacent to the city border. The expansion area was not only designated to accommodate housing but also employment centers with good access to both railway stations and highway exits (e.g., north of the Danube Canal and along the southern tangential motorway). Large exurban, car-oriented, shopping centers were built in this period (e.g., Shopping City Süd, which opened in 1976), leading to retail blight in the inner city (Lichtenberger, 1993). The result was worsening roadway congestion, parking problems, air pollution, noise, and traffic injuries and fatalities.

In terms of housing, architect Harry Glück's social housing projects (so-called "fully adequate housing") with ample green roofs and sports facilities, located along public transport lines, were a trademark of the era. Affordable for a majority, they were also well-liked by developers due to their low resident turnover and low maintenance costs. However, Glück's *Wohnpark Alt-Erlaa* project was less popular. Modeled after Le Corbusier's *Ville Radieuse*, it was one of the largest residential complexes in Austria, packing 9000 people in three blocks of skyscrapers. Located to the south east of the city center, it was considered a flagship self-sufficient satellite town, compete with public transport and social infrastructure (Lichtenberger, 1993). Detractors criticized its high-rise and standardized architecture. Amsterdam and Stockholm also embarked on similar modernistic experiments (see below).

In the 1970s and 1980s, Vienna experienced a wave of urban renewal to counter urban deterioration, which was becoming visible in the cityscape of the center. Here urban renewal took a gentler form than the demolition and rebuilding works occurring elsewhere. The hallmark of this era was a planning tool called "area care center." Dense, industrial neighborhoods in need of housing upgrades were targeted for intervention. Renovations were sensitive to the local social and physical structures. Generally, planning sought to provide an integrated package of mass transit, shopping centers, pedestrian zones, parks, social service facilities and attractive layouts for the apartment buildings and their immediate surroundings. Hundertwasser's expressionist architecture is also associated with this stage of urban renewal. The extension of public transport lines in Vienna was slower than in Amsterdam and Stockholm—partly due to a lack of cooperation between the City of Vienna and Austrian Railways. On the other hand, the development of a new road network was slow too, but this had the beneficial side effect of containing car traffic (Lichtenberger, 1993). Transport plans envisioned the construction of urban highways (*autobahns*) but widespread public opposition—including demonstrations—blocked nearly all these proposals. The main exception was the 18km *Südosttangente*, a cross-town motorway (A23) in the south-eastern part of the city, which at its closest passes 5km from the historic city center (Buehler et al., 2017).

One major TOD project was built during the period: UNO City. Located on the left bank of the Danube River along the U1 underground line, UNO City consisted of three large office buildings visually aligned with St. Stephen's Cathedral. It was built with the intention of creating a symbolic architectonic showpiece to reinforce Vienna's status as a world city. Completed in 1979, it was the last project built almost entirely by the state and implemented through a top-down, rational approach (Novy et al., 2001). This type of planning was encouraged by the fact that all mayors of Vienna have been Social Democrats since 1945, and all transport ministers were Social Democrats until 2010, when a Green became transport minister and vice-mayor (Buehler et al., 2017).

During the 1980s, social-democracy began to establish new forms of urban governance in line with the neo-liberal political restructuring of other European countries. Municipal socialism began to transform into municipal capitalism. Within the context of an increasingly internationalized and deregulated economy, political affiliations and corporatist and clientelist networks became less relevant. Rents were deregulated and, as a result, urban land values became more sensitive to location and accessibility. Forms of old and new urban governance were articulated into a hybrid ensemble, which was physically expressed through large urban development projects. In contrast with the publicly-funded TODs of the past, new urban development projects were planned as public–private partnerships. In 2000, the national government allowed Vienna to divert housing funds to infrastructure projects, which signaled a defeat of the corporatist model (Novy et al., 2001).

Similar to Amsterdam and Stockholm, Vienna's TOD focus shifted to inner city areas from the 1980s onward. Part of the shift was driven by the desire of city leaders to promote Vienna's image as an internationally competitive city and a gateway to Eastern Europe, and motivate the private sector to implement this vision. Architectural competitions and international workshops began to take place in order to create a public sphere for business. After the Cold War, many firms operating in post-communist countries chose Vienna as a convenient location for their headquarters. Easily accessible and visible locations along the U-Bahn were particularly popular choices. Meanwhile, three sites near underground stations, U3

Ottakring, U3 *Simmering*, and U6 *Siebenhirten*, experienced densification and diversification. High-rise towers became increasingly important elements of the Viennese skyline, which until then had been defined by church roofs and six-story apartment buildings (Novy et al., 2001).

More recently, two sites in the urban periphery—*Liesing* and *Aspern Seestadt*—are undergoing transformation according to TOD principles. *Liesing* is currently dominated by highways, large shopping centers, unattractive apartment blocks, and low-density development. Renewal plans for the area include housing for 20,000 additional residents and office space to accommodate 10,000 new jobs. *Aspern Seestadt* (under development) is embedded within the existing urban structure of Vienna's *Donaustadt* district, in close proximity to a national park and a lake. Plans for *Aspern Seestadt* seek to accommodate 24,000 new residents and 20,000 new jobs in greenfield development in order to create a multifunctional city of the future and the high-tech center of the Centrope region. The proposed new amenities combine green urbanism and TOD elements: half of the total available area is reserved for public open spaces, with streets, squares, gardens, and cycle lanes. The lake with its landscaped shoreline, promenade, and surrounding park is the centerpiece of the development. An efficient, high-capacity public transport link (an extension of the U2 line) has been put in place prior to the overall development. In the future the station will become a multimodal node, with long-distance trains also stopping there (Schremmer, 2014). The 60 km corridor between Vienna and Bratislava presents further opportunities for TOD creation. The twin capitals are combining efforts to improve infrastructure at the same time as retaining green space along the corridor.

Administratively, these contemporary TODs are an expression of a new forms of entrepreneurial governance. While marking a break with traditional corporatism, they represent an elitist approach with coopted public participation. The approach is also in line with the deeply entrenched hierarchical structure of Vienna. The key actors involved include real estate businesses, international investors, and public opinion leaders (Novy et al., 2001).

3.2 Amsterdam

Amsterdam has a dense multimodal public transport system based on metro, tram, bus, and bicycle. Its metropolitan region is an exemplar of relatively successful, albeit complex, development control which has attracted interest from planners around the world (Pojani and Stead, 2015b). However, the regional spatial structure has not been achieved without tensions between Amsterdam and the neighboring municipalities, where perceptions of Amsterdam as an arrogant domineering player striving to annex surrounding territories have been felt (Alexander, 2002). This can be seen as a consequence of specific decision-making approaches.

In the postwar period, the city expanded out from its historic fan-shape. The expansion was based on the spatial concept of "lobe city": a series of built-up urban extensions along public transport corridors, alternating with wedges of open space at walking and cycling distance (Bertolini, 2005). During the 1970s, the inner city remained the epicenter of development while the overspill housing was accommodated in regional growth centers in the lobes (Alexander, 2002). Many new housing projects built in the 1950s, 1960s and 1970s took the form of multi-story apartment blocks. While their scale grew over time, they remained smaller than in Vienna and Stockholm. A substantial number of townhouses were built as well during this period. Housing construction and transportation planning were strongly connected.

In the early 1980s, the underlying doctrine of planning in Amsterdam began to move away from lobed urban development to interconnected metropolitan centers, reflecting the growing importance of new, peripherally-located TOD nodes which concentrated population and social and economic activity and were not unilaterally reliant on the central city. The largest of these nodes was Almere, a new town of about 200,000 people, located north-east of Amsterdam, which became a municipality in 1984 (following the national "concentrated deconcentration" and *Vinex* policies, mentioned earlier). Many middle-class residents relocated to Almere and other suburban satellites in search of larger owner-occupied housing, while an influx of non-European immigrants boosted the city's population (Salet, 2005).

Another important node which originates from this era is IJburg, a housing expansion site for 18,000 dwelling units, built on six artificial islands raised from the IJ Lake. Amsterdam had sought to develop it since 1978, but construction only started 20 years later after much discussion and deliberation. Construction is ongoing at the time of writing. The area is connected to Amsterdam via tram but the line did not reach IJburg until 2000, after the first bridge was put in place. With the arrival of the tram, IJburg can also be considered as a TOD location. However, its "island" location with limited connections to the city is the root of transport bottlenecks (Alexander, 2002).

In the 1990s and 2000s, interest in urban living revived, and the traditional inside-out expansion policy was exchanged for an outside-in approach. The City of Amsterdam regained population to reach about 800,000. The compact city approach made a comeback. At the same time, the concept of "urbanity" came to the fore, which was to be achieved through better urban design (Bertolini and Salet, 2003). However, with decentralization of planning powers, conflicting views and tensions between the City of Amsterdam and the province (*Provincie Noord-Holland*) surfaced. The City believed that it deserved a majority of transportation and housing funding, while the province adopted a view that development should be spread around the regional transit network, not just in the city (Salet, 2005).

Within Amsterdam, an attempt to establish a central business district in the city along the shores of the IJ River did not materialize (Salet, 2005). Several secondary nodes emerged. *Zuidas*, an interchange station located in the south of the city, became a major redevelopment node. The success of the area has been ascribed to the availability of large amounts of office space, a concentration of prestigious law firms, the proximity to the Schiphol airport, an international allure, and excellent accessibility by car (including the necessary parking facilities). These traits are absent from the central city, which is highly accessible by train only. However, the general quality of the *Zuidas* urban environment, especially its public spaces, is mediocre. The area remains largely mono-functional and dominated by high-rise office buildings—similar to *La Défense* in Paris or *Docklands* in London. A railway ring and a highway sever the area functionally and visually from the rest of Amsterdam. Generous public investments to upgrade *Zuidas*' urban design have not been forthcoming because they would demand a hard political choice in favor of one location in one city which would signify a break with the Dutch tradition of distributing investments and benefits (Bertolini and Salet, 2003; Bertolini and Spit, 1998).

Schiphol Airport, one of the busiest airports in Europe, became another extremely important node. Located about 9 km southwest of Amsterdam, the airport area has attracted a range of activities including offices, conference centers, hotels, warehouses, and retail outlets which employ 50,000 people (Alexander, 2002).

An attempt was made to develop other urban TOD nodes which would be specialized in terms of land-use, including *Amstel*, *Sloterdijk*, and *Bijlmer*. Initially, the businesses that located in these nodes, which are also accessible via road, benefited from proximity to the regional labor markets (Bertolini, 2005). However, these mono-functional places are currently considered less attractive to businesses, as witnessed by high office vacancy rates. Their aesthetic quality, with modernist buildings, lacks variety. While relatively convenient for office workers in terms of access, these spaces are empty after working hours. Their look is perhaps "too American" for the taste of the Dutch public, accustomed to historic buildings, tree-lined canals, and intimate squares with cozy cafés (Pojani and Stead, 2014b). Small-scale professional services, retail shops, and entertainment and cultural venues remain attached to Amsterdam's convivial and nearly car-free historic city (Bertolini, 2005), while the attempts to promote TOD in *Amstel*, *Sloterdijk*, and *Bijlmer* resulted in less attractive urban environments in the eyes of the public.

The current situation does not bode well for the implementation of contemporary TOD in the Amsterdam region. Although a highly knowledgeable "TOD lobby" has formed, it has failed to reach a wider audience and frame the TOD concept for the planning community. Local planners are searching for (a) ideas related to the urban design of areas in the immediate proximity of train stations, and (b) financial tools that would make TOD viable without substantial investment from the public sector (Pojani and Stead, 2014a).

The economic crisis in the first decade of the 21st century has been particularly problematic for the City of Amsterdam which found itself owning a large amount of land away from TOD zones. Before being able to develop TOD sites, the city needed to find a way of disposing of its current stock of land. While train station areas were seen as convenient work places, families and individuals did not perceive them as high-status living environments. Because bicycle use is widespread, the standard distance for non-motorized travel to train stations is much higher than in TODs in other countries (Pojani and Stead, 2015a). Despite these difficulties, many Dutch planners are still positive about the future of TOD in the Amsterdam region and view it as one of the most efficient urban and regional development policies (Pojani and Stead, 2014b).

3.3 Stockholm

While planning at the regional scale is generally weak in Sweden, Stockholm is arguably a leading example of coordinated rail transit and urban development. In the postwar period, the city was transformed from monocentric to a polycentric transit-dependent metropolis. Although the term TOD has not been used, TOD has been a guiding concept of Stockholm's (and other

Swedish regions') regional development for many decades (Qviström and Bengtsson, 2015). While no longer a cornerstone of planning, TOD is still present in planning visions for the future (Höjer et al., 2007, 2011; Qviström, 2015).

The Stockholm metropolis has a star-shaped form. About half of its 800,000 inhabitants live in central neighborhoods, while the rest is spread among several master-planned satellite communities. Built after WWII, these satellites were radially linked to the core by a regional rail system (*Tunnelbana*), currently 106 km long. The historic island city (*Gamla Stan*) has been preserved as a tourist center (Strong, 1971). The satellites are not necessarily self-contained, nor balanced in terms of jobs and housing. Despite the fact that car ownership rates are high in the Stockholm region, and car use has steadily grown over the years, car commuting is relatively low and rail use is high compared to many other European cities (Höjer et al., 2007). Many of the new towns' residents and workers commute by train because of the well-developed rail network and pedestrian-friendly designs in the proximity of stations (Cervero, 1995; Gullberg and Kaijser, 2004; Höjer et al., 2007).

Industrialization, economic growth, and urbanization following WWII did not result in very high levels of sprawl, car dependence, and highway-oriented development in Stockholm. Rather, the settlement pattern and the rail network became more strongly connected. The first plan that laid the ground for urban development in Stockholm after WWII was Sven Markelius' General Plan of 1945–52, which envisioned a series of dense satellite centers where most residents would be within walking distance of a train station. These satellites would be placed "like pearls on a necklace" along the rail lines. This deconcentrated structure was continued in a political decision of 1969 to control Stockholm's growth and "overpopulation." In addition to the planners' efforts in orchestrating and coordinating land-use and transportation, postwar TOD was made possible because of the Swedish tradition of public land ownership and the commitment of the Swedish government to improving urban housing. As in Vienna and Amsterdam, land consolidation was in favor of TOD in the sense that, much postwar public housing could be accommodated around train stations (Bourne, 1975; Cervero, 1995; Höjer et al., 2007; Strong, 1971).

The first generation of new satellite towns, including Vällingby, Farsta, Skärholmen, Jârva, and Täby, was designed and built between 1950 and 1970 based on a policy called ABC. It should be noted that the Swedish ABC policy was very different from the Dutch one (see above) in that it provided guidance on the local land-use mix rather than on regional location. The formula was: A = *Arbete* (jobs), B = *Bostad* (housing), C = *Centrum* (services). Each new town contained 80,000–100,000 residents with 10,000–15,000 housed within 1 km of each subway station. This density was estimated to be large enough for the station to be profitable (Strong, 1971). Between 75% and 90% of new suburban housing was multi-family, in the form of large modernist blocks, initially much praised but later vilified. Such a large share of multi-family housing construction in Stockholm was unique among European capitals at the time. While aesthetically dull by contemporary standards, Vällingby became the prototype of the application of the ABC policy within Sweden and gained an international reputation (Gullberg and Kaijser, 2004; Höjer et al., 2007). Between the satellite cities were farms, canals, or forest land (Strong, 1971).

Planners sought to avoid dormitory environments by distributing jobs (industry and offices) and services (shops and civic buildings) to the satellites in proportion to the residential population. Public ownership of land allowed this to occur. Tax incentives were also used to attract non-residential uses to new towns. The resulting towns were only "half-contained": half of the working inhabitants would commute out of town and half of the workforce would be drawn in from elsewhere. This was seen as positive because it allowed for a bi-directional flow of passengers rather than overloading the transit system in one direction only (Cervero, 1995; Gullberg and Kaijser, 2004).

The rail system was developed in parallel with the suburbs. Its construction was crucial for regional development as the center of Stockholm was largely located on islands, which were poorly connected to the suburbs by roads. The existing tramways were discontinued in 1967 (when driving on the right side of the street was introduced in Sweden). At the outset—before the new settlement pattern had taken form—the rail system incurred huge operational deficits. To help counter deficits and supply passengers for the new system, higher densities were planned in suburban TOD areas and neighborhood centers. In addition, the main commercial and civic centers were placed in station areas. Pedestrian and bicycle paths were separated from automobile traffic throughout the towns. In addition to the regional railway, new motorways were built in order to connect the suburbs to the inner city (Cervero, 1995).

The second generation of new satellite towns, including Spånga, Kista, and Skärpnack, was designed and built between 1970 and the late 1980s. These new towns broke with the ABC tradition as the monumentality and dreariness of housing in the earlier suburbs came under sharp criticism. Each town was planned or evolved as a more specialized community. A mostly residential community, Spånga, attracted a large number of low-income industrial workers often of non-European origin; it is now an ethnically mixed town. Kista emerged as a technopolis (i.e., Sweden's Silicon Valley), whereas Skärpnack's design followed New Urbanist principles of human scale, including mid-rise apartments, narrow streets, sidewalk cafés, and other neotraditional elements. While multi-family housing construction continued, the rhythms were much slower and nearly matched single-family housing construction rates. In the second generation of new towns, very small shares of workers live and work in the same community. Many residents commute to inner city neighborhoods. Conversely, a large portion of the suburban workforce lives in central urban areas and commutes outward. Overall, the new satellites are heavily dependent on the rest of the region. Rail serves a large share of work commuting but car use is higher than in the first generation suburbs. In addition to master-planned satellites, this period also witnessed some scattered, low-density development but to a much lesser degree than North America (Cervero, 1995).

Starting in the late 1980s, the planning focus (an aspect of the *planning environment*) in Stockholm shifted from greenfield new town construction to brownfield redevelopment in existing urban areas. Infill development became an explicit policy in Stockholm's 1999 City Plan. This strategy was a response to a population decline in the inner city, which had been driven by the suburbanization of upper-income households that desired spacious housing. Two infill TOD projects stand out from this period: Ericsson Globe and the Southern Station project. Ericsson Globe (originally known as Stockholm Globe Arena) is a spectacular indoor sports arena built near a *T-Bana* station just outside the city. The arena is combined with commercial and office space. The Southern Station project has a housing focus. A large apartment complex was built on the site of the old station while the station itself was modernized. The project, designed in a post-modern style by Spanish architect Ricardo Bofill, comprises a large semicircular building enclosing a neighborhood park. Both projects attracted worldwide attention and helped spark Stockholm's urban renaissance (Gullberg and Kaijser, 2004; Höjer et al., 2007).

Notwithstanding these efforts, deteriorating transport infrastructure and traffic congestion in the inner city emerged as major concerns in the 1990s. Support for roads resurrected (Newman and Thornley, 1996). With the rise of neoliberal economic policies, municipalities were placed under political pressure to sell publicly-owned land to the highest bidder, setting aside other considerations such as land-use or social mix (Schmitt, 2015). In contrast to earlier policies to contain Stockholm's physical and economic growth, a sentiment emerged that "the Stockholm region is the country's engine" and needed to be modernized and made more efficient (Newman and Thornley, 1996). In a climate of market orientation and governmental retreat (Khakee, 1996), the national government appointed a special mediator, Bengt Dennis, the governor of the Bank of Sweden, to garner stakeholder support for a package of traffic investments in the region. The "Dennis package" proposed the construction of a new ring road and a new high-speed tram line around the city and the introduction of tolls along new motorways. These proposals proved to be extremely controversial. Opponents, including the environmental lobby, argued that the package's overarching goal was economic growth, for which the improvement of car access was set as a precondition. In view of the strong opposition, as well as rising construction costs at the time, the Dennis package was shelved. A considerably abridged version was adopted later (Gullberg and Kaijser, 2004). By now, the majority of the ring road had been built. Around the same time, efforts were made to redevelop the Stockholm Central Station area by inserting new buildings and services and refurbishing public spaces (Bertolini and Spit, 1998).

The new millennium found Stockholm without a clear TOD policy despite urban sustainability having a prominent role in planning discourse and the property management division of the national railway company (SJ) lobbying for development around railway stations (Bertolini and Spit, 1998). Overall, the capital's visions for the future are uncertain and conflicting, while the automobile lobby has gained ground. Individual development projects have come to dominate the development scene. Their siting often appears to be accidental rather than based on careful planning and coordination with public transport (Gullberg and Kaijser, 2004). Various new projects have been built along regional motorways and offer ample parking. This laissez-faire approach has blurred the previously sharply defined borders of the inner city (Höjer et al., 2007). TOD is seen as one of several complementary tools which could potentially be adopted but by no means the leading one (Qviström and Bengtsson, 2015).

One flagship example of TOD-influenced brownfield redevelopment stands out—*Hammarby Sjöstad*. It covers 160 ha and houses 20,000 inhabitants. Constituting a marriage of TOD and green urbanism, *Hammarby Sjöstad* is a "new town/in town." Active transport rates are very high, and the environmental footprint of its inhabitants is claimed to be approximately one-third lower than the footprint of residents of Stockholm's suburbs. The town is considered to be a desirable place to live relative to the inner city and the early new towns. Although this development has been criticized as a driver of gentrification, local planners are actively promoting this model abroad (Cervero and Sullivan, 2011; Höjer et al., 2007; Schmitt, 2015).

4. CONCLUSION

The chapter has demonstrated that TOD, albeit called by other names or not named at all in policy, has been an intrinsic principle of planning in Austria, the Netherlands, and Sweden and in their respective capitals since WWII. Far from being a recent North American invention, TOD has its roots in Europe and dates back many decades. Clearly, the enthusiasm with which TOD in its recent embodiment has been received in the United States and Canada has done much to highlight and promote the term in Europe.

In the early postwar period, entire new satellite towns or lobes were developed around the peripheral stations of the rail systems of Vienna, Amsterdam, and Stockholm. This period reflected the economic prosperity and the popular desire to suburbanize in that era. In later years, in parallel with the urban revival movement, TOD efforts were transposed to the inner cities, in new brownfield redevelopments. In both cases (earlier suburban and later urban TODs), the national, regional, and local governments played a major role in steering development toward public transit stations and lines—or in servicing existing housing developments with public transport.

The discourses contained in policy documents in Austria, the Netherlands, and Sweden express support for sustainable and resilient urban and regional development, and include reference to various TOD principles (without referring explicitly to TOD). At the same time, changing political priorities and administrative reform have led to a decline of the status and role of planning, especially at the national and regional levels, which is increasingly framed as a time-consuming and cost-intensive activity. In various cases, the interests of developers are placed ahead of strategic efforts to structure cities and regions in a more environmentally sustainable manner. This situation currently limits the extent to which cities can promote TOD in practice, and may pose a key barrier for TOD in the future.

Notwithstanding the intensity of interactions and the internationalization of planning ideas, efforts to transfer policy and practice from Austria, the Netherlands and Sweden have rarely resulted in specific actions or hard outcomes (see also Pojani and Stead, 2015b). Contextual differences in culture, social setup, language, physical patterns, planning legislation, and financial resources form barriers to transfer. Where transfer has occurred, the imported policies or programs have been adopted to the local context. Adoption is of course a necessary strategy in almost all cases—replication is rarely considered to be a useful option, as the more critical literature on policy transfer and best practices is keen to emphasize (e.g., Evans, 2009a,b).

Although policy transfer and learning are relatively limited on the specific issue of TOD, studying practice elsewhere can nevertheless help practitioners, politicians and academics to understand their "home" situation better and to consider their own practices and knowledge in a different light or with a more critical eye. However, this is unlikely to result in the simple replication of physical developments seen in Vienna, Amsterdam or Stockholm.

REFERENCES

Ache, P., 2015. Netherlands. disP Plan. Rev. 51 (1), 56–57.

Alexander, E., 2002. Metropolitan regional planning in Amsterdam: a case study. Town Plan. Rev. 73 (1), 17–40.

Alpkokin, P., 2012. Historical and critical review of spatial and transport planning in the Netherlands. Land Use Policy 29 (3), 536–547.

Anderton, C., Goedman, J., 2008. The Netherlands. In: Ryser, J., Franchini, T. (Eds.), International Manual of Planning Practice. ISOCARP, The Hague, pp. 230–236.

Bertolini, L., 2005. Cities and transport: exploring the need for new planning approaches. In: Albrechts, L., Mandelbaum, S. (Eds.), The Network Society: A New Context for Planning. Routledge, London, pp. 67–80.

Bertolini, L., Salet, W., 2003. Planning concepts for cities in transition: regionalization of urbanity in the Amsterdam structure plan. Plan. Theory Pract. 4 (2), 131–146.

Bertolini, L., Spit, T., 1998. Cities on Rails: The Redevelopment of Railway Station Areas. Spon, London.

Bertolini, L., Curtis, C., Renne, J., 2012. Station area projects in Europe and beyond: towards transit oriented development? Built Environ. 38 (1), 31–50.

Bourne, L., 1975. Urban systems: strategies for regulation. In: A Comparison of Policies in Britain, Sweden, Australia, and Canada. Clarendon Press, Oxford.

Buehler, R., Pucher, J., Altshuler, A., 2017. Vienna's path to sustainable transport. Int. J. Sustain. Transp. 11 (4), 257–271.

Burtenshaw, D., Bateman, M., Ashworth, G., 1981. The City in West Europe. John Wiley & Sons, Chichester.

Calthorpe, P., 1993. The Next American Metropolis. Princeton Architectural Press, New York.

Cavallo, R., 2007. The railway and the Dutch City. OverHolland 5, 6–10.

Cervero, R., 1995. Sustainable new towns: Stockholm's rail-served satellites. Cities 12 (1), 41–51.
Cervero, R., Sullivan, C., 2011. Green TODs: marrying transit-oriented development and green urbanism. Int. J. Sust. Dev. World Ecol. 18 (3), 210–218.
Dangschat, J., 2015. Austria. disP Plan. Rev. 51 (1), 18–19.
Evans, M., 2009a. New directions in the study of policy transfer. Policy Stud. 30 (3), 237–241.
Evans, M., 2009b. Policy transfer in critical perspective. Policy Stud. 30 (3), 243–268.
Faludi, A., van der Valk, A., 1994. Rule and Order: Dutch Planning Doctrine in the Twentieth Century. Springer, Amsterdam.
Gerrits, L., Rauws, W., de Roo, G., 2012. Dutch spatial planning policies in transition. Plan. Theory Pract. 13 (2), 336–341.
Gullberg, A., Kaijser, A., 2004. City-building regimes in post-war Stockholm. J. Urban Technol. 11 (2), 13–39.
Höjer, M., Gullberg, A., Pettersson, R., 2007. Images of the Future City: Time and Space for Sustainable Development. Springer, Dordrecht.
Höjer, M., Gullberg, A., Pettersson, R., 2011. Backcasting images of the future city: time and space for sustainable development in Stockholm. Technol. Forecast. Soc. Chang. 78, 819–834.
Khakee, A., 1996. Urban planning in China and Sweden in a comparative perspective. Prog. Plan. 46, 91–140.
Lichtenberger, E., 1993. Vienna: Bridge Between Cultures. Belhaven Press, London and New York.
Newman, P., Thornley, A., 1996. Urban Planning in Europe: International Competition, National Systems and Planning Projects. Routledge, London and New York.
Novy, A., Redak, V., Jäger, J., 2001. The end of red Vienna: recent ruptures and continuities in urban governance. Eur. Urban Reg. Stud. 8 (2), 131–144.
Persson, C., 2013. Deliberation or doctrine? Land use and spatial planning for sustainable development in Sweden. Land Use Policy 34, 301–313.
Pojani, D., Stead, D., 2014a. Dutch planning policy: the resurgence of TOD. Land Use Policy 41, 357–367.
Pojani, D., Stead, D., 2014b. Ideas, interests, and institutions: explaining Dutch transit-oriented development challenges. Environ. Plan. A 46 (10), 2401–2418.
Pojani, D., Stead, D., 2015a. Transit-oriented *design* in the Netherlands. J. Plan. Educ. Res. 35 (2), 131–144.
Pojani, D., Stead, D., 2015b. Going Dutch? The export of sustainable land-use and transport planning concepts from the Netherlands. Urban Stud. 52 (9), 1558–1576.
Qviström, M., 2015. Putting accessibility in place: a relational reading of accessibility in policies for transit-oriented development. Geoforum 58, 166–173.
Qviström, M., Bengtsson, J., 2015. What kind of transit-oriented development? Using planning history to differentiate a model for sustainable development. Eur. Plan. Stud. 23, 2516–2534. https://doi.org/10.1080/09654313.2015.1016900.
Roodbol-Mekkes, P.H., van der Valk, A.J., Korthals Altes, W.K., 2012. The Netherlands spatial planning doctrine in disarray in the 21st century. Environ. Plan. A 44 (2), 377–395.
Rubitzki, I., Schrenk, M., 2008. Austria. In: Ryser, J., Franchini, T. (Eds.), International Manual of Planning Practice. ISOCARP, The Hague, pp. 2–14.
Rydén, E., Palmér, K., Wirén, E., 2008. Sweden. In: Ryser, J., Franchini, T. (Eds.), International Manual of Planning Practice. ISOCARP, The Hague, pp. 294–302.
Salet, W., 2005. Amsterdam and the north wing of the Randstad. In: Kreukels, A., Salet, W., Thornley, A. (Eds.), Metropolitan Governance and Spatial Planning: Comparative Case Studies of European City-Regions. Routledge, London, pp. 175–188.

Schmitt, P., 2015. Sweden. disP Plan. Rev. 51 (1), 72–73.
Schremmer, C., 2014. Vienna, smart urban development. In: Report. Institute for the Environment and Regional Development, Vienna.
Schulman, M., Böhme, K., 2000. New dynamics in a municipal-based planning system: spatial planning in Sweden. Built Environ. 26 (1), 72–81.
Schwanen, T., Dijst, M., Dieleman, F.M., 2004. Policies for urban form and their impact on travel: the Netherlands experience. Urban Stud. 41 (3), 579–603.
Shetter, W., 1988. The Netherlands in Perspective: The Organization of Society and Environment. Martinus Nijhoff, Leiden.
Spaans, M., 2006. Recent changes in the Dutch planning system: towards a new governance model? Town Plan. Rev. 77 (2), 127–146.
Strong, A.L., 1971. Planned Urban Environments: Sweden, Finland, Israel, The Netherlands, France. The John Hopkins Press, Baltimore and London.
Van Duinen, L., 2013. Mainport and corridor: exploring the mobilizing capacities of Dutch spatial concepts. Plan. Theory Pract. 14, 211–232.
Waterhout, B., Othengrafen, F., Sykes, O., 2012. Neo-liberalization processes and spatial planning in France, Germany, and the Netherlands: an exploration. Plan. Pract. Res. 28 (1), 141–159.

CHAPTER FIVE

Transport Policy in the Era of Ridehailing and Other Disruptive Transportation Technologies

Giovanni Circella*,†,1, Farzad Alemi*
*Institute of Transportation Studies, University of California, Davis, CA, United States
†School of Civil and Environmental Engineering, Georgia Institute of Technology, Atlanta, GA, United States
[1]Corresponding author: e-mail address: gcircella@ucdavis.edu

Contents

Abstract

Transportation is changing at an unprecedented pace. New transportation options provided by shared mobility providers are expanding the set of travel alternatives and they account for an increasing percentage of total trips. In particular, ridehailing services, such as those provided by Uber and Lyft, have become a popular option for trips in cities and metropolitan areas of North America. Understanding the impacts of these mobility services on the use of other travel modes and other components of travel behavior is not easy. In this chapter, we analyze the use of ridehailing using data from the California Millennials Dataset, a rich dataset that contains information on individual attitudes, residential location, vehicle ownership, travel behavior and the adoption of emerging transportation services from approximately 2000 millennials and members of the preceding Generation X in California. We find that users of ridehailing are predominantly well-educated independent millennials or young Gen Xers, who do not have children and live in urban neighborhoods. These travelers also tend to use ridehailing more frequently. Suburban residents who live with their families are less likely to use Uber/Lyft frequently, though their likelihood of using ridehailing increases if they make long-distance trips by plane. We find that single-user ridehailing replaces the use of public transit, walking and bicycling, and, to some extent, the use of a private vehicle. Only a minority of travelers increases public transportation use, e.g., through using ridehailing for first-/last-mile access to public transportation terminals. Based on the results from this research, we urge planners and policy makers to regulate these services to maximize societal benefits through a combination of pricing and other

Advances in Transport Policy and Planning, Volume 1
ISSN 2543-0009
https://doi.org/10.1016/bs.atpp.2018.08.001

policies that lead to the integration of ridehailing with other transportation options, expand travel options for those that do not own a car, increase the shared used of vehicles, and support the use of public transportation and active travel modes.

Keywords: Shared mobility, Travel behavior, Transport policy, Ridehailing, Autonomous vehicles

1. INTRODUCTION

Transportation is changing at an unprecedented pace. The increased availability of locational data and the continuously-increasing number of information and communication technology (ICT) solutions, and in particular smartphone-based applications, are transforming transportation supply and demands in many ways. Among other effects, they provide opportunities for the introduction and deployment of a wide range of transportation services and for reinventing vehicle ownership models.

Among the new technology-enabled transportation options, modern shared-mobility services merge the advantages of mobile communications and instant reservations with the principles of the sharing economy. In doing so, they separate access to transportation services from the fixed costs of auto ownership and provide cheaper options than driving one's own car to several groups of travelers (Davidson and Webber, 2017). These technology-enabled services can affect travel behavior in multiple ways, e.g., they increase the number of available options for a trip, reduce travel uncertainty, increase the attractiveness of living in zero- (or low-)vehicle households, and potentially increase the efficiency of transportation.

Shared-mobility services range from carsharing, including fleet-based round-trip and one-way services such as Zipcar and Car2Go or peer-to-peer services such as Turo, to ridesharing services, including dynamic carpooling such as Carma and ridehailing such as Uber and Lyft, as well as bikesharing services. The availability of these technology-based services has significantly increased in the past few years, though it still varies considerably across cities and regions (Hallock and Inglis, 2015; Shaheen et al., 2016). The range of these services is expected to evolve even faster in the near future thanks to the integration of multiple transportation services, smartphone apps and technological platforms.[a]

[a] In the future, the integration of other technologies, including autonomous and connected vehicles, will lead to big changes in the field of "mobility as a service" (MaaS), including the convergence of carsharing and ridehailing services into fleets of shared automated vehicles that are accessible "on demand."

One of the most rapidly growing—and controversial—forms of shared-mobility services is ridehailing, also known as ride-sourcing, on-demand ride services, or transportation network companies (TNCs), such as Uber and Lyft in the U.S. market. Didi, Grab, and Ola are the other major providers of ridehailing services mainly serving the markets of China, South Asian countries, and India, respectively. Ridehailing services are similar to taxi services in that they connect travelers requesting a ride with the network of available drivers through a smartphone application. They are different from dynamic ridesharing services such as Carma in the United States or BlaBlaCar in Europe, because drivers who participate in the latter only offer rides to other travelers (with similar destinations) along the route of a trip the driver would be taking anyway. Instead, ridehailing drivers "chauffeur" passengers to their destination, independently from the drivers' own travel needs.

The availability and popularity of these services are quickly growing. So do their impacts on transportation demand and traffic congestion. For example, a study of ridehailing in San Francisco showed that the share of total trips made with Uber and Lyft (approximately 170,000 trips per day) exceeds 15% of all trips inside the city of San Francisco on a typical weekday (SFCTA, 2017), which is equivalent to 20% of total vehicle miles traveled (VMT) inside San Francisco, and 6.5% of total VMT including both intra- and inter-city trips. The rapid growth in the adoption and frequency of use of ridehailing poses significant challenges to transportation planners and policy makers. According to some estimates, the combined ridership of Uber, Lyft and taxis is likely to surpass local bus ridership in the United States by the end of 2018, making them among the largest urban transportation providers (Schaller, 2018). However, to date, the factors affecting the use of these services and their impacts on the other components of travel behavior and vehicle ownership are still largely unexplored.

Understanding how ridehailing, and shared mobility more in general, is changing travel behaviors today, and how autonomous shared-mobility services will change them in the future, is not easy. Recent studies of shared mobility suggest that the impacts of shared-mobility services vary significantly depending on the types of services available, the local context in which the services are provided, the characteristics of the users, and the differences among various subsets of the population. Further, several reasons limit transportation researchers in their ability to answer these questions including (1) the lack of data on users of shared mobility, the nature of the use, and the resulting changes in travel behavior; (2) the uncertainty over the evolution and maturation of shared-mobility services and their impacts over time; and (3) the heterogeneity in their impacts owing to differences in the local context and the characteristics of the users.

Despite this limited knowledge, transportation planners and policy makers are called to regulate this dynamic sector and make important decisions on transportation investments in a quickly changing landscape. This book chapter helps closing (at least partially) this gap, through discussing the findings that are available, to date, from the literature and from the research carried out by its authors, and discussing conclusions that are relevant to transportation policy. Specifically, we discuss the factors that affect the adoption and frequency of use of ridehailing among various sociodemographic groups and in various geographic contexts, using data collected in California, and the limitations that prevent travelers from (or reduce their likelihood of) using these services. Further, we discuss the impacts that the use of these services has on other components of travel behavior, and in particular on the use of other modes of transportation such as driving a personal vehicle, riding public transit and/or walking and bicycling. We discuss findings available from the analysis of the California Millennials Dataset, a detailed mobility dataset collected in California among young adults (millennials) and members of the preceding Generation X, as the first round of data collection in a panel study of emerging transportation trends and adoption of technologies (Circella et al., 2018). Based on the insights from these analyses, we discuss policy goals (and areas for policy implementation) on how to govern the evolution of transportation and help prepare cities and regions for a future increasingly dominated by demand-responsive and technology-based transportation services, which have the potential to revolutionize the way we travel, organize our schedules and engage in activities.

2. TRANSPORTATION AT THE TIME OF SHARED MOBILITY

Limited information exists on the changes brought by the introduction of technology-based shared-mobility services, and their impacts on travel behavior and mode choice. Recent studies suggest that the impacts of shared mobility may significantly vary depending on the types of services that are implemented, the local context in which the services are provided, the characteristics of the users, and the differences among various subsets of the population. For example, researchers found mixed, even contradictory, results about the impact of carsharing on public transit:

Firnkorn and Müller (2011) as well as Costain et al. (2012) showed that carsharing can complement the use of public transit, while Le Vine et al. (2014) observed that one-way carsharing is mostly used in place of public transportation. The same is true about the impacts of bikesharing programs. Bikesharing tends to increase transit use for those living in the urban periphery, where access to public transportation by walk is limited, but it decreases transit use for individuals in the urban core (Buck et al., 2013; Martin and Shaheen, 2014).

Ridehailing (also known as ride-sourcing, on-demand ride services or transportation network companies, or TNCs) is probably the fastest growing form of shared mobility and is causing huge disruptions to the transportation sector. The studies that investigate the adoption of ridehailing and the impacts of these services on various components of travel behavior are still limited due to the limited availability of data and lack of robust approaches that can capture the causal relationship between the use of these services and other components of travel behavior. Most studies, to date, are based on either descriptive statistics of the self-reported behavioral changes, or other proxy variables such as Google trend data that are used to measure the intensity of use of Uber/Lyft. Further, many of the existing studies ignore the potential heterogeneity associated with the use and the impacts of ridehailing on other means of transportation among various groups of users, they do not control for the effects of various confounders/covariates and only report aggregate results (e.g., sample means for these variables). Other relevant issues with these studies are the use of convenience or other non-representative samples, as in the case of studies that focus on university students, and the focus on large metropolitan areas. Little information has been collected, to date, on the use of these services in smaller cities and/or in suburban/rural areas. Thus, it is difficult to extrapolate the findings from the existing studies and generalize them to the entire population. Additional difficulties associated with these studies are the on-going maturation of ridehailing services and their impacts over time (Circella et al., 2018).

The adoption of ridehailing can affect travel behavior in a number of ways, e.g., increasing the number of available options for a trip, providing a flexible alternative to driving, or enhancing public transportation efficiency through integrating first- and last-mile access/egress and providing rides when public transit is not safe/available (Circella et al., 2016, 2018; Shaheen et al., 2015, 2018; Taylor et al., 2015). Thus, the use of ridehailing can affect many transportation-related decisions, including activity patterns, mode choice, vehicle miles traveled, and vehicle ownership. For example, in one study, about 40% of Uber/Lyft users in San Francisco reported that they reduced their driving due to the adoption of ridehailing (Rayle et al., 2014). Patrons of such services may also use them as a substitute for or as a complement to the use of public transit (Babar and Burtch, 2017; Clewlow and Mishra, 2017; Feigon and Murphy, 2018; Hampshire et al., 2017). In the longer term, users may dispose of one or more of their vehicles and turn to ridehailing as their primary means of travel (Hampshire et al., 2017; Henderson, 2017). Other technology-enabled transportation services, such as carsharing, are sometimes credited with similar effects on auto ownership (Mishra et al., 2017; Roberts, 2017). However, as carsharing currently accounts for a smaller percentage of total trips (than ridehailing), its impacts on travel behavior and vehicle ownership are more limited.

It is not yet clear the extent to which ridehailing affects vehicle miles traveled (VMT). Whether or not ridehailing increases total VMT depends on the balance of competing forces: on one hand, these services divert non-driving trips to a driving mode, and add new types of VMT for dead-head repositioning of vehicles. On the other hand, these services reduce personal vehicle dependency and cruising for parking. Henao (2017) evaluated the changes in total VMT by providing a ride to more than 300 Uber and Lyft riders in Denver, Colorado. The author found that total VMT increased by approximately 85%, when accounting for all factors including dead-heads and the potential substitution (or eventual complementarity) effects on the use of other modes. Similarly, Schaller (2017) reported that in 2016 the use of Uber/Lyft contributed to a 3.5% increase in VMT in New York City and a 7% increase in Manhattan, western Queens, and Western Brooklyn. Schaller (2018) suggested that even pooled ridehailing services, such as UberPOOL and Lyft Line, which are increasingly available in large American cities, contribute to an increase in total VMT.

Uber and Lyft are more often used for short trips: data from the ridehailing operators in five U.S. metro areas showed that the average Uber/Lyft trips are between 2 and 4 miles (Feigon and Murphy, 2018), suggesting potential impacts on the use of non-motorized modes (i.e., walking and bicycling). Little is known about the impact of this door-to-door services on walking and biking, but it is expected that Uber/Lyft might affect the adoption of these modes in either direction. In the analysis of our data from California, we showed that about 25% of millennials and 12% of Gen Xers who used ridehailing would have walked or biked in the absence of these services (Alemi et al., 2018a). We also found that the use of ridehailing increases walking and bicycling for some individuals—e.g., if instead of driving for an entire trip/tour, a user walks on one leg and returns by Uber/Lyft, or walk for part of the trip, before catching a ride with these services—but to a smaller extent. Henao (2017) showed that out of 311 respondents, about 12% of them would have walked or biked if Uber/Lyft was not available. In another study, Hampshire et al. (2017) found that the temporary halting of Uber/Lyft led to a small increase (about 2.5%) in the use of non-motorized modes, suggesting that the substitution effect of ridehailing on walking and biking is prevalent.

The changes in individuals' travel behavior can create a number of societal and economic challenges or opportunities: ridehailing may contribute to improving equity, e.g., providing access to those who do not have access to a vehicle. In other contexts, it may expedite gentrification and dividedness. Or it can help decrease traffic fatalities, e.g., providing alternatives to driving, and avoiding drinking and driving. Depending on the circumstances, ridehailing can amplify or attenuate negative transportation-related externalities, including traffic congestion and greenhouse gas (GHG) emissions. For example, Henao (2017) reported that about 19.5% of Uber/Lyft riders used ridehailing to avoid the difficulty of searching and paying for parking. The largest impact of ridehailing on parking is expected to occur at large event locations (e.g., stadium, concerts), as well as airports and dense urban neighborhoods, where parking costs and search time are often prohibitive. Cortright (2016) confirmed this issue and showed that the growth in the use of Uber/Lyft is highly correlated with parking prices. The reduction in the demand and cruising for parking can ultimately affect traffic congestion and transportation emissions. On the other hand, cruising of vacant ridehailing vehicles or the use of parking space for these vehicles while they wait for a passenger can worsen traffic conditions and generate additional demand for parking in certain locations. More research is required to better understand these impacts.

3. ADOPTION OF RIDEHAILING

This chapter builds on a large research effort undertaken to investigate the relationships among individual attitudes, lifestyles, residential location, travel behavior and vehicle ownership, the adoption of shared mobility, and the aspiration to purchase and use a vehicle vs use other means of transportation among young adults (millennials) and older adults in California. As part of the study, we collected a rich dataset in fall 2015 with a detailed online survey that was administered to a sample of 2400 California residents, including millennials (i.e., young adults, 18–34 year old in 2015) and members of the preceding Generation X (i.e., middle-age adults, 35–50). The data collection is part of a longitudinal study of emerging transportation trends in California, designed with a rotating panel structure, with additional waves of data collection in 2018 and during the following years. In the first wave of data collection, we used an online opinion panel and a quota sampling approach to recruit respondents from each of the six major regions of California and three dominant neighborhood types (urban, suburban and rural). The six regions are the San Francisco Bay Area (identified by the boundaries of the San Francisco's Metropolitan Transportation Commission, or MTC), the Greater Los Angeles Area (following the boundaries of the Southern California Association of Governments, or SCAG), Sacramento (following the boundaries of the Sacramento Area Council of Governments, or SACOG), San Diego (following the boundaries of the San Diego Association of Governments, or SANDAG), the Central Valley of California (including the eight counties in the central San Joaquin River valley) and the Rest of California and Others (including the remaining predominantly rural, mountain and coastal regions in the state). We controlled for sociodemographic targets including household income, gender, race and ethnicity, and presence of children in the household in the data collection, and used a combination of cell weighting and the iterative proportional fitting (IPF) raking approach to reduce the sample non-representativeness of the population of California. For additional information on the survey content, data collection and data processing, see Circella et al. (2016, 2017b, 2018).

Fig. 1 shows the proportion of users that have used ridehailing (either in their hometown or while traveling away from home) in California, by neighborhood type. The following Fig. 2 shows the distribution of users vs non-users by geographical region in the state. Even if ridehailing has been introduced to the market more recently than other shared-mobility services such as carsharing and bikesharing, it already accounts for a larger proportion of total trips, and the proportion of individuals that report they have already used ridehailing is higher than the proportions of users of other shared-mobility services (Circella et al., 2018). Fig. 3 summarizes the distributions of the use of ridehailing in the hometown and when traveling away from home for millennials and the members of the preceding Generation X.

In order to investigate the way the adoption of ridehailing varies among different segments of the population, we estimated a model of the adoption

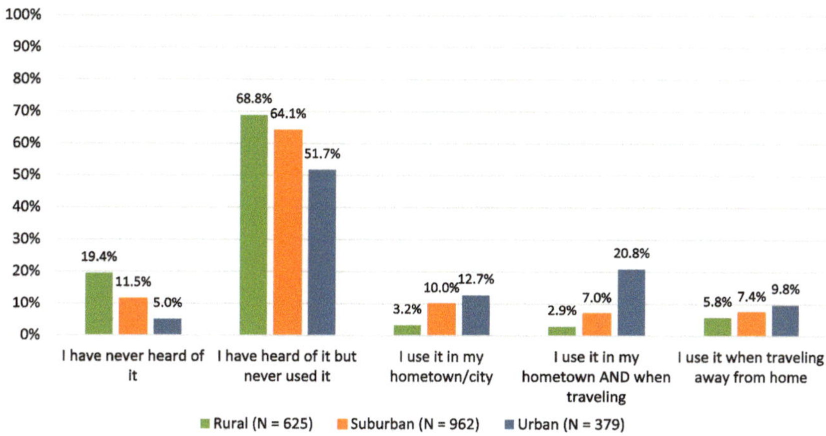

Fig. 1 Awareness and use of ridehailing (Uber/Lyft) by neighborhood type ($N = 1966$).

of Uber/Lyft,[b] and investigated the impact of sociodemographics, built environment characteristics, individual lifestyles and personal attitudes on the likelihood of using these services. We found that better-educated and higher-income older millennials are more likely to adopt ridehailing, in line with the findings from previous studies based on descriptive statistics (e.g., Feigon et al., 2016; Rayle et al., 2014; Taylor et al., 2015). This seems also consistent with the other travel choices of the members of the millennial generation, who tend to more often live in zero-/lower-vehicle owning households, drive less and use non-motorized means of transportation more often compared to the previous cohorts at the same age (Blumenberg et al., 2016; Frändberg and Vilhelmson, 2011; Kuhnimhof et al., 2012), likely due to a combination of (a) generational differences in lifestyles and individual attitudes, (b) period effects and economic conditions, and (c) stage in life cycle and residential location. We also found that individuals who do not work nor study and those of Hispanic origin are less likely to use ridehailing. Not surprisingly, those who have previously used taxis and carsharing services are more likely to use ridehailing. For more details on the model estimation, and a more complete discussion of the model results, see Alemi et al. (2018a).

To test for the impact of individual attitudes and preferences on the adoption of on-demand ride services, we also incorporated factor scores as explanatory variables in the adoption model. The rate of adoption of ridehailing was found to be significantly higher among individuals with

[b] Additional details on the model estimation and complete results are available in Alemi et al. (2018a).

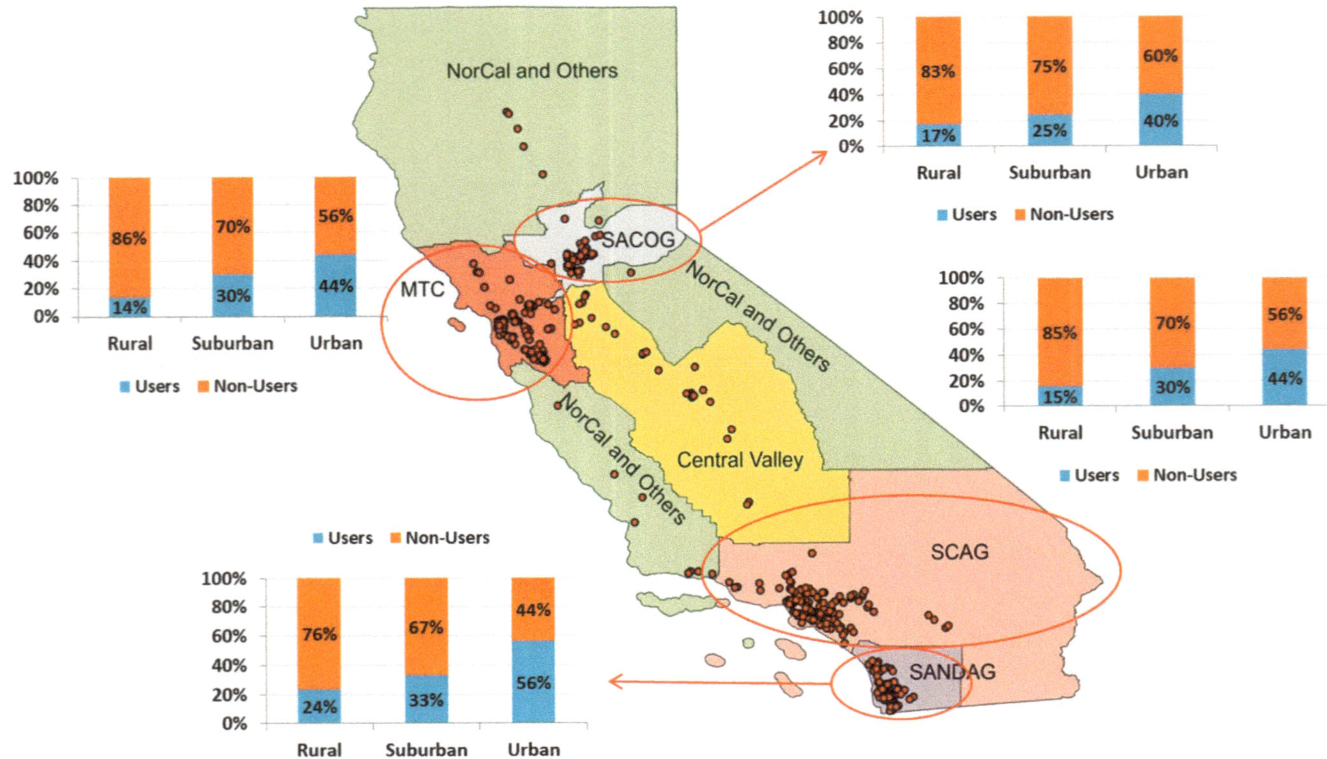

Fig. 2 Adoption of ridehailing by region of California and neighborhood type ($N = 1707$).

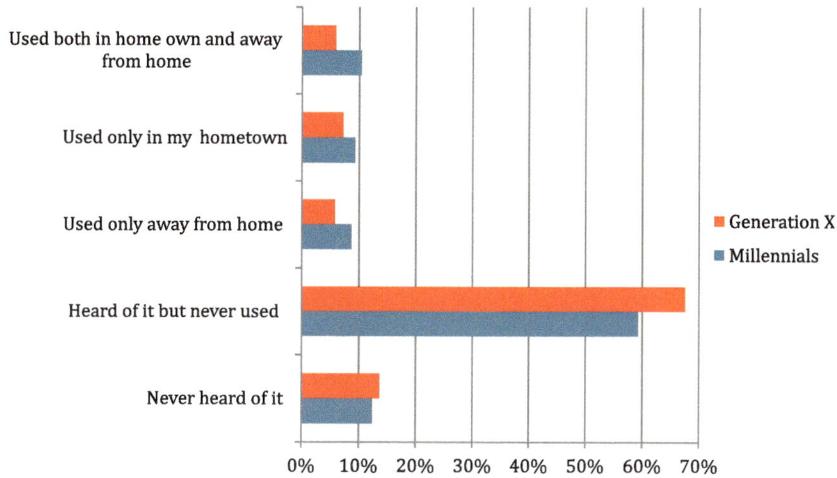

Fig. 3 Awareness and use of Uber and Lyft by age group ($N_{\text{Millennials}}=1073$, $N_{\text{Gen X}}=888$).

more positive attitudes toward technology embracing, pro-environmental policies, and seeking variety in life. These attitudes are consistent with a profile of young, dynamic, and variety-seeking users of these services.

The inclusion of attitudinal variables in the adoption model improved its goodness of fit while it only had a small impact on the coefficients and statistical significance of the other explanatory variables in the model, with the only exception of age. The inclusion of the attitudinal variables in the model reduces the magnitude of the estimated coefficients for the age group-related variables, thus signaling the fact that the apparent impact of age and generation on the adoption of these technological transportation services can be more properly explained in terms of lifestyles, individual preferences and stage in life. Because these attitudes are correlated with age, when models do not explicitly control for individual attitudes and lifestyles, their effects are attributed to the age group variables (which act as a proxy for these other unobserved variables in explaining these behaviors).

Further, individuals with higher familiarity with modern technologies (e.g., use of smartphones to access information on transportation services, and use of carsharing), and frequent long-distance travelers (in particular those that travel often by plane) are more likely to use ridehailing. Studying the adoption of ridehailing while controlling for both individual attitudes and the adoption of information and communication technologies (e.g., smartphone use) allows us to further separate the role of these variables from age. Overall, the adoption of ridehailing is found to be affected both by technology-savviness, which is accounted for by the technology-related attitudes and the use of smartphones, and by the stage in life and residential location, which affect the likelihood that an individual finds herself in situations that are more conducive to the use of Uber and Lyft. Previous studies on ridehailing have suggested an important role of the built environmental characteristics on affecting the adoption of ridehailing. In our analyses, we found that living in urban neighborhoods is associated with a higher likelihood of being an Uber/Lyft user. Among various built environment characteristics, the degree of land use mix, regional auto accessibility, and public transit availability and quality have the strongest impacts on the adoption of ridehailing (Alemi et al., 2018a).

In order to better understand the factors that affect the use of on-demand ride services, we employed a latent-class choice model to control for individuals' taste heterogeneity and variations (Alemi et al., forthcoming; Circella et al., 2018). In the model, we jointly estimate the adoption of ridehailing and stochastically segment individuals based on their socioeconomic and demographic attributes, such that those who put similar weight on the various factors influencing their decision regarding the use of these services are grouped together.

The latent-class choice model comprises two models: (1) the class membership model and (2) the class-specific choice model. We defined our latent classes such that represent the variations in individual lifestyles, whereas the factors affecting the adoption of on-demand ride services are tested in the class-specific choice models of the adoption of Uber/Lyft.

Similar to our binary model of ridehailing adoption that we previously discussed, we divided the explanatory variables available in the dataset into four main categories: (1) Sociodemographic variables; (2) Built environmental variables; (3) Technology adoption and the use of social media; and (4) Long-distance travel and number of vehicles in the households. After testing several solutions with different numbers of latent classes and model specifications, the final solution which provided the best performance, in terms of model fit and interpretability of the results, includes three latent classes. In the latent-class model, we model class membership based on individuals' lifestyles and their stage in life. Fig. 4 summarizes the main characteristics of the members of the three classes. The class that is largely composed of higher educated independent millennials (i.e., millennials who have already established their own households) has the highest

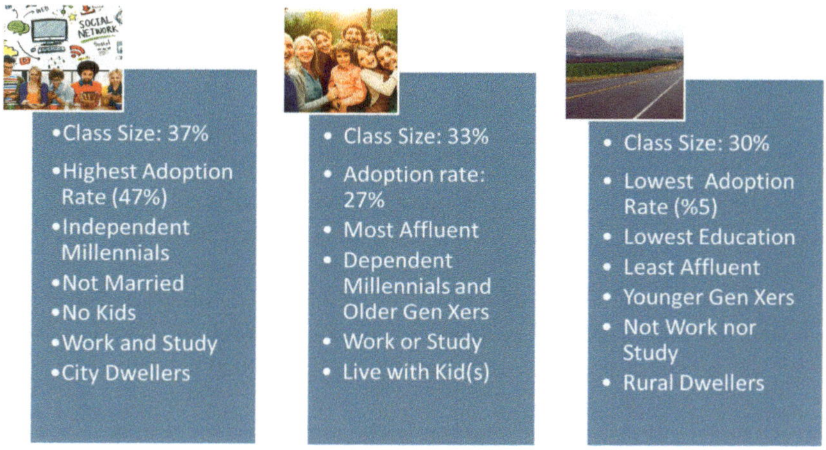

Fig. 4 Characteristics of the latent classes of Uber and Lyft users.

adoption rate, while the adoption of ridehailing is lowest among the members of a class that is largely composed of less affluent individuals with lower education.

Independent millennials (i.e., those who have already established their household and do not live with their parents) are grouped mainly in Class 1 (37% of total respondents in the sample): the members of this class are usually not married and tend to live in households without kids. This class has the highest number of individuals who both work and study at the same time. Individuals in Class 2 (33% of total respondents) tend to be more affluent and are usually *dependent* millennials (e.g., young adults that still live with their family of origin) or older members of the Generation X. In most cases, individuals in this class live in households with children below 18 years old. The high frequency of long-distance trips, especially when made by plane, increases the likelihood of using ridehailing among the members of this class, who often live with their families in suburban locations and use these services to access major transportation facilities and terminals. Individuals with the lowest education level and who are the least affluent are more likely to belong to Class 3 (30% of total respondents). This class has the highest share of younger members of the Generation X and a large share of individuals who do not work or study. Additional information and details on the model estimation can be found in Alemi et al. (forthcoming) and Circella et al. (2018).

Key findings: Adoption of Uber/Lyft

- Higher-educated older millennials (between 25 and 34, in 2015) are more likely to use ridehailing than other groups.
- Greater land-use mix and more central urban locations are associated with higher adoption of Uber and Lyft.
- Higher adoption is observed among individuals who make a large number of long-distance trips, and in particular those who travel more frequently by plane.
- The degree of familiarity with ICT and other technology-enabled transportation services positively affects the adoption of Uber/Lyft.
- Those who have previously used taxis and carsharing are more likely to use ridehailing.
- The rate of ridehailing adoption is significantly higher among individuals with stronger *technology-embracing*, *pro-environment*, and *variety-seeking* attitudes.

Few studies have investigated the factors affecting the frequency of use of ridehailing services. A recent study from the Pew Research Center (2016) showed that out of the 15% respondents in their sample who reported that they have used ridehailing ($N=4787$), only 3% and 12% reported that they use it on a daily and weekly basis, respectively. The research confirmed that younger adults tend to use Uber/Lyft more frequently. Similarly, Feigon et al. (2016) showed that the most frequent ridehailing users live in middle-income households (annual income of $50,000 to 75,000). Both studies showed that frequent users of Uber/Lyft are more likely to live in households with a lower-than-average number of vehicles per driver and to rely on other means of transportation, including public transit or active travel modes.

Using the information in the California Millennials Dataset, we estimated (a) an ordered probit model with sample selection and (b) a zero-inflated ordered probit model to understand the factors affecting the frequency of use of ridehailing (Alemi et al., 2018b). For the purposes of this analysis, we classified individuals as *non-users*, *low-frequency users* (i.e., those who use the service less than once a month) and *high-frequency users* (i.e., those who use the service at least once a month). The results of both models indicate that sociodemographic variables are good predictors for the adoption of ridehailing, and not for the frequency of use of these transportation services. Among the various built environment variables that were controlled for, we find that land use mix and activity density impact the frequency of use of these services. The impact of other built environment variables, including the geographic region where the individual lives and public transit quality and connectivity were only significant in the adoption model. However, the impacts of some of these built environment attributes might have been masked by to the coarse classification of the frequency categories used for this study or, more importantly, by the confounding effects of variables such as mobility/modality styles and other factors affecting individuals' residential location, with which they are correlated. Individuals who use a smartphone in connection to their travel (in particular those who use a smartphone to find new places and to navigate in real time) are more likely to adopt and use these technology-based services more frequently.

Interestingly, though not entirely surprisingly, the results of our analyses indicate that there is competition among various shared-mobility services. Those who have used carsharing (e.g., Zipcar) before are also more likely to adopt ridehailing. However, frequent users of carsharing tend to use ridehailing less frequently. Among various travel-related decisions, we found that frequent long-distance travelers (in particular those with higher shares of long-distance leisure trips made by plane) and individuals who live in zero-vehicle households tend to use ridehailing more often. We also found that the frequency of Uber/Lyft use decreases among individuals who evaluate the preference to use (have) their own vehicle as a strongly limiting factor in using these services (Alemi et al., 2018b).

Key findings: Frequency of use of Uber/Lyft

- About 17% and 15% of millennials use ridehailing less than once a month and at least once a month, respectively. These shares decrease to 14% and 8%, respectively, for the members of Generation X.
- Individuals who live in a zero-vehicle household are more likely to use Uber/Lyft with higher frequency.
- Frequent long-distance travelers (by plane, in particular) use Uber/Lyft more often.
- Land-use mix and activity density (i.e., population and job density) impact the frequency of use of ridehailing.
- Individuals who frequently use smartphone apps to determine destination and route choice are more likely to both adopt ridehailing and use it more often.
- There is competition among shared-mobility services: carsharing users are more likely also to use ridehailing (compared to those who do not use carsharing), but frequent users of carsharing tend to use Uber/Lyft less frequently.

4. IMPACTS OF RIDEHAILING ON THE USE OF OTHER TRAVEL MODES

Ridehailing services are contributing to revolutionizing transportation in particular in more central urban areas. In addition to understanding what factors affect the likelihood of using these services, planners and policy makers have great interest in the impacts that the adoption and use of ridehailing have on the use of other travel modes. In this section, we briefly discuss how the use of on-demand ride services affects the use of other means of transportation using the data collected in California as part of the same research project.

Recent studies indicate that the impact of shared-mobility services, and ridehailing in particular, on other means of transportation vary based on the type of services, the local context, and the characteristics of the users (Circella et al., 2016; Taylor et al., 2015). For example, 40% of TNC users in San Francisco reported that they reduced their driving due to the adoption of ridehailing (Rayle et al., 2014). Further, depending on local circumstances, travelers may use these services as a substitute for or as a complement to the use of public transit. For example, a survey of 4500 users of shared-mobility services revealed that frequent users of shared mobility tend to use public transit more often and are more multimodal than non-users. Some of this relationship may be due to the correlation of both behaviors with other variables and various characteristics of the individuals and their households, such as low-car ownership or more accessible residential locations. A study carried out by Feigon et al. (2016) found that the majority of trips made by ridehailing occurs between 10 p.m. and 4 a.m., when public transit either runs very infrequently or does not run at all. This finding suggests a complementarity effect. On the other hand, public transit may lose its riders as the share of ridehailing increases: A study of seven large U.S. metro areas showed that these services tend to substitute 6% and 3% of the trips that would have been otherwise made by bus and light rail, respectively (Clewlow and Mishra, 2017). However, it is not yet clear the extent to which the adoption of ridehailing causes an increase (or decrease) in transit use, as opposed to both of those conditions being caused by other variables (such as residential location, individual preferences, age/stage in lifecycle, and vehicle ownership).

In this study, we analyzed the self-reported behavioral changes in response to the use of ridehailing (Alemi et al., 2018c) and employed a latent classification approach to classify the self-reported impacts that the last ridehailing trip had on the use of other travel modes (Circella et al., 2018). Very interestingly, we find that, compared to other survey respondents, frequent users of ridehailing more often report that they are considering reducing the number of vehicles in their household (Circella et al., 2018). Further, the latent-class analysis of self-reported behavioral changes provides more meaningful and scientifically interesting results against the noisy background compared to other approaches (e.g., descriptive statistics of self-reported changes). The preliminary results of this analysis are presented in Fig. 5. As shown in the figure, three rather well-defined latent classes were identified in this latent-class analysis:

(a) The first class (which accounts for 53% of individuals who used Uber/Lyft in the sample) predominantly comprises younger independent millennials who tend to live in urban neighborhoods with high walk and transit accessibility. The members of this class travel frequently using a combination of travel options (i.e., they are rather multimodal) and use ridehailing more often compared to the members of all other classes. The use of ridehailing affects their use of other modes of transportation: the members of this class reported that they have reduced their amount of driving, as well as their use of public transportation and active modes as a result of the use of ridehailing.

(b) The members of the second class mainly include suburban dwellers who live in vehicle-sufficient households (i.e., the ratio of cars per household driver is the highest for the members of this class). The members of this class are highly car-dependent individuals who also report the strongest attitudes toward vehicle use and ownership. The members of this class also tend to be among the most frequent air travelers, which leads to the speculation that ridehailing is often adopted as a replacement for other modes as a way to travel to/from the airport. This class accounts for approximately 37% of ridehailing users in our data: they used ridehailing as a perfect substitute to the use of a personal vehicle.

(c) The last class also includes individuals who predominantly live in the suburbs with low public transportation and walk accessibility. This group largely comprises older Gen Xers that have more pro-environmental attitudes. However, the members of this class report that they like biking more than the other classes and they also tend to be surprisingly multimodal, when possible, despite the low accessibility of the locations where they live. This tiny class of individuals

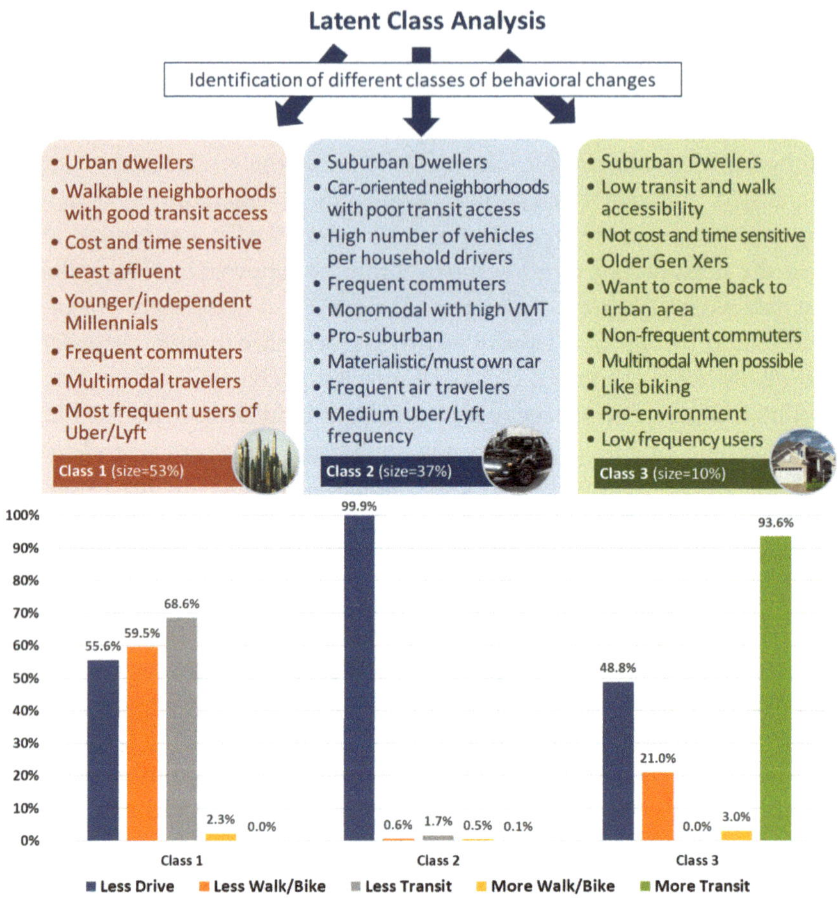

Fig. 5 Latent classes of ridehailing users and impacts on the use of other travel modes.

(which accounts for only 10% of the individuals who reported that they have used ridehailing in our sample[c]) reported that the use of ridehailing led to an increase in the use of public transportation. The members of this class reported that they reduced their driving and use of active modes but they increased their use of public transportation through using Uber/Lyft as an access mode to public transportation stations and stops.

[c] The percentage of ridehailing trips made by the individuals in this class is even lower than that, as the users in this class tend to use Uber/Lyft rather infrequently.

Key findings: Impacts of ridehailing on the use of other travel modes

- Many respondents report that the use of Uber/Lyft reduces their use of a personal car. Ridehailing also substitutes for some trips that would be otherwise made by transit or active modes.
- Somewhat concerning from the perspective of environmental sustainability and the promotion of active lifestyles, a larger proportion of millennials reduced their amount of walking and biking as the result of the use of ridehailing.
- Compared to other survey respondents, frequent users of ridehailing more often report that they are considering reducing the number of vehicles in their household.
- Users can be grouped into three well-defined latent classes, based on the self-reported behavioral changes associated with the use of ridehailing.
- The largest class of users in our sample is mainly composed of independent millennials who live in walkable neighborhoods with high transit accessibility, and are multimodal travelers. Ridehailing has mixed effects on these users, contributing to reducing the use of personal cars, transit and active modes.
- Ridehailing substitutes for the use of a personal vehicle among the members of the class composed of affluent suburban dwellers with positive attitudes toward car ownership and use, and high VMT.
- The use of Uber/Lyft increases the use of public transit (e.g., providing access to transit stations) among a group of predominantly suburban dwellers who live in less accessible areas but try to be multimodal when possible and have pro-environmental attitudes. This group only includes few users, who use ridehailing occasionally.

5. RIDEHAILING AND THE FUTURE OF TRANSPORTATION

This study provides initial insights into the factors that affect the adoption and frequency of use of ridehailing services, such as Uber/Lyft, a fast-growing form of shared mobility that is quickly changing transportation. Through the analysis of data collected in California among millennials and members of the previous Generation X, we find that the initial single-passenger ridehailing services to some extent tend to reduce the amount of driving among both frequent and non-frequent users, and also substitute for trips that would have otherwise been made by public transportation or active modes. The substitution effect is stronger among the frequent users of Uber/Lyft, who are more likely to live in zero-/lower-vehicle households and are more multimodal. Thus, the net VMT impacts of single-passenger services are uncertain but most likely positive, given that reduced trips by private vehicles are offset by the use of ridehailing vehicles, a reduction in public transportation use and some deadheading by Uber/Lyft drivers. Other studies also affirm that single-passenger services have non-trivial effects on VMT, contributing to an overall increase in the total vehicle miles traveled on U.S. roads (Clewlow and Mishra, 2017; Schaller, 2017, 2018).

The results from our study highlight the importance of properly regulating this sector in order to minimize the negative externalities associated with the use of new transportation services such as ridehailing and maximize their potential benefits. The experience from the last few years has shown that letting the market self-regulate has led to an increasing role of ridehailing as a reliable transportation option in central urban areas, often in direct competition with the use of other travel options, including public transportation, walking and bicycling. Ridehailing is a popular travel option, in particular, among younger travelers who live in central locations, often live in households that own zero or few vehicles, and largely rely on non-car transportation options. This puts ridehailing in direct competition with the use of other modes, including public transportation, walking and bicycling, and, to some extent, carsharing.

One apparent benefit is that frequent users of on-demand ride services report that they are more willing to dispose of one or more of their household's vehicle(s). However, the direction of this relationship is not clear: in the next stage of this research we plan to better explore this topic by estimating joint models of the adoption of ridehailing and other components of travel behavior, and testing alternative causality structures to explore the relationships between the adoption of these services and individuals' changes in travel behavior and vehicle ownership over time through the analysis of longitudinal data.

The findings from this study help planners and policy makers better understand how shared-mobility services are transforming transportation, what factors limit/encourage their use, and how their adoption affects the use of other modes of transportation. Particularly challenging is the issue of public transportation. Single-traveler ridehailing services inevitably divert some passengers from public transportation, undermining an important public service. Our study and others provide some insights into this phenomenon, but the effects are still uncertain due to large variability across demographic groups, transit service levels, and limited data availability.

Moving forward, some opportunities exist to align societal benefits with the expansion of these technological services. Shared mobility can be integrated with public transportation to provide better overall service, with lower economic and environmental costs, especially since public transportation is often called upon to offer services in lightly populated areas that could be served at lower cost by a variety of demand-responsive services. Many U.S. public transportation operators have started partnering with Uber, Lyft and others to reduce their costs of providing the service and improve accessibility (Polzin and Sperling, 2018). In some cases, they themselves are offering demand-responsive services in vans and small buses on routes with lower demand (as in the case of *microtransit*) to complement the fixed-route services provided along major transportation corridors.

It is of the outmost importance to establish the right pricing mechanisms to incentivize the use of these services under certain circumstances, e.g., when connecting to/from a major transportation hub as a first-/last-mile access solution, while discouraging their use in situations where they directly compete with mass transit and generate additional traffic congestion in the central core of cities. Further, the use of appropriate pricing mechanisms can be used to promote higher-occupancy of vehicles, e.g., promoting shared rides instead of single-occupant ridehailing.

The role (and impacts) of ridehailing will likely become even more relevant as the society transitions toward a future dominated by autonomous vehicles and *mobility as a service* (*MaaS*) solutions, which provide increased access to transportation without the fixed costs of auto ownership. Ridehailing has already contributed to reducing the cost per mile of accessing on-demand transportation. The marginal cost to provide a ride will be further reduced as TNC fleets increasingly transition to fleet of electric vehicles, putting additional pressure on public transportation and the use of other means of travel. In the future, vehicle automation will allow reducing the marginal cost to access these services through reducing (or eliminating) the cost of labor. There will be increasing need to coordinate policy making and incentives in order to harvest the potential benefits of these services, while reducing the negative effects. Some public benefits would be achieved by promoting the pooling services (e.g., UberPOOL and Lyft Line) and integrating these options with other transportation services, such as public transportation.

Pooling services may have positive, neutral, or negative impacts, depending on what other modes of transportation the use of these services replaces and the extent to which the pooled services actually carry multiple passengers (and/or require additional driving miles to pick up/drop off the various passengers). The potential benefits may expand to societal, environmental and economic benefits, such as reduced road infrastructure costs, greenhouse gas emissions, and parking demand. However, adequate policies including trip fees, introduction of congestion pricing and public transit priority should be considered to help cities manage ridehailing demand, and manage the limited street space (Schaller, 2018). Uber and Lyft executives widely assert that they are strongly committed to pooling services as a way to increase ridership, revenue, and profits (Sperling et al., 2018). To achieve successful pooling services and achieve the goal of increased transportation sustainability (and efficiency), policy makers need a better understanding of who might use pooling services and what incentives and policies would be most effective at encouraging them to do so. More research is needed to determine the price elasticity for various groups of travelers (by trip purpose) and to understand individuals' willingness to share rides with strangers. As discussed by Sperling et al. (2018), the public sector can support pooling services in various forms, for instance, by giving priority access and/or rights of way to pooling services as a way to lower travel times.

In addition to understanding the factors affecting the adoption and frequency of use of ridehailing, there is interest in understanding the degree to which current Uber/Lyft users will continue to use ridehailing as they transition to later stages of life and as they move to other residential locations (Taylor et al., 2015). The emergence of other technology-enabled transportation services, such as pooled ridehailing, and the future introduction of autonomous and connected vehicles raise questions about the eventual permanence of the observed travel patterns and how shared mobility will continue to reshape transportation in future years.

Ridehailing services are already offered in a variety of forms. In the future, they will likely operate without drivers, providing one of the first applications of driverless vehicles on the market, with either a traditional "pay-as-you-ride" model or a subscription plan business model. When driverless vehicles become available, the challenges of managing travel will become even more complex. Autonomous vehicles (AVs) have the potential to dramatically change future travel demand. They may lead to, among other effects, safer roads, reduced congestion, increased network capacity, improved travel comfort and increased utility of traveling by personal vehicles, and reduced parking requirements. However, the future and the promised benefits of vehicle automation are far from certain, and more research is needed to fully understand the upcoming opportunities and challenges that will arise. Limited information exists, to date, on the potential effects associated with the additional travel demand induced by the enhanced features of autonomous vehicles, but some empirical evidence in this area of research points to a substantial increase in car travel and VMT (Harb et al., 2018; Malokin et al., 2015). Accordingly, several interventions will be required to ensure that future transportation services move in the right direction, and the deployment of these transportation technologies do not further contribute to car dependence and negative externalities of transportation (Circella et al., 2017a). Governing this dynamic field, at a time of changing technologies and evolving travel behaviors, will be a primary challenge that planners and policy makers will have to face in the next few years.

ACKNOWLEDGMENTS

This chapter builds on the results from a study funded by the National Center for Sustainable Transportation (NCST), which receives funding from the USDOT and Caltrans through the University Transportation Centers program. The authors would like to thank Caltrans, the NCST and USDOT, for their support of university-based research in transportation. The authors also would like to thank Patricia L. Mokhtarian, Susan Handy, Dan Sperling, Rosaria Berliner, Kate Tiedeman, Yongsung Lee and Ali Etezady for their contributions to the survey design, data collection and data analyses in the project.

REFERENCES

Alemi, F., Circella, G., Handy, S.L., Mokhtarian, P.L., 2018a. What influences travelers to use uber? Exploring the factors affecting the adoption of on-demand ride services in California. Travel Behav. Soc. 13, 88–104.

Alemi, F., Circella, G., Mokhtarian, P.L., Handy, S.L., 2018b. In: On-Demand Ride Services in California: Investigating the Factors Affecting the Frequency of Use of Uber/Lyft. Presented at the Transportation Research Board 97th Annual Meeting, Washington DC, January 2018.

Alemi, F., Circella, G., Sperling, D., 2018c. Limitations to the Adoption of Uber and Lyft in California and Impacts on the Use of Other Travel Modes. Presented at the Transportation Research Board 97th Annual Meeting, Washington DC, January 2018.

Alemi, F., Circella, G., Handy, S.L., Mokhtarian, P.L., What makes travelers use Uber: exploring the latent constructs behind the use of on-demand ride services in California. J. Choice Model. forthcoming.

Babar, Y., Burtch, G., 2017. Examining the Impact of Ridehailing Services on Public Transit Use. September 25, 2017. Available at https://ssrn.com/abstract=3042805. [Accessed 14 July 2018].

Blumenberg, E., Ralph, K., Smart, M., Taylor, B., 2016. Who knows about kids these days? Analyzing the determinants of youth and adult mobility in the U.S. between 1990 and 2009. Transp. Res. A Policy Pract. 93, 39–54.

Buck, D., Buehler, R., Happ, P., Rawls, B., Chung, P., Borecki, N., 2013. Are bikeshare users different from regular cyclists? A first look at short-term users, annual members, and area cyclists in the Washington, DC region. Transp. Res. Rec. 2387, 112–119.

Circella, G., Fulton, L., Alemi, F., Berliner, R.M., Tiedeman, K., Mokhtarian, P.L., Handy, S., 2016. In: What Affects Millennials' Mobility? PART I: Investigating the Environmental Concerns, Lifestyles, Mobility-Related Attitudes and Adoption of Technology of Young Adults in California. Project Report, National Center for Sustainable Transportation. University of California, Davis, May 2016. Available at http://ncst.ucdavis.edu/wp-content/uploads/2014/08/05-26-2016-NCST_Report_Millennials_Part_I_2016_May_26_FINAL1.pdf. [Accessed 14 July 2018].

Circella, G., Ganson, C., Rodier, C., 2017a. Keeping Vehicle Use and Greenhouse Gas Emissions in Check in a Driverless Vehicle World. 3 Revolutions Policy Briefs, University of California, Davis. April 2017. Available at https://3rev.ucdavis.edu/wp-content/uploads/2017/04/3R.VMT-GHG.final_-1.pdf. [Accessed 14 July 2018].

Circella, G., Alemi, F., Tiedeman, K., Berliner, R.M., Lee, Y., Fulton, L., Mokhtarian, P.L., Handy, S., 2017b. In: What Affects Millennials' Mobility? PART II: The Impact of Residential Location, Individual Preferences and Lifestyles on Young Adults' Travel Behavior in California. Project Report, National Center for Sustainable Transportation. University of California, Davis, March 2017. Available at https://ncst.ucdavis.edu/wp-content/uploads/2015/09/NCST_Report_Millennials_Part_II_2017_March_31_FINAL.pdf. [Accessed 14 July 2018].

Circella, G., Alemi, F., Tiedeman, K., Handy, S., Mokhtarian, P.L., 2018. The Adoption of Shared Mobility in California and Its Relationship with Other Components of Travel Behavior. Project Report, National Center for Sustainable Transportation, University of California, Davis. March 2018. Available at https://ncst.ucdavis.edu/project/the-adoption-shared-mobility-in-california-and-relationship-with-other-components-travel-behavior/. [Accessed 14 July 2018].

Clewlow, R.R., Mishra, G.S., 2017. Disruptive Transportation: The Adoption, Utilization, and Impacts of Ride-Hailing in the United States. Institute of Transportation Studies, University of California, Davis. Research Report UCD-ITS-RR-17-07.

Cortright, J., 2016. Cities and The Price of Parking. Available at http://cityobservatory.org/cities_and_the-price-of-parking. [Accessed 14 July 2018].

Costain, C., Ardron, C., Habib, K.N., 2012. Synopsis of Users' behaviour of a Carsharing program: a case study in Toronto. Transp. Res. A Policy Pract. 46 (3), 421–434.

Davidson, T., Webber, M.E., 2017. Using Only Uber or Lyft Is Cheaper than Owning a Car for 25% of Americans—Here's How to Know If You Apply. Business Insider. Available at http://www.businessinsider.com/uber-or-lyft-could-be-cheaper-than-owning-a-car-2017-10. [Accessed 14 July 2018].

Feigon, S., Murphy, C., 2018. Broadening Understanding of the Interplay Between Public Transit, Shared Mobility, and Personal Automobiles. Pre-publication draft of TCRP Research Report 195, Transportation Research Board, Washington, D.C.

Feigon, S., Murphy, C., Shared-Use Mobility Center, 2016. Shared Mobility and the Transformation of Public Transit. TCRP Report 188. Transportation Research Board; Washington, D.C.

Firnkorn, J., Müller, M., 2011. What will be the environmental effects of new free-floating Car-sharing systems? The case of car2go in Ulm. Ecol. Econ. 70 (8), 1519–1528.

Frändberg, L., Vilhelmson, B., 2011. More or less travel: personal mobility trends in the Swedish population focusing on gender and cohort. J. Transp. Geogr. 19 (6), 1235–1244.

Hallock, L., Inglis, J., 2015. The Innovative Transportation Index: The Cities Where New Technologies and Tools Can Reduce Your Need to Own a Car. Available at http://www.uspirg.org/sites/pirg/files/reports/Innovative_Transportation_Index_USPIRG.pdf. [Accessed 14 July 2018].

Hampshire, R.C., Simek, C., Fabusuyi, T., Di, X., Chen, X., 2017. Measuring the Impact of An Unanticipated Suspension of Ride-Sourcing in Austin, Texas. Available at https://ssrn.com/abstract=2977969. [Accessed 14 July 2018].

Harb, M., Xiao, Y., Circella, G., Mokhtarian, P.L., Walker, J., 2018. Projecting travelers into a world of self-driving vehicles: estimating travel behavior implications via a naturalistic experiment. Transportation (accepted).

Henao, A., 2017. Impacts of Ridesourcing—Lyft and Uber—on Transportation Including VMT, Mode Replacement, Parking, and Travel Behavior. Doctoral Dissertation for Department of Civil and Environmental Engineering, University of Colorado Denver.

Henderson, P., 2017. Some Uber and Lyft riders Are Giving up Their Own Cars: Reuters/Ipsos Poll. Reuters. Available at https://mobile-reuters-com.cdn.ampproject.org/c/mobile.reuters.com/article/amp/idUSKBN18L1DA. [Accessed 14 July 2018].

Kuhnimhof, T., Armoogum, J., Buehler, R., Dargay, J., Denstadli, J.M., Yamamoto, T., 2012. Men shape a downward trend in Car use among young adults—evidence from six industrialized countries. Transp. Rev. 32 (6), 761–779.

Malokin, A., Circella, G., Mokhtarian, P.L., 2015. How Do Activities Conducted while Commuting Influence Mode Choice? Testing Public Transportation Advantage and Autonomous Vehicle Scenarios. Presented at the Transportation Research Board 94th Annual Meeting, Paper No. 15-1179, Washington DC, January 2015.

Martin, E.W., Shaheen, S.A., 2014. Evaluating public transit modal shift dynamics in response to Bikesharing: a tale of two US cities. J. Transp. Geogr. 41, 315–324.

Mishra, G.S., Mokhtarian, P.L., Clewlow, R.R., Widaman, K.F., 2017. Addressing the joint occurrence of self-selection and simultaneity biases in the estimation of program effects based on cross-sectional observational surveys: case study of travel behavior effects in carsharing. Transportation 1–29. https://link.springer.com/content/pdf/10.1007/s11116-017-9791-1.pdf.

Pew Research Center, 2016. Shared, Collaborative and on Demand: The New Digital Economy. May 2016. Available at http://www.pewinternet.org/files/2016/05/PI_2016.05.19_Sharing-Economy_FINAL.pdf. [Accessed 14 July 2018].

Polzin, S.E., Sperling, D., 2018. Upgrading Transit for the Twenty-First Century. In: Three Revolutions: Steering Automated, Shared, and Electric Vehicles to a Better Future. 2018. Island Press, pp. 109–129.

Rayle, L., Shaheen, S., Chan, N., Dai, D., Cervero, R., 2014. App-Based, On-Demand Ride Services: Comparing Taxi and Ridesourcing Trips and User Characteristics in San Francisco. Working Paper, University of California Transportation Center (UCTC). Available at https://www.its.dot.gov/itspac/dec2014/ridesourcingwhitepaper_nov2014.pdf. [Accessed 14 July 2017].

Roberts, A., 2017. Car-sharing companies hit speed bumps as demand slows, ride-hailing grows. Wall Street J. Retrieved from, https://www.wsj.com/articles/car-sharing-companies-hit-speed-bumps-as-demand-slows-ride-hailing-grows-1500024601. [Accessed 14 July 2018].

San Francisco County Transportation Authority (SFCTA), 2017. TNCs Today: A Profile of San Francisco Transportation Network Company Activity. November 2017, Available at http://www.sfcta.org/sites/default/files/content/Planning/TNCs/TNCs_Today_112917.pdf. [Accessed 14 July 2018].

Schaller, B., 2017. Unsustainable? The Growth of App-Based Ride Services and Traffic, Travel and the Future of New York City. Report by Schaller consulting, Brooklyn NY. February 2017. Available at http://schallerconsult.com/rideservices/unsustainable.pdf. [Accessed 14 July 2018].

Schaller, B., 2018. The New Automobility: Lyft, Uber and the Future of American Cities. Report by Schaller Consulting, Brooklyn NY. July 2018. Available at http://www.schallerconsult.com/rideservices/automobility.htm. [Accessed 27 July 2018].

Shaheen, S., Chan, N., Bansal, A., Cohen, A., 2015. Shared Mobility—A Sustainability and Technology Workshop: Definition, Industry Development and Early Understanding. White paper from University of California, Berkeley Transportation Sustainability Research Center. Available at http://innovativemobility.org/wp-content/uploads/2015/11/SharedMobility_WhitePaper_FINAL.pdf. [Accessed 14 July 2018].

Shaheen, S., Cohen, A., Zohdy, I., 2016. Shared Mobility: Current Practices and Guiding Principles. Report No. FHWA-HOP-16-022 (April 2016). Available at https://ops.fhwa.dot.gov/publications/fhwahop16022/fhwahop16022.pdf. [Accessed 14 July 2018].

Shaheen, S., Totte, H., Stocker, A., 2018. Future of Mobility White Paper. Institute of Transportation Studies, UC Berkeley. Available at https://escholarship.org/uc/item/68g2h1qv. [Accessed 14 July 2018].

Sperling, D., Brown, A., Chase, R., Dunne, M.J., Pike, S., Polzin, S.E., Shaheen, S., Taylor, B.D., Tillemann, L., van der Meerand, E., 2018. Three Revolutions: Steering Automated, Shared, and Electric Vehicles to a Better Future. Island Press.

Taylor, B.D., Chin, R., Melanie, C., Dill, J., Hoel, L.A., Manville, M., Polzin, S., et al., 2015. Between Public and Private Mobility: Examining the Rise of Technology-Enabled Transportation Services. Special Report 319. Transportation Research Board: Committee for Review of Innovative Urban Mobility Services. Transportation Research Board; Washington, D.C.

Le Vine, S., Adamou, O., Polak, J., 2014. Predicting new forms of activity/mobility patterns enabled by shared-mobility services through a needs-based stated-response method: case study of grocery shopping. Transp. Policy 32, 60–68.

CHAPTER SIX

An Empirical Investigation of the Reward Incentive and Trip Purposes on Departure Time Behavior Change

Ali Arian*, Alireza Ermagun†,1, Xiaoyu Zhu‡, Yi-Chang Chiu§
*Department of Civil Engineering and Engineering Mechanics, The University of Arizona, Tucson, AZ, United States
†Mississippi State University, Department of Civil and Environmental Engineering, Starkville, MS, United States
‡Metropia Inc., Tucson, AZ, United States
§Department of Civil Engineering and Engineering Mechanics, The University of Arizona, Tucson, AZ, United States
[1]Corresponding author: e-mail address: aermagun@cee.msstate.edu

Contents

Abstract

Incentives, as one of the travel demand management strategies, are deployed to eliminate or temporally and spatially shift trips away from congested periods and corridors. This study analyzes the impact of incentives on departure time for seven main trip purposes in order to further provide a personalized incentive scheme to achieve an optimal manner at the system wide level. We compare two consecutive incentive schemes,

Advances in Transport Policy and Planning, Volume 1
ISSN 2543-0009
https://doi.org/10.1016/bs.atpp.2018.07.001

each lasting for over a 1-year period, to understand how effectively these incentive scenarios influence the departure time of seven trip purposes. The data used in this research were collected by the Metropia app, one of the first reward-based travels demand management smartphone applications, and include 364,966 trips conducted by 2270 users between May 2015 and May 2018. Four accelerated failure time models are conducted to explain the time to observe a departure event and the acceleration factors for various trip purposes under two incentive scenarios. The results suggest that peak hour travelers may be open to behavioral incentives that promotes non-peak hour departure time. The incentives, however, may need to be tailored based on time of the day and the purpose of the trip. The findings highlight that traveling for recreation, errands, and work is the most sensitive trip purposes to the incentives in the morning peak hour. However, in the evening peak hour, traveling for other trips, errands, and school becomes the most sensitive trip purposes. These results can facilitate the design of incentives tailored to a specific individual and trip, to incentivize lasting and meaningful behavioral changes.

Keywords: Travel behavior, Pricing, Smartphone-app, Peak-hour, Departure time, Incentive

1. INTRODUCTION

Planning agencies have attempted to deploy travel demand management (TDM) strategies in most metropolitan regions to eliminate or temporally and spatially shift trips away from congested periods and corridors. These strategies cover congestion pricing, incentives to shift travel to off-peak periods or alternative non-congested corridors, flexible work hours, telecommuting, transit subsidies, and ridesharing programs. With the global proliferation of mobile technology, the smartphone has become widely utilized as a tool of TDM strategies (Ermagun et al., 2017). This mobile framework allows for agencies and researchers to intervene and deliver timely information to influence users' behavior through their smartphones. The ability to collect and disseminate location-based information, including trips, travel time, money spent, and activities conducted through this platform, has created the opportunity to make these interventions even more personalized.

A number of incentive-based mobile app schemes have been implemented in the transportation sector. Although there is documented evidence regarding the impacts of such schemes, there is a need for additional insight into the impacts of incentives on traveler behavior as research has shown trips with different activity purposes exhibit inconsistent flexibility in departure or arrival time (Bhat and Steed, 2002; Lemp and Kockelman, 2010;

Mannering et al., 1994). As a result, offering the same amount of incentive for different trip purposes might not be effective or financially efficient. However, most of the implemented incentive schemes for influencing departure time provide a static amount of incentive regardless of how much the trip is shifted or what time of day (including peak hours) the shift happens.

This research presents a straightforward approach for comparing incentive designs associated with behavioral interventions, where incentive design refers to how an agency might deliberately structure incentives in order to trigger behavioral changes to shift departure times. These comparisons can be done across possible incentive scenarios as well as across various trip purposes to determine which scenario might be the most impactful for individuals or a specific population. By systematically comparing incentive designs, resources can be employed in an optimal manner that is most probable to succeed.

The remainder of the study is structured as follows. First, we evaluate the literature spanning the fields of departure time modeling and incentive-based travel behavior programs. Second, we lay out the methodological approach with a particular focus on the relationship between incentive and trip purpose relative to departure time. Third, we provide an in-depth discussion about the data collection process and its characteristics. This is followed by a discussion of results focusing on the behavioral psychology that drives travelers' choices when they are presented with a certain type of assigned incentive within two scenarios. The conclusion focuses on the theoretical and practical implications for transportation policy and opens an alley up for future work.

2. LITERATURE REVIEW

2.1 Departure Time Choice

Departure time decision is one of the most important travel behaviors that plays a key role in travel planning and traffic operation in large urban areas, especially during the peak hours of congestion. There are numerous research efforts focused on the departure time problem attempting to understand the rationality and uncertainty behind these decisions in order to make better predictions for travel behavior, improve traffic control, and manage travel demand using pricing or incentives.

The behavioral decisions for departure time are primarily influenced by perception of travel time, cost, arrival time, the personality and habit of travelers, and other trip related factors, such as trip purpose. Bhat and Steed (2002) studied the effects of individual and household socio-demographics, employment attributes, and trip-related characteristics on departure time choice. Mannering et al. (1994) investigated the determinants of commuter flexibility and the influence of pre-trip traffic information on changing routes and departure times for the morning trip to work. Travel time reliability, measured as travel time variability, was then studied as one of the important factors to avoid unexpected delays (Arellana et al., 2012). Furthermore, psychological factors such as attitude toward being on time and toward changes in trip conditions were introduced by Arellana et al. (2012). Later on, psychological factors and studies from the perspective of behavioral psychology emerged within the study of travel behavior. For example, the intention to arrive on time, to have short travel times, and to have low travel costs was analyzed with the Theory of Planned Behavior (Thorhauge et al., 2016).

In the literature, there have been some methodologies focusing on departure time choice modeling. For example, Mahmassani and Chang (1986) presented a modeling framework to investigate the dynamic properties of a system of commuters located along a highway facility. Bhat (1998) built a mixed multinomial logit structure for home-based social–recreational trips. Mannering (1989) investigated routes and departure times for morning trips to work using an ordered logit probability approach, and a Weibull duration model with a heterogeneity correction term. Jou et al. (2008) studied dynamic commuter departure time choices under uncertainty. Continuous departure time models, however, have begun appearing over the last two decades. Bhat and Steed (2002) built a continuous-time model of departure time choices for urban shopping trips using Gamma mixing distributions with a nonparametric hazard setting. Lemp and Kockelman (2010) used Bayesian estimation with a continuous logit model and a continuous cross-nested logit model.

2.2 Incentive-Based Strategies

With this understanding of the factors that influence departure time decisions, figuring out how to motivate people to alter their behavior became another issue for researchers. Recent work has suggested that financial and social incentives, such as those via mobile frameworks, may have greater effects on some individuals (Jariyasunant et al., 2015; Merugu et al., 2009). One might hypothesize that social incentives that provide a "carrot" rather than a "stick" might be more effective in encouraging driving alternatives.

The incentives, intrinsic and extrinsic, can be in the form of travel feedback, monetized lottery/rewards, messages in environmental contributions, or transit tickets/discounts. In the Netherlands, rewards are well-recognized as extrinsic motivation for discouraging rush-hour driving (Ben-Elia and Ettema, 2011a,b), by providing individuals credits ranging from 3€ to 7€ for not driving during peak hours. Reward drawing based on a pyramid structure was studied in an experiment in Bangalore by incentivizing the commuters to travel at less congested times (Merugu et al., 2009). During an 8-day temporary freeway closure in Osaka, Japan, some travelers in their 20s were offered a 1-month free bus ticket and were observed to have used the bus more frequently even after the freeway reopened (Fujii and Kitamura, 2003). According to a longitudinal study in Germany, which offered the incentive of a pre-paid bus ticket, bus usage increased by 35% and trips finished by car decreased by 13% (Bamberg et al., 2003). In Melbourne, Australia, an early bird ticket program was proposed to alleviate the rail overcrowding issue during the peak hours and proved to be effective (Currie, 2011).

3. ANALYSIS METHODOLOGY

Generally, departure times mark the beginning of a trip, or the end of the preceding activity. The aim of this study is to describe the distribution of departure times and understand how incentives and activity type affect it. In order to avoid inconsistent results, peak hour has been chosen as the fixed original time, and all departure times are calculated with respect to it in minutes. The peak hours that are of interest in this study and targeted by the incentive profiles are 8:00 AM and 4:30 PM. For example, departure times at 7:30 AM and 8:30 AM both will be translated to 30 min. The same holds true for PM; departure times at 4:00 PM and 5:00 PM will be replaced by 30 min. This transformation is shown in Fig. 1.

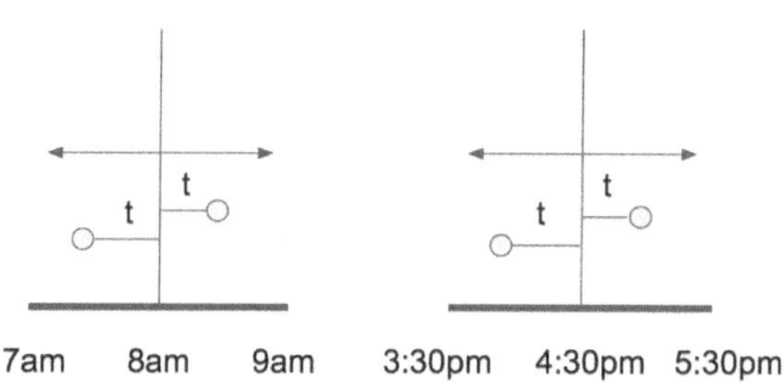

Fig. 1 Definition of departure time from peak hour in the morning and afternoon.

In this study, an Accelerated Failure Time model was implemented. Considering t as a non-negative random variable representing the duration from the original time point (midnight) to the departure time, most generic forms of an Accelerated Failure Time make a linear relation between the natural log of t with the covariates of an individual, as shown in Eq. (1):

$$\log(t) = \beta X + \sigma w \tag{1}$$

where β is a vector of parameters to be estimated, X is a set of covariates, σ is the standard deviation of the transformed t, and w is an unobserved heterogeneity term that is assumed to be independent of t. Considering this, T can be defined as the duration during which an individual does not take a trip, and the cumulative distribution function $F(t) = Pr[T < t]$ gives the probability of having an event before some transpired time t. Therefore, the associated density function $f(t)$ represents the trip's departure time probability during a day. Moreover, the integration of $f(t)$ between t_1 and t_2 shows the probability that a person takes a trip between times t_1 and t_2.

Literature has considered different distributions for w, the unobserved heterogeneity term, in fully parametric models. A variety of duration distribution alternatives are available, including gamma, exponential, Weibull, log-logistic, and log-normal. To select the best distribution, the Akaike Information Criterion (AIC) is used as a standard of measurement. The lower the AIC is, the better the fit a model becomes. The results of the AIC test nominated the Weibull distribution as the best distribution for our survival time analysis. With the assumption that w follows the extreme value distribution, T has a Weibull density (Mudholkar et al., 1996). Considering λ and α as parameters of the Weibull density:

$$f(\lambda, \alpha) = \alpha t^{\alpha-1} \lambda \exp(\lambda t^{\alpha}) \tag{2}$$

where $\lambda = \exp(X\beta^*)$, $\alpha = \frac{1}{\sigma}$ and $\beta^* = \frac{-\beta}{\sigma}$. In this notation λ is known as the acceleration factor. This parameter indicates how the survival times are differently accelerated for different levels of a covariate. Substituting λ in the formulation, the likelihood of a departure at time t for an individual i can be written as Eq. (3):

$$f(X_i, \alpha, \beta^*) = \alpha t^{\alpha-1} \exp(X_i\beta^*) \exp(-t^{\alpha} \exp(X_i\beta^*)) \tag{3}$$

Trips in our data are assumed to be independent, as carpooling trips and the trips that are made with one car (such as family trips) are excluded from this data set. As a result, the joint likelihood for n trips can be stated as Eq. (4):

$$l(t|\, X_i, \alpha, \beta^*) = \prod_{i=1}^{n} \alpha t^{\alpha-1} \exp\left(X_i\beta^*\right) \exp\left(-t^{\alpha} \exp\left(X_i\beta^*\right)\right) \tag{4}$$

4. EMPIRICAL STUDY DATA

This section first discusses the data collected by the Metropia app, followed by going through the entire process that users experience when using the app, including earning points and redeeming them for rewards. Next, an explanation of how the app incentivizes its users (vehicle drivers in this study) to trigger behavior changes of their departure time is provided. Two different point scheme scenarios were tested during the study period. As mentioned earlier, this research further postulates that departure time choice behavior is influenced by various trip purposes. Certain types of trips may have different rigid departure or arrival requirements, which allows for less flexibility in departure time shift. Without deploying a traditional survey, a method to infer each users' trip purpose using their trajectory data was developed. This approach is demonstrated in the latter part of this section. Finally, a summary of variables used for the modeling process is described.

4.1 Data Collection Process

Metropia[a] is one of the first reward-based travel demand management platforms that offers users incentives in the forms of points if they choose a less congested time and route. The Metropia app, using prediction methods combined with rewards, incentivizes drivers to change their departure time to balance traffic load and reduce congestion. The platform provides accurate travel time predictions from a queried origin-destination using different data sources and leveraging prediction methods. Considering travel time and network wide traffic situations, the app proposes various reward points for different departure times. This information is displayed to the driver such that all options are visible and the driver can consume the information. Fig. 2 shows the process of proposing reward points to a driver. In case the driver wants to leave at a later time based on the proposed rewards

[a] http://metropia.com

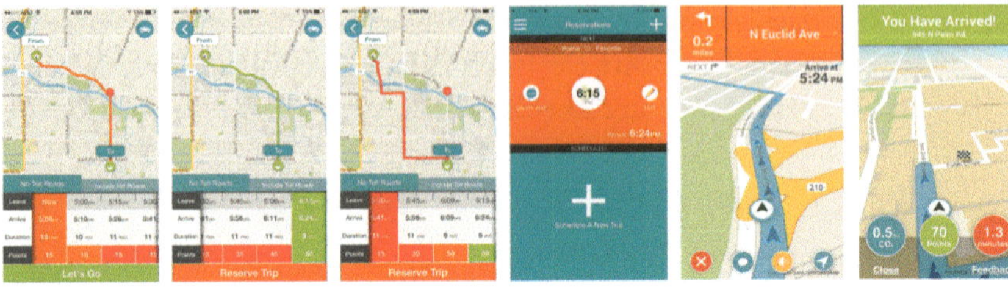

Fig. 2 User flow in the app from observing points, scheduling, and finishing a trip.

and travel time, the driver can schedule (or "reserve") for that time. This design allows drivers to make departure time decisions considering all options and reward points. The points offered and earned by user/driver can be redeemed for different gift cards and donation options. At the time of this study, every 200 points are valued at one US dollar.

The goal of the app and its backend algorithms is to influence its users to collectively reduce demand during peak hours and for congested routes. The app was first deployed in late 2014, with the goal of developing an innovative platform to evaluate Active Travel Demand Management (ATDM) programs. The Metropia app's user engagement process also offers an opportunity to evaluate the effectiveness of incentives in influencing each user's departure time.

As shown in Fig. 2, the four-step user experience provided by the Metropia app proceeds as follows:

Step 1 (Discover): A Metropia user provides the travel destination to be completed in the near future. Metropia's server-based models then use both real-time and historical data to analyze (in space and time) where available capacity exists for this trip and estimate the mPoints to be awarded for each departure time and route. If a departure and route is found be more beneficial to the system as a whole, a higher number of mPoints are allocated to that option. This accurate prediction helps a driver decide whether to leave now or later, bearing in mind the likely congestion status.

Step 2 (Reserve): The driver then makes a pledge for a specific route and departure time and the system promises a certain reward. The reward is in a form of points and points follow a temporal profile that is generally set up with a minimal point value during the peak of the AM and PM peak hours and a maximal value during the shoulder of the AM and PM peak hours. These points are displayed on the Metropia app (see the second image from the left in Fig. 3). Once the user selects a specific time slot and press the

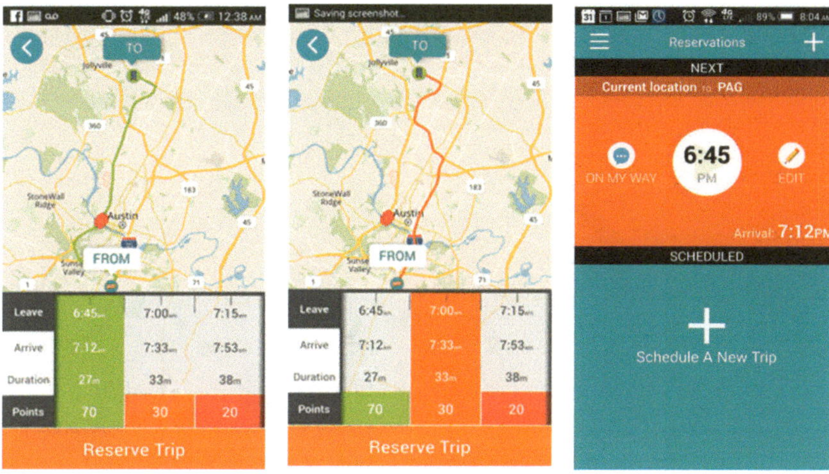

Fig. 3 Metropia driver use case: reserve.

"Reserve" button on the phone, the Reserve step records such an action and reward agreement.

If the user selects and reserves a future time slot, then the App will stay at the Standby page (the third image from the left in Fig. 3). Ten minutes before the scheduled departure, the App will play a ringtone as the reminder. When the user enters and starts the vehicle and ready to embark the trip, the Metropia App turns into a turn-by-turn navigation App.

Step 3 (Validate): Once the trip commences, Metropia becomes a navigation app that provides audio turn-by-turn navigation guidance for the user to follow the reserved route to their final destination. During the trip, the App transmits the GPS location data back to the system for the system to verify if the user leaves at the promised time slot and follows the Metropia recommended route. The user is awarded the reserved points once the majority of the route being followed is completed (Fig. 4).

Step 4 (Reward Redemption): The earned points can be redeemed for various discounted products and services, freebies, lotteries, or even charity donations. Users can access their personal dashboard using their mobile device or computer to access their performance, their mPoint total and other personalized information. Fig. 5 shows the redemption page in which several gift cards are listed with face value and redemption point requirements listed.

Users of the app are recruited through different marketing strategies, such as social media marketing campaigns, maintaining a booth at different

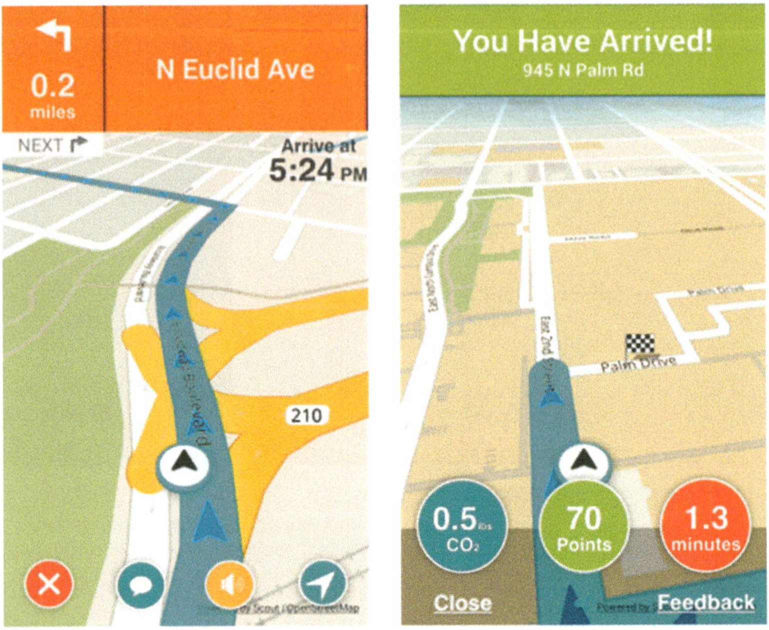

Fig. 4 Metropia driver use case: in-trip and validation.

events, and others (Arian and Chiu, 2017). Therefore, the sample of users used in this study can be said to be representative of a target city population. The data used in this study are a sample collected across Tucson, Arizona and Austin, Texas. In total, considering weekdays, the data set includes 364,966 trips collected from 2270 users over 3 years (May 2015–May 2018).

4.2 Participants

As it mentioned earlier, the total number of 2270 users are selected for this study which is a random sample from all the app's users. The socio-demographic information is not typically collected by Metropia. We, however, conducted a survey among 700 active users in fall 2017 to get insights regarding the socio-demographic information of the users. Table 1 summarizes the socio-demographic information of 700 selected users.

4.3 Departure Time Pattern

The departure time of each trip is counted as the moment that users hit the start button on the app, and the app then switches to the navigation mode. Generally speaking, most urban areas and cities experience no congestion during the weekends. Therefore, this study is mainly interested in weekday

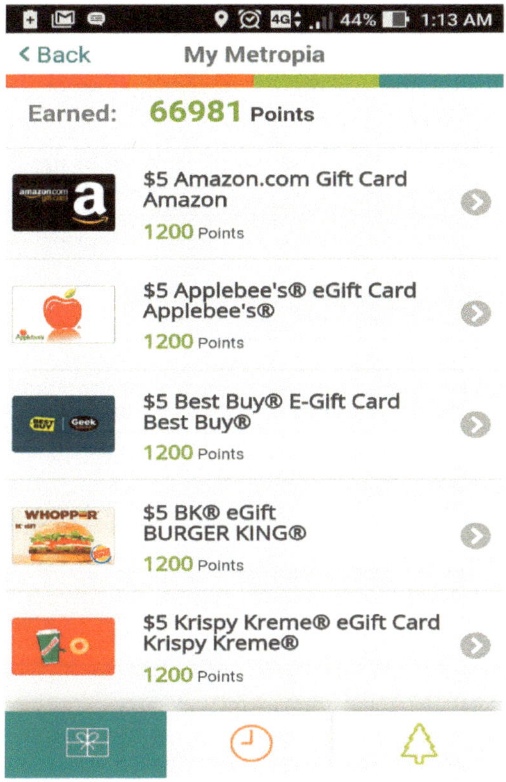

Fig. 5 Metropia gift card redemption page.

patterns of departure times, as it looks to explore strategies to mitigate gridlocks and disperse trips from peak hours. The pattern of hourly departure time distribution is presented in Fig. 6.

4.4 Point Scheme and Scenarios

As mentioned earlier, the point scheme is designed to incentivize users to shift their travel departure time away from peak hours. Initially, a point profile mimicking the congestion level of the entire city was deployed. This point profile fluctuated based on the ratio of the predicted travel time to the free flow travel time of the trip (aka the TTI index). Moreover, the amount of points was locked to a flat number of 10 points between 10:00 PM and 5:00 AM. This point profile, with an hourly average shown in Fig. 7, is referred to as Scenario 1 in this research. For morning peak hour trips, users were incentivized to leave earlier with the maximum daily point

Table 1 Socio-Demographics of Sample of Metropia App Users

Variable	Description	Count	Avg.	Std.
HH_employee	1 = one, 2 = two, 3 = three, 4 = four or more	–	1.87	0.89
HH_kids_under_18	1 = one, 2 = two, 3 = three, 4 = four or more	–	0.95	1.19
HH_size	1 = one, 2 = two, 3 = three, 4 = four or more	–	2.86	1.1
Age	18–25 years old	139	–	–
	26–30 years old (1 = yes, 0 = otherwise)	150	0.19	0.39
	31–35 years old (1 = yes, 0 = otherwise)	151	0.19	0.39
	36–45 years old (1 = yes, 0 = otherwise)	194	0.24	0.43
	46–55 years old (1 = yes, 0 = otherwise)	109	0.13	0.34
	56–65 years old (1 = yes, 0 = otherwise)	58	0.07	0.26
	Over 66 years old (1 = yes, 0 = otherwise)	9	0.01	0.1
Gender	Female	438	–	–
	Male (1 = yes, 0 = otherwise)	354	0.44	0.5
	Prefer not to answer (1 = yes, 0 = otherwise)	18	0.02	0.15
Driving_years	Less than 1 year (1 = yes, 0 = otherwise)	34	0.04	0.2
	At least 1 year but less than 3 years (1 = yes, 0 = otherwise)	43	0.05	0.22
	At least 3 years but less than 5 years (1 = yes, 0 = otherwise)	39	0.05	0.21
	At least 5 years but less than 10 years (1 = yes, 0 = otherwise)	72	0.09	0.28
	10 years or longer	622	–	–
Commute_type	Commute to school	65	–	–
	Commute to both work and school (1 = yes, 0 = otherwise)	165	0.2	0.4
	Commute to work (1 = yes, 0 = otherwise)	535	0.66	0.47
	I am not a commuter (1 = yes, 0 = otherwise)	45	0.06	0.23

Table 1 Socio-Demographics of Sample of Metropia App Users—cont'd

Variable	Description		Count	Avg.	Std.
Income	Less than $39,999 (1 = yes, 0 = otherwise)		214	0.26	0.44
	$40,000–$74,999 (1 = yes, 0 = otherwise)		287	0.35	0.48
	$75,000–$99,999 (1 = yes, 0 = otherwise)		128	0.16	0.36
	$100,000–$199,999		140	–	–
	$200,000 or more (1 = yes, 0 = otherwise)		41	0.05	0.22
Degree	Some high school (1 = yes, 0 = otherwise)	High school (1 = yes, 0 = otherwise)	32	0.04	0.19
	High school graduate (1 = yes, 0 = otherwise)		51	0.06	0.24
	Some college, no degree (1 = yes, 0 = otherwise)	Undergraduate	165	0.2	0.4
	Associate degree		82	–	–
	Bachelor degree (1 = yes, 0 = otherwise)		289	0.36	0.48
	Masters (1 = yes, 0 = otherwise)	Graduate (1 = yes, 0 = otherwise)	162	0.2	0.4
	Doctorate (1 = yes, 0 = otherwise)		29	0.04	0.19
City	Tucson (1 = yes, 0 = otherwise)		341	0.42	0.4
	El Paso (1 = yes, 0 = otherwise)		163	0.2	0.49
	Austin		306	–	–

value (70) offered. Similarly, trips during the evening peak were intended to be pushed back to mainly after 6:00 PM. This point scheme was deployed from May 2015 to July 2016.

In July 2016, a new point profile was deployed. This change was aimed at evaluating the effectiveness of a new strategy and observing the reaction of users and their response to the new incentive. In this new profile, more

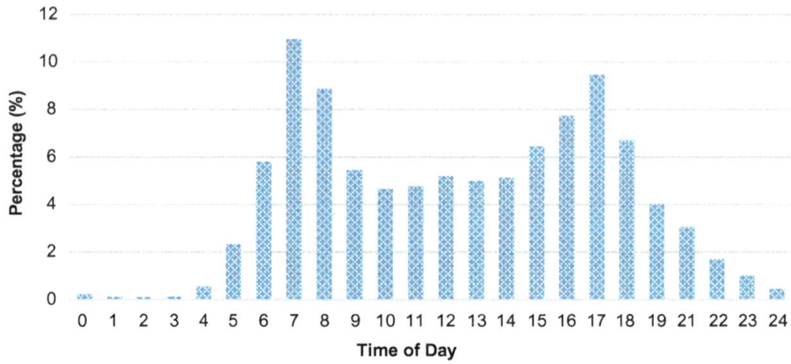

Fig. 6 Departure time of the trips during the study period over weekdays.

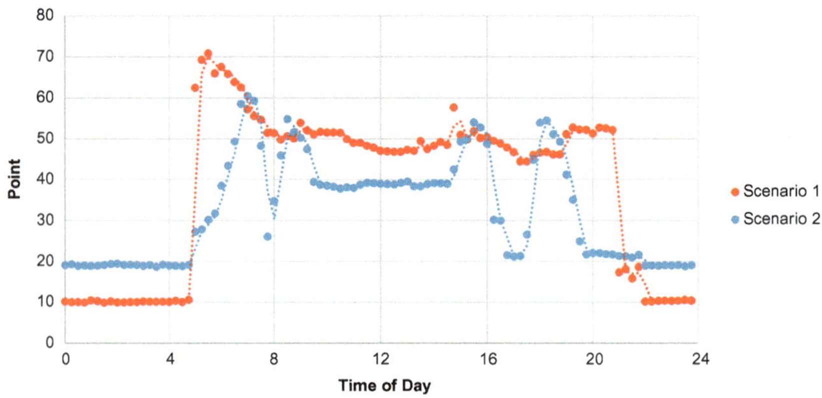

Fig. 7 Point profile of point offering for different time of a day.

points were added to the shoulders of peak hours and relatively lower point values were assigned to the most congested time periods in the morning and evening. As shown in Fig. 7, for trips departing between 7:45 AM to 8:15 AM and 16:45 PM to 17:45 PM, 25 and 20 points were offered, respectively. This new point profile, named Scenario 2, can help shed more light on the hypothesis that it is easier to start a trip earlier or later to avoid a peak hour. This topic is discussed in Section 5.

4.5 Inferring Trip Purposes

One of the major contributions of this study is to examine how departure choice behavior is affected by the trip purpose without a traditional survey. The idea is to infer trip purposes from the raw GPS coordinates of the trip's origin and destination locations. To improve the quality of this inference

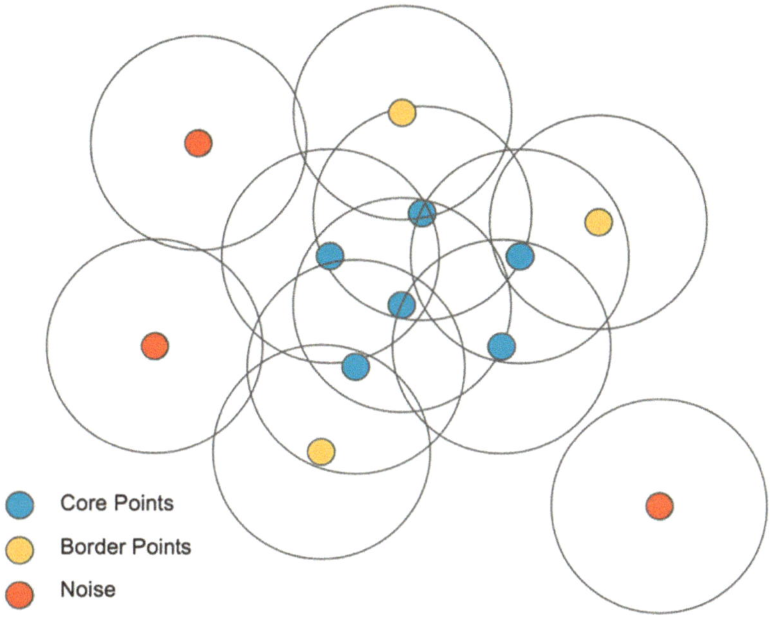

Fig. 8 Folding GPS points to different groups by DBSCAN method.

we focus on frequently visited locations rather than occasional trips. This approach helped us to cluster locations together and has a more accurate reverse geocoding. For this purpose, we performed a density-based spatial clustering of applications with noise (DBSCAN) algorithm on destination locations of each individual to filter out occasional trips as noises and cluster trips with the same destinations. Fig. 8 shows how the DBSCAN method categorizes points to core points, border points, and noises within a cluster. In the data set, 26,652 locations among all users were identified with the maximum of 155 destination clusters for a user. Arian et al. (2017) provided more detailed description of this process.

Each important location of users was tagged with a proper activity type or trip purpose in a process. The overall accuracy of this inference was reported at 79% with the highest performance in trips with purpose of Home (86%) and lowest for trips with the purpose of Pick-Up or Drop-Off (44%) (Arian, 2018).

4.6 Variable Specifications

Several types of variables in the departure-time choice models were considered. These include trip-related characteristics, reward structure related attributes, and trip purpose related variables.

Table 2 Variables Description

Variable	Definition
Departure time	A continuous value between 0 and 60 representing departure time
Trip duration	Duration of a trip until the trip is manually or automatically ended by the app
Rev-TTI index	A value between 0 and 1 derived from dividing travel time at free flow conditions by travel time of the trip at departure time
Incentive	A value between 5 and 100 representing the amounts of points a user has earned
Work	1: if trip purpose is going to work; 0: otherwise
Home	1: if trip purpose is going to home; 0: otherwise
School	1: if trip purpose is going to school; 0: otherwise
Running errands	1: if trip purpose is running errands; 0: otherwise
Pickup dropoff	1: if trip purpose is pick up drop off; 0: otherwise
Recreational	1: if trip purpose is recreational activities; 0: otherwise
Others	1: if trip purpose is others; 0: otherwise

Trip-related characteristics include the departure time of the trip as a continuous variable calculated from midnight, trip duration in minutes, and the TTI index of the trip at departure time. The TTI index value is derived from the ratio of the predicted travel time at the departure time to the travel time of the same trip at free flow conditions. In this research we use reverse value of TTI as one of the parameters. The reward structure related attributes include the exact points earned for the specific trip and the point scheme scenario as discussed above. The trip purpose related variables are inferred as discussed above, with seven dummy variables indicating the purpose of the trip. The definition of each variable is listed in Table 2.

5. RESULTS AND DISCUSSIONS

As discussed in the preceding sections, two distinct incentive scenarios were offered to Metropia users for both the morning and evening peak hours. This section attempts to explore how and to what extent the users responded to the provided incentives. Users only experience the information of the time up until the occurrence of departure. To handle this time-to-event outcome, accelerated failure time (AFT) models were deployed, as this research was primarily interested in understanding the time-to-event and not the probability of departing. Many parametric survival methods are accelerated failure time models, which provide the "acceleration factor" as an alternative to the hazard ratio measurement and are able to meet this study's needs. In this model, increasing a descriptive variable with a positive coefficient sign will decrease the time-to-event. As alluded to previously, we consider the time-to-event as the absolute value of the difference between the departure time and peak hour. Consequently, a positive correlation (acceleration factor more than one) between independent variables and dependent variable indicates closer departure time to the peak hour; while, a negative correlation (acceleration factor less than one) specifies further departure time from the peak hour. Four different parametric models were developed to not only explore the impacts of the incentives on departure time, but also to unravel how users respond to incentives at different times of the day in different scenarios. The description of the models is provided as follows:

- *Model 1:* This model targets morning peak hour departure times, when Scenario 1 is implemented. In this model, the departure time falls between 7:00 AM and 9:00 AM.
- *Model 2*: This model targets evening peak hour departure times, when Scenario 1 is implemented. In this model, the departure time falls between 3:30 PM and 4:30 PM.
- *Model 3*: Similar to Model 1, this model analyzes morning peak hour departure times, when Scenario 2 is implemented. Hence, the departure time falls between 7:00 AM and 9:00 AM.
- *Model 4*: Similar to Model 2, this model analyzes evening peak hour departure times, when Scenario 2 is implemented. Hence, the departure time falls between 3:30 PM and 4:30 PM.

Tables 3 and 4 outline the results of Scenario 1 and Scenario 2, respectively. The models include the interaction of the incentive variables with different trip purposes, while the trip duration and TTI index are controlled within the models. The interaction terms enable this research to seek whether and to what extent users respond to the incentives across different trip purposes. It should be emphasized that the models developed in this research do not aim to model or predict travel departure time, but rather to investigate the impacts of the incentives on shifting travel departure times for different trip purposes.

Table 3 Results of the Survival Analysis in Scenario 1 for Morning and Evening Peak Hours

	Model 1			Model 2		
Variable	**Coefficient**	***z*-Test**	**AF**	**Coefficient**	***z*-Test**	**AF**
Rev-TTI	0.0571	15.21	1.058	−0.0781	−28.18	0.924
Trip duration	−0.0088	−2.58	0.991	0.0224	7.85	1.022
Incentive × work	0.0077	1.24	1.007	0.0094	4.56	1.009
Incentive × home	0.0078	1.77	1.007	0.0109	2.91	1.011
Incentive × school	0.0048	1.01	1.004	0.0313	12.21	1.031
Incentive × errands	0.0297	6.42	1.030	0.0041	1.35	1.004
Incentive × PickDrop	0.0026	0.51	1.002	0.0269	8.47	1.027
Incentive × recreational	−0.014	−2.49	0.986	0.0126	3.94	1.012
Incentive × others	−0.0008	−0.23	0.999	0.0066	2.56	1.006
Constant	3.459	19.31	–	4.3721	16.61	–
Shape parameter	1.5665	22.11	–	1.6082	29.64	–
No. observations	36,083			32,044		

Table 4 Results of the Survival Analysis in Scenario 2 for Morning and Evening Peak Hours

	Model 3			Model 4		
Variable	**Coefficient**	***z*-Test**	**AF**	**Coefficient**	***z*-Test**	**AF**
Rev-TTI	0.064	14.55	1.066	−0.0058	−3.35	0.994
Trip duration	−0.0031	−2.21	0.996	−0.012	−7.14	0.988
Incentive × work	0.0023	0.97	1.002	0.0186	10.65	1.018
Incentive × home	0.0089	5.07	1.008	0.0454	12.72	1.046
Incentive × school	0.0323	16.10	1.032	0.0155	8.67	1.015
Incentive × errands	0.0019	0.94	1.002	−0.0077	10.38	0.992
Incentive × PickDrop	0.0081	3.72	1.008	0.0486	16.26	1.049
Incentive × recreational	−0.0387	−19.65	0.962	0.039	10.92	1.039
Incentive × others	0.005	3.21	1.005	−0.014	−8.09	0.986
Constant	4.0061	26.33	–	3.4834	19.53	–
Shape parameter	1.7453	49.30	–	1.5842	42.8	–
No. observations	161,973			134,866		

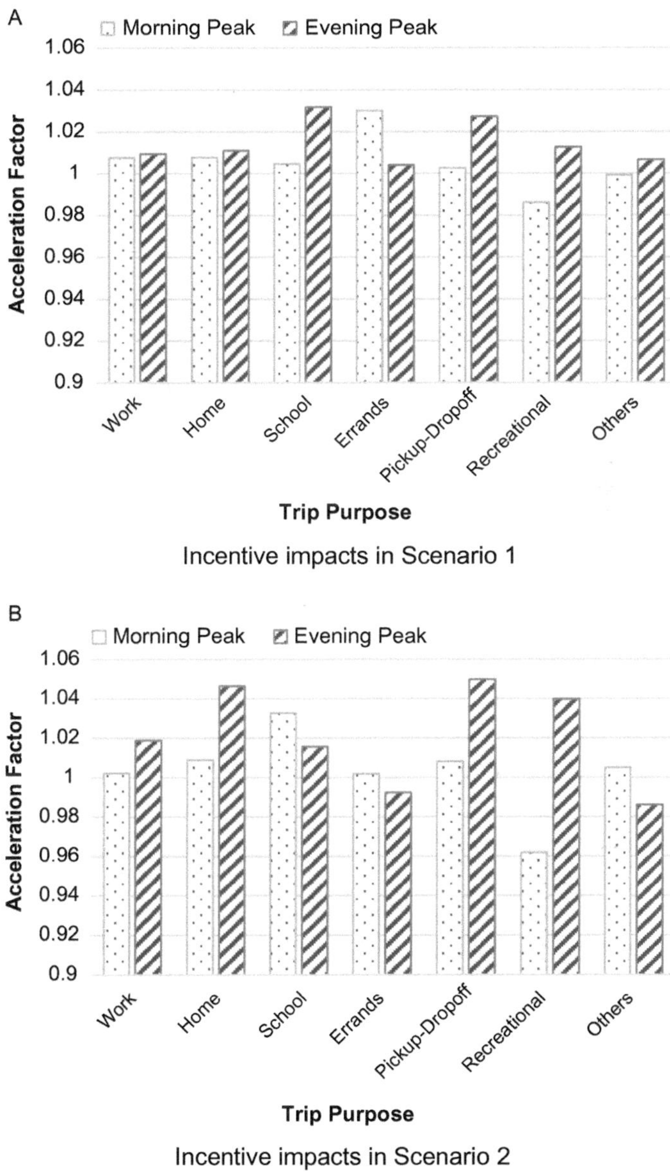

Fig. 9 Acceleration factor analysis corresponding to 200 units (one US dollar) incentive.

To give a sense of the magnitude of shift to departure time when Metropia offers incentives, the acceleration factors are simulated in response to a 200 unit (one US dollars) increase in incentives for both scenarios. Fig. 9 depicts the results of the analysis.

From the Scenario 1 analysis, the research found a positive correlation between the time-to-departure during the morning peak hours and the interactions of the incentive variable with all trip purposes except recreational and others. The sensitivity of response, however, varies according to the trip purpose. Looking at Fig. 9A (the light dotted pattern), it is observed that an increase in the amount of incentives for recreational trips has a lower acceleration factor than other travel purposes during the morning peak. It is inferred that users are more willing to depart earlier in their recreational trips to earn more points. The reasoning might be: unlike work and home trips that are mandatory routine trips, recreational trips have more flexibility in which departing earlier or later is much feasible. More precisely, the results of the acceleration factor analysis indicate that offering 200 units ($US 1) worth of incentive accelerates the departure time by 0.98 and 0.99 times in recreational and others trip purposes, respectively. This acceleration, however, equals 1.007 in work and home trip purposes and equals 1.004 in school trip purposes.

Investigating the response to incentives during evening peak hours reveals a slightly different result. Looking at Fig. 9A (the dark-shaded pattern), it is found that an increase in the amount of incentives does not push the departure time in the desirable way, but in the trips with purpose of errands has a stronger impact on the departure time than other travel purposes. The results of the acceleration factor analysis demonstrate that offering 200 units ($US 1) worth of incentive accelerates the departure time by 1.31 and 1.27 times in school and pick-up or drop-off trip purposes, respectively. The school trip purpose is the least elastic trip purpose in the evening peak hour.

As for Scenario 2, comparing the coefficient with the Scenario 1 shows a higher effect in both the morning and evening rush hours. Similar to Scenario 1, during the morning rush hour, users are more willing to change departure and gain more points in recreational trip purposes. Measuring the acceleration factor, it is found that offering 200 units (one US dollar) worth of incentive accelerates the departure time by 0.962 in this trip purpose, which is lower than Scenario 1 (higher effect). This acceleration ranges between 1.002 and 1.032 for other trip purposes. During the evening rush hour, unlike Scenario 1, incentive policies have more impacts on shifting the departure time and it actually changed departure of errands and the others trips when compared to other travel purposes. As shown in Fig. 9B, a 200 unit (one US dollar) increase in the incentive accelerates the departure time by 0.992 and 0.986 in the school and other trip purposes, respectively.

Comparing Scenario 1 and Scenario 2, it can be determined that the incentive policy in Scenario 2 had a larger impact on shifting the departure time than Scenario 1. It is speculated that the difference comes from the pattern of implementation, as the magnitude of incentives is equal in both scenarios. As shown in Fig. 7, the highest amounts of incentives are offered at 6:15 AM in Scenario 1, which is shifted to 8:00 AM in Scenario 2, which is fairly close to the morning peak hour. The short gap between the peak hours and the offered departure time might result in an uncertainty about getting stuck in traffic, and consequently discouraging users from changing their departure time.

6. CONCLUSION

This research evaluated the effectiveness of two incentive scenarios that were proposed for Metropia app users over 3 years. The results suggest that peak hour travelers may be open to behavioral incentives that promote non-peak hour departure time. The incentives, however, may need to be tailored with consideration of time of day and travel purpose. As far as the policy implementation is concerned, we found that the second scenario has a higher success rate of changing departure time of the users than the first scenario. Lower average of acceleration factors is an evidence of this success. We speculate that the superiority of the second scenario is rooted in the fact that the second scenario offers a minimum amount of incentive at the most congested time while it retaliates with the highest amount of points in the shoulders that have 30 min time difference with the prior. Consequently, the relative point difference would be very obvious for users and departure time change would be appealing if users have the flexibility in their schedule. However, the first scenario generally tries to shift users from a wider congested time span to a very early morning (for morning trips) and very late afternoon (for the afternoon trips). Findings, such as those presented herein, may facilitate the design of incentives tailored to specific individuals or groups with similar characteristics. Such tailoring has the potential to increase the probability of incentivizing lasting and meaningful behavioral change.

ACKNOWLEDGMENTS

The authors acknowledge the partial financial support from Department of Energy, ARPA-E, TRANSNET program, DE-AR0000614. The authors are solely responsible for the viewpoints expressed and conclusions made in this paper.

REFERENCES

Arellana, J., Daly, A., Hess, S., de Dios Ortúzar, J., Rizzi, L., 2012. Development of surveys for study of departure time choice. Transp. Res. Rec. J. Transp. Res. Board 2303, 9–18. https://doi.org/10.3141/2303-02.

Arian, A., 2018. Exploring Travel Behavior Change Opportunities Through a Spatial-Temporal Dimensioned Persuasion Framework. The University of Arizona.

Arian, A., Chiu, Y.-C., 2017. Evaluating the promotion of innovative mobility options with an agent-based modeling and simulation approach. Transp. Res. Rec. J. Transp. Res. Board 2645, 176–183.

Arian, A., Ermagun, A., Chiu, Y.-C., 2017. In: Characterizing activity patterns using co-clustering and user-activity network. Intelligent Transportation Systems (ITSC), 2017 IEEE 20th International Conference on IEEE.

Bamberg, S., Ajzen, I., Schmidt, P., 2003. Choice of travel mode in the theory of planned behavior: the roles of past behavior, habit, and reasoned action. Basic Appl. Soc. Psychol. 25 (3), 175–187.

Ben-Elia, E., Ettema, D., 2011a. Changing commuters' behavior using rewards: a study of rush-hour avoidance. Transp. Res. Part F Traffic Psychol. Behav. 14 (5), 354–368. https://doi.org/10.1016/J.TRF.2011.04.003.

Ben-Elia, E., Ettema, D., 2011b. Rewarding rush-hour avoidance: a study of commuters' travel behavior. Transp. Res. Part A Policy Pract. 45 (7), 567–582. https://doi.org/10.1016/J.TRA.2011.03.003.

Bhat, C.R., 1998. Accommodating flexible substitution patterns in multi-dimensional choice modeling: formulation and application to travel mode and departure time choice. Transp. Res. Part B Methodol. 32 (7), 455–466. https://doi.org/10.1016/S0191-2615(98)00011-3.

Bhat, C.R., Steed, J.L., 2002. A continuous-time model of departure time choice for urban shopping trips. Transp. Res. Part B Methodol. 36 (3), 207–224. https://doi.org/10.1016/S0191-2615(00)00047-3.

Currie, G., 2011. Free fare incentives to shift rail demand peaks—medium-term impacts. In: Transportation Research Board 93rd Annual Meeting (No. 11-0739) Retrieved from, https://trid.trb.org/view/1091561.

Ermagun, A., Fan, Y., Wolfson, J., Adomavicius, G., Das, K., 2017. Real-time trip purpose prediction using online location-based search and discovery services. Transp. Res. Part C Emerg. Technol. 77, 96–112.

Fujii, S., Kitamura, R., 2003. What does a one-month free bus ticket do to habitual drivers? An experimental analysis of habit and attitude change. Transportation 30 (1), 81–95. https://doi.org/10.1023/A:1021234607980.

Jariyasunant, J., Abou-Zeid, M., Carrel, A., Ekambaram, V., Gaker, D., Sengupta, R., Walker, J.L., 2015. Quantified traveler: travel feedback meets the cloud to change behavior. J. Intell. Transp. Syst. 19 (2), 109–124. https://doi.org/10.1080/15472450.2013.856714.

Jou, R.-C., Kitamura, R., Weng, M.-C., Chen, C.-C., 2008. Dynamic commuter departure time choice under uncertainty. Transp. Res. Part A Policy Pract. 42 (5), 774–783. https://doi.org/10.1016/J.TRA.2008.01.017.

Lemp, J.D., Kockelman, K.M., 2010. The continuous cross-nested logit model: formulation and application for departure time choice. Transp. Res. Part B Methodol. 44 (5), 646–661. https://doi.org/10.1016/J.TRB.2010.03.001.

Mahmassani, H.S., Chang, G.-L., 1986. Experiments with departure time choice dynamics of urban commuters. Transp. Res. Part B Methodol. 20 (4), 297–320. https://doi.org/10.1016/0191-2615(86)90045-7.

Mannering, F.L., 1989. Poisson analysis of commuter flexibility in changing routes and departure times. Transp. Res. Part B Methodol. 23 (1), 53–60. https://doi.org/10.1016/0191-2615(89)90023-4.

Mannering, F., Kim, S.-G., Barfield, W., Ng, L., 1994. Statistical analysis of commuters' route, mode, and departure time flexibility. Transp. Res. Part C Emerg. Technol. 2 (1), 35–47. https://doi.org/10.1016/0968-090X(94)90018-3.
Merugu, D., Prabhakar, B.S., Rama, N.S., 2009. An incentive mechanism for decongesting the roads: a pilot program in Bangalore. In: Proc. of ACM NetEcon Workshop, Retrieved from, http://citeseerx.ist.psu.edu/viewdoc/download?doi=10.1.1.208.6965&rep=rep1&type=pdf.
Mudholkar, G.S., Srivastava, D.K., Kollia, G.D., 1996. A generalization of the Weibull distribution with application to the analysis of survival data. J. Am. Stat. Assoc. 91 (436), 1575–1583. https://doi.org/10.1080/01621459.1996.10476725.
Thorhauge, M., Haustein, S., Cherchi, E., 2016. Accounting for the theory of planned behaviour in departure time choice. Transp. Res. Part F Traffic Psychol. Behav. 38, 94–105. https://doi.org/10.1016/J.TRF.2016.01.009.

CHAPTER SEVEN

Institutional Influences on the Development of Urban Freight Transport Policies by Local Authorities

Emine Zehra Akgün*, Jason Monios†,1
*Transport Research Institute, Edinburgh Napier University, Edinburgh, United Kingdom
†Kedge Business School, Marseille, France
[1]Corresponding author: e-mail address: jason.monios@kedgebs.com

Contents

Abstract

Urban freight transport (UFT) provides the last mile delivery of goods, return of unwanted or recyclable goods and the removal of waste. Despite such benefits, freight vehicles often cause adverse impacts on the economy, environment and society such as air pollution, reduced mobility, congestion and road casualties. Local authorities implement various regulations and initiatives to mitigate the problems caused by freight vehicles and to decrease conflicts between various road users. The aim of this chapter is to investigate how institutional influences on local authorities determine urban freight transport policy, paying particular attention to three pressure factors (coercive, normative and mimetic) that cause institutional isomorphism. The empirical study compares three countries (Scotland, England and Sweden) based on data collected from 11 cities, each exhibiting different levels of intervention in terms of

Advances in Transport Policy and Planning, Volume 1
ISSN 2543-0009
https://doi.org/10.1016/bs.atpp.2018.07.004

UFT policy. Our findings showed that the impact of normative and mimetic factors on local authorities is more intense than the impact of coercive factors, with social pressure generally being stronger than national government mandate. The case cities in England and particularly Scotland demonstrated a limited vision when incorporating urban freight in their local transport planning, being reluctant to enforce restrictions on users in order to meet urban freight goals. By contrast, evidence from Sweden suggests that a better relationship between public and private stakeholders makes it easier to implement freight policies in partnership.

Keywords: Urban freight transport, City logistics, Policy, Institutional isomorphism

1. INTRODUCTION

The aim of this chapter is to investigate how institutional influences on local authorities determine urban freight transport (UFT) policy. Commercial freight vehicles provide the last mile deliveries of goods, return of unwanted or recyclable goods and the removal of waste. Therefore, UFT is one of the important factors keeping cities functioning. The importance of freight transport in urban areas has grown in parallel to the increasing population of cities and economic growth (Browne et al., 2012).

UFT consists of activities such as loading and unloading, parking, storage and consolidation, which require significant use of urban space (Dablanc, 2007). These activities require a certain degree of interaction between different stakeholders, who can be public authorities (national, regional or local), retailers (e.g., shops, hotels, restaurants), and other road users such as buses, cars, bikes and pedestrians. Each stakeholder has different needs and objectives concerning space, mobility, accessibility and safety and sometimes these objectives contradict each other.

Despite its benefits, UFT often comes into question due to the adverse impacts that freight vehicles cause on the environment. Road transport is the dominant mode of freight distribution in cities. Although the share of freight vehicles compared to nonfreight vehicles in overall road traffic is relatively low, they produce a disproportionate contribution to emissions, congestion, and road casualties (Kin et al., 2017; Lindholm and Blinge, 2014). In addition, UFT contributes to reduced mobility and accessibility in urban areas as goods vehicles occupy road capacity as well as pavements (Dablanc et al., 2013; Kin et al., 2017). Public authorities implement various regulations and initiatives to mitigate the problems caused by freight vehicles. Local authorities (i.e., municipalities or city councils) are the primary organizations that are responsible for enforcing policies on local roads. Local policies aim to decrease conflicts between various road users by providing space for different transport modes, increasing mobility and accessibility for vulnerable road users.

Facing such challenges and conflicting stakeholder demands, there are many influences on the transport policies eventually implemented by local authorities, and UFT is no exception. Policies are not chosen simply by their necessity or effectiveness but also to some degree by institutional influences according to what is expected by various stakeholders and what is done in other cities. Yet very little research has addressed the institutional component of UFT. Rose et al. (2016) applied the theory of institutional isomorphism (DiMaggio and Powell, 1983) to explore the coercive and mimetic pressures on logistics service providers. The coercive pressures identified come from the constrained space and finite resources of the urban transport environment, leading to management challenges across the public and private sectors. They concluded that freight operators represent a lower priority for public authorities; thus in order to overcome this problem the operators face mimetic pressures to work with the public sector in certain authorized ways in order to be considered legitimate members in the urban sphere.

In order to explore the institutional influences on UFT policy, this chapter also uses the theoretical perspective of institutional isomorphism, but in contrast to the study of Rose et al. (2016) applying it to private operators, this study addresses the public sector side, using empirical data from an analysis of 11 local authorities in three countries: Scotland, England and Sweden. Local authorities are core units of decision making when it comes to the organization of traffic and roads at the city level and they are under the influence of various factors when planning and organizing particular elements, including freight. They implement their policies while trying to keep local, regional and national requirements in balance, while also interacting with many other public and private organizations, particularly freight transport operators and users.

Institutional theory concerns the fact that organizations are heavily influenced by their institutional environment. The institutional structure of this environment can lead to the emergence of particular forms of organizational structure as well as being related to the development and implementation of individual policies which are seen as legitimate and acceptable. Some of this behavior is derived not purely from the policy goals but from a desire on behalf of the organization to gain legitimacy. The theory of institutional isomorphism developed by DiMaggio and Powell (1983) suggests that particular pressures lead organizations to resemble each other.

The pressure factors fall under three categories: coercive, normative and mimetic. In this chapter, the isomorphism is not just the organizational form but also how they are represented in the policies that are selected.

Each of these factors influences local authorities' decisions concerning to what extent they will involve UFT in their local planning and which policies they will implement to mitigate related problems, and, importantly, how interventionist they will be. The empirical element of this chapter is based on interviews and document analysis across the 11 cities. Their institutional environment, organizational structure, policy development process and current UFT policies were analyzed according to the three pressures that lead to institutional isomorphism, in order to determine whether these cities have indeed adopted similar organizational forms and policy choices, and which of the three influences were strongest.

2. DESIGNING POLICY FOR THE URBAN FREIGHT TRANSPORT SECTOR

Local authorities introduce policies to prevent all road users from potential threats caused by vehicle traffic in cities and to provide a prosperous and safe environment for residents, workers and visitors (Lindholm and Blinge, 2014). Local authorities regulate road traffic concerning particular issues such as road safety, transportation of dangerous goods, air quality standards, freight deliveries during particular hours (e.g., night-time delivery bans). Economic activities and the geographical clustering of these activities heavily affect the traffic flow coming into and going out of cities, and there is a risk that interferences between different systems may make one or more system dysfunctional. For instance, illegal parking in loading-only bays or cycle lanes is a very common problem, which constrains the mobility of different road users.

Local authorities need to establish their local transport strategies and plans by considering the complex nature of the multiple transport systems. Despite the fact that local authorities increasingly recognize UFT in transport planning (Browne et al., 2012), policy makers in general have paid limited attention to designing specific UFT policies (Lindholm and Blinge, 2014). Passenger transport is generally prioritized over freight transport in cities, and when freight is considered it is at the national and international levels (Savy, 2012). Local authorities require advanced knowledge concerning how logistics systems work at the urban level, what transport requirements exist for various delivery operations (e.g., vehicle routing, demand planning, and delivery schedules) and demand patterns of customers. They need knowledge in order to implement effective freight policies and to be able to incorporate the needs of other transport systems (Lindholm and Blinge, 2014). The lack of attention is not particular only to local authorities but also national and regional authorities often lack dedicated bodies that deal with freight transport related issues in cities (van Duin and Quak, 2007).

According to Cui et al. (2015), centralized national governments can make decisions concerning transport policies, planning and investments, which are insensitive to local transport issues. On the other hand, historically, national governments have an indirect influence on UFT through infrastructure and maintenance, land use policies and sometimes even providing funding for projects (Wittlöv, 2012). In recent years, public authorities have increased their understanding and awareness through putting more effort into data collection, cooperating with other stakeholders and participating in national and international projects (Ballantyne and Lindholm, 2014; Ballantyne et al., 2013; Lindholm and Browne, 2013). The awareness of public authorities in developing effective freight and logistics increases in connection with the increasing awareness of the benefits of logistics as well as the adverse effects of road transport. Logistics as a sector supports local economies and ensures that people living in cities receive goods and services at the right time and place. However, freight vehicles are also sources of air pollution, road casualties and congestion.

There are various policy actions that have been taken in order to assess the challenges of urban traffic including freight vehicles; however, these policies aim to restrict freight vehicles either for a period of time or on an ongoing basis such as time window restrictions, size restrictions and route maps (i.e., showing recommended and mandatory routes for vehicles). Even though these types of restrictions are becoming more common, they may not reflect the rapidly changing dynamics of urban economies and cities in the long run and they may have adverse effects on cities' economies as well as the environment (Macharis and Kin, 2017). This is mainly because consumers and markets are constantly going through changes that affect consumption patterns (e.g., increased variety of products, free shipping) and delivery patterns (e.g., same day or next day deliveries) (Kin et al., 2017). This situation causes many commercial vehicles with very low fill rates to drive in cities, adding to the existing problems concerning congestion and air pollution.

Considering these changes and the challenges of urban areas, public authorities should be able to take further steps toward implementing policies that aim to improve UFT and to reduce adverse effects caused by UFT. Public authorities enforce policies such as time window restrictions or size restrictions and they often do not undertake any deep consultation with other stakeholders such as freight operators or receivers before implementing such policies. On the other hand, if public authorities (both local and national level) want to implement effective freight-focused policies, they need to involve other stakeholders in data acquisition (Gatta and Marcucci, 2016) and the policy design process (Stathopoulos et al., 2012), and they need to create partnerships that guarantee long-term relations and mutual understanding (Lindholm and Browne, 2013). Such early stakeholder involvement can lead public authorities to have a better understanding of the needs of freight operators and receivers. In addition, public authorities can communicate their objectives with operators and receivers concerning society, environment and the economy more clearly. It also helps public authorities to understand potential consequences of planned policies on logistics operations of other stakeholders.

As local authorities shift their perspectives more toward implementing freight-focused and effective policies, there are various types of policies developed either by local authorities or developed as a result of a partnership between public institutions and private organizations. Each of these policies aims to address one or more UFT challenges. Clean air policies, low emission vehicles, consolidation solutions, designated loading and unloading zones, road pricing systems, real time information systems, shared use of public transport infrastructure and developing night-time delivery schemes are policies which are being observed in different cities. Yet Kiba-Janiak (2017) showed how different cities can be located at different points along a spectrum according to how "mature" they are in terms of taking an active role in UFT policy, with many cities only implementing very few or basic policies.

3. INSTITUTIONAL THEORY AND INSTITUTIONAL ISOMORPHISM

Institutions are emergent and higher order factors above the individual level (Amenta and Ramsey, 2010). Institutions are made of governance structures, social arrangements, norms and rules. They are bounded by informal constraints such as sanctions, customs and traditions and also by formal rules such as constitutions and laws (North, 1991). Various political, economic, cultural and social aspects shape behaviors, perceptions and choices of institutions. Their existence is based on certain economic and social motivations. North (1991, p. 97) stated the economic reason as "Together with the standard constraints of economics they define the choice set and therefore determine transaction and production costs and hence the profitability and feasibility of engaging in economic activity." Institutions also evolve over time. As they evolve, the direction of economic and social change within them takes different forms toward growth, stagnation or decline.

Organizational theorists consider that institutions are the results of human activities but they are not outcomes of conscious design (DiMaggio and Powell, 1991a,b). Neo-institutional theorists have had a strong influence on organizational analysis and form the basis of the theoretical approach taken in this chapter (drawing on DiMaggio and Powell, 1983; Meyer and Rowan, 1977). Yet both old and new institutionalism include many common aspects such as viewing institutionalization as a state dependent process. In this process, governments limit organizations' choices that they can pursue and organizations become less instrumentally rational. However, the structural emphasis of new institutionalism is on the symbolic role of formal structure, including interorganizational influences, conformity, and persuasiveness of cultural accounts rather than the functions that they are intended to perform (DiMaggio and Powell, 1991a,b). When it comes to organizational dynamics, new institutionalism identifies a reduction in variety, emphasis on homogeneity of organizations, and highlights stability as well as persistence of institutionalized components (DiMaggio and Powell, 1983; Zucker, 1977).

Neo-institutionalists argue that an organization's survival depends on its fit with the cultural environment and its ability to gain social legitimacy. This means that an organization's success depends on whether it adopts structures that are considered as rational and legitimate in the external environment. Organizations mirror environmental beliefs about what a legitimate organization of that type should look like. Such actions can lead to institutional isomorphism, which can be defined as a process of developing the same organizational forms. DiMaggio and Powell (1983, pp. 63–64) explain reasons that pave the way toward isomorphism as "Structural change in organizations seems less and less driven by competition or need for efficiency. Instead, we contend, bureaucratization and other forms of organizational change occur as a result of processes that make organizations more similar without necessarily making them more efficient." Neo-institutionalism emphasizes the prevailing influence of institutions on human behavior through rules, norms and beliefs, which fall under three categories and each category triggers its own isomorphism process; these are regulations, normative controls and cognitive controls.

Regulations or regulatory institutions are an explicit form of institutional control. They constrain behaviors through rules, laws, and behavior inducements such as incentives and punishments. These pressure factors cause coercive isomorphism (DiMaggio and Powell, 1983), where isomorphism occurs as a direct response to government mandate. The second established institutional control is normative. Normative controls guide what organizations should and should not do, or how they should and should not appear. Normative control involves informal rules and guidelines, but they are just as influential on organizational behavior as laws and regulations, because they guide behaviors of organizations through a logic of appropriateness, sense of duty or awareness of what should be done. According to DiMaggio and Powell (1983, p. 70), normative isomorphism stems primarily from professionalization, which has been described as "collective struggle of members of an occupation to define the conditions and methods of their work." Normative isomorphism drives compliance by social obligations and its indicators are certifications and accreditation. According to the principles of isomorphism, organizations are rewarded for their similarity to other organizations in their sector. Such acknowledgement makes it easier for organizations to be in a transaction with other organizations, to attract skilled stuff and to be recognized as reputable and legitimate. The third and the last type of institutional control is cognitive control, leading to mimetic isomorphism (DiMaggio and Powell, 1983). Mimetic pressure occurs when an organization faces circumstances containing environmental uncertainty, ambiguity and complexity (DiMaggio and Powell, 1983). In addition, compliance with cognitive institutions occurs because other types of behaviors are inconceivable and cognitive beliefs are perceived as the natural and taken for granted ways of doing things. As a result, organizations intend to model themselves after similar organizations in their sector which they think to be more successful as well as more legitimate.

This study focuses on public organizations, more specifically on local authorities (i.e., municipalities or city councils). Local authorities are responsible for implementing local transport strategies in their territories (urban and suburban areas). Existing literature focuses on the active role of public organizations in the institutionalization process of other organizations rather than evaluating them as the objects of institutional pressure (Frumkin and Galaskiewicz, 2004). Collaboration, relationship building, and interaction among public and private institutions have begun to be addressed in the urban freight transport literature but so far, very few studies have analyzed the institutional aspect of UFT (cf. Rose et al., 2016). This chapter applies the concept of institutional isomorphism to explore coercive, normative and mimetic influences in UFT.

Coercive pressure in UFT comes from formal institutions such as national governments or other regulatory institutions (i.e., European Commission). These institutions set formal and informal requirements. Formal requirements such as national targets (e.g., compulsory air quality management) exert external pressure on local authorities. Informal requirements aim to encourage local authorities to implement policies and provide funding available (e.g., funding calls by regional or national authorities). Sometimes, coercive pressures can also be internal to a local authority, such as lack of resources.

Factors that create normative pressure in terms of UFT are more about moral requirements and "doing the right thing." One major stream of pressure comes from the public, through voting and lobby groups. While much of this influence relates to passenger rather than freight transport, often passenger policies will still affect UFT (e.g., pedestrianization, cycle lanes). Local businesses and freight forwarders will also lobby local authorities to improve the transport for them, for instance, reducing congestion and increasing the number of loading bays, but at the same time, they will be lobbying local authorities to be less interventionist. In addition, safety and environmental concerns influence transport decisions and the requirements concerning safety and environment put pressure on local authorities to limit traffic flows and/or incentivize greener engines.

Mimetic UFT pressures influence the creation process of policy heavily, as strong pressures exist for local authorities to copy policy from elsewhere, often without sufficient proof that it is suitable. Some of these influences result from the desire to copy already legitimized policies that can head off potential criticism, especially when supported by good PR channels and the use of accreditation procedures. Economic development is another strong pressure, whereby all cities face pressure to be choosing UFT policies based on economic gain, providing jobs and making the city attractive for business.

4. THREE COUNTRY CASE STUDIES

The topic of this study is exploratory in nature; therefore, a methodology of qualitative case studies was selected. The main motivation behind the case selection was to analyze different countries with different institutional dynamics. The choice of the first two cases was made after a detailed review of transport plans and strategies at local, regional and national levels in England and Scotland.[a] It was identified that they have various differences regarding how they regulate urban freight transport in their own territories. It is also known from the existing literature that Sweden is one of the most proactive countries dealing with UFT. From the perspective of transport maturity introduced by Kiba-Janiak (2017), each of the three countries can be located on different positions on a scale concerning how mature they are in terms of implementing freight-focused policies in their cities.

The data for the case studies were obtained via documentary analysis across the 3 countries and interviews at 11 cities.[b] In Scotland and England, where local authorities have less responsibility for UFT compared to Sweden, some regional transport organizations are active in this role (e.g., freight partnerships, regional transport partnerships). Therefore, on the recommendation of the local authorities contacted, these regional organizations were also interviewed.[c] In total, semi-structured interviews were completed face-to-face or on the phone with 15 different public authorities (see Table 1). The documentary analysis included transport policy at national, regional and local levels in order to understand the policy context and influences, and the interviews asked local and regional authority officers about how they constructed transport policies, what challenges they faced, how they dealt with conflicting stakeholder demands and what policies they eventually implemented in their cities. The interviews too place between December 2016 and February 2017, and all interviews were recorded and transcribed. The influences on UFT policy selection and implementation were identified from analyzing both sources of data and then classified under each of the three types of institutional pressure.

[a] England and Scotland are treated as two different countries instead of being mentioned as the United Kingdom; due to the devolved political situation in the United Kingdom, transport responsibilities are devolved to the Scottish level. There are also differences in local and regional governance, which reflect on transport planning and transport implementation. For instance, in some areas England has combined authorities, which consist of the combination of neighboring cities. In Scotland, the city councils produce Local Transport Strategies (LTS) while English councils produce Local Transport Plans (LTP).

[b] For Scotland and Sweden, the four biggest cities (in terms of population) were chosen; however, one of the cities from Sweden chose not to participate in the study. In the case of England, London was excluded from the list because of its unique nature and large size and the next four biggest cities were selected. All case cities are major hubs with regards both to population and also economic wealth. The final list of cities was: Sweden (Stockholm, Gothenburg, Malmö), England (Greater Manchester, Bristol, Birmingham, Newcastle) and Scotland (Edinburgh, Glasgow, Dundee, Aberdeen).

[c] Each of these regional organizations has only one major city within its boundaries, which are the cities we analyzed in our research, and who advised us to include them. Therefore, while they are technically regional bodies aiming to improve transport coordination across a region, from the UFT perspective they are dealing with the cities listed in the table.

Table 1 The List of Interviewed Authorities and Positions of the Interviewees

Country	City	Level	Authority	Position
Scotland	Aberdeen	Local	Aberdeen City Council	Senior Engineer for Transport Strategy
		Regional	North East of Scotland Transport Partnership (NESTRANS)	Transport Strategy Manager
	Edinburgh	Local	Edinburgh City Council	Senior Project Manager
		Regional	South East of Scotland Transport Partnership (SEStran)	Head of Programmes
	Glasgow	Local	Glasgow City Council	Technical Officer for Transport
		Regional	Strathclyde Partnership for Transport (SPT)	Senior Transport Planner
	Dundee	Local	Dundee City Council	Head of Road and Transport
England	Bristol	Local	Bristol City Council	Strategic Projects Team Manager and Transport Planner
	Birmingham	Local	Birmingham City Council	Transport Officer
	Newcastle	Local	Newcastle City Council	Transport Planner
		Regional	North East Freight Partnership	Senior Specialist Transport Planner
	Manchester	Local	Transport for Greater Manchester (TfGM)	Chief Executive Officer
Sweden	Malmö	Local	Malmö City Municipality	Project Leader
	Stockholm	Local	Stockholm City Municipality	Transport Planner
	Gothenburg	Local	Gothenburg City Municipality	Project Manager

This section presents the key features of each of the case countries investigated in this study. The cross-case analysis then explores the similarities and differences between and across the three countries in order to determine the institutional influences on these policy environments. Key features of each case are presented in Table 2.

Table 2 Key Features of Each Case Country

Country		**Scotland**	**England**	**Sweden**
Population (million)		5.4	55.3	10.1
Cities analyzed in this research		• Edinburgh • Glasgow • Aberdeen • Dundee	• Greater Manchester • Birmingham • Bristol • Newcastle upon Tyne	• Stockholm • Gothenburg • Malmö
Maturity in terms of UFT		Beginner	Medium	Advanced
Main UFT challenges	Air quality	x	x	
	Congestion	x	x	x
	Accidents	x	x	
	Noise	x	x	x
	Parking space	x	x	
	Decreased quality of urban life	x	x	x
Main UFT policies	Time restrictions	x	x	x
	Weight restrictions	x	x	x
	Air quality management	x	x	x
	Urban consolidation centers		x	x
	Certification/accreditation schemes	x	x	
	Congestion charge			x
	Night-time delivery	x		x

4.1 Scotland

Scotland is the second largest country in the United Kingdom with a population of 5.4 million (NRS, 2018). In general, in Scotland, UFT has been given very little attention. Efforts to make UFT specific policies remain very local and only a couple of initiatives have been established that are concerned with increasing the efficiency of freight deliveries in the city centers. One of the reasons is that Scotland has less urban population in comparison to England.

According to the policy documents, congestion and air pollution are the most significant problems concerning general traffic and UFT in Scotland. According to the latest National Transport Strategy published in 2016, Transport Scotland aims to tackle congestion in order to improve journey times and to reduce the level of emissions to improve air quality. Some Scottish cities suffer from through traffic, which contributes to congestion problems in cities; however, the national government works on projects to build city bypasses around these cities (Aberdeen City Council, 2016; Transport Scotland, 2018a). Some concerns noted are the rising trend in e-commerce and increasing number of size restrictions on freight vehicles which increase the number of goods vehicles as well as their distance traveled in cities (Department for Transport, 2016; RAC Foundation, 2014). The distance traveled by light goods vehicles (up to 3.5 tons) on all Scottish roads increased from 5460 to 6979m km between 2005 and 2015, while the distance traveled by heavy goods vehicles (up to 40 tons) on all Scottish roads decreased from 2637 to 2504m km (Transport Scotland, 2016a,b). The increasing number of light goods vehicles in cities also causes noise pollution and increases the chance of interference between freight vehicles and road users, which may lead to road casualties.

Scotland has a very limited amount of policies specifically dedicated to UFT issues. Restrictions related to parking, loading, time window and size are the most common policies applied. Size restrictions are only applied due to constructional constraints such as narrow and historic streets or weak bridges. Freight Quality Partnerships and Regional Transport Partnerships have a mediating role in implementing UFT policies together with the city councils. Traffic signaling and freight route maps for truck drivers are two particular policies, which are implemented as a collaboration between the city councils and the regional transport partnerships. By 2018, Scotland will introduce low emission zones (LEZs) gradually. LEZs are going to be implemented based on a national framework but each city council will implement their own setups (Transport Scotland, 2018b).

4.2 England

England is the largest country in the United Kingdom with a population of 55.3 million (ONS, 2018). According to policy documents, local authorities in England aim to create environments for enabling the efficient supply of goods and services as efficient logistics activities will support businesses to receive goods that they need to produce wealth and value. An efficient system is also important to attract more businesses to locate in England. Retailing (including supermarkets, fashion, bars, restaurants and hotels) and service businesses (i.e., banking, insurance, other finance related companies) comprise the majority of the economic activity in England but there are still some production facilities that require constant flow of goods in and out such as automotive. Some of the cities in England consider UFT as one of the main sectors that contributes to the economy on local and regional levels and creates job opportunities. Therefore, these cities promote the establishment of logistics clusters to attract companies in the logistics sector.

Air pollution and congestion are the most significant problems, according to the documentary analysis from England. Congestion partly occurs due to the increasing number of light goods vehicles. This situation occurs as a consequence of size restrictions in place. E-commerce is another factor that contributes to the increasing number of vehicles and distances traveled in cities by light goods vehicles (Department for Transport, 2016). Similar to Scotland, there is a significant increase in distance traveled by light goods vehicles. According to Department for Transport (2017), vehicle miles increased from 22.2 to 41.7bn in England between 1993 and 2016. An increasing trend can also be observed in the distance traveled by heavy goods vehicles. Between 1993 and 2016, vehicle miles increased from 13 to 14.4bn in England. Congestion becomes critical especially when freight deliveries and passenger transport are concentrated at particular hours of the day. In some cases, cities in England need to accommodate through traffic, which occurs due to a lack of ring roads. There are also problems concerning road safety and noise pollution; however, they are considered less pressing problems.

The city councils in England implement various policies in order to tackle traffic related problems. Parking restrictions, loading/unloading restrictions and time restrictions are in place in order to prevent particular geographical areas from congestion during particular hours of the day. The city councils declared Air Quality Management Areas (AQMAs) to monitor air pollutants such as particulate matter. As air pollution becomes a life-threatening problem in the cities in England, other bigger cities are getting prepared to introduce clean air zones, where polluting vehicles that are not compliant with Euro engine standards will not be permitted. The current policies in place such as restrictions do not provide permanent solutions for congestion problems caused by freight vehicles as long as the number of vehicles that travel to cities remains the same or increases. In addition, most of the existing policies do not directly aim to mitigate problems caused by UFT but focus on general traffic problems.

Overall, England presents a reasonably progressive agenda concerning UFT policies. The city councils are planning and developing UFT policies and initiatives that will enable freight operators to make deliveries that are more efficient (Transport for Greater Manchester, 2016; West of England Partnership, 2011). The councils and the government also promote the use of low emission vehicles. Some cities in England implement consolidation centers that aim to decrease the number of heavy goods vehicles to enter congested areas by offering consolidation operations, some even with electric vehicles (Paddeu, 2017). The city councils work on developing delivery service plans and guidance on how to design dedicated loading-only zones. Delivery service plans aim to promote use of bicycles and electric vehicles for freight transport in urban areas and establishing subregional freight facilities and economic centers in order to cluster trade and logistics related activities in centralized places, which will enable companies to consolidate goods.

4.3 Sweden

Sweden has a population of 10.1 million (SCB, 2018). UFT is considered one of the most important contributors to the local economies in Swedish cities. Sweden has a longer history of dealing with UFT related problems than either England or Scotland. Therefore, some of the problems that are common in other countries do not pose threats in the case of Sweden. For instance, emission levels do not pose a significant problem on the local roads in Sweden in comparison to air quality problems on regional and national roads that are passing through the city. The main reason is that Sweden has a longer history to promote the use of zero and low emission vehicles that operate within the city. The most significant problem concerning UFT is that current size restrictions and time restrictions on heavy goods vehicles leads to the increase in the number of light goods vehicles and results in congestion in the city centers. It is identified that the distance traveled by light goods vehicles increased from 3606 to 9089 m km between 1990 and 2017 (Trafik Analys, 2017). The same data show an increase in the distance traveled by heavy goods vehicles from 3656 to 4912 mkm between 1990 and 2017 (Trafik Analys, 2017).

Sweden has a larger portfolio of UFT focused policies than the other two countries. They implement time window restrictions and size restrictions in connection with the time window restrictions, with various additional current and planned UFT policies. The policies that they implement are based on factors such as establishing stakeholder engagement groups, initiating safe and efficient logistics, promoting energy efficient vehicles and data collection for implementing policies that are more efficient. For instance, the city of Stockholm implements off-peak deliveries. They initiated the project to mitigate congestion problems that occur during the day, which leads to inefficient deliveries. As they also want to promote safe and efficient logistics, they allow hybrid delivery and waste collection vehicles to make deliveries during off-peak hours to decrease the chance of interference between vehicles and other road users (cf. Koutoulas et al., 2017). In order to tackle congestion, Stockholm and Gothenburg implement congestion charging. Swedish cities also implement urban consolidation centers (UCCs) to serve various geographical areas and for various services. For instance, there are particular schemes which are specifically developed for city center deliveries and construction deliveries. In this way, they can promote use of low emission vehicles as well as fewer numbers of vehicles driving into the populated city centers.

5. CROSS-CASE ANALYSIS AND INSTITUTIONAL DISCUSSION

This section compares the three country cases according to the three dimensions of institutional isomorphism: coercive, normative and mimetic. The key influences are summarized in Table 3.

5.1 Coercive Influences

In this study, five types of coercive pressure were identified: target monitoring, technology standards, institutional change, lack of resources and project participation.

Formal institutions such as national governments are primary sources of coercive pressure in UFT, acting as an external force on local authorities. Governments and local authorities work toward increasing accessibility and mobility to create attractive and liveable cities, identifying their objectives and targets around these aims. However, problems such as air pollution have become a significant barrier to achieving environmental objectives. In recent

Table 3 Summary of Institutional Influences on Each Case

Country		Scotland	England	Sweden
Coercive influences	National government target monitoring[a]	x	x	
	Technology standards	x	x	x
	Institutional change		x	
	Lack of resources	x	x	x
	Project participation	x	x	x
Normative influences	National government policy	x	x	x
	Public opinion	x	x	x
	Industry lobby groups	x	x	x
Mimetic influences	Dedicated UFT personnel			x
	Certification and accreditation	x	x	
	Becoming attractive cities	x	x	x

[a]National government monitoring in Scotland and England is only related to air quality in cities, not specifically from the UFT perspective.

years, governments moved forward from just acknowledging road freight transport as a challenge to societal and environmental well-being to actively searching for mitigation strategies. Encouragement for UFT policies from the national level can be considered a coercive pressure but often they do not impose any statutory requirements; therefore, it becomes more of a normative pressure (and is discussed in the next section). However, close monitoring of targets from the national level does appear in the United Kingdom as a coercive pressure, but only in one specific instance relating to air quality. UK government mandates the implementation of AQMAs in cities where air pollution levels are higher than accepted levels. Cities in England and Scotland with AQMAs are the only examples within the sample, which experience close monitoring of targets as a coercive pressure. Concerning other KPIs identified in Sweden, England and Scotland, there is no pressure from upper level organizations to monitor the local authorities' targets.

Technology standards are another type of coercive pressure. Almost all case cities aim to incentivize the use of low or zero emission vehicles in freight as well as passenger transportation in their policy documents. However, they do not dictate to the private sector to switch to low emission vehicles completely but they implement measures such as LEZ/environmental zones to constrain use of vehicles that produce high emissions. It is observed that cities in Sweden use technological tools to develop other solutions such as advance-booking system for loading/unloading bays and producing trip generation models in order to estimate the number of vehicles coming into the city in future. Such differentiation may occur due to the fact that Swedish cities implemented the use of low emission vehicles earlier than other case cities in England and Scotland. Therefore, they started earlier to investigate the existence of other technological standards in order to advance UFT in their city.

Another formal coercive pressure is stability and alterations in institutions. It has a great influence on isomorphism in local authorities. The city councils in England evinced a high level of institutional change. In recent years, the cities in England started to form combined authorities according to the Cities and Local Government Devolution Act 2016. Combined authorities are defined as "a legal body set up using national legislation that enables a group of two or more councils to collaborate and take collective decisions across council boundaries" (Local Government Association, 2016, p. 4). Greater Manchester (GM) was one of the earliest combined authorities in England. Transport for GM mentioned that alteration in their governance structure provided by combined authority status enabled them to follow up their targets and KPIs, which individual local authorities cannot manage to do due to shortages in financial and human resources. In addition, other cities such as Newcastle (North East Combined Authority), Birmingham (West Midlands Combined Authority) and Bristol (West of England Combined Authority) have become parts of other combined authorities. These authorities became more powerful concerning policy-making and wealthier in terms of acquiring required resources for implementing policies.

Local authorities can also experience coercive pressure due to budget limitations. These factors are highly influential on local authorities' decisions concerning to what extent they will involve freight transport in their local planning and which policies they will implement to mitigate related problems. All local authorities in England and Scotland and two out of three in Sweden mentioned lack of resources as one of the primary reasons for lacking dedicated UFT departments, lacking freight-focused policies and lacking KPIs. In order to tackle budget issues, as noted above, local authorities in England started to establish combined authorities, which are entitled to combine power and access more financial resources. In addition, EU projects and national calls enable local authorities to obtain required resources to develop freight solutions.

An increasing participation by cities in EU projects provided an opportunity for local authorities to obtain more financial resources for UFT policy measures. All 11 sample cities in this study are involved in at least one EU project. Project participation is considered here as a coercive pressure, where they believe that they need to be involved in such projects, first in order to obtain additional funds, and second, to be able to keep up with current trends in freight, urban mobility and sustainability. It was observed in the interviews that local authorities consider such projects as a venue not only for implementing a new policy measure but also as a venue for exchanging knowledge.

5.2 Normative Influences

Normative pressure comes primarily but not exclusively from external sources. This study identified three normative pressures: national government, public opinion and industry lobby groups.

Encouragement for UFT policies from the national level can be considered a coercive pressure (as discussed above) but often they do not impose any statutory requirements; therefore, it becomes more of a normative pressure. For example, the UK national government recently published the Freight Carbon Review 2017. This study presents potential measures that can be implemented in order to mitigate adverse impacts of freight transport such as synchronized collaboration, use of UCCs and rescheduling deliveries to off-peak hours. Other national and international level reports such as the Scottish National Transport Strategy (2016), Cleaner Air for Scotland (2015) or the European Union's White paper on Roadmap to a Single European Transport Area (2011) reflect on local transport planning and how freight is elaborated in transport planning. The national governments' targets as well as EU objectives affect all case countries, even when they are not mandatory. Air quality became a top priority for all case countries because air pollution has hazardous impacts on health and the environment and road freight transport is one of the significant contributors to air pollution. Aside from AQMA for air quality mentioned above as a coercive pressure in the United Kingdom, the rest exist only as normative pressures, because local authorities are not forced to apply them. In Sweden, normative pressure arises either from national level objectives similar to England and Scotland or from other public authorities on the national level. For instance, Sveriges kommuner och Landsting (SKL) is an association that represents local authorities in Sweden. Among various areas of interest, urban freight is one of the topics that the association works on. SKL published a handbook for freight distribution in Swedish Cities, which is a manual that the municipalities in Sweden can use to support the process of creating sustainable UFT systems (SKL, 2018). The handbook does not have statutory power but may create normative pressure on local authorities to take actions toward establishing public–private cooperation and planning policies to tackle challenges of UFT operations.

Local authorities also experience normative pressure through informal groups and organizations such as public and lobby groups. Local authorities react to this pressure by doing the "right" things for society as well as the environment. Societal well-being and businesses are the two main pressure factors. Societal well-being is concerned with quality of life in cities. Improved environment, safety, security, and quality of the transport system are the determinants of quality aspects in cities, crucial to city residents. From the perspective of transport, public opinion demands clean air, safe and secure places where intrusion of vehicles is avoided. Public opinion is a big determinant because the public elects mayors and other local politicians and creates pressure through lobbying groups and awareness campaigns. The three most important issues which political campaigns emphasize heavily concerning transport are mobility, accessibility and safety in the cities. It is important for the public to see that politicians are working on issues that are directly related to individuals; for instance, decreasing the number of road casualties, providing accessible public transport and enabling people to use other transport modes such as cycling.

All three countries are influenced by normative pressure from public opinion, yet differences were identified concerning how they react. Scotland and combined authorities in England prioritize more public transport and mobility of individuals compared to the attention given to freight policies in transport planning. Sweden provides a more balanced approach toward transport planning and the local authorities acknowledge the fact that the public needs to be informed about the importance of freight in the city. The local authorities in Sweden stated that it is crucial to develop methods and implement policies which enable all transport modes and people to exist together without compromising mobility, safety and accessibility.

Normative pressure from the freight industry and local businesses forms the other side of the coin. The pressure factors can arise from different angles. First, they ask for less intervention from local authorities, but they also desire investment for a high-quality transport system, based on quality infrastructure, availability of parking space and proper signaling systems. Collaboration and partnership are two primary topics when it comes to building relationships between public authorities and the private sector. From the interviews, it was found that partnership and information sharing are more important in Sweden than in England and Scotland. All case countries mention the importance of collaboration with freight operators and businesses during the interviews and in their local transport plans. However, local authorities in Sweden actually work on more projects that require public–private partnerships. Through such processes, public authorities and other stakeholders must come to an agreement about financial and operational issues. If they cannot agree on these matters, this will not lead them to collaborate on developing projects. UCC projects provide a good example for goal agreement and collaboration between public and private stakeholders. For instance, in Scotland, there is no working UCC model. Despite multiple attempts, businesses and freight operators are not interested in getting involved in a project. In comparison, numerous projects were identified in Sweden and England. Combined authorities in England have taken some steps forward in order to understand how supply chains work in the city context, particularly in Greater Manchester. In addition, transport bodies in combined authorities are involved in training sessions together with truck drivers concerning cyclists' safety. Sweden has the most collaborative projects and studies among the three case countries. They are actively involved with private industry through consolidation centers, off-peak deliveries and freight networks.

5.3 Mimetic Influences

The last category of institutional pressures consists of mimetic pressures. Mimetic influences lead authorities to mimic the organizational structure or policies of others, which presents a shared logic and hence greater legitimacy for their actions as a buffer against potential criticism. The three main mimetic pressures identified in this research were dedicated UFT personnel or department, certification and accreditation schemes and the motivation to become attractive cities.

In terms of organizational structure, since there is no dedicated department or personnel for freight transport in English and Scottish councils, different departments come together occasionally to work on urban freight projects. When different departments come together to work on the same project, it becomes easier to develop communication channels. However, when there is no dedicated personnel or department dealing with UFT, awareness and knowledge concerning freight and logistics in cities do not build up in an efficient way. Relevant departments come together and work on a project as one of the many other projects on which they are working at any given time. This does not enable local authorities to deepen their knowledge concerning urban freight. This is how English and Scottish local authorities act when they build relationships and transfer ideas and policies. Sweden has a different picture. Sample cities have at least one or two people dealing specifically with UFT on the local level.

Local authorities want to gain legitimacy by transferring and adapting policies from other places. One way to gain legitimacy can be through certification and accreditation. This is one of the most common ways to gain legitimacy in Scotland and England. Local authorities often participate in fleet recognition and safety schemes (e.g., ECO Stars, CLOCS, FORS) in order to collaborate with the private sector and prove that they take necessary actions to think and act according to environmental concerns such as decreasing emissions and preventing road casualties. In Sweden, there is no similar certification or accreditation program. The case cities in Sweden control emission levels through environmental zones. In addition, some of the local authorities adjust their public procurement activities by introducing transport provisions in their contractual requirements with their suppliers. They take these actions for promoting energy efficient and sustainable transport.

As much as private companies compete in the market, there exists also competition between local authorities as well. Institutional isomorphism in the context of local authorities can also be explained by competition, as they want to earn titles such as the most liveable cities, the most environmental cities or the most sustainable cities. Policies, regulations and initiatives that are implemented by local authorities aim to make cities more attractive for everybody who works, lives or visits the city. A high-quality transport system is also a crucial part of economic activity and increasing economic activities attracts more business. Local authorities have a responsibility to ensure that adequate infrastructure for transport, delivery, parking, loading and unloading is provided. Therefore, an increasing need of mobility for all traffic users and making required improvements cause mimetic pressure on local authorities. At the same time, transport policies need to be aligned with other policies such as land use and city planning. Space is a scarce resource in city centers, which is shared by many users with conflicting interests. It is a challenging task to find an optimal solution, which would meet everybody's objectives and there is no single solution which fits in all cases. Therefore, policy makers and planners from different sectors need to be aware of each other's tasks and responsibilities.

6. CONCLUSION

The first conclusion from this research was to identify the principal types of coercive, normative and mimetic pressures operating in UFT policy, as listed in Table 3. Almost all of these were operating in all three case countries, although with some differences in government structure and interaction between the national, regional and local levels. All local authorities in all three countries face the same pressure to keep city centers functioning smoothly, increase economic activity and undertake necessary improvements to transport infrastructure. The latest trends indicate that decreasing the number of private cars and freight vehicles on city roads and prioritizing public transport are the obligatory components of attractive and sustainable cities.

The second conclusion is to explore how, even in the presence of similar influences, the three countries are revealed to be on a different point on the scale of maturity in terms of UFT policy (Kiba-Janiak, 2017). Thus, isomorphism is identified in cities of the same country, with a clear difference between each of the three countries. There appears to be some influence at work on the national level, as several differences were identified between Sweden and the other two countries. Local authorities in Sweden react more strongly to public opinion for greener transport, but on the other hand, they also make the public more aware of the importance of UFT. A crucial difference is that they have dedicated personnel for UFT, unlike the other two countries. This department or people need to cooperate with other departments to develop projects and policies. However, dedicated departments and personnel also have the responsibility to deepen UFT knowledge and share this information to inform other departments about how UFT is relevant to their tasks and why it is necessary to consider freight when implementing policies for other transport modes. Having said that, a change to larger authorities in England has been positive for UFT as they have larger resources and power to act, which leaves Scotland as the country of the three with the weakest institutional structure in terms of UFT policy.

In terms of the policies implemented (Table 2), all local authorities in the study were willing to implement some restrictions (such as weight-based restrictions); however, these may be considered "soft" restrictions in comparison to the other types that require businesses to pay fees or upgrade their vehicle fleets. Yet, certain differences also emerged, with Sweden the most likely of the three countries to implement stronger restrictions, while Scotland was the least likely, hesitating to upset the freight sector by proposing restrictions such as congestion charging or the requirement to deliver during off-peak times. The hesitation of Scottish authorities may also arise from their previous experiences. In 2005, Edinburgh wanted to introduce congestion charging; however, it was rejected by a public referendum. According to Rye et al. (2008), negative coverage by newspapers, disagreement on objectives and the complexity of the scheme leading to public misunderstanding were the main reasons for the "no" vote. This confirms the view that each of the three countries is on a different point on the scale of maturity in terms of UFT policy.

Since local authorities (and the regional and national layers that lie behind them) remain reluctant to enforce restrictions on users in order to meet UFT goals, it suggests a higher influence of normative and mimetic factors compared to coercive. Considering the fact that local transport plans are very much driven by national transport strategies, the same goals arise in local transport plans as well, yet effective policies to achieve these goals are lacking in many cases, partly due to a lack of coercive influence. UFT continues to have lower priority compared to other policy areas, and local authorities in England and particularly Scotland demonstrate a limited vision when incorporating freight issues in their transport planning. One way forward could be for local authorities in future to move beyond consideration of restrictive measures that they do not want to implement, and instead focus on participatory and collaborative measures based on the agreement of different stakeholders, which requires a deeper understanding of the institutional influences as elaborated in this chapter. Evidence in Sweden suggests that a better relationship between the public and private stakeholders makes it easier to implement restrictive measures in partnership rather than through top-down imposition.

As noted above, while collaboration, relationship building and interaction among public and private institutions have begun to be addressed in the UFT literature, so far, very few studies have analyzed the institutional aspect of UFT (cf. Rose et al., 2016). Some existing literature focuses on the active role of public organizations in the institutionalization process of other organizations rather than evaluating them as the objects of institutional pressure (Frumkin and Galaskiewicz, 2004). This study therefore contributes to knowledge of UFT by explaining how institutional factors influence public authorities in the process of choosing and implementing policies to regulate UFT. It is particularly important that public authorities are aware of constraining factors (e.g., lack of resources, public opinion) and their capabilities (e.g., dedicated personnel, certification and accreditation). Another contribution from the study is to demonstrate that differences in institutional environment lead to different levels of success in UFT policy implementation. This was reflected in the differences across the three countries, for example, the normative difference in Sweden, where UFT is viewed more positively and there is greater collaboration between stakeholders, and the coercive influence of a changing institutional structure for managing UFT in England through combined authorities with greater resources. Thus UFT policy analysis is not simply about the actual policies chosen but to what degree their institutional environment will influence the outcome of the same policy in a different city or country. This provides the motivation for future research in this field.

REFERENCES

Aberdeen City Council, 2016. Local Transport Strategy. [Online] Accessed in June 2018. https://www.aberdeencity.gov.uk/sites/default/files/Local%20Transport%20Strategy%20%282016-2021%29.pdf.

Amenta, E., Ramsey, K.M., 2010. Institutional theory. In: Leicht, K.T., Jenkins, J.C. (Eds.), Handbook of Politics. Springer, New York, pp. 15–39.

Ballantyne, E.E.F., Lindholm, M., 2014. Identifying the Need for Freight to Be Included in Local Authority Transport Planning. In: Gonzalez-Feliu, J. (Ed.), Sustainable Urban Logistics: Concepts, Methods and Information Systems. Springer, Berlin Heidelberg, pp. 37–48.

Ballantyne, E.E.F., Lindholm, M., Whiteing, A., 2013. A comparative study of urban freight transport planning: addressing stakeholder needs. J. Transp. Geogr. 32, 93–101.

Browne, M., et al., 2012. Reducing social and environmental impacts of urban freight transport: a review of some major cities. Procedia. Soc. Behav. Sci. 39, 19–33.

Cui, J., Dodson, J., Hall, P.V., 2015. Planning for urban freight transport: an overview. Transp. Rev. 35 (5), 583–598.

Dablanc, L., 2007. Goods transport in large European cities: difficult to organize, difficult to modernize. Transp. Res. Part A Policy Pract. 41 (3), 280–285.

Dablanc, L., Giuliano, G., Holliday, K., Obrien, T., 2013. Best practices in urban freight management: lessons from an international survey. Transp. Res. Rec. J. Transp. Res. Board 2379, 29–38.

Department for Transport, 2016. Road Use Statistics GB 2016. [Online] Accessed in June 2018. https://www.licencebureau.co.uk/wp-content/uploads/road-use-statistics.pdf.

Department for Transport, 2017. Traffic Volume-Miles. [Online] Accessed in June 2018. https://www.gov.uk/government/statistical-data-sets/tra01-traffic-by-road-class-and-region-miles#table-tra0103.

DiMaggio, P.J., Powell, W.W., 1983. The iron cage revisited: collective rationality and institutional isomorphism in organizational fields. Am. Sociol. Rev. 48 (2), 147–160.

DiMaggio, P.J., Powell, W.W., 1991a. The New Institutionalism in Organizational Analysis, 17th ed. University of Chicago Press, Chicago, IL.

The organization of societal sectors: propositions and early evidence. DiMaggio, P.J., Powell, W.W. (Eds.), 1991b. The New Institutionalism in Organizational Analysis. The University of Chicago Press, Chicago, pp. 108–140.

Frumkin, P., Galaskiewicz, J., 2004. Institutional isomorphism and public sector organization. J. Public Adm. Res. Theory 14 (3), 283–307.
Gatta, V., Marcucci, E., 2016. Stakeholder-specific data acquisition and urban freight policy evaluation: evidence, implications and new suggestions. Transp. Rev. 36 (5), 585–609.
Kiba-Janiak, M., 2017. Urban freight transport in city strategic planning. Res. Transp. Bus. Manag. 24, 4–16.
Kin, B., Verlinde, S., Macharis, C., 2017. Sustainable urban freight transport in megacities in emerging markets. Sustain. Cities Soc. 32, 31–41.
Koutoulas, A., Franklin, J.P., Eliasson, J., 2017. Assessing nighttime deliveries in Stockholm, Sweden. Transp. Res. Rec. J. Transp. Res. Board 2605, 54–60.
Lindholm, M.E., Blinge, M., 2014. Assessing knowledge and awareness of the sustainable urban freight transport among Swedish local authority policy planners. Transp. Policy 32, 124–131.
Lindholm, M., Browne, M., 2013. Local authority cooperation with urban freight stakeholders: a comparison of partnership approaches. Eur. J. Transp. Infrastruct. Res. 13 (1), 20–38.
Local Government Association, 2016. Combined Authorities: A Plain English Guide. [Online] Accessed in June 2018. https://www.local.gov.uk/sites/default/files/documents/combined-authorities-plai-fb6.pdf.
Macharis, C., Kin, B., 2017. The 4 A's of sustainable city distribution: innovative solutions and challenges ahead. Int. J. Sustain. Transp. 11 (2), 59–71.
Meyer, J.W., Rowan, B., 1977. Institutionalized organizations: formal structure as myth and ceremony. Am. J. Sociol. 83 (2), 340–363.
National Records of Scotland, 2018. Mid-Year Population Estimates Scotland, Mid-2017. [Online] Accessed in June 2018. https://www.nrscotland.gov.uk/files//statistics/population-estimates/mid-17/mid-year-pop-est-17-publication.pdf.
North, D.C., 1991. Institutions. J. Econ. Perspect. 5 (1), 97–112.
ONS, 2018. Office for National Statstics. [Online] Available at https://www.ons.gov.uk/peoplepopulationandcommunity/populationandmigration/populationestimates. (Accessed 18 December 2017).
Paddeu, D., 2017. The Bristol-Bath Urban freight Consolidation Centre from the perspective of its users. Case Stud. Transp. Policy 5 (3), 483–491.
RAC Foundation, 2014. Van travel trends in Great Britain. [Online] Accessed in June 2018. https://www.racfoundation.org/assets/rac_foundation/content/downloadables/van_report_aecom_100414.pdf.
Rose, W.J., Mollenkopf, D.A., Autry, C.W., Bell, J.E., 2016. Exploring urban institutional pressures on logistics service providers. Int. J. Phys. Distrib. Logist. Manag. 46 (2), 153–176.
Rye, T., Gaunt, M., Ison, S., 2008. Edinburgh's congestion charging plans: an analysis of reasons for non-implementation. Transp. Plan. Technol. 31 (6), 641–661.
Savy, M., 2012. Urban freight: a comprehensive approach. In: Wolmar, C. (Ed.), Urban Freight for Livable Cities. Gothenburg, Volvo Research and Education Foundation, pp. 24–30.
SCB, 2018. Statistics Sweden. [Online] Available at http://www.scb.se/en/finding-statistics/statistics-by-subject-area/population/population-composition/population-statistics. (Accessed 18 December 2017).
Scottish Government, 2015. Cleaner Air for Scotland: The Road to a Healthier Future. [Online] Accessed in June 2018. http://www.gov.scot/Resource/0048/00488493.pdf.
SKL, 2018. Trafikverket. [Online] Available at https://www.trafikverket.se/contentassets/347f069e6d684bfd85b85e3a3593920f/handbok_for_godstransporter_i_den_goda_staden.pdf. (Accessed 10 January 2018).

Stathopoulos, A., Valeri, E., Marcucci, E., 2012. Stakeholder reactions to urban freight policy innovation. J. Transp. Geogr. 22 (1), 34–45.
Trafik Analys, 2017. Trafikarbete på svenska vägar 1990-2017. [Online] Accessed in June 2018. https://www.trafa.se/vagtrafik/trafikarbete/.
Transport for Greater Manchester, 2016. Greater Manchester Freight and Logistics Transport Strategy. Transport for Greater Manchester, Manchester.
Transport Scotland, 2016a. National Transport Strategy. [Online] Accessed in June 2018. https://www.transport.gov.scot/media/10310/transport-scotland-national-transport-strategy-january-2016-final-online.pdf.
Transport Scotland, 2016b. Scottish Transport Statistics. [Online] Accessed in June 2018. https://www.transport.gov.scot/publication/scottish-transport-statistics-no-35-2016-edition/sct01171871341-08/.
Transport Scotland, 2018a. Aberdeen Western Peripheral Road. [Online] Accessed in June 2018. https://www.transport.gov.scot/projects/aberdeen-western-peripheral-route-balmedie-to-tipperty/document-library/.
Transport Scotland, 2018b. Building Scotland's Low Emission Zones: A Consultation. [Online] Accessed in June 2018. https://www.transport.gov.scot/media/39673/low-emission-zones-consultation.pdf.
van Duin, J., Quak, H.J., 2007. City logistics: a chaos between research and policy making? A review. In: Brebbia, C.A. (Ed.), Urban Transport XIII: Urban Transport and the Environment in the 21st Century. WIT Press, Southampton, pp. 135–146.
West of England Partnership, 2011. Joint Local Transport Plan. [Online] Accessed in June 2018. https://s3-eu-west-1.amazonaws.com/travelwest/wp-content/uploads/2015/05/joint-local-transport-plan.pdf.
Wittlöv, A., 2012. Urban freight transport: challenges and opportunities. In: Wolmar, C. (Ed.), Urban Freight for Livable Cities. Gothenburg, Volvo Research and Educational Foundation, pp. 12–23.
Zucker, L., 1977. The role of institutionalization in cultural persistence. Am. Sociol. Rev. 42 (5), 726–743.

FURTHER READING

Dablanc, L., 2009. Freight Transport for Development Toolkit: Urban Freight. The World Bank, Washington, DC.

CHAPTER EIGHT

Europe's Freight Transport Policy: Analysis, Synthesis and Evaluation

Paulus T. Aditjandra[1]
Newcastle University Business School, Newcastle upon Tyne, United Kingdom
[1]Corresponding author: e-mail address: paulus.aditjandra@ncl.ac.uk

Contents

Abstract

This book chapter maps the changing nature of European Union (EU) surface freight transport policy since 2000. Over this period the policy, based on the liberalization of the Single European Market in the 10 years before 2000, changed from purely national to supranational, on a pan-European scale. This period saw the expansion of the EU to the East and the changing make-up of the Union and the Commission and witnessed how the political nature of the policy adapts. The research is the first accessible, objective and independent review of overall EU surface freight policy.

The review show that, by 2011, intervention, modal shift and intermodalism have been replaced by "smart," "green," and "integrated" themes, alongside economic

Advances in Transport Policy and Planning, Volume 1
ISSN 2543-0009
https://doi.org/10.1016/bs.atpp.2018.07.006

competitiveness and growth. The key change is that policy now looks to separate mobility from its negative effects; for example, behavioral change orientation programs, such as road pricing for freight, have declined in importance. Innovative technology, by contrast, is the chosen tool of the current EU freight policy to meet ambitious emission reduction targets, led by the decarbonization of road haulage. The tension between technocracy and explicit political intent is evident in the development and is discussed. Successful and unsuccessful freight policies are also drawn, discussed and concluded.

Keywords: European Union, Transport policy, Transportation policy, Freight, Logistics, Railways, Maritime, Urban freight, Sustainability

1. INTRODUCTION

The objective of this book chapter is to build an organized resource that looks into the development of European Union (EU) freight transport policy with reference to how it has changed and how it is likely to change in the future. The methodology adopted was a literature review of the different sources, categorizing the core policy documents of the EU as primary and concurrent commentary and review of the policies as secondary, including those commissioned by the EU and others. The mapping of the changing nature of EU freight policy between 2001 and 2011 and beyond, in this research identifies trends that have and will lead to the shaping of future European freight transport policy.

The GDP of the EU in 2015 was circa €14,600 billion (European Union, 2017)—larger than the USA (Eurostat, 2016). With 6.9% of the world's population, the EU's trade with the rest of the world accounts for around 20% of global exports and imports. It is the world's biggest exporter and the second-biggest importer. Around two-thirds of EU countries' total trade is done with other EU countries. The United States is the EU's most important trading partner, followed by China. In 2014, the EU's exports of goods were 15.0% of the world exports and 14.8% of imports (European Union, 2017).

Estimates put the share of the freight transport logistics market in Europe at close to 7% of GDP between 2008 and 2012 (Ecorys et al., 2015). Over recent years, the logistics industry has had growth rates above the average of European economies. For example, intra- and extra-EU trade has risen by 55% in value since 1999 (European Commission, 2007a). This growth has come about through European integration, liberalization and the relatively low cost of freight transport, which has led to changes in production and trade patterns, inside the EU and globally (European Commission, 2007a). For example, an introduction of the mega vessels in the shipping industry and the race of the companies to be efficient and competitive led to surplus in carrying capacity and consequently lower freight rates. These changes has affected the global freight distribution system due to technology, infrastructure, transport modes and terminals that all related to attributes such as gateways, corridors, hinterlands, regulation, governance, value chains and labor (Rodrigue and Notteboom, 2010).

In this context the role of freight transport policy is a crucial component of the planning, practice and sustainability of freight logistics (Islam et al., 2013a). Many of those policies have been introduced at local or national level first before then promoted at European and pan-European in various ways. The following are relevant here: *regulations* and *decisions*—which have a direct effect; *directives*—a legislative act of the EU that requires member states to achieve a particular result without dictating the means; and *communication*—an opinion or recommendation which has no legal effect (Borchardt, 2010). Through many of those legal documents, freight policies have been leveraged in EU countries to reach expected impact such as making logistics activities in supply chains greener and sustainable (for further detail, please see: McKinnon et al., 2015, Psaraftis, 2016 and Grant et al., 2017).

The European Commission is one of the main institutions of the EU representing and upholding the interests of the EU as a whole. It drafts proposals for new European laws and manages the implementation of policies and the spending of funds. The European Commission divides its activities into Directorates General (DG), and it should be noted that, from 2001 to 2010, both transport and energy were managed within DG Transport and Energy (DG TREN), which was split in 2010 into DG Mobility and Transport (DG MOVE) and DG Energy (DG ENER). While the rationale was an increased focus on climate change, it must be noted that the split was more organizational than policy based, and therefore it can be assumed no effects for this analysis.

While air transport is within the same building as the rest of DG TREN/MOVE, it is noted that effectively air transport is separate from what is referred to as "surface transport"; this paper follows that division, addressing only surface modes. It is unclear whether this division led to different priority given to air vs surface transport modes; however, recent report demonstrated that the air transport sector has been more advanced in research and development than others (SETRIS, 2016).

Review reported in this book chapter is complementary to other reviews of policy and/or research into the systemization of policy evaluation, such as the review on electric mobility policies (Leurent and Windisch, 2011); the development of an urban transport sustainability index (Zito and Salvo, 2011) and the development of a decision support framework for intermodal transport policy (Macharis et al., 2011; Meers and Macharis, 2015). It differs in its focus on a time series qualitative evaluation of EU policy at top level, over a decade, which complements the more focused and local work of the above mentioned papers and others that focus at the local, urban, or sector level.

The chapter is structured hereafter as: analysis of source documents; timeline and analysis of key policies; selected areas of focus where certain modal, thematic or geospatial areas are addressed; commentary of successful and unsuccessful policy and conclusion. This work builds on Zunder et al. (2012) and expands it in analysis of freight policy paper beyond 2010, i.e., Mid-term review of White Paper; and analysis of successful and unsuccessful freight policy.

2. METHODOLOGY

The methodology adopted was to review literature from different sources, categorizing the core policy documents of the EU as primary and the concurrent commentary and review of the policies as secondary, including those commissioned by the EU and others. The primary sources are in many cases highly candid; indeed, many are opening dialogues with wider society, the European Parliament and the Council of Ministers. Secondary sources were often specifically focused, for example, at the concern of a trade association or political group about a single issue, or on the benefit of a certain historical distance; however, they may also lack the "unspoken" or ephemeral content which inform politics in any society. This chapter looks to review the two types of source, using the secondary materials to confirm and contradict, or simply to add a better understanding and contextualization of the primary material, so as to develop a holistic view of the policies, their development and their context within the wider evolution of the EU. For the primary sources, the collected data were drawn from the European Commission web portal (http://ec.europa.eu). For the secondary data, Scopus (http://www.scopus.com) and ScienceDirect http://www.sciencedirect.com) were used as bibliographic databases, together with the Google search engine. Keywords such as "EU," "freight," transport policy" and the combination of the three in turn were used, to collect the data. This was then complemented by the expert knowledge of the author, peer reviewers and various sources to cross check for completeness or redundancy.

This methodology is sound as a social research tool for the study of qualitative data and, as that data are accumulated into later analysis and new sources over time, a "tertiary" body of data will emerge that is further removed from the events and the actors, such as textbooks, or retrospectives, reviews or revisions of history. It is understood, since the events are still contemporaneous, such tertiary data are yet to be created and the primary/secondary split is therefore adequate (Barton, 2005; Heaton, 2008).

3. LITERATURE REVIEW FINDINGS

A complete reference of collected papers based on the above approach is tabulated in the Appendix. From all the sources collated, 52 are primary. These are mainly "communication" documents, 37 of which were published between 2001 and 2011 and the 2015 Mid-term review of the 2011 Transport White Paper. The remaining sources are secondary.

From the 52 primary papers, 14 describe general transport issues, covering passenger as well as freight; 8 describe freight issues in general, covering road, rail and maritime; 9 specifically address rail, including rail freight; 3 cover maritime; 5 road freight (including 2 on Intelligent Transport System—ITS); 3 the internalization/externalization of cost; 5 are on intermodal issues (including 3 on combined transport); and 2 on urban mobility.

The secondary sources can be divided into seven themes, namely: general transport studies; rail (freight), Intermodal, Port and maritime freight, Road and Intelligent Transport Systems (ITS), (Trans-European Transport Network (TEN-T) and urban freight studies. The general studies include a number of text books and articles about transport planning, global supply chain, green logistics, freight scenarios modeling, energy demand trend and transport policy evaluation. Fig. 1 illustrates the key pillars of EU freight transport policy under discussion.

A word counting analysis was undertaken to identify of what has changed between the 2001 White Paper (European Commission, 2001), the 2006 Mid-term review Paper (European Commission, 2006) and the 2011 White Paper (European Commission, 2011a), using a few key terms that represent EU policies over time. In 2001, "modal-shift" is used once in the document, though it is described in alternative terms from the start; however, the 2006

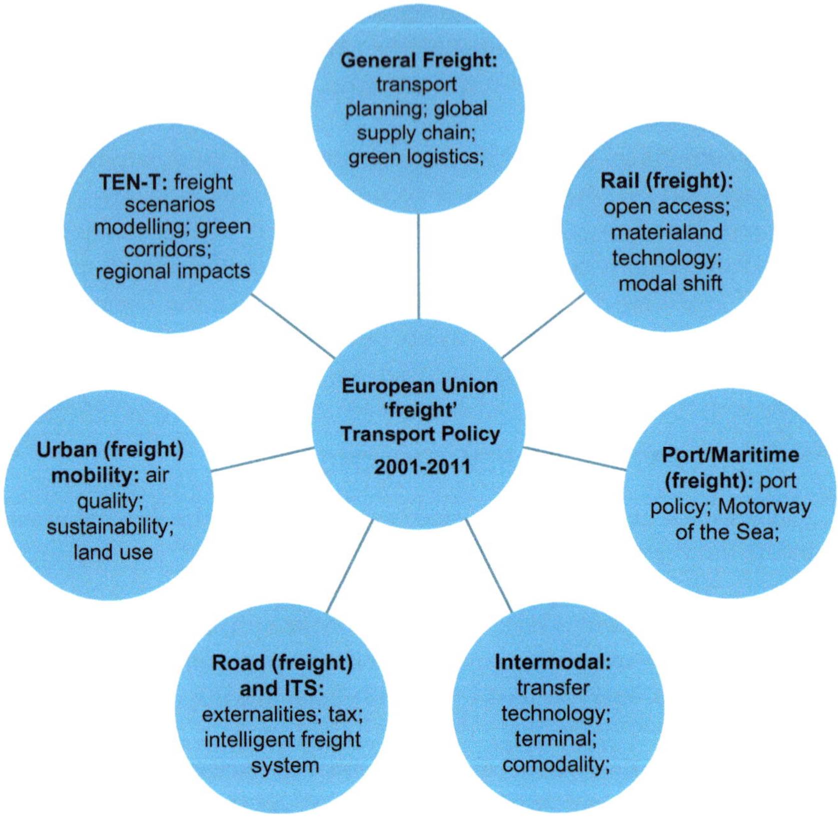

Fig. 1 Key pillars of EU freight transport policy under discussion.

and 2011 papers no longer mention it. The use of "Intermodality" changes and disappears over time, having been mentioned 28 times in 2001, only once in 2006 and not at all in 2011. "Co-modality" was introduced and mentioned four times in 2006 but by 2011 is mentioned only once.

The word "smart" is only found once in 2001, whereas in 2006 and 2011 it appears 13 times each. Whereas in the 2001 paper, "smart" is only used in "smart protection device," in 2006 and 2011 "smart" is used to represent "smart mobility," "smart funding/pricing," "smart infrastructure/ticketing," "smart vehicle," etc. The word "green" has also expanded in use from 2001, when it is used to explain "greenhouse gas emissions" (11 times) or "green paper" (6 times); by 2006 and again in 2011, the use of green is less for "greenhouse gas emissions" (4 times in 2006 and twice in 2011) but more for "green truck," "green aircraft," "green propulsion"—13 times each.

It is also drawn to attention of the declining word use pattern of "innovative" and the increasing use of "innovation." The interpretation is that, while in 2001 many endeavors were deemed "innovative," by 2011 they could be defined as innovation. The word "innovative" appeared 22 times in 2001, 3 times in 2006 and 4 times in 2011; the word "innovation" appeared 6 times in 2001, 10 times in 2006 and 19 times in 2011.

In 2015, Mid-term review of 2011 White Paper on transport was published and it can be drawn that the 2011 Transport White Papers objectives are still deemed relevant.

3.1 Timeline and Key Policies

Before the 1990s the EU made little transport policy; it is in the last decade of the 20th century that the area starts to receive focus, in parallel with—and caused by—the completion of the single European market on 1st January 1993, with the free movement of goods, services, people and money. A key element in the process of European integration is the establishment of Trans-European Networks (TENs), as the infrastructural investment policy to connect peripheral states of the existing Community, as well as improving efficiency for the congested central regions. The origin of TENs dates back to as early as 1951, in the Treaty establishing the European Coal and Steel Community and then being integrated into the Treaty of Rome founding the European Economic Community in 1957 (Böttcher, 2006). The 1996 Single Market Review concluded that the reorganization of the distribution process generated, led to logistic cost reductions between 1987 and 1992 of as much as 29%. The largest cost reductions were in transport, where firms reported up to a 50% cost reduction and the average number of days from order placement to receipt declined from 21 days to 15 (European Commission, 1996). The key EU transport policy milestones before 2001 can be seen in Table 1.

These are the roots of the period addressed in this paper, and already there are themes that shall continue, albeit with changing names and emphasis, over time. The degree to which continuity, or change can be seen, is often disguised by the apparent similarities in policies.

The transport policy from the beginning of the 1990s up to 2000 was marked by two significant changes: the new environmental debate and the challenge of sustainable development. While environmental issues, such as noise, visual intrusion and pollution, had been a concern of the

Table 1 EU Transport Policy Milestones Before 2001

Year	Document Typology	Issues
1957	Treaty of Rome	EU formation
1970	Regulation 1107/70/EEC	State aid to modernize combined transport
1975	Directive 75/130/EEC	Exemption of road transport quota/permit
1982	Directive 82/603/EEC	Taxation for vehicle used in combined transport
1991	Directive 91/440/EEC	Railway policies development
1992	EC COM (92) 494 final	Common transport policy toward single market Europe
1993	Single European Market, free movement of goods, serviced, people and money	
1993	EC Decision 93/45/CEE followed by 93/628/EEC	Combined transport scheme that promote the development of the Trans-European Transport Network (TEN-T)
1995	EC Green Paper COM (95) 691	Pricing policies in transport (mainly road)
1996	EC White Paper COM (96) 421	A strategy for revitalizing the Community's railways, introducing market forces into rail, integration of national systems
1996	EC Decision 1692/92/EC	Community guidelines for the development of the TEN-T
1997	EC COM 97/243	Intermodality
1997	EC COM 97/223	Transport telematics
1998	EC White Paper COM (98) 466	Infrastructure charging policy

transportation development (Greene and Wegener, 1997), the new debate was broader and included the global issue of climate change, use of non-renewable resources and general quality of life (Banister, 2002) and the human response to those changes (Banister, 2008). Alongside this is an EU infrastructure development program, in response to the extending of EU economic integration and to the increasing competitive pressures, which consequently demand a solid, reliable, supra-regional transport system, named the trans-European transport network (TEN-T) (Vickerman, 1995). The EU definition of sustainable development is "a development for meeting the needs of present generations without jeopardising the ability of future generations to meet their own needs—in other words, a better quality of life for everyone, now and for generations to come" which is very much echoing the Brundtland (1987) that aimed to inform United Nations of the risk of climate change and the need of pursuing a low-carbon economy. By 2009, EU has formulated sustainable transport agenda that include key policy developments such as the Green Transport Package, Directives and proposals for a new Directives that aim to take account of all aspects of sustainability (such as emissions, noise, land occupancy and biodiversity) (European Commission, 2009). The next sections discuss these developments within the context of freight. The rail freight policy aspects have been covered exclusively in Islam et al. (2013a), this chapter looks freight policies beyond just rail.

4. ANALYSIS OF KEY POLICY PAPERS EFFECTING FREIGHT

4.1 2001 White Paper "European Transport Policy for 2010: Time to Decide"

Post 2000, the key milestone of common transport policy was the White Paper "European Transport Policy for 2010: Time to Decide" (European Commission, 2001). One of the main messages is the recognition of the increasing demand for transport that cannot be answered by building new infrastructure, but that the transport system needs optimization to meet the demands of both enlargement of the EU and sustainable development.

The document reviews the problems derived from the growth of road transport demand, including distorted competition (between different transport modes); traffic congestion; environmental pollution; public health; and road accidents. It identifies the need for integration of all modes of transport, as envisioned in the Treaty of Rome. It identifies the need for better usage and integration between sea, inland waterways and rail, which are seen as under-utilized, and provides the opportunity to reduce road congestion and air pollution.

The tone was judgmental, the words "blame" and "culprit" appeared and, although the approach adopted was interventionist, a direct "dirigiste" control of transport was considered, before being dismissed. Key phrases are: "Shifting the balance between modes of transport"; "Regulated competition"; and "Tightening up controls and penalties."

There were many measures to be taken at the EU level up until 2010 with key freight issues such as transport infrastructure investments; road, rail and maritime for goods improvements; freight integrator; multimodal corridors giving priority to freight included (please see Islam et al., 2013a, pp. 8–12, for longer list of issues).

Two major aims were modal-shift and decoupling economic growth from transport growth, using interventionist policies. What is of note is why, since it appears that the document places the means to the ends first and makes the tools the objective. The end goals were reducing congestion (estimated at 0.5% of Community GDP at that time); reducing energy dependency on imported fossil fuels; reducing carbon emissions; and reducing pollutants. The means chosen were to suppress transport growth, while allowing continued economic growth, and to discriminate against road. It was fair to say "… there are politically motivated policy moves within the EU to find ways of switching as much freight as possible from road onto the rail, and to a lesser extent onto the waterways network..." (Lowe, 2005). The document states that infrastructure and start-up funds should be exclusively focused on rail or intermodal projects, rather than road, which most member states have favored. This had, however, already been acknowledged, even before the launch of the White Paper, as the TENs promotion of "interconnection" and "intermodality" favored high speed rail networks (Sichelschmidt, 1999) and great efforts have been made to advance rail priority projects characterized by high cost, large scale and a cross-border nature (Janic and Reggiani, 2001).

The 2001 White paper states that road haulage is gaining unfair advantage and practicing unsafely; "one might ask what factors are sustaining, indeed encouraging, the expansion of road transport over middle and long distances, where alternative solutions are available. Part of the answer lies in the perpetuation of practices that distort competition. The ending of these practices will call, not so much for further regulation, as for effective enforcement of the existing regulations by tightening up and harmonising penalties."

Another clear theme is the message that infrastructure needs to be funded and that new, harmonized charging mechanisms are needed to internalize the external costs. Also that funds generated should be held at a supranational level, to supplement the existing but deficient TEN-T scheme. Noticeably, in 2001 this is seen only as an infrastructure-funding tool, rather than having a demand management role.

In 2004, the EU saw its biggest enlargement to date, when Cyprus, the Czech Republic, Estonia, Hungary, Latvia, Lithuania, Malta, Poland, Slovakia and Slovenia joined the Union. On 1 January 2007, Romania and Bulgaria became the EU's newest members. These changes were apparent, as the Commission had already started to include new nationalities, and discussions started to address new concerns such as accessibility, the need for growth and a lower priority for the environmental concerns of what came to be called the EU "mid-west." The extension of the TEN-T programme to connect EU-25, and subsequently EU-27, turns out to be relevant to this call. By 2005, 30 priority projects were reported, that connect 65,100 km of motorways; 212,800 km of rail lines (including 110,458 km electrified); 42,709 km navigable inland waterways; 70,000 km of maritime coast; and 1239 ports—at an estimated cost of up to €600 billion, representing 0.16% of EU GDP. The additional economic growth this would bring was estimated at 0.23% of GDP (European Commission, 2005). The deployment of Intelligent Transport System (ITS), European Rail Traffic Managements System (ERTMS), Vessel Traffic Management Information System (VTMIS), Air Traffic Management (ATM) and Global Navigation Satellite System (GNSS) are some of the main features included in the TEN-T programme, demonstrating the Commission's plans to stimulate the use of telematics—new technologies combining telecommunications and informatics—in order to facilitate "intelligent" guidance of traffic flows, with the aim of improving capacity utilization of infrastructure networks (Böttcher, 2006; Sichelschmidt, 1999). It is important to note that most, if not all, of the TEN-T projects were aimed at addressing passenger as well as freight demand, with some of the projects focused on unlocking freight bottlenecks.

4.2 2006 Mid-term Review "Keep Europe Moving—Sustainable Mobility for Our Continent"

The 2006 mid-term review of the 2001 White Paper is a key document in that, born of a new Commission representing an enlarged 25 nation EU; it represents a different political agenda. In 2005 the neglected Lisbon Agenda (not to be confused with the Treaty of Lisbon) was refocused on actions that promote growth and jobs within the objective of sustainable development. This re-emergence of growth, combined with new member states many of which had adopted liberal economic policies post Communism, changed the emphasis. By 2006 the Commission said "Whereas pollution, land use and congestion are of major concern in the densely populated and industrialised 'midwest', for other Member States accessibility is still the key concern. The diversity may in certain policy areas require more differentiated solutions, leaving room for local, regional and national solutions whilst ensuring a Europe-wide internal transport market."

The review clearly states its objectives as goals, not methods. These are high level of mobility to people and businesses; protect the environment; ensure energy security; minimum labor standards (improving working conditions to attract employment to the sector); innovate for increased efficiency and sustainability; and connect internationally. This is contextualized within the Lisbon Agenda, enlargement, and energy policy.

Crucially it abandons decoupling stating that, despite slower economic growth than predicted, freight volumes will increase roughly in line with GDP from 2000 to 2020—circa 50%. Road congestion, previously predicted to reach 1% of GDP by 2010, is already at that level by 2006, and although NOx and particulates have fallen due to technological improvement, carbon emissions continue to grow. The review states that: "The 2001 White Paper measures will, however, have only minor effects on these environmental trends." The key change is that, rather than decoupling economic and transport growth, mobility itself must be disconnected from its negative side effects. In this phrase policy shifts to a goal based exercise, whereas in 2001 it was a task based one. Interestingly, a study identified that decoupling of road freight and GDP has begun, but it was argued the net environmental benefits were likely to be quite modest (McKinnon, 2007). The emphasis of decoupling transport demand growth from GDP growth has shifted to decoupling demand growth from negative effects, such as greenhouse gas emissions, as it was identified that the objective of 2001 White Paper has not been achieved for freight (Steer Davies Gleave, 2009). Recent observation revealed that technological changes, transition to more service-oriented economies and efficiency objectives can explain the decoupling trends (Alises and Vassallo, 2015).

The important concept that emerges from this time is co-modality: "the efficient use of different modes on their own and in combination will result in an optimal and sustainable utilisation of resources." This concept removes the explicit bias against road. In future talk was of "achieving shifts to more environmentally friendly modes where appropriate" and "all modes must become more environmentally friendly, safe and energy efficient." Intermodalism wasn't finished, but it had become just one of many options.

Other developments of wider note are the continuance of most themes from 2001, the rising importance of safety and security post 9/11, urban transport where 80% of Europeans live, the addition of demand management in charging—the "user pays" principle—discussions, the use of soft/smart measures to release infrastructure capacity, and increased interest in Intelligent Transport Systems (ITS).

The 2006 review also announced significant policy work to come, in the area of freight transport, reversing a tendency for freight to be an afterword and focusing specifically upon it (Jarzembowski, 2007), especially via the rapid introduction of ERTMS (European Rail Traffic Management System), RIS (River Information Services) and Galileo (the European satellite based global navigation system). The adoption of ITS in freight will provide the means to achieve transparency in logistics networks, before, during and after operations, achieving better planning as well as monitoring performance to identify successes and failures (Ruijgrok, 2008).

4.3 2007 Freight Transport Agenda

The short document of EU's freight transport agenda (European Commission, 2007b)—just seven pages—prompts positive will toward logistics and competitiveness, stating that transport of freight is "essential to economic activity and quality of life...." The opening page refers to the expected growth in goods transport 2000–2020 not as a negative but as an accepted fact requiring policy to secure efficiency and sustainability. The key issues are again congestion, climate change targets, fossil fuel dependency, safety and security and, in addition, the growing difficulty in attracting qualified staff. The nature of European transport logistics as a global competitor is emphasized, plus the need to both trade and compete with neighbors.

Co-modality is key once again and a wide range of policy initiatives is proposed:

- Freight Transport Logistics Action Plan (FTLAP);
- Communication on a freight-oriented rail network;
- Communication on a European Ports Policy;
- the commencement of consultation on maritime space and Motorways of the Sea;
- a focus on corridors;
- the promotion of innovative technologies;
- the simplification of transport chains; and
- the reinforcement of quality.

The role of the EC is seen as facilitative, creating framework conditions, technical standardization, political and financial support and the promotion of best practice. This is a market friendly document incorporating all modes, innovation as a tool for sustainability, green freight corridor based recognition of TEN-T priority projects at a holistic level and demand led.

4.4 2007 Freight Transport Logistics Action Plan (FTLAP)

European Commission (2007a) is a communication paper between EU government and EU logistics industry, primarily to achieve sustainable and competitive mobility, and also a cleaner environment, security of energy supply, transport safety and security. Written after extensive consultation for the 2006 mid-term review, it is a document based not in DG TREN, but in the actors and stakeholders of freight transport and logistics sector. Six pillars of action toward the industry were enacted:

1. *E*-Freight and Intelligent Transport Systems (ITS) (a paper-free, electronic flow of information associating the physical flow of goods with paperless trail built by information and communication technology (ICT) including radio frequency identification technology (RFID) and Galileo satellite positioning system);
2. Sustainable quality and efficiency (efforts to enhance the attractiveness of logistics professions through, for example: cross-border staff mobility; performance benchmarking; and logistics institute and industry initiatives);
3. Simplification of transport chains (establishing a one stop shop for all administrative procedure in all modes, through, for example: legislative proposal, to facilitate the secure integration of transport modes in the logistics chain);
4. Vehicle dimensions and loading (modification of the standards for vehicle weight on European intermodal loading units that can be used for all surface modes);
5. Green transport corridors for freight (prioritizing freight within the TEN-T framework where industry is encouraged to rely on co-modality and on advanced technology in order to accommodate rising traffic volumes sustainably);
6. Urban freight transport logistics (allowing cities to lead the action plan through, for example: best practice exchanges and the development of benchmarks).

The FTLAP led to a wide range of activity. Vehicle weights and measures became controversial with the introduction in Europe of 60 ton trucks (so-called "gigaliners"), with concerted opposition from the rail sector, politicians, and environmentalists, and support from certain member states and other environmentalists (UIC et al., 2007, 2014). The e-Freight initiative led to the Freightwise Framework, which was incorporated into the Universal Business Language 2.1 (Cisternino, 2010). The possible initiative on liability became the debate over the Rotterdam Rules and has probably been superseded by them (CLECAT, 2009; ICS, 2009). The green corridors and benchmarking initiatives have seen some research activities: BE LOGIC (2008–2011; example of outputs can be seen in Islam et al. (2013b)) and SUPERGREEN (2010–2013; a book was written as reported in Psaraftis, 2016) that led to the development of TEN-T Comprehensive and Core Network Corridors policy (European Commission, 2013). The revision of the European Intermodal Loading Unit (EILU) from the previous disastrous standards of 2003 has resulted in an industry led ILU-code standard and registry (UIRR, 2011). An observation that monitors the on-going FTLAP has identified both direct and indirect progress made by all the above themes, with vehicle dimensions, green corridors and urban freight impacting "green logistics" the most (TRT - Trasporti e Territorio, 2010).

4.5 2007 Toward a Rail Network Giving Priority to Freight

The communication document shows how freight policy is intertwined with wider transport policy. Key policy was a strategy for the revitalization of the railways in Europe against a backdrop of decline, through the separation of infrastructure and operations and the opening of the market to competition. The EU used directives in this area, possibly due to the almost exclusive state ownership of rail at the beginning of the period, and these were delivered in railway packages, 2001, 2004 and 2007, with varying success (Zunder et al., 2013). Please see Islam et al. (2013a), pp. 8–12 for detail analysis of the progress made within rail freight policy sector. Additionally, Aditjandra et al. (2016b) reviewed intensively the state of rail freight research within EU funding and policy framework.

4.6 2007 Communication on a European Ports Policy

Whereas the FTLAP was about facilitation and was industry focused and the rail freight policy was about directives and harrying member states, the communication on EU ports policy was nuanced. Maritime is important: "more than 1,200 merchant ports dot some 100,000 km of European coasts; several hundred others punctuate the 36,000 km of our inland waterways. They are key points of modal transfer and are of vital interest to handle 90% of Europe's international trade (by cargo volume) and they handle 40% of the tonne-kilometres carried out in intra-Community trade." The nuancing is due to the fact that the ownership, operation, and work practices are heterogeneous, with mixes of public and private ownership of ports, terminals, operations, etc. Since the sector is seen as efficient, attractive to inward investment and functioning, the Commission has adopted a more liberal approach, delegating responsibility to member states, or industry, in such areas as port performance, hinterland connections (where bottlenecking of ports needs addressing), and the relationships between ports and local cities—a relationship which is often conflicted. It chooses to take collaborative action on waste and emission reduction and in increasing the transparency of public financing, while the simplification of short sea shipping is where it sees itself in a lead role, addressing the problem that a vessel traveling between two EU ports is subject to more complex and time-consuming procedures than a truck, since the vessel is judged to have left and re-entered the EU. It sees e-maritime, counterpart to e-Freight, as key to increased port logistics efficiency, and again proposes quality indicators for port operation. The social dimension is noticeable here, addressing the training shortfall and the poor health and safety record in ports. The communication ends with a call to all public and private stakeholders to support this approach, perhaps confirming that the complexity and success of the sector requires policy to be inclusive and yet light touch. A study review of EU port policy toward the adoption of "Motorways of the Sea" (as part of the TEN-T programme) identified that, despite embracing safety, environmental protection and security to promote the competitiveness of EU ports and a modal shift from road, other measures are also needed, due to the lack of cohesion among distinct individual policy areas, the rejection of the ports package, and the shift to security focus following 9/11 (Psaraftis, 2005). Recent observation identified the heterogeneity of the current port regulation and governance across EU countries that could benefit from commonalities (Ferrari et al., 2015).

Much work has also been done on inland waterways, in such programs as Navigation and Inland Waterway Action and Development in Europe (NAIADES) and River Information Systems (RIS). The promotion of Inland Waterway Transport (IWT) as part of modal shift strategy has been notable, with significant intermodal growth. However, it was argued that a major factor is the family-driven nature of the barge industry, with independent skippers offering services to barge operators which in turn lead to strong competition with an elevated customer focus (Notteboom, 2007). This is in marked contrast to the railway industry, run traditionally by national railway companies. Notwithstanding the optimism about IWT modal shift, it was argued that the waterborne freight sector is more fragmented than the rail industry (Woodburn and Whiteing, 2010), mainly due to its characteristics of restricted geographical coverage.

4.7 2009 Maritime Transport Policy

The Agenda began consultation and review of "maritime transport space without barriers" and progress on Motorways of the Sea (MoS). In 2009, this and other factors led to the communication: "Strategic goals and recommendations for the EU's maritime transport policy until 2018." This is both a recap of maritime policy since the 2001 White Paper and a parallel document to the 2011 White Paper. It is economics-led, with the introduction focusing on growth, prosperity and competitiveness; support for energy and environmental policies, is secondary. It is said to have been written as part of a continuous dialogue with experts from member states and senior shipping professionals and is an analytical trends study.

The tone is commercial and internationalist, looking to press the EU case in the world maritime arena. One goal is formal observer status in the IMO, leading to membership. There is a growing understanding that Europe now controls entire areas of maritime space and can look to extend the Single Market onto the high seas. Under TEN-T 2007–2013, the EU has assigned approximately €40m for MoS, co-funding projects in Sweden, Germany, Belgium, Poland and Denmark, among others. In addition, several MoS projects received funding under the EU Marco Polo programme, which targets private industry projects. There is evidence that, at the European level, MoS has very limited competitive edge against road or rail, due to the fact that seaway-equivalent infrastructure is treated unfairly (Baird, 2007) although recent study concludes an emerging positive output from MoS (Aperte and Baird, 2013). Although this was hampered by the continuing Global Economic Crisis that causes many governments to put less priority to its development (Brooks et al., 2017).

4.8 2011 White Paper Roadmap to a Single European Transport Area

The 2011 White Paper appeared to targeted 10 goals with over 100 individual initiatives (European Commission, 2011a). This was written alongside the "Roadmap for moving to a competitive low carbon economy in 2050" which was a communication paper to reach higher commitment to EU's climate action based on innovative solutions on resources efficiency policies (European Commission, 2011b).

Importantly, like the 2001 paper, this one states that the transport system is unsustainable. Given EU targets to reduce greenhouse gases (GHGs) by 60% by 2050 (relative to 1990), the current system cannot endure. The solutions to be proposed are trailed by the telling phrase: "Since the first big oil crisis 40 years ago ... the transport system has not fundamentally changed."

The goals are not yet stated and yet methods are being unfolded: "new technologies for vehicles and traffic management will be key..."; "it is crucial that European transport continues to develop and invest to maintain its competitive position." Whereas the 2001 paper looked to break transport growth from economic growth, in 2011 the challenge is to "break the ...system's dependence on oil without sacrificing its efficiency and sacrificing mobility...use less and cleaner energy." This is elaborated upon: improve the energy efficiency of all vehicles; optimize logistics chains with limited modal shift where technology cannot achieve the desired effect; use transport and infrastructure more efficiently with ICT, ITS, etc. Almost tucked away are demands for the full development of an integrated rail market; removal of the final restrictions on road cabotage and abolition of barriers to short sea shipping.

This is a technocrats' White Paper; the route to reducing energy use and increasing mobility will be technology. While some, e.g., Hillman (2004) would argue that rebound effects and the inherent problems with a technology solution will not work, the paper's authors are clearly pinning their flag to the mast of energy efficiency through technology, with the added benefit of global competition in the low carbon economy—the view more closely linked to Stern (2010), albeit without a carbon tax.

On the other hand, a move toward full application of "user pays" and "polluter pays" principles is present, but this need not in and of itself address longer term economic intervention in climate change and carbon. As both Stern and Hillman argue, modern economics is badly suited to very long term investment decisions, since discounted interest rates simply fail to adequately function over a 50 or 100 year horizon. In the short and medium term, private and public sector engagement is present, to eliminate distortions including harmful subsidies. These short, medium and long terms can be referred to Keynes' witty comment that "in the long run we are all dead" (Keynes, 1924). Economics is seen more as a way to generate revenues and ensure financing for future transport investment.

The flow through 10 years of policy development is sound; in each area the understanding that road is the mode of choice for short distances is offset by the wish for rail freight to grow along green corridors that combine all modes, co-modally. Issues such as air quality, that are unique to transport in urban areas, where most citizens will increasingly dwell, are succinctly described. An understanding of ports is there, with the need or opportunity for a single maritime space without internal borders. Some less than successful ideas are no longer mentioned within a new vision of the TEN-T network as a "core network," such as the freight prioritized rail network, or the freight integrator concept (politely dismissed by the industry already fulfilling that role).

Other "old" issues are still strong, even after 10 years of being refused by member states. The call for internalization of externalities, the pooling of infrastructure charging funds and a comprehensive harmonization of fuel taxes are repeated from 2001. In addition, the discriminatory taxing of transport items, such as company cars, is targeted. It is also of note that in 2011 freight is an integral and equal partner in the document; not a tokenistic addition, nor a separate area, but integrated holistically into all policies and statements. However, the most noticeable theme is technological advance. This includes both the development and deployment of new and sustainable fuels and propulsion systems, and ICT, through deployment of the European Global Navigation Satellite System (Galileo) and improvement of the multimodal transport information, management and payment system.

The goals are listed and they are ambitious. The potential impact is undeniable; the political difficulty of achieving them enormous. Here listed are just those covering surface freight transport:

Developing and deploying new and sustainable fuels and propulsion systems: Halve the use of "conventionally-fuelled" cars in urban transport by 2030; phase them out in cities by 2050; achieve essentially CO2-free city logistics in major urban centers by 2030.

Optimizing the performance of multimodal logistic chains, including by making greater use of more energy-efficient modes: 30% of road freight over 300 km should shift to other modes such as rail or waterborne transport by 2030, and more than 50% by 2050, facilitated by efficient and green freight corridors. To meet this goal will also require appropriate infrastructure to be developed. A fully functional and EU-wide multimodal TEN-T "core network" by 2030, with a high quality and capacity of comprehensive network by 2050 and a corresponding set of information services. By 2050, connect all core network airports to the rail network, preferably high-speed; ensure that all core seaports are sufficiently connected to the rail freight and, where possible, inland waterway system.

Increasing the efficiency of transport and of infrastructure use with information systems and market-based incentives; deployment of equivalent land and waterborne transport management systems; deployment of the European Global Navigation Satellite System (Galileo). By 2020, establish the framework for a European multimodal transport information, management and payment system. By 2050, move close to zero fatalities in road transport. In line with this goal, the EU aims at halving road casualties by 2020. Make sure that the EU is a world leader in safety and security of transport in all modes of transport.

Move toward full application of "user pays" and "polluter pays" principles and private sector engagement to eliminate distortions, including harmful subsidies, generate revenues and ensure financing for future transport investments.

Following the launch of the White Paper, some research activity (i.e., TRANSFORUM http://www.transforum-project.eu) was conducted to collect key stakeholders views on addressing the goals. Those that engaged with freight roadmap include the formulation of "long distance freight" that can be supported with policies such as large scale investment in new infrastructure and more efficient use of existing infrastructure (Akerman et al., 2014). The city related freight is dealt with "urban transport" roadmap where low carbon city logistics, technological substitution of conventional fuels and less car dependent alternatives were considered as key policy drivers (Gudmundsson et al., 2014).

4.9 2015 Mid-term Review of 2011 White Paper

Between March and June 2015, an open consultation of the 2011 White Paper was advertised by the Commission to provide an input to the progress made. This process has invited a number of key stakeholders with various backgrounds such as industry associations, private and public sector, research organizations, consultants and central public authority (European Commission, 2015). The general conclusion of the consultation review was that the 2011 White Paper objectives are still relevant and worth to pursue despite still little progress made (toward the goals set 2011) due to, for example, technology development (automation and digitalization); governments commitment to improve and maintain national transport systems and infrastructures; negotiations of cleaner technologies deployment; and sustainable urban mobility planning (SUMP) enforcement (IET UK and ITS UK, 2015; PTEG, 2015; POLIS, 2015). Although some organizations objected the generalized approach such as SUMP, some considered that it was too early to assess the ability to attain the 2050 White Paper targets. The consultation has successfully generated a number of enquiries for further finance and investment mechanism toward supporting various organizations' interests. For freight, this simply means support for the adoption of rail and inland waterway freight, electric truck use, and city logistics innovation.

5. SYNTHESIS OF EUROPE'S FREIGHT POLICY

Since the launch of the 1992 Common Transport Policy, freight transport has witnessed a number of definitions that can be seen as key milestones in the progress of understanding transport modality terms. Multimodal (1992 White Paper) was defined as a combination of two or more transport modes for freight, also called combined transport. Intermodal (2001 White Paper) was defined as the transportation of freight in an intermodal container or vehicle, using multiple modes of transport. These definitions were introduced to deliver the realization of integrated transport systems in the EU (Janic and Reggiani, 2001). Co-modal (2006 Mid-term review Paper) was introduced and was defined as an efficient use of different transport modes to obtain a sustainable and optimum resources allocation. Finally, in the 2011 White Paper, Multimodal was re-launched with a new definition—a transport operation for both freight and passengers carried out using different modes of transport. The period also witnesses the evolution from the improvement of individual mode performance (e.g., combined transport, railway deregulation and short sea shipping to a focus on co-modality, the efficient of one, several or all modes concurrently to achieve the most sustainable and efficient system. This ties in well with the adoption of TEN-T as the backbone of European economic growth (e.g., dedicated railfreight and motorways of the sea—MoS); door-to-door supply chain design; and the green multimodal corridors approach. Fig. 2 illustrates the overview of freight transport definition by EU Policy.

One of the extensive reviews of EU Transport Policy since the launch of the Common Transport Policy has concluded that progress has been made toward meeting European economic, social and environmental sustainability goals (Steer Davies Gleave, 2009). The particular agenda for freight has been the recommendation of full road liberalization and the adoption of new, cleaner technologies in the transport market. Safety and security are the key social objectives, largely considering passenger transport, rather than

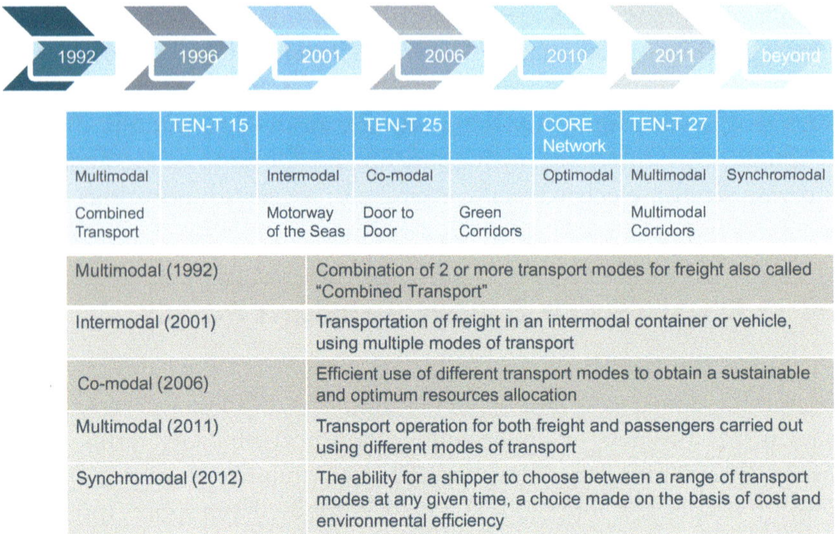

Fig. 2 Freight transport definition by EU Policy since 1992 Common Transport Policy.

freight, albeit the improvement of road safety and conditions for transport workers certainly touch on the freight sector's welfare.

For freight, the 2001 White Paper can best be summarized by the words by "regulation," "modal shift" and "decoupling" and the 2011 White Paper "smart," "green" and "integrated."

The bridge between the two papers is the 2006 mid-term review, partially initiated by the obvious failings in modal shift and the intermodalist agenda of 2001, but also by the accompanying shift of political approach, as the new member states re-emphasized concepts of growth and jobs in the revitalized Lisbon Agenda. The TEN-T policy to reinforce the supra-regional transport infrastructure has played a role in delivering and addressing the "interconnectivity" and "interoperability" agenda. "Interoperability" mainly refers to the use of standardized and compatible infrastructure, technology, facilities and equipment and the characteristics of vehicles, while "interconnectivity" concerns the horizontal co-ordination of transport modes for an integrated door-to-door transport service (Janic and Reggiani, 2001). For freight, the economic focus on competitiveness and the interest shown by the German Presidency of the Council of Europe have led to extensive examination and planning of freight transport logistics that has raised the role of freight in the common transport policy since 2007.

A more market-led approach, influenced by the 2004 EU expansion into the East, and also a more urban approach have developed a more nuanced understanding of the relative merits of the different modes; road is now an equal partner in policy and indeed the focus now is on making road carbon free, rather than avoiding it. Different areas of freight policy have become attuned to the sectors; rail freight continues to be "Commission versus recalcitrant states," using directives to drive liberalization and corridors across Europe, whereas ports policy recognizes the relative success of a heterogeneous sector, and applies a light touch. In urban freight the Commission applies the principle of subsidiarity, acknowledging the leading role of cities and, on the broader maritime scene, the Commission sees its role as an international champion.

It is noticeable that, throughout this period, road has been remarkably absent from policy; this is to some extent because the advances in road came before this period, and also that what changes been seen—e.g., changes in working time and the introduction of digital tachographs—have been carried out under health and safety policy, not transport. However, the final paper proposes a highly significant change: the decarbonization of road transport itself.

Some policies have never fully taken hold; the period sees repeated attempts to solve the issue of infrastructure charging—how it is levied, harmonization, who holds the funds, etc. Motorways of the Seas has survived as policy from 2001 to 2011, with no appreciable sign of take up, and indeed the TEN-T network itself has had to be redefined, from a core network to a comprehensive network.

The drift from "innovative" to "innovation" maybe a semantic artifact, but it may also represent two possible changes. First, in a progressive sense the innovative developments in 2001 may have matured and become innovations by 2011, but perhaps it also shows a shorter term focus on results, is an innovation closer to deployment than something which is innovative? For researchers who have seen the EU Framework Programmes move to a shorter terms impact led approach under Horizon 2020, the difference may have resonances, or perhaps one English speaker simply nuances phrases differently to another?

It remains to be fully seen just how the ambitious goals of 2011 will be treated by the wider community of stakeholders. At 2015 mid-term review, the goals were still seen as good objectives and bear expectation of more investment made from various stakeholders to achieve those objectives. It can be said at least that the 2001 goals were partially achieved; some key policies deemed failed (please see the following section for some examples and discussion), but were conveniently redefined in 2006. There is a strong tradition of dialogue between European policy makers and research academics, such as the review prepared for the meeting of the European Conference of Ministers of Transport in May 2006 (May, 2009; May and Crass, 2007) and as such it is appropriate to speculate on why some policies thrive and others wither. One significant reason may well be that many transport policies since the 2001 White Paper have been largely oriented toward behavioral change, and aimed more at passenger transport than freight, e.g., road user charging, Eurovignette, congestion charge. The 2011 White Paper's focus on technological change demonstrates an EU policy shift away from such behavioral change. Amendment in style is observed, from dirigiste to facilitative, and a huge step-change in the call for decarbonization of road, which will almost certainly require some form of intervention.

Lastly it is noticeable that the change over the period is in some senses one from a political policy document to a technocratic policy document. This tension in government, and especially the European Union between explicit political intent and implicit reliance on technology or metrics (Godard, 1997; Kurki, 2011) may be positive in that the acceptance of the single European Market as a liberal economic model is likely to be supported by commercial actors, and freight is primarily a commercial activity, but it is also possible that by removing political intent, and not replacing it with a strong commercial mechanism, that dependence on technology alone will not deliver the very ambitious goals and objectives. These goals and objectives, despite basing them in climate change science, are inherently political, and as such an apolitical European Commission would be in danger of being blown this way and that as popular politics blows hot and cold on what are potentially life changing policies for the future.

6. SUCCESSFUL AND UNSUCCESSFUL FREIGHT POLICIES

Freight transportation has long been developed to optimize goods movement between points of production and points of consumption. The relationship between the cost of transport and the level of demand for freight can be explained by a case of production and consumption of market goods (Kanafani, 1983; Kawamura, 2016). Substantial transportation economics studies have attempted to assess the impacts of distance, time and elasticities on freight flows (Button, 2010). Those impacts can be quantified further through four core elements according to Hesse and Rodrigue (2004):

1. transport cost (metrics: distance, time, composition, transhipment, decomposition);
2. the organization of the supply chain (number of suppliers, number of distribution centers, number of parts/variety of components);
3. the transactional environment (competition, (sub-)contracting, inter-firm relationships, power issues, (de-)regulation; and
4. physical environment (infrastructure supply, road bottlenecks and congestion, urban density, urban adjustments).

Building on the freight transport geography typology above, forecasting demand model for freight has been paramount interest for transport policy makers (Chow et al., 2010). The demand for freight is determined by factors such as:

- economic growth (e.g., GDP) with gross output or added value of a region;
- resources, goods and services (e.g., products, cultural trade and tourism services);
- the supply of transport infrastructure and services (e.g., capacities, speed, safety, comfort) and technology (e.g., ITS);
- vehicle technology (e.g., containerization, automation, handling and interchange systems) and packaging of goods;
- the spatial structure of cities or region;
- the ongoing economic process of globalization with intermodal and combined transport (i.e., free market zones); and
- the design of spatial organization of inventories, warehousing and just-in-time (JIT) practices.

Source: Tavasszy, 2008; Tsekeris and Tsekeris, 2011

The above indicators have been used to influence many freight transport policies in Europe toward sustainable development goals as discussed in the previous sections. At the global level, those policies are influenced with trends such as: globalization; deregulation and privatization; broader focus to enable better co-ordination of investments toward efficiency of transport networks; and social and political issues, such as environmental externality and social equity (Slack et al., 2017). The key transport policy actions in Europe, which based on social-market economy, have been pretty much in line with those trends with four key pillars:

1. The planning and the promotion of new infrastructure (e.g., TEN-T dedicated freight lines, Reggiani et al., 2000;
2. Competition and regulation policies (e.g., trucking industry, railfreight, ports);

3. The environment policy (e.g., Euro vignette, Euro level emission standard); and
4. The safety policy (i.e., fatalities rate).

Those policies were argued sound and consistent but unbalanced with successful competition in sectors dominated by private firms (i.e., road freight and air) but less in sectors under policy makers' control (i.e., TEN-T, railways, ports) (Ponti et al., 2013). Furthermore, the environment and the road safety policies have been considered successful while modal shift (road to rail) and social protection of workers have remained a concern (Ponti et al., 2013). Such transport policies can be classified as strategical, tactical and operational as typically adopted in transport planning (Anthony, 1965; Armstrong and Hax, 1977; Assad, 1980). While there are only a few strategical level policies as discussed above, there are many well-known transport policies at tactical and operational level such as at urban level.

Assessing quantitative information on freight transport policies is not easy task as there are many variables which have to be considered such as transport cost, transport time, reliability, frequency, ICT applications, cargo security and safety, traffic safety and bottlenecks, and national/regional/local transport policies, many of which are not easy to be captured from the vast majority of companies and therefore the conclusion is limited to certain extent (please see Psaraftis, 2016, for further detail and Aditjandra et al., 2012, for review at national level). Simplified quantification is of course possible and efforts made to model and to optimize global green supply chain network design is well documented (see, for example: Elhedhli and Merrick, 2012; Govindan et al., 2015; Rezaee et al., 2017; Sundarakani et al., 2010; Wang et al., 2011) but the target user or beneficiary is generally limited to individual company (i.e., car manufacturers, office furniture, etc.). At individual company operational level, quantification for impact is more straightforward, for example, Dekker et al. (2012) reported that typically up to 5% CO_2 emissions and between 3% and 5% cost reduction can be achieved via vehicle routing package. Moreover, container ships lowering their speed from 26 to 18 knots reduce their fuel use by 30% (Dekker et al., 2012).

For long distance freight, the most discussed policies are related to environmental consideration for road (where considered suitable to cover urban distance level), rail (medium distance) and sea (long distance) freight (Rodrigue and Notteboom, 2013). One of the arguments made was on speed reduction in maritime transportation to reduce emissions (popularly known as slow steaming) which was argued not necessarily giving solution, especially for transport of high value goods (Psaraftis, 2016, p. xvii). Another was on low sulfur marine fuels policy in Northern Europe (SECA—Sulfur emission control area) which was argued to be of limited impact (Cullinane and Bergqvist, 2014) and need to be supported with Euroviognette for road transport charging to be successful (Holmgren et al., 2014). Moreover, modal shift from sea to road were evidenced from the forest industry in Sweden (Bergqvist et al., 2015). For rail transportation, the current state of challenges is more on technological and its deployment within different settings (that raises issues of compatibility and costs) and therefore dedicated framework of Shift to Rail has been the key policy and act as the sole finance mechanism of European rail research to improve the rail system in Europe and beyond (more discussion can be seen in Aditjandra et al., 2016b). The potential benefit of cross continent rail freight as opposed to sea freight has been deemed as good opportunity at present time (Leonardi et al., 2017) and started to be seriously considered and modeled (Wiegmans and Janic, 2018). Alongside the technological development, the success of long distance freight would very much depends on international logistics and thus international business, management and governance that touches political economy to influence any meaningful change.

Example of quantification of long distance strategic freight policy is the opening of Rotterdam-Genoa rail freight corridor (via TEN-T finance mechanism) where dedicated double track freight railway "Betuweroute" segment has increased the share market of the railfreight by 70% in 2010, as compared by 45% in 2009, due to active tariff policy, the electrification of the Port Railway Line, and the stretch between node and shunting center (OECD, 2014). The shift to the corridor optimizes the flow of freight to benefit the region's economy as well as the environmental (pollution) impact (RailFreight.com, 2017). Some €4.5 billion public fund was used to build the 160 km dedicated route for the rail freight, avoiding built-up areas, no crossings, 10 km/h, and electrified at 25 KV and serving 10 trains per hour in each direction (Peijs, 2006).

Observations for urban freight policies include the concern for the widespread adoption of urban distribution/consolidation centers (for addressing efficiency) (Allen et al., 2012) and road pricing (for addressing congestion and environmental problems) (Demir et al., 2015) where experience of big European cities on road freight pricing can be considered ineffective (Zunder et al., 2016). Some of those issues can be associated with gaps between those working in freight modeling and those working in policy or business and management related issues (Browne and Goodchild,

2013; Leonardi et al., 2014) and fragmented studies in the field of logistics and management (Lagorio et al., 2016). Additionally, gaps between academic sector research vs industry research can also be blamed (McKinnon et al., 2014). It was argued that what academic sector research wants is not necessarily the interest of industry research priority. It can be said that it is more of trial and error for successful or unsuccessful adopted freight policies. Many of those policies are well promoted toward various key stakeholders—especially city authorities—in EU cities and regions with examples of successful as well as unsuccessful implementation (please see full coverage of the best practices as reported in CIVITAS WIKI consortium, 2015). For the private sector, such as logistics service providers, cost-effective systems of goods distribution should follow the trend in a new Europe, where strategies for large/small to medium-sized providers have been geared toward influencing market diversity, consumer choice, jobs and prosperity (Browne et al., 2017).

Quantifying the impact of urban freight policies is not straightforward exercise and this is especially true with different interest of city logistics stakeholders. For example, strategical policy such as Freight Quality Partnership is not easily measured despite the benefit obtained toward, for example, good communication between city stakeholders in finding best solutions for addressing urban freight issues. A combination adoption of UCC and electric vehicles in Central London demonstrates 20% reduction of travel distance and 54% reduction in CO_2 in Central London (Browne et al., 2011). Recent effort to quantify urban freight policy impacts using combination policy of urban consolidation center, electric vehicle and freight partnership in Newcastle, North East England, demonstrates the potential emission reduction up to 43% (Aditjandra et al., 2016a).

Despite all the above issues and the fact that modern logistics tend to increase road transport volume (Browne et al., 2017) due to the importance of value-conscious customer (Christopher, 2017), freight which operate to ensure the lifeblood of cities and regions has always survived in its own right. Best practices of freight policies have been well acknowledged (see, for example: FP7 BESTFACT (2015, 2012); INTERREG IVC SUGAR (2011)), and well spread across global cities and regions via multinational companies' logistics and supply chains and also recently supported via EU funded projects (see, for example: FP7 TURBLOG (2010), FP7 VIAJEO PLUS (2015, 2016), IEE SMARTSET (2014)). Freight and logistics is quite a progressive research field and any innovative development toward new trends (i.e., e-commerce, automated vehicle, physical internet, etc., for further detail, please see Financial Times, 2018) will receive quick response from the sector where best practices can be drawn. The issues arose when the best practices adopted for different situation without taking into account many other factors that can contribute to the success or failure of any measures used. Recent freight study shows the complexity of (urban) freight policies and measures that can be mapped in a framework of policies' taxonomy (Aditjandra and Zunder, 2018). Many of the lessons learned from the above projects were that no single freight policy would work equally well in two different places. They are bounded by geographic, built environment, economic, social, cultural, political scopes and so forth to characterize a distinctive place and belong to communities who have nurtured those places over time since those places were discovered for its own unique characteristics and resources.

ACKNOWLEDGMENTS

The book chapter has emerged from an earlier paper presented at the Transportation Research Board (TRB) 91st Annual Meeting, January 22–26, 2012, Washington, D.C., USA. Since that date it has been substantially revised, having benefited from comments from this conference and reviews on related work. The script presents extended analysis and new discussion to support the contribution to transport policy and planning research. Thanks to Tom Zunder and Dewan Islam for inputs to the earlier versions. Thanks also to Humberto Moyano for the insightful meeting in Gijón in spring 2012 that inspired the development of the key EU freight transport definition; and to Sergio Barbarino for the insightful talk about Kenyan's bean in Gothenburg, SUPERGREEN Final meeting, January 2013.

APPENDIX

Primary documents (European Commission's publication)

No	Year	Policy Area	Document
1	2016	Mid-term review	The implementation of the 2011 White Paper on Transport "Roadmap to a Single European Transport Area—towards a competitive and resource-efficient transport system" five years after its publication: achievements and challenges—SWD (2016) 226 final
2	2011	White Paper	Roadmap to a Single European Transport Area—Towards a competitive and resource efficient transport system
3	2011	White Paper	Commission Staff Working Document Accompanying the White Paper—Roadmap to a Single European Transport Area—SEC (2011) 391 final

Continued

No	Year	Policy Area	Document
4	2011	General	A roadmap for moving to a competitive low carbon economy in 2050. COM (2011) 112 final
5	2010	Freight	Towards an integrated system—freight focus. Research contributing to integration and interoperability across Europe. Transport Research Knowledge Centre
6	2010	ITS	Deployment of Intelligent Transport Systems in the field of road transport and for interfaces with other modes of transport. Directive 2010/40/EU
7	2010	Rail	IMPACT ASSESSMENT Accompanying document to the Proposal for a DIRECTIVE OF THE EUROPEAN PARLIAMENT AND OF THE COUNCIL establishing a single European railway area (Recast). SEC(2010) 1043 final
8	2010	Rail	COMMUNICATION FROM THE COMMISSION concerning the development of a Single European Railway Area
9	2009	General	A sustainable future for transport—Towards an integrated, technology-led and user-friendly system. European Commission Directorate-General for Energy and Transport
10	2009	Maritime	Strategic goals and recommendations for the EU's maritime transport policy until 2018
11	2009	Road	Road Freight Transport Vademecum
12	2009	General	Mainstreaming sustainable development into EU policies: 2009 Review of the EU Strategy for Sustainable development. COM (2009) 400 final
13	2008	Freight	Statistical coverage and economic analysis of the logistics sector in the EU
14	2008	Taxes and charges	Strategy for the internalisation of external costs COM (2008) 435 final
15	2008	Road	FINAL REPORT Effects of adapting the rules on weights and dimensions of heavy commercial vehicles as established within Directive 96/53/EC
16	2008	Rail	Rail Noise Abatement COM (2008) 432
17	2008	General	Greening Transport Inventory COM (2008) 433 final. Brussels
18	2007	Freight	The EU's freight transport agenda: Boosting the efficiency, integration and sustainability of freight transport in Europe. COM (2007) 606 final

No	Year	Policy Area	Document
19	2007	Freight	Freight Transport Logistics Action Plan. COM (2007) 607 final
20	2007	Freight	Freight Transport Logistics Action Plan IMPACT ASSESSMENT
21	2007	Rail	Towards a rail network giving priority to freight. COM (2007) 608 final
22	2007	Port/ Maritime	Communication on a European Ports Policy. COM (2007) 616 final
23	2007	Maritime	Report on the Motorway of the Sea State of play and consultation. SEC (2007) 1367
24	2007	Urban	Green Paper: Towards a new culture for urban mobility. COM(2007) 551 final
25	2007	Rail	Monitoring development of the rail market COM (2007) 609
26	2006	Mid-term Review	Keep Europe moving—Sustainable mobility for our continent Mid-term review of the European Commission's, 2001 Transport White Paper. COM (2006) 314 final
27	2006	General	RENEWED EU SUSTAINABLE DEVELOPMENT STRATEGY. 10917/06
28	2006	General	After Enlargement: Voting Behaviour in the Sixth European Parliament
29	2006	Freight	Freight Transport Logistics in Europe—the key to sustainable mobility. COM (2006) 336 final
30	2006	Rail	Policy effectiveness of rail. EU policy and its impact on the rail system
31	2006	Intermodal	Intermodal freight terminals. In search of efficiency to support intermodality growth
32	2006	Urban freight	Urban freight transport and logistics. An overview of the European research and policy
33	2006	Rail	REPORT FROM THE COMMISSION TO THE EUROPEAN PARLIAMENT, THE COUNCIL, THE EUROPEAN ECONOMIC AND SOCIAL COMMITTEE AND THE COMMITTEE OF THE REGIONS on the implementation of the first railway package

Continued

No	Year	Policy Area	Document
34	2005	TEN-T	Trans-European Transport Network TEN-T priority axes and projects 2005
35	2005	Road	PARTICULATES—Final Publishable Report (Characterisation of Exhaust Particulate Emissions from Road Vehicles)
36	2001	General	White Paper—European Transport Policy for 2010: Time to Decide. COM(2001) 370 final
37	2001	Freight	Freight intermodality. Results from the transport research programme
38	2001	Freight	RESEARCH RESULTS PAPER 10 OF 10 FREIGHT INTERMODALITY
39	1998	Taxes and charges	White Paper "Fair payment for infrastructure use: a phased approach to a common transport infrastructure charging framework in the EU." COM (98) 466
40	1997	Intermodal	Intermodality and intermodal freight transport in the European Union. A Systems approach to freight transport. Strategies and actions to enhance efficiency, services and sustainability. COM (97) 243 final
41	1997	ITS/Road	COMMUNITY STRATEGY AND FRAMEWORK FOR THE DEPLOYMENT OF ROAD TRANSPORT TELEMATICS IN EUROPE. COM (97) 223 final
42	1996	General	The 1996 Single Market Review. SEC (96) 2378
43	1996	Rail	White Paper "A strategy for revitalising the Community's railways' introducing market forces into rail, integration of national systems." COM (96) 421
44	1996	TEN-T	Decision 1692/96/EC on Community guidelines for the development of the trans-European transport network (TEN-T)
45	1995	Taxes and charges	Green Paper "Towards fair and efficient pricing in transport." COM (95) 691
46	1993	Combined transport	Council Decision 93/45/CEE concerning the granting of financial support for pilot schemes to promote combined transport
47	1993	TEN-T	93/628 EEC: Council Decision of 29 October 1993 on the creation of a trans-European combined transport network
48	1992	General	The Future Development of the Common Transport Policy. COM 92/494 (final)

No	Year	Policy Area	Document
49	1991	Rail	Council Directive 91/440/EEC. 29 July 1991. EC on the development of the railways
50	1982	Combined transport	Directive 82/603/EEC. Taxation for vehicle used in combined transport
51	1975	Combined transport	Regulation 1107/70/EEC. State aid to modernise combined transport
52	1957	General	Treaty of Rome. EU formation

Secondary documents (research papers and or review of the policy)

No	Year	Type of Document	Area of Research	Document
1	2012	Conference proceedings	Rail	Robinson, M., Carruthers, J., O'Neill, C., Ingleton, S. and Grasso, M. (2012) Transport of DE-LIGHT: The Design and Prototyping of a Lightweight Crashworthy Rail Vehicle Driver's Cab. Procedia—Social and Behavioural Sciences 48: 672–681
2	2012	Conference proceedings	Green freight corridors	Aditjandra PT, Zunder TH, Islam DMZ, Vanaale E. (2012) Investigating Freight Corridors Towards Low Carbon Economy: Evidence from the UK. Procedia: Social and Behavioral Sciences, Special Issue: TRA Conference 2012, 48: 1865–1876
3	2012	Article	Maritime	Aperte, X.G. and Baird, A.J. (2012) Motorway of the sea policy in Europe. Maritime Policy & Management. July 2012, 1–17, iFirst
4	2012	Article	ITS; Co-modality	Zunder, T., Westerheim, H., Jorna, R. and Pedersen, J.T. (2012) Is it possible to Manage and Plan Co-Modal Freight Transport Without a Centralised System? International Journal of Applied Logistics 3(2): 25–39

Continued

No	Year	Type of Document	Area of Research	Document
5	2011	Report	Rail	IBM (2011) Rail Liberalisation Index 2011. A study conducted by IBM Deutchland GmbH in collaboration with Prof.Dr.Dr.Dr.h.c. Christian Kirchner, Humboldt-University, Berlin. Brussels
6	2011	Presentation	Rail (including passenger)	Nash, C. (2011) How Effective is EU Rail Policy? Institute for Transport Studies, University of Leeds. Presentation given at Transport Economic Group meeting 27 April 2011 London
7	2011	Book	General	Helmreich, S. and Keller, H. (editors) (2011) FREIGHTVISION—Sustainable European Freight Transport 2050. Forecast, Vision and Policy Recommendation. Springer
8	2010	Book	Freight and Logistics	McKinnon, A., Cullinane, S., Browne, M. and Whiteing, A. (editors) (2010) Green Logistics Improving the environmental sustainability of logistics
9	2010	Book	General	TRT—Trasporti e Territorio (2010) Logistics as an instrument for tackling climate change study. European Parliament Directorate-general for internal policies Policy Department B: Structural and Cohesion Policies Transport and Tourism
10	2010	Presentation	General	Capros PP, Mantzos DL, Tasios N, Vita AD, Kouvaritakis N. (2010) EU energy trends to 2030—UPDATE 2009. Brussels
11	2010	Conference Proceedings	Urban freight	Clean Urban Transport Conference Proceedings on Urban Freight Transport and Logistics (2010) 16–17 November. Brussels
12	2010	Report	Rail	New Europe (2010) Rail Freight Liberalization: A New Europe Policy Report. Issue 868. 17 November 2010

No	Year	Type of Document	Area of Research	Document
13	2010	Article	Port and Maritime	Pallis, A., Vitsounis, T., De Langen, P. (2010) Port Economics, Policy and Management: Review of an Emerging Research Field. Transport Review 30(1): 115–161
14	2010	Book	Intermodal	Seidelmann, C. (2010) 40 years of road-rail combined transport in Europe—from piggyback traffic to the intermodal transport system. International Union of combined road-rail transport companies UIRR scrl. Brussels
15	2010	Article	Road	Santos, G., Behrendt, H., Maconic, L., Shirvanic, T., and Teytelboym, A. (2010) Part I: Externalities and economic policies in road transport. Research in Transportation Economics 28(1): 2–45
16	2010	Article	Road	Santos, G., Behrendt, H., Teytelboym, A. (2010) Part II: Policy instruments for sustainable road transport. Research in Transportation Economics 28(1): 46–91
17	2009	Report	General/ Forecasting tools	Petersen M.S., Enei R., Hansen C.O., Larrea E., Obisco O., Sessa C., Timms P.M., Ulied A. (2009) TRANSvisions—Final Report on Transport Scenarios with a 20 and 40 year Horizon
18	2009	Report	General (mainly passenger)	Steer Davies Gleave (2009) Evaluation of the Common Transport Policy (CTP) of the EU from 2000 to 2008 and analysis of the evaluation and structure of the European transport sector in the context of the long-term development of the CTP. Final Report prepared for European Commission DG-TREN. August 2009. www.steerdaviesgleave.com

Continued

No	Year	Type of Document	Area of Research	Document
19	2009	Article	Road/ITS	Giannopoulos, G. (2009) Towards a European ITS for freight transport and logistics: results of current EU funded research and prospects for the future. European Transport Research Review 1(4): 147–161
20	2009	Report	Rail	PwC—PriceWaterhouseCoopers (2009) Amendments to the rail access legislation in the framework of the recast of the 1st railway package. March 2009. EC DG-TREN
21	2009	Article	Maritime	Verhoeven, P. (2009) European ports policy: meeting contemporary governance challenges. Maritime Policy & Management 36(1): 79–101
22	2009	Report	Rail	Castagnetti, F. (2008). New Opera Final report. (France Castagnetti, Ed.) (p. 188). Brussels: THE EUROPEAN FREIGHT AND LOGISTICS LEADERS FORUM(F&L)
23	2009	Article	Rail	Dablanc, L. (2009) Regional policy issues for rail freight services. Transport Policy 16: 163–172
24	2009	Article	ITS	Crainic TG, Gendreau M, Potvin J-Y. (2009) Intelligent freight-transportation systems: Assessment and the contribution of operations research. Transportation Research Part C: Emerging Technologies 17(6): 541–557
25	2008	Book	General	Ben-Akiva, M., Meersman, H. and E. vand de Voorde (editors) (2008) Recent Developments in Transport Modelling: Lessons for the Freight Sector
26	2008	Book	Urban freight	Hesse, M. (2008) The City as a Terminal the Urban Context of Logistics and Freight Transport. Ashgate. Hampshire. England

No	Year	Type of Document	Area of Research	Document
27	2008	Presentation	General	Capros PP, Mantzos DL (2008) Papandreou V, Tasios N. EUROPEAN ENERGY AND TRANSPORT TRENDS TO 2030—UPDATE 2007. Luxembourg
28	2008	Presentation	Road and Rail	Woodburn, A., Allen, J., Browne, M., Leonardi, J. (2008) The Impact of Globalisation on international Road and Rail Freight Transport Activity Past trends and future perspectives
29	2008	Article	Urban freight	Dablanc L. (2008) Urban Goods Movement and Air Quality Policy and Regulation Issues in European Cities. Journal of Environmental Law 20(2): 245–266
30	2008	Article	Urban freight	Behrends, S.,Lindholm, M. and Woxenius, J. (2008) The Impact of Urban Freight Transport: A Definition of Sustainability from an Actor's Perspective. Transportation Planning and Technology 31(6): 693–713
31	2007	Article	General	McKinnon, A. (2007) Decoupling of Road Freight Transport and Economic Growth Trend in the UK: An Exploratory Analysis. Transport Reviews 27(1): 37–64
32	2007	Article	General	Shaheen, S. and Lipman, T. (2007) Reducing Greenhouse Emissions and Fuel Consumption—Sustainable Approaches for Surface Transportation. IATSS Research 31(1): 6–20
33	2007	Article	General	Jarzembowski, G. (2007) European Transport Policy in a Broader Perspective. Intereconomics, September/October 2007, pp.: 281–284

Continued

No	Year	Type of Document	Area of Research	Document
34	2007	Book	Urban freight	Allen, J., Thorne, G. and Browne, M. (2007) BESTUFS Good Practice Guide on Urban Freight Transport. European Commission FP6 for Research and Technological Demonstration. BESTUS.NET Best Urban Freight Solutions. PTV AG, Karlsruhe, Germany
35	2007	Article	Tax and charges	Runhaar, H. and van der Heijden, R. (2005) Public Policy intervention in freight transport costs: effects on printed media logistics in the Netherlands. Transport Policy 12: 35–46
36	2007	Article	Rail	Woodburn, A. (2007) Appropriate indicators of rail freight activity and market share: A review of UK practice and recommendations for change. Transport Policy 14: 59–69
37	2007	Article	Intermodal/ Maritime	Notteboom, T. (2007) Inland waterway transport of containerised cargo: from infancy to a fully fledged transport mode. Journal of Maritime Research IV(2): 63–80
38	2007	Article	Maritime	Baird, A.J. (2007) The economics of Motorway of the Sea. Maritime Policy & Managament. August 2007, 34(4): 287–310
39	2007	Article	Urban freight	Dablanc, L. (2007) Goods transport in large European cities: Difficult to organize, difficult to modernize. Transportation Research Part A 41(3): 280–285
40	2007	Book Section	General	Meunier, S. and McNamara, K. (2007) The State of the European Union Making History: European Integration and Institutional Change at Fifty in Making History: European Integration and Institutional Change at Fifty (The State of the European Union)

No	Year	Type of Document	Area of Research	Document
41	2006	Article	TEN-T	Böttcher, B. (2006) The trans-European transport network (TEN-T): history, progress and financing. Komunikácie/ Communication 6(1): 51–54
42	2005	Book	General	Banister, D. (2005) Unsustainable transport—City transport in the new century. Routledge Taylor and Francis Group. London and New York
43	2005	Book	Intermodal	Vrenken, H., Macharis, C. and Wolters, P. (2005) Intermodal Transport in Europe. European Intermodal Association (EIA). Brussels, Belgium
44	2005	Article	Maritime	Psaraftis, H. (2005) EU Port s Policy: Where do we Go from Here? Maritime Economics and Logistics 7: 73–82
45	2005	Book	Intermodal/ Road	Lowe, D. (2005) Intermodal Freight Transport. Oxford. Elsevier Butterworth-Heinemann
46	2005	Article	Urban freight	Anderson, S., Allen, J. & Browne, M. (2005) Urban logistics—how can it meet policy makers sustainability objectives? Journal of Transport Geography 13(1): 71–81
47	2004	Article	Intermodal	Bontekoning, Y.M., Macharis, C. and Trip, J.J. (2004) Is a new applied transportation research field emerging?—A review of intermodal rail-truck freight transport literature. Transportation Research Part A 38: 1–34
48	2004	Article	General	Eberlein B, Kerwer D. (2004) New Governance in the European Union: A Theoretical Perspective. JCMS: Journal of Common Market Studies 42(1): 121–142

Continued

No	Year	Type of Document	Area of Research	Document
49	2002	Book	General	Banister, D. (2002) Transport Planning. 2nd Edition. Taylor & Francis. London & New York
50	2001	Book	General	Brewer, A.M., Button, K.J. and Hensher, D.A. (editors) (2001) Handbook of Logistics and Supply-Chain Management. Elsevier Science Ltd. Oxford, UK
51	2001	Article	General	Janic, M., Reggiani, A. (2001) Integrated transport systems in the European Union: an overview of some recent developments. Transport Reviews 21(4): 469–497
52	2000	Book	General	Banister, D., Stead, D., Steen, P., Akerman, J., Dreborg, K., Nijkamp, P. and Schleicher-Tappeser, R. (2000) European Transport Policy and Sustainable Development
53	1997	Article	General	Banister, D., Watson, S. and Wood, C. (1997) Sustainable Cities—transport, energy and urban form. Environment and Planning B 24(1): 125–143
54	1999	Article	TEN-T	Sichelschmidt, H. (1999) The EU programme "trans-European networks"—a critical assessment. Transport Policy 6: 169–181
55	1998	Book section	Urban freight	Browne, M. and Allen, J. (1998) The impact of sustainability policies on urban freight transport and logistics systems in (eds.: Meersman, H., van de Voorde, E., Winkelmans, W) World Transport Research: Selected Proceedings of the 8th World Conference on Transport Research
56	1995	Article	TEN-T	Vickerman, R.W. (1995) The regional impacts of Trans-European networks. The Annals of Regional Science 29: 237–254

No	Year	Type of Document	Area of Research	Document
57	1987	Book	General	World Commission on Environment and Development (1987) Brundtland report—Our Common Future. Oxford University Press. Oxford

REFERENCES

Aditjandra, P., Zunder, T., 2018. Developing a multi-dimensional poly-parametric typology for city logistics. In: Taniguchi, E., Thompson, R.G. (Eds.), City Logistics 2: Modelling and Planning Initiatives. John Wiley & Sons, Inc., pp. 143–163

Aditjandra, P., Zunder, T.H., Islam, D.M.Z., Vanaale, E., 2012. Investigating freight corridors towards low carbon economy: evidence for the UK. Procedia Soc. Behav. Sci. 48, 1865–1876.

Aditjandra, P.T., Galatioto, F., Bell, M.C., Zunder, T.H., 2016a. Evaluating the impacts of urban freight traffic: application of micro-simulation at a large establishment. EJTIR 16 (1), 4–22.

Aditjandra, P., Zunder, T.H., Islam, D.M.Z., Palacin, R., 2016b. Green rail transportation: improving rail freight to support green corridors. In: Psaraftis, H.N. (Ed.), Green Transportation Logistics: The Quest for Win-Win Solutions. Springer International Publishing Switzerland, Cham, pp. 413–454.

Akerman, J., Schippl, J., Nelldal, B.-L., Czermanski, E., Vesela, J., Edelmann, M., Schotte, D., Reichenbach, M., 2014. FP7 TRANSFORUM D6.2 Long-distance Freight Roadmap, Cologne: FP7 European Commission. Rupprecht Consult GmbH, Köln, Germany.

Alises, A., Vassallo, J.M., 2015. Comparison of road freight transport trends in Europe. Coupling and decoupling factors from an input-output structural decomposition analysis. Transp. Res. Part A Policy Pract. 82, 141–157.

Allen, J., Browne, M., Woodburn, A., Leonardi, J., 2012. The role of urban consolidation centres in sustainable freight transport. Transp. Rev. 32 (4), 473–490.

Anthony, R.N., 1965. Planning and Control Systems: A Framework for Analysis. Harvard Graduate School of Business Administration, Boston.

Aperte, X.G., Baird, A.J., 2013. Motorways of the sea policy in Europe. Marit. Policy Manag. 40 (1), 10–26.

Armstrong, R.J., Hax, A.C., 1977. A Hierarchical Approach for a Naval Tender Job Shop Design. Addison Wesley, Boston.

Assad, A.A., 1980. Modelling of rail networks: toward a routing/makeup model. Transp. Res. Part B 14 (1–2), 101–114.

Baird, A.J., 2007. The economics of motorways of the sea. Marit. Policy Manag. 34 (4), 287–310.

Banister, D., 2002. Transport Planning, second ed. Spon Press, New York.

Banister, D., 2008. The sustainable mobility paradigm. Transp. Policy 15 (2), 73–80.

Barton, K.C., 2005. Primary sources in history: breaking through the myths. Phi Delta Kappa Int. 86 (10), 745–753.

Bergqvist, R., Turesson, M., Weddmark, A., 2015. Sulphur emission control areas and transport strategies—the case of Sweden and the forest industry. Eur. Trans. Res. Rev. 7 (10), 1–15.

BESTFACT, 2012. BESTFACT project deliverable. In: Ruesch, M., Bohne, S. (Eds.), FP7 BESTFACT deliverable 2.1 main challenges in freight logistics. European Commission FP7, Zurich.

BESTFACT, 2015. In: Permala, A., Eckhardt, J. (Eds.), FP7 BESTFACT deliverable D3.2: recommendation and policy tools. European Commission FP7, Espoo, Helsinki.
Borchardt, K.-D., 2010. The ABC of European Law. Publications Office of the European Union, Luxembourg.
Böttcher, B., 2006. The trans-European transport network (TEN-T): history, progress and financing. Communications 6 (1), 51–54.
Brooks, M.R., Cullinane, K.P.B., Pallis, A.A., 2017. Revisiting port governance and port reform: a multi-country examination. Res. Transp. Business Manag. 22, 1–10.
Browne, M., Goodchild, A., 2013. Modelling approaches to address Urban Freight's Challenges: A comparison of the United States and Europe. In: International Freight and Logistics Consortium Consisting of European Commission, The US Department of Transportation's Research and Innovative Technology Administration, and The Transportation Research Board, (Eds.), City logistics research, A Transatlantic Perspective. The National Academies of Sciences, Engineering, Medicines, Washington D.C., pp. 77–92.
Browne, M., Allen, J., Leonardi, J., 2011. Evaluating the use of an urban consolidation centre and electric vehicles in central London. IATSS Res. 35 (1), 1–6.
Browne, M., Allen, J., Woodburn, A., 2017. Developments in Western European Strategies. In: Waters, D., Rinsler, S. (Eds.), Global Logistics: New Directions in Supply Chain Management. Kogan Page & The Chartered Institute of Logistics and Transport, London/Philadephia/New Delhi, pp. 395–418.
Brundtland, H., 1987. Report of the World Commission on Environment and Development: Our Common Future. United Nations.
Button, K., 2010. Transport Economics, third ed. Edward Elgar Publishing Ltd., Cheltenham, UK
Chow, J.Y., Yang, C.H., Regan, A.C., 2010. State-of-the art of freight forecast modelling: lessons learned and the road ahead. Transportation 37 (6), 1011–1030.
Christopher, M., 2017. New directions in logistics. In: Waters, D., Rinsler, S. (Eds.), Global Logistics: New Directions in Supply Chain Management. London/Philadelphia/New Delhi, Kogan Page & The Chartered Institute of Logistics and Transport, pp. 1–12.
Cisternino, R., 2010. Universal Business Language For Corporate Managers 1.1. UBL XML.org.
CIVITAS WIKI consortium, 2015. In: Stefanelli, T., di Bartolo, C., Galli, G., Pastori, E., Quak, H. (Eds.), Making urban freight logistics more sustainable www.eltis.org www.civitas.eu Available at: http://www.eltis.org/resources/tools/civitas-policy-note-making-urban-freight-logistics-more-sustainable.
CLECAT, 2009. RE: 2008—United Nations Convention on Contracts for the International Carriage of Goods Wholly or Partly by Sea—the "Rotterdam Rules," Brussels. European Association for Forwarding, Transport, Logistics and Customs Services.
Cullinane, K., Bergqvist, R., 2014. Emission control areas and their impact on maritime transport. Transp. Res. Part D Transp. Environ. 24, 1–5.
Dekker, R., Bloemhof, J., Mallidis, M., 2012. Operations research for green logistics—an overview of aspects, issues, contributions and challenges. Eur. J. Oper. Res. 219 (3), 671–679.
Demir, E., Huang, Y., Scholts, S., van Woensel, T., 2015. A selected review on the negative externalities of the freight transportation: modeling and pricing. Transp. Res. Part E Logist. Transp. Rev. 77, 95–114.
Ecorys, Fraunhofer, TCI, Prognos, AUEB-RC/Translog, 2015. Fact-finding Studies in Support of the Development of an EU Strategy for Freight Transport Logistics Lot 1: Analysis of the EU Logistics Sector. European Commission.
Elhedhli, S., Merrick, R., 2012. Green supply chain network design to reduce carbon emissions. Transp. Res. Part D Transp. Environ. 17 (5), 370–379.

European Commission, 1996. The 1996 Single Market Review. European Commission, Luxembourg.
European Commission, 2001. White Paper European Transport Policy for 2010: Time to Decide, Brussels. European Commission.
European Commission, 2005. Trans-European Transport Network—TEN-T Priority Axes and Projects. Office for Official Publications of the European Communities, Luxembourg.
European Commission, 2006. Keep Europe Moving—Sustainable Mobility for our Continent: Mid-Term Review of the European Commission's 2001 Transport White Paper. European Commission.
European Commission, 2007a. COM (2007) 607 Final—Freight and Logistics Action Plan. Commission of the European Communities, Brussels.
European Commission, 2007b. COM (2007) 606 Final: The EU's Freight Transport Agenda: Boosting the Efficiency, Integration and Sustainability of Freight Transport in Europe. European Commission, Brussels.
European Commission, 2009. COM (2009) 400 Final: Mainstreaming Sustainable Development in EU Policies: 2009 Review of the European Union Strategy for Sustainable Development. European Commission, Brussels.
European Commission, 2011a. White Paper on Transport—Roadmap to a Single European Transport Area—Towards a Competitive and Resource Efficient Transport System. Publications Office of the European Union.
European Commission, 2011b. SEC (2011) 391 Final: Commission Staff Working Document: Accompanying the White Paper—Roadmap to a Single European Transport Area—Towards a Competitive and Resource Efficient Transport System. European Commission, Brussels.
European Commission, 2013. The Core Network Corridors—Trans European Transport Network 2013. European Commission, Brussels.
European Commission, 2015. Public Consultation Mid-Term Review of the White Paper on the European Transport Policy. European Commission, Brussels.
European Union, 2017. Facts and Figures about the EU. European Commission.
Eurostat, 2016. In: Strandell, H., Wolff, P. (Eds.), The EU in the world 2016 edition. Publications Office of the European Union, Luxembourg, Available at http://ec.europa.eu/eurostat.
Ferrari, C., Parola, F., Tei, A., 2015. Governance models and port concessions in Europe: commonalities, critical issues and policy perspectives. Transp. Policy 41, 60–67.
Financial Times, 2018. Special Report Transport & Logistics. Financial Times. Available at: https://www.ft.com/reports/transport-logistics.
Godard, O., 1997. Social decision-making under scientific controversy, expertise, and the precautionary principle. In: Integrating Scientific Expertise Into Regulatory Decision Making. National Experiences and European Innovations, pp. 39–73. Available at: http://hal.archives-ouvertes.fr/docs/00/62/40/27/PDF/PRECCON3-97.pdf.
Govindan, K., Jafarian, A., Nourbakhsh, V., 2015. Bi-objective integrating sustainable order allocation and sustainable supply chain network design with stochastic demand using a novel robust hybrid multi-objective metaheuristic. Comput. Oper. Res. 62, 112–130.
Grant, D.B., Trautrims, A., Wong, C.Y. (Eds.), 2017. Sustainable Logistics and Supply Chain Management: Principles and Practices for Sustainable Operations and Management, second ed. Kogan Page.
Greene, D.L., Wegener, M., 1997. Sustainable transport. J. Transp. Geogr. 5 (3), 177–190.
Gudmundsson, H., Schippl, J., Leiren, M.D., Brand, R., Sorenson, C.H., Anderton, K., Reichenbach, M., 2014. FP7 TRANSFORUM D6.2 Urban Transport Roadmap. FP7 European Commission, Cologne.

Heaton, J., 2008. Secondary analysis of qualitative data: an overview. Hist. Soc. Res. 33 (3), 33–45.
Hesse, M., Rodrigue, J.-P., 2004. The transport geography of logistics and freight distribution. J. Transp. Geogr. 12 (3), 171–184.
Hillman, M., 2004. How We Can Save the Planet. Penguin Books.
Holmgren, J., Nikopoulou, Z., Ramstedt, L., Woxenius, J., 2014. Modelling modal choice effects of regulation on low-sulphur marine fuels in Northern Europe. Transp. Res. Part D Transp. Environ. 28 (2014), 62–73.
ICS, 2009. The Convention on Contracts for the International Carriage of Goods Wholly or Partly by Sea (the "Rotterdam Rules"). International Chamber of Shipping.
IET UK & ITS UK, 2015. Response: Mid-Term Review of the 2011 White Paper on Transport. Institution of Engineering and Technology/Intelligent Transport Systems, UK.
Islam, D.M.Z., Meier, J., Aditjandra, P., Zunder, T.H., Pace, G., 2013a. Logistics and supply chain management. Res. Transp. Econ. 41 (1), 3–16.
Islam, D.M.Z., Zunder, T.H., Jorna, R., 2013b. Performance evaluation of an online benchmarking tool for European freight transport chains. BIJ 20 (2), 233–250.
Janic, M., Reggiani, A., 2001. Integrated transport systems in the European Union: an overview of some recent developments. Transp. Rev. 21 (4), 469–497.
Jarzembowski, G., 2007. European transport policy in a broader perspective. Intereconomics 42 (5), 281–284.
Kanafani, A., 1983. Transportation Demand Analysis. McGraw-Hill, New York.
Kawamura, K., 2016. Transport economics and pricing. In: Bliemer, M.C.J., Mulley, C., Moutou, C.J. (Eds.), Handbook on Transport and Urban Planning in the Developed World. Edward Elgar, Cheltenham, UK/Northampton, USA, pp. 231–253.
Keynes, J.M., 1924. A Tract on Monetary Reform Reprinted. Macmillan and Co., Limited, London.
Kurki, M., 2011. Democracy through technocracy? Reflections on technocratic assumptions in EU democracy promotion discourse. J. Interv. State Build. 5 (December 2013), 211–234.
Lagorio, A., Pinto, R., Golini, R., 2016. Research in urban logistics: a systematic literature review. Int. J. Phys. Distrib. Logist. Manag. 46 (10), 908–931.
Leonardi, J., Browne, M., Allen, J., Zunder, T., Aditjandra, P., 2014. Increase urban freight efficiency with delivery and servicing plan. Res. Transp. Bus. Manag. 12, 73–79.
Leonardi, J., Woodburn, A., Allen, J., Browne, M., 2017. International road and rail freight transport activity. In: Waters, D., Rinsler, S. (Eds.), Global Logistics: New Directions in Supply Chain Management. London/Philadephia/New Delhi, Kogan Page & The Chartered Institute of Logistics and Transport, pp. 376–394.
Leurent, F., Windisch, E., 2011. Triggering the development of electric mobility: a review of public policies. Eur. Transp. Res. Rev. 3 (4), 221–235.
Lowe, D., 2005. Intermodal Freight Transport. Elsevier Butterworth-Heinemann, Oxford.
Macharis, C., Caris, A., Jourquin, B., Pekin, E., 2011. A decision support framework for intermodal transport policy. Eur. Transp. Res. Rev. 3 (4), 167–178.
May, A., 2009. Improving decision-making for sustainable urban transport: an introduction to the distillate research programme. Eur. J. Transp. Infrastruct. Res. 9 (3), 184–201.
May, A., Crass, M., 2007. Sustainability in transport: implications for policy makers. Transp. Res. Rec. J. Transp. Res. Board 2017, 1–9.
McKinnon, A., 2007. Decoupling of road freight transport and economic growth trends in the UK: an exploratory analysis. Transp. Rev. 27 (1), 37–64.
McKinnon, A., Plessis-Fraissard, M., Ricci, A., 2014. Consultation of the Horizon 2020 Advisory Groups Response of the Transport Advisory Group June 2014, Brussels. European Commission.

McKinnon, A., Browne, M., Whiteing, A., Piecyk, M. (Eds.), 2015. Green Logistics: Improving the Environmental Sustainability of Logistics, third ed. Kogan Page Publishers.

Meers, D., Macharis, C., 2015. Prioritization in modal shift: determining a region's most suitable freight flows. Eur. Transp. Res. Rev. 7 (23), 1–12.

Notteboom, T., 2007. Inland waterway transport of containerised cargo: from infancy to a fully-fledged transport mode. J. Marit. Res. 4 (2), 68–80.

OECD, 2014. The Competitiveness of Global Port-Cities. OECD Publishing.

Peijs, K., 2006. Developing European freight corridors—making the Rotterdam—Geno rail freight corridor a success for the European economy. In: CER (Ed.), Competition in Europe's rail freight market. Eurail press, Community of European Railway and Infrastructure Companies—CER, Bruxelles, pp. 65–78.

POLIS, 2015. White Paper on Transport Midterm Review Polis Position Paper. POLIS European Cities and Regions Networking for Innovative Transport Solutions, Brussels.

Ponti, M., Boitani, A., Ramella, F., 2013. The European transport policy: its main issues. Case Studies Transp. Policy 1 (1–2), 53–62.

Psaraftis, H.N., 2005. EU ports policy: where do we go from here? Marit. Econ. Logist. 7 (1), 73–82.

Psaraftis, H.N. (Ed.), 2016. Green transportation logistics—the quest for win-win solutions. Springer.

PTEG, 2015. Consultation Response: Mid Term Review of the European Commission Transport White Paper 2011–2020 Progress 2010–2013. Urban Transport Group, Leeds.

RailFreight.com, 2017. 10 Years and Counting for Dutch Betuweroute Freight Line. RailFreight.com. https://www.railfreight.com/corridors/2017/06/16/10-years-and-counting-for-dutch-betuweroute-freight-line. accessed on 27 June 2018.

Reggiani, A., Cattaneo, S., Janic, M., Nijkamp, P., 2000. Freight transport in Europe—policy issues and future scenarios on trans-border alpine connections. IATSS Res. 24 (1), 48–59.

Rezaee, A., Dehghanian, F., Fahimnia, B., Beamon, B., 2017. Green supply chain network design with stochastic demand and carbon price. Ann. Oper. Res. 250 (2), 463–485.

Rodrigue, J.P., Notteboom, T., 2010. Comparative North American and European gateway logistics: the regionalism of freight distribution. J. Transp. Geogr. 18 (4), 497–507.

Rodrigue, J., Notteboom, T., 2013. Containerized freight distribution in North America and Europe. In: Bookbinder, J.H. (Ed.), Handbook of global logistics. vol. 181. Springer, pp. 219–246.

Ruijgrok, C., 2008. Intelligent freight transport systems: opportunities and practice. In: Ben-akiva, M.E., Meersman, H., van de Voorde, E. (Eds.), Recent Developments in Transport Modelling: Lessons for the Freight Sector. Emerald Group Publishing Ltd., Bingley, pp. 231–241

SETRIS, 2016. SETRIS project deliverable. In: Aditjandra, P., Palacin, R. (Eds.), SETRIS D1.5 EC-funded research contribution to road-mapping of long distance transport. EU Horizon 2020, Newcastle upon Tyne.

Sichelschmidt, H., 1999. The EU programme "trans-European networks"—a critical assessment. Transp. Policy 6 (3), 169–181.

Slack, B., Notteboom, T., Rodrigue, J.-P., 2017. The nature of transport policy. In: Rodrigue, J.-P. (Ed.), The Geography of Transport Systems. Dept. of Global Studies & Geography, Hofstra University, New York, USA, New York.

SMARTSET, 2014. SMARTSET project deliverable. In: Kocak, N., Clark, A. (Eds.), IEE SMARTSET deliverable 6.4: preliminary evaluation results & recommendations. Intelligent Energy Europe (IEE), Gothenburg.

Steer Davies Gleave, 2009. Evaluation of the common transport policy (CTP) of the EU from 2000 to 2008 and analysis of the evolution and structure of the European transport sector in the context of the long-term development of the CTP. Steer Davies Gleave, London.

Stern, N., 2010. A Blueprint for a Safer Planet: How We can Save the World and Create Prosperity. Vintage Books.

SUGAR, 2011. SUGAR project deliverable. In: Dablanc, L. (Ed.), SUGAR: City logistics best practices: a handbook for authorities. European Regional Development Fund, Bologna.

Sundarakani, B., de Souza, R., Goh, M., Wagner, S.M., Manikandan, S., 2010. Modeling carbon footprint across the supply chain. Int. J. Prod. Econ. 128 (1), 43–50.

Tavasszy, L., 2008. In: Freight Modeling: An Overview of International Experiences (with Discussion). TRB Conference: Freight Demand Modelling: Tools for Public-Sector Decision Making. Transportation Research Board, Washington D.C., pp. 47–55.

TRT—Trasporti e Territorio, 2010. Directorate-general for internal policies: policies department B: structural and cohesion policies: transport and tourism. In: Maffii, S., Pastori, E., Galli, G., Moizo, A. (Eds.), Logistics as an instrument for tackling climate change study. European Parliament, Brussels.

Tsekeris, T., Tsekeris, C., 2011. Demand forecasting in transport: overview and modeling advances. Econ. Res. Ekonomska Istraživanja 24 (1), 82–94.

TURBLOG, 2010. TURBLOG project deliverable. In: Timms, P. (Ed.), Deliverable 1: a worldwide overview on urban logistic interventions and data collection techniques. European Commission FP7, Lisbon.

UIC, CER, UNIFE, 2007. Rail Freight? What the Admission of Mega-trucks, Paris. International Union of Railways (UIC), the Community of European Railways and Infrastructure Companies (CER), and the European Rail Industry (UNIFE).

UIC, CER, UNIFE, 2014. Mega-Trucks Versus Rail Freight?Paris. International Union of Railways (UIC), the Community of European Railways and Infrastructure Companies (CER), and the European Rail Industry (UNIFE).

UIRR, 2011. Issuance of the ILU-Code Begins Today. Press release, July, p. 1.

VIAJEO PLUS, 2015. VIAJEO PLUS project deliverable. In: Aditjandra, P., Rosenquist, M., Timms, P. (Eds.), FP7 VIAJEO PLUS deliverable 7.1: best solutions on innovative logistics. European Commission FP7, Gothenburg.

VIAJEO PLUS, 2016. VIAJEO PLUS project deliverable. In: Rosenquist, M., Aditjandra, P., Timms, P., Galindo Leal, A., Chen, H., Chengliang, T. (Eds.), FP7 VIAJEO PLUS deliverable 7.2: global innovative urban logistics R&D and policy trends report. European Commission FP7, Gothenburg.

Vickerman, R.W., 1995. The regional impacts of trans-European networks. Ann. Reg. Sci. 29, 237–254.

Wang, F., Lai, X., Shi, N., 2011. A multi-objective optimization for green supply chain network design. Decis. Supp. Syst. 51, 262–269.

Wiegmans, B., Janic, M., 2018. Analysis, modelling, and assessing performance of supply chains served by long distance freight transport corridors. Int. J. Sustain. Transp. 1–16. https://doi.org/10.1080/15568318.2018.1463419.

Woodburn, A., Whiteing, A., 2010. Transferring freight to "greener" transport modes. In: McKinnon, A. et al., (Ed.), Green Logistics—Improving the Environmental Sustainability of Logistics. Kogan Page, pp. 124–139.

Zito, P., Salvo, G., 2011. Toward an urban transport sustainability index: an European comparison. Eur. Transp. Res. Rev. 3 (4), 179–195.

Zunder, T.H., Aditjandra, P., Islam, D., 2012. In: Europe's freight transport policy, White Paper 2001 to White Paper 2011. Proceedings of the 91st Annual Meeting of the Transportation Research Board, Washington D.C.

Zunder, T.H., Islam, D.M.Z., Mortimer, P.N., Aditjandra, P., 2013. How Far Has Open Access Enabled the Growth of Cross Border Pan European Rail Freight? A case study. Research in Transportation Business & Management.

Zunder, T.H., Aditjandra, P., Islam, D.M.Z., Tumasz, M.R., Carnaby, B., 2016. Urban freight distribution. In: Bliemer, M.C.J., Mulley, C., Moutou, C.J. (Eds.), Handbook on Transport and Urban Planning in the Developed World. Edward Elgar, Cheltenham, UK/Northampton, USA, pp. 106–129.

CHAPTER NINE

Greenhouse Gas Emissions and Transport Planning: Toward a New Era?

Silvio Nocera*,[1], Alberto Dianin[†], Federico Cavallaro*,[†]
*Department of Architecture and Arts, IUAV University of Venice, Venice, Italy
[†]Eurac Research, Institute for Regional Development, Bolzano, Italy
[1]Corresponding author: e-mail address: nocera@iuav.it

Contents

Abstract

Reducing carbon emissions is a relevant aspect that helps achieving sustainability in transport planning. However, most of the mobility plans have not yet adopted a shared methodology to internalize these emissions and to make them one of the parameters

ISSN 2543-0009
https://doi.org/10.1016/bs.atpp.2018.07.009

able to influence the final choices on the policies and measures to be taken. In particular, it is extremely complex to quantify and to assign a unitary economic value to GHG emissions. The present paper dwells upon this issue, presenting the methodologies currently in use and the vast degree of scientific and economic uncertainty that characterizes them. Through an extensive review of the plans and the urban strategies adopted (mostly in Europe), we analyze the current stand of transport policy for carbon emissions, drawing some conclusions and possibly inspiring some food for thought for possible future perspectives to control the effects of this issue in the long run.

Keywords: GHG emissions, Urban mobility planning, Transport measures, Paradigm change

1. INTRODUCTION

In the last 10 years, the international community has increased its efforts in order to reduce greenhouse gas (GHG) emissions from all civil sectors. European countries agreed on new climate and energy targets for the year 2030 (EC, 2014). They include a minimum 40% cut in GHG emissions compared to 1990 levels, the use of at least 27% of renewable energy and the improvement in energy efficiency. At international level, the 21st Conference of the Parties to the United Nations Framework Convention on Climate Change (UN, 2015) set the ambitious objective to limit global warming to less than 2°C, committing participating countries to reduce their GHG emissions accordingly.

The transport sector continues to be one of the main GHG contributors: it counts for roughly 26% of overall GHG emissions in Europe, with an increase by 22% between 1990 and 2014 (EEA, 2016), which makes it the only growing sector. Most of the emissions from transport are produced at urban level, where transport contributes to about 40% of overall emissions (Glaeser and Kahn, 2010). Hence, it is legitimate to think that sustainable urban mobility plans (SUMPs) can play a main role toward their reduction (EU, 2017). The environmental awareness of SUMPs is linked to their capacity to set solid goals in terms of decrease in emissions, to define appropriate measures and to monitor them with accurate evaluations. However, this approach has been found not common in transport planning (Nocera and Cavallaro, 2014): an analysis of selected mobility plans at European level explained the methodological and practical obstacles, which result in a sort of ancillary role assigned to carbon evaluation. Only a limited number of plans mentioned GHGs in the part that describes the expected effects of the measures. Hence, mobility plans were found still far from a real inclusion of the carbon component.

In some terms, this chapter may be seen as the follow-up of that analysis, also according to the changed international framework mentioned above. More precisely, it focuses on the planning process followed by SUMPs, exploring their growing degree of GHG awareness in proposing specific objectives and measures. However, mutatis mutandis, this approach can be easily extended to other transport externalities (e.g., noise and air local pollution, congestion, accidents), thus contributing to include them actively into the planning phase and allowing a fairer evaluation of transport externalities (Ricard-AEA, 2014).

The chapter is structured as follows: after this introduction, Section 2 recaps briefly the main theoretical and practical issues that have led to the difficulties in internalizing the carbon component into the planning phase. A selection of examples confirms this general perspective (Section 3). Section 4 illustrates some recent innovative plans that have included an evaluation of GHG for the selection of the most appropriate measures. Section 4.1, which ends the contribution, is a discussion on possible future perspectives of carbon policy in transport, in order to make it not a niche limited to few experimental plans, but rather a common practice in contemporary transport planning.

2. THEORETICAL DIFFICULTIES IN DEALING WITH GHG EMISSIONS MOBILITY PLANS AND GHG EMISSIONS

The inclusion of a fair carbon evaluation in urban mobility plans is a complex issue, based on two main phases. The first one is the estimation of the quantity of GHG that is expected to be reduced, according to the specific transport measures that are to be introduced. The second phase is the economic valuation of the carbon social benefit deriving from such reduction. Each of the two phases is characterized by the presence of several uncertainties,[a] which make traditional methods of evaluation not efficient and do not allow a proper inclusion of this component into the appraisal. The interval of the unitary values found in the scientific literature is incredibly vast, ranging from −10.00 to 7243.73 US$/tC (Tol, 2013) and it does not allow a proper assessment of the impacts. As a consequence, mobility

[a] In Nocera et al. (2018), we have proposed a taxonomy that identifies three main groups of uncertainties. They are, respectively, the technical, economic and decisional ones and affect the decisional-making process noticeably. Interested readers may refer to this paper for a further discussion about this theme.

plans generally include GHG reduction as one of the overall goals, but do not quantify and evaluate the impacts of specific measures.

To overcome this issue, a dynamic approach is required, which does not aim at forecasting the future condition, but rather at developing strategies to face the assumption that future is largely uncertain. In this framework, a compromise between analytical and intuitive approaches has to be achieved. The development of alternative scenarios may be a valid solution for these problems (Vanston and Vanston, 2004). A scenario is not a forecast of the future condition, but rather a "representation of visions/images of the future and courses of development organised in a systematic and consistent way" (EC, 2008). A scenario is based on given hypotheses, which are crossed with the initial situation, thus leading to the future sequence of events that the hypotheses imply. In this sense, scenarios can be seen not as a static snapshot of future condition, but rather as a logical consequence of events (Banister, 2004). For GHG purposes, a carbon cost-benefit approach can be proposed (Fig. 1).

This approach can be a valid solution to deal with GHG emissions in mobility plans; nevertheless, its adoption is still rather limited, as witnessed by the numerous examples of mobility plans presented in the next subsection.

3. PRACTICAL CONSEQUENCES FOR MOBILITY PLANS

This section defines the carbon approach adopted by different mobility plans in selected European countries, proposing a clustering operation according to different geographical contexts. Together with the next section, the aim is to show differences between old and more recent SUMPs in terms of inclusion of the GHG component. In this section, samples deal only marginally with carbon issues, despite their theoretical initial interest for the topic. An analysis at the national scale is here proposed for those countries where SUMPs or equivalent forms of plans have become—or are becoming—a widespread tool, including France, UK, Germany, Austria and Italy. Some examples from Eastern and Northern Europe and extra-European contexts are grouped into three general clusters, without national distinction. In the first case, Eastern Europe SUMPs (even though available) are not as common as in the previous cases. In the second case, plans adopted in Northern Europe present common aspects. In the last case, the difference between the European context and other continents (where SUMPs are not adopted) is sufficient to reveal a different approach. Even if this analysis does

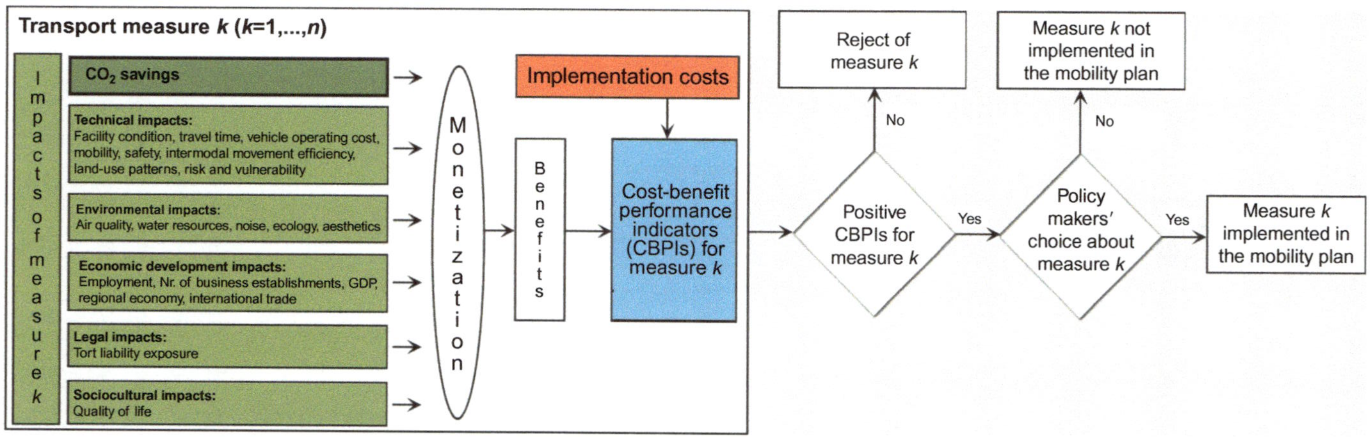

Fig. 1 A carbon cost-benefit approach to deal with GHG emissions in mobility plans. *Source: Nocera S., Tonin S., Cavallaro F., 2015a. Carbon estimation and urban mobility plans: opportunities in a context of austerity. Res. Transport. Econ. 51, 71–82. doi: 10.1016/j.retrec.2015.07.009.*

not claim to be comprehensive, it represents an exemplificative picture of the current condition of European mobility plans and some extra-European tools, with reference to GHG emissions.

3.1 France

In France, the *Plan de Déplacements Urbains* (PDUs) is a mandatory form of mobility planning for all cities with more than 100,000 inhabitants, while for smaller cities it is realized on a voluntary basis. PDUs have the main objective to coordinate the different transport modes and to promote more sustainable solutions of mobility. To reach this general target several actions are suggested, regarding different spheres, such as the management of road traffic, the development of sustainable public transport solutions, the regulation of parking, the improvement or development of information systems and integrated ticketing and the regulation of freight transport. However, these plans do not have to indicate to which extent these measures can contribute to the abatement of GHG emissions. The PDU of Paris (CRI, 2012) tries partially to fill this gap, by including an annex with an analysis of the past trends about pollutant emissions, including also GHGs. Nevertheless, this past trend is not extended to future forecasts. The only mention of future emissions pertains to the reduction of unitary emissions from cars by the improvement of the vehicle performances. Indeed, this is a technological aspect, which is valid for each context and it is not part of a specific territorial analysis. Other PDUs confirm a similar approach: the PDUs of Lille Metropole, valid from 2010 to 2020 (Lille Métropole Communauté urbaine, 2011), and Strasbourg (Strasburg.eu and Communautè Urbaine, 2012), indicate only very general objectives (−40% of GHG reduction in the former case, −24% by 2025 in the latter one), without any description of the related measures, nor a quantitative explanation regarding how to reach this goal.

3.2 United Kingdom

In the United Kingdom, the attention given to carbon emissions is often extensive in the first part of the documents, when the general challenges are identified and the objectives of the plan are set. On the other hand, GHG emissions become a secondary aspect, when this issue has to be addressed practically. Examples of this approach are given by the Local Transport Plan 2015–31 for the Oxfordshire (Oxfordshire County Council, 2015a), the Cambridgeshire Local Transport Plan for 2011–31

(Cambridgeshire County Council, 2015) and the Nottingham Local Transport Plan: Strategy 2011–26 (Nottingham City Council, 2011). In the case of the Oxfordshire, the plan contains a chapter that deals with the reduction of emissions, by proposing several measures considered useful for this aim, as minimizing the need to travel, increase walking and cycling, influencing travel choice, promoting low emission vehicles and reducing the foot print of the plan's operations. However, this list does not include any numerical contribution. Even the integrative Strategic Environmental Assessment (Oxfordshire County Council, 2015b) does not contain any quantitative estimation about carbon abatements. The plan for the Cambridgeshire and the Nottingham Local Transport Plan (NLTP; Nottinghamshire County Council, 2011) presents a similar structure; it can be even considered emblematic. Being composed by two documents (the Local Transport Plan Strategy 2011–26) and the Implementation Plan (first version: 2011–15; second version: 2015–18), it covers the whole county and is valid from April 1, 2011 to March 31, 2026. In addition, the County Council contributes with further thematic assessments, such as the Strategic Environmental Assessment. NLTP offers preliminary relevant room to the issue of GHG emissions: the reduction of carbon emissions is even defined as being at the "heart of this strategy." A change toward more sustainable and greener modes is encouraged, since road transport is found to contribute for 21% of total GHG emissions in UK. A specific section of the document ("Low Carbon and Resilient Transport") is devoted to this topic, presenting four potential strategies to reduce carbon emissions: to influence and reduce travel demand, to improve operational efficiency, to use sustainable cars, and to improve transport resilience. Given such premises, a wide discussion about the carbon implications deriving from the different measures should be the logical consequence. However, the plan does not provide any quantitative information regarding the expected GHG reduction according to the different strategies. The only available data deal with previous measurements of specific interventions, such as the mention of 774 tons of CO_2 saved thanks to the use of three new ethanol busses. Not surprisingly, the final part of the plan, which sets the outcomes, re-introduces GHG issues in a very generic way, proposing the reduction of carbon emission, without specifying the quantities. The last Annual Monitoring Report implemented by the City Council (Nottingham City Council, 2017), which is an integrative part of the plan, points out the general trend regarding carbon emissions from transport. The survey shows that from 2011 to 2016 carbon emissions have only partially decreased until 2013, but the value registered in 2016 is quite similar to the 2011 values (66,000 against 67,000 tons). This evaluation confirms the discrepancy between the intentions expressed in the plan and the actual carbon efficiency of the measures. Obviously, results cannot be interpreted only as a consequence of the initial lack of quantitative data, but undoubtedly the absence of a structured approach to address the issue has contributed to this condition.

3.3 Germany

In Germany, mobility plans propose commonly the reduction of GHG emissions as one on the main goals, sometimes providing also the targets for the long-term period. These general targets are sometimes matched with specific policies or scenarios that provide quantitative information, even if with a limited extension. Our analysis has taken into account the Urban Transport Development Plan 2025 for the city of Berlin StEP (Senatsverwaltung für Stadtentwicklung und Umwelt, 2014), the Sustainable Urban Mobility Plan Bremen 2025 (Freie Hansestadt Bremen, 2008), the Frankfurt Urban Development Report (Stadt Frankfurt am Main, 2012), the Hamburg Mobility Plan (Freie und Hansestadt Hamburg, 2012), the Hannover Masterplan Mobilität 2025 (Landeshauptstadt Hannover, 2011), the Mobilität 2020 (Stadt Leipzig, 2013), and the Transport Development Plan of Munich (City of Munich, 2006). The SUMP of Bremen is a significant example. This plan provides a wide framework of objectives, including the reduction of GHG emissions, the analyses of the current situation with many different focuses (transport modes, urban structure, parking demand, walking and cycling behavior, etc.). Then, it builds five different scenarios within a framework of evaluation based on 16 parameters (including emissions and noise). However, carbon emissions are joint with local air pollutants and no quantitative figures are proposed to justify the appropriateness of a given scenario to the paradigm of sustainability. In the plan of Berlin, the issue of GHG emissions is explicitly cited and analyzed. The role of the air transport is considered crucial to the overall emissions since this sector increased its GHG emissions by 160% between 1990 and 2007. Considering this fact, the plan underlines the difficulties to control the negative effects of this mode on the territory of its own competence. At the same time, StEP shows a high awareness about historical trends of other modes, highlighting that GHG emissions by the road and rail traffic decreased between 1990 and 2007, respectively, by 7% and 40%. In addition, a general forecast is also proposed, which consists in an expected reduction of emissions: from the ca. 2.6 Mio tons in 2006 to 1.6 Mio tons in 2025.

This overall target is supported by the introduction (and description) of measures that can contribute to the trend registered so far, as the increasing of e-mobility, the enforcement of multimodality and alternative transport modes and the optimized management of the local traffic—the latter is expected alone to obtain a reduction of emissions by 20%. However, all these measures are described only from a very general and theoretical perspective, without specifications about how such data are obtained.

3.4 Austria

In the neighboring Austria, the plan of Vienna STEP 2025 (Urban Development Vienna, 2014), was adopted by the City Council in 2014. Developed according to the Climate Protection Programme (City of Vienna, 2010), it aims at including several aspects: fairness, healthiness, compactness, eco-friendliness, robustness and efficiency. The last three aspects are strictly connected with the abatement of GHG emissions. Some quantitative aspects are included, as the general goal to decrease carbon emissions by 20% in 15 years, passing from 2.1 Mio tons in 2010, year used as benchmark, to 1.7 Mio tons in 2025. This objective is considered reachable thanks to the growth of cycling and shared forms of transport: indeed, by 2025 80% of householders is expected to own a bike, 40% of them will have a bike-sharing station within 300 m, and 50% of them has a car-sharing station within 500 m. These forecasts are supported by the historical trend of carbon emissions, which has shown a constant increase in emissions until 2005 (1999: 1871 kt, 2005: 2219 kt), followed by a slow but constant decrease (2010: 2141 kt, 2011: 2072 kt and 2012: 2062 kt). Compared to the previous mobility plan (Winkel, 2006), the updated version seems more aware about environmental issues, even if the evaluations remain quite general and are not related to specific measures.

3.5 Italy

In Italy, the old *Piano Strategico per la Mobilità Sostenibile* of Rome (Comune di Roma, 2009) does not ignore the environmental issues, but at the same time it does not provide any contribution regarding GHG emissions. It proposes a scenario based on the simplistic hypothesis of the cars circulating in future, and no relationship between measures and results is included. Anyway, currently the new SUMP of Rome is under development and new changes may be required (Roma Capitale, 2018). The condition of Pescara is different. In this city, a PUMS (Comune di Pescara, 2017) has been recently developed and approved. The plan proposes three general strategic aims (including the improvement of the environmental quality) and a list of specific objectives for each of them, including the reduction of air pollution. This approach confirms a general awareness about the theme; at the same time, the plan deals with this issue only partially, since no quantitative forecasts are provided. Similarly, the PUMS of Turin (Città di Torino, 2010) was adopted in 2011, and it should have been sided by periodic observations on its effects (including those regarding carbon emissions). However, these observations are practically integrated neither by a forecast of future results nor by quantitative consequences. At the moment, several Italian municipalities are developing new PUMS (about 60 all over the country; Italian PUMS observatory). This opens new possibilities for a more coherent inclusion of environmental aspects.

3.6 Eastern Europe

In the countries of Eastern Europe the condition is rather similar. The Budapest Transport Development Strategy (BMT) 2014–30 (BKK Centre for Budapest Transport, 2014) is developed by the Centre for Budapest Transport (BKK), and is sided by the Strategic Environmental Assessment, which evaluates the consistency between the environmental objectives of the city and the indications proposed by the BMT. The development strategy presents a method (based on a problem tree) that is clear and straightforward. Firstly, a wide analysis of the current condition is presented, including the GHG emissions. Secondly, a general goal is set, which expresses the desirable role of transport in the next years. Thirdly, strategic objectives are identified; among them achieving a liveable urban environment. Finally, four main areas of intervention are listed: more connections, attractive vehicles, better services, and efficient governance. Among them, only the second area deals (even though in a marginal way) with GHG emissions, considering the effects granted by a renovation of the vehicular fleet. Another example is the St. Petersburg Transport Strategy for 2011–25 (Russian Federation, 2011). In 2011, the transport in St. Petersburg was perceived as inadequate compared to the standards of the main European cities, because of the high levels of congestion, the lack of quantity and quality of PT, and the huge environmental and safety impacts produced: it has been estimated that transport was responsible for 80% of pollutant gasses produced by the city. However, the strategy for reducing air and noise pollution is based on the generic principle of transport efficiency, with consequent beneficial environmental effects. As a matter of fact, any quantitative evaluations are missing. The last example is "The transportation system of Warsaw: sustainable development strategy up to the year 2015 and successive years" (Capital city of Warsaw, 2010), adopted by the Capital City of Warsaw City Council. This plan represents one of the first updated tools for the management of transport in Poland. A SWOT analysis identifies the main issues and field of action, but in this tool no specific mention about carbon issues is provided.

3.7 Northern Europe

In the countries of Northern Europe, a specific attention to climate issues may be seen; the cities of Malmö (SUMP of Malmö; Malmö stad, 2016), Helsinki (Helsinki city plan – Vision 2050; City of Helsinki, 2013), and Stockholm (Urban Mobility Strategy; City of Stockholm, 2012) are significant examples. In the case of Stockholm, the Urban Mobility Strategy is sided by the action plan for climate and energy 2010–20 (City of Stockholm, 2010). This document represents a positive example, including both historical trends, and expected future results, fixing the target of reducing GHG emissions by 3.0 tons per capita by 2015 thanks to strategical actions and technologic developments. On the other hand, the mobility plan considers environmental issues among the initial targets, aiming at reducing road traffic emissions by 30% by 2030, and at reaching a traffic free from fossil fuel by 2050. These ambitious goals are supported by a strong vision about the future development of the city, but not supported by an estimation of the GHG contribution deriving from the adoption of the measures.

3.8 Extra-European countries

Finally, some experiences from the extra-European context allow a broader understanding of the phenomenon, even in those countries where GHG emissions and mobility have not often been object of dedicated analyses. In this international context, several examples of plans can be mentioned, which are characterized by a lack of operational aspects related to GHG emissions. Obviously the analysis can be only emblematic of a general approach and could be extended also to other contexts (e.g., China, USA). This absence of attention to carbon emissions is particularly evident and mismatched in cities that are known for paying high attention to the transport initiatives. Singapore, for instance, has developed its Land Transport Masterplan (Land Transport Authority of Singapore, 2013), reserving limited space to the policies that should increase the awareness of citizens regarding environmental issues. The main initiative proposed is the update of the Carbon Emissions-based Vehicle Rebate, which assigns to new cars with emission rate lower than 160 g CO_2/km the minimum Additional Registration Fee (ARF) available for their vehicular category; while for the ones with emission rate higher than 211 g CO_2/km, a proportional higher ARF is set. In South Africa, the Comprehensive Integrated Transport Plan 2017–20 of Cape Town (TDA Cape Town, 2017) presents a similar approach: quantitative and economic evaluations are missing and only a brief part is dedicated to emissions (i.e., by proposing the renovation of PT feet with electric busses, and the growing share of cycling and walking). A higher attention is considered for long-term strategies, but still without any numeric value. A third example is provided by the Canadian city of Toronto. The Transportation Master Plan Report (City of Toronto, 2017) reserves a low attention to GHG emissions, without any information regarding its active inclusion and quantification. Indeed, this tool focuses mainly on specific measures such as street network development, transversal street sections, transit transport, cycling, walking, traffic analysis, but no relations with their carbon implications are provided. In this case, GHG reduction is even not considered as one of the general objectives of the plan.

Most of the examples described in this section share a vague approach toward the issue of GHG emissions (Table 1). This condition makes their inclusion into urban mobility plans complicated and makes even harder the construction of a consistent process from the initial assumptions (which often consider carbon emissions as a main objective) to the concrete actions that have to be adopted. However, the increasing global importance of this issue is slowly suggesting a change of paradigm, as visible from some recent cases presented in the next section.

4. A DEVELOPING TREND IN URBAN MOBILITY PLANS

The international efforts to reduce carbon emissions (recalled in the introduction) together with the increased awareness of the civil society have recently produced some consequences in the transport field, also at the local scale. Indeed, the ancillary condition of GHG emissions shown in the previous section has been slowly replaced by alternative approaches. This section presents some case studies that in the last 5 years have tried to address carbon issues with a more rigorous methodology, in most cases based on alternative scenarios.

Table 1 An Overview of Selected Mobility Plans and Their Inclusion of GHG Evaluations

				GHG Analysis		
Country	**City or Region**	**Adoption**	**Expected Validity**	**Past Values**	**General Forecast**	**Contribution of Measures**
Austria	Vienna	2014	2014–25	✓	✓	~
Canada	Toronto	2017	2017–31	~	✗	✗
France	Paris	2012	—	✓	✗	~
France	Lille	2010	2010–20	✓	✓	✗
France	Strasburg	2012	2012–20	✓	✓	✗
Germany	Bremen	2008	2008–25	~	~	~
Germany	Berlin	2014	2014–25	✓	✓	~
Hungary	Budapest	2014	2014–30	✓	~	~
Italy	Rome	2009	—	~	~	✗
Italy	Pescara	2017	—	~	~	✗
Italy	Turin	2011	—	✓	✗	✗
Poland	Warsaw	2011	2010–25	~	✗	✗
Russia	St. Petersburg	2011	2011–25	~	✗	✗
Singapore	Singapore	2013	2030	~	~	~
South Africa	Cape Town	2017	2017–20	~	~	✗
Sweden	Stockholm	2012	2010–20	✓	~	~
UK	Oxfordshire	2015	2015–31	~	✗	✗
UK	Nottingham	2011	2011–26	✓	~	✗

Legend: ✓: complete or almost complete info; ~: partial info; ✗: absent or almost absent info.

4.1 The CHP 2025 of Copenhagen

The CHP 2025 Climate Plan of Copenhagen was adopted by the City Council in 2012 (The City of Copenhagen, 2012a), and updated in 2016 with data regarding registered trends (in the period 2012–16) and relative fixed projections. It is in line with the well-known tradition of the city to include environmental aspects, thanks to dedicated tools such as the Copenhagen Climate Plan (The City of Copenhagen, 2009), the eldest case presented here. Both the cited documents aim at making the city carbon neutral by

2025. In this framework, the mobility plays a crucial role, confirmed by the important space reserved to it in the CHP 2025 Climate Plan, and by numerous initiatives, such as the "City of Cyclist" (The City of Copenhagen, 2013) and the Bicycle strategy 2011–25 (The City of Copenhagen, 2012b). Focusing on the last version of the CHP 2025 (updated in 2016), the plan confirms a constant decreasing trend in emissions (The City of Copenhagen, 2016): if in 2005 emissions amounted to about 2.3 Mio tons, in 2015 they decreased to about 1.0 Mio tons. To this historical data, the plan adds a solid estimation of future targets and expected decreases. Indeed, by 2025 it is expected that mobility will contribute to the overall carbon reduction by 11% (equal to −135,000 tons of GHG emitted). This aim is reachable thanks the initiative "green mobility," where four main fields should contribute to the overall goal with a fixed percentage of the total: "City of Cyclist," 30%; "New fuels," 18%; "Public transport," 22%; "ITS and mobility planning"; 30%. Cycling is considered the best measure to reduce GHG emissions (−40,000 tons per year compared to the levels of 2010). This, in turn, generates a reduction of car as favorite transport mode from 34% to 25%. Alternative fuels such as electricity and hydrogen may contribute to a reduction of 30,000 tons. PT and Intelligent Traffic Control (ITC) will guarantee a further reduction of 30,000 and 35,000 tons, respectively: the former thanks to a growing use (+20%) and environmental-friendly technologies; the latter thanks to traffic management, optimization of traffic signals and eco-driving. These features (summarized in Table 2) make Copenhagen an important reference in dealing with carbon issues.

Table 2 Decrease in GHG Emission by 2025 in Copenhagen Thanks to Four Mobility Initiatives

Copenhagen CHP—Year 2025			
Field	**Expected Consequences**	**Expected Decrease in GHG Emissions**	
City of Cyclist	35% of work and study commutes by bike. Reduction of car share from 34% to 25%	−40,000 t CO_2	−30%
New fuels	Both light and heavy vehicles adopting new fuels (about 30/40% of total)	−30,000 t CO_2	−18%
Public transport	+20% of PT share. Growing environmental-friendly technologies	−30,000 t CO_2	−22%
ITS and planning	Traffic management. Optimization of traffic signals. Eco-driving	−35,000 t CO_2	−30%

4.2 PMU of Barcelona

The Urban Mobility Plan of Barcelona (Ajuntament de Barcelona, 2013), valid from 2013 to 2018, is the second eldest case presented and can be considered as a pioneering experience. As declared by the Agencia de Ecología Urbana de Barcelona (2012), its main focus is the sustainability. The solution found to reach this goal is the implementation of the "Superblocks" (defined as a new model of mobility that reshapes the typical road network), and the compliance with European regulatory parameters of environmental quality. Therefore, for this plan, the concept of sustainability covers a wide range of qualitative and quantitative aspects, including the town design. The plan is based on the definition of three mobility scenarios, which represent different strategies. The first scenario (E_S1) focuses on the urban-shape theme of the Superblocks. The use of this grid determines the new form of PT service and generates more pedestrian areas inside the Superblocks themselves; the consequence is a decrease by 14% of private vehicles. The second scenario (E_S2) introduces also the requirement of respecting the European standards regarding air quality in all measurement stations of the city. To achieve this standard, a decrease by 30% of private mobility has to be obtained. Finally, the scenario E_S3 adds a further condition: a higher technological development of vehicles by the year 2018. Including this parameter, the percentage of GHG reduction by private vehicles decreases to 21%, since this development covers a compensatory role. Moreover, a different modal share is assigned to every scenario. For each of them, different quantitative results are provided, including those regarding GHG emissions. According to these results, the third one (E_S3) is considered as the most reliable one and consequently it is adopted as basis for the PMU.

First, the overall expected decrease (22.6% compared to 2011) is declared. Subsequently, a specific analysis of Superblock is carried out. The emissions of CO_2 forecasted for the year 2017 are equal to 121,423 kg/day, significantly lower than those registered in the year 2013 (156,011 kg/day). This expectation in the decrease is partially due to the technologic development of vehicles foreseen by the scenario E_S3, and by the different number of kilometers covered by vehicles with the new configuration. A final comprehensive assessment of the impacts on the environment is proposed by the Plan, with a sub-section dedicated to carbon emissions (2.7.1). To calculate them, the Corinair/Copert model (Emisia, 2018) is used, so as to assign to each vehicular category a consumption and emission rate (kg CO_2/km). Furthermore, to make the assessment more precise, the vehicular fleet is organized according to the different types of fuels and euro classes. For the scenario

Table 3 GHG Emissions Forecasted by 2017 in the Scenarios Proposed by the PMU of Barcelona

PMU of Barcellona—Year 2017			
Scenario	**Variation of Private Vehicles (Relative Value) %**	**GHG Emissions (Absolute Value) t CO_2/1000 km**	**Emission (Relative Value) %**
E_S1	−14%	669	−13.7%
E_S2	−30%	537	−30.8%
E_S3	−21%	608	−21.6%
Registered data (year 2017)	+2.1%	Not available	Same as in 2014

E_S1 (−14% of private vehicle share), the amount of CO_2 emissions is 669 t/1000 km; for the E_S2 (−30%), 537 t/1000 km; and for the E_S3 (−21%), 608 t/1000 km (Table 3). Each emission value is displayed in a diagram that shows the share of each vehicular class according to the fuel. These expected figures regarding the modal share can be compared to registered values. The report *Dades bàsiques de mobilitat* (Ajuntament de Barcelona, 2017) showed for the year 2017 an increase in the use of private vehicles equal to 2.1% compared to 2013, with consequences in terms of growth of GHG emissions. This difference between forecasted and registered values reveals some difficulties of SUMPs in achieving effective results. In this case, such figures are due to difficulties in applying the measures planned, which are the basis of the scenarios (e.g., the Superblock model is still an on-going process).

4.3 SUMP 2025plus of Dresden

The mobility plan of Dresden, adopted in 2014 (Landeshauptstadt Dresden, 2014) is carried out by the city of Dresden jointly with the local Environmental Office. This last body has been involved in order to address the issues regarding GHG emissions, air quality and noise pollution. The objectives of the SUMP assign a prominent role to the environmental guidelines proposed by the clean air law (as regards the limits of GHG emissions), by the EU Environmental Noise Directive, the City of Dresden Clean Air Plan, the City of Dresden 2030 Integrated Energy and Climate Protection Concept, and The Noise Reduction Master Plan (Landeshauptstadt Dresden, 2014). This legislative framework determines four general criteria that characterize the SUMP. One of them is specifically referred to the environment, since it proposes the achievement and maintenance of a high level of sustainability by rising the efficiency of integrated transport systems and by reducing the use on natural rescues. Subsequently, some measurable criteria are proposed for the year 2025, in order to make the objectives quantifiable:

- The modal share of sustainable transport modes has to reach at least 59% of all movements.
- The road traffic should be lower than that forecasted in the scenario "Baseline forecast 2025."
- The road traffic of the central ring should be lower than in "Baseline forecast 2025" at least by 5%.
- In 2025, the GHG emissions produced by road traffic should be lower by 30% than in 2010.

The SUMP elaborates five different scenarios (Table 4) and chooses the one that fits better with the specific criteria mentioned above. The first and second scenarios propose, respectively, the absence of the SUMP (Baseline forecast 2025) and the inclusion of only some measures proposed by the

Table 4 Scenarios Proposed by the Plan of Dresden to Achieve the Main Objectives

Dresden—SUMP 2025plus

Expected Results of Each Scenario for the Objectives Set by the Plan (Relative Value)					
Objective	**Baseline**	**Anyway**	**Scenario A**	**Scenario B**	**Scenario C**
The modal share of sustainable transport modes has to reach at least 59% of all movements	n.a.	60.7%	60.0%	63.2%	66.6%
The road traffic should be lower than that forecasted in the scenario "Baseline forecast 2025"	n.a.	−0.3%	+12.5%	−4.9%	−7.2%
The road traffic of the central ring should be lower than in "Baseline forecast 2025" at least by 5%	n.a.	−3.1%	+4.3%	−1.7%	−7.5%
In 2025, the GHG emissions produced by road traffic should be lower by 30% than in 2010	−16.5%	−16.8%	−6.1%	−20.6%	−33.1%

authorities responsible for road-building (Anyway case 2025). The others include a broader implementation of transport measures. "Scenario A" adds some measures regarding new road and PT infrastructures; "Scenario B" focuses on the short-range mobility in order to save environmental resources; "Scenario C" is a further improvement of the previous scenarios, assuming an important change in citizens' travel behavior, due to higher mobility costs, greater environmental awareness and changed lifestyles. A quantitative analysis of GHG emissions is then carried out. Forecasted traffic trends of motorized vehicles feed this estimation, based on data collected by more than 60 measurements conducted since 1994. Future traffic estimations are proposed, and combined with emission factors provided by HBEFA 3.1 (Infras, 2017). Compared to the current levels, the first scenario "Baseline forecast 2025" grants a saving of emissions by 16.5% in 2025, higher than the "Anyway forecast 2025" (16.8%) and scenario A (6.1%), but lower than the scenario B (20.6%), and C (33.1%). This analysis is matched with other specific objectives, in order to find out the ones that provide the best results at the aggregate level.

The result of this analysis is a comparative table that crosses the scenarios with objectives and measures, revealing how much each scenario satisfies all the five objectives and how easily they can be implemented. At the end of this process, the City Council of Dresden has chosen the scenario B as basis for its SUMP (equal to −20.6% of GHG reduction). Despite the lower score obtained, if compared to the scenario C, it has been found out that this result is influenced by a behavioral prediction considered not directly controllable. This approach, even if it has not selected the most virtuous plan in terms of GHG emissions, has taken them into account as one of the main criteria of the plan.

4.4 PUMS of Milan

The *Piano Urbano della Mobilità Sostenibile* (PUMS) of Milan (Comune di Milano, 2015a) has been implemented in the year 2015 with the active involvement of the local municipality and Agency for Mobility, Environment and Territory. This PUMS gives large attention to GHG evaluation, being part of a specific section (8.6) dedicated to the improvement of environmental sustainability. Four macro objectives are proposed, in order to cover wide and conceptual fields: sustainable mobility; equity, safety and social inclusion; environmental effectiveness; innovation and economic efficiency. The decrease in GHG emissions produced by mobility is explicitly associated to the third one. As in other plans described in this section, the development of some alternative scenarios contributes to understand the implications deriving from their adoption. This process has been flanked by the elaboration of a sustainable environmental assessment (Comune di Milano, 2015b). To elaborate the scenarios, several technical elements have been taken into account: besides the four objectives mentioned above, also the contributions arisen from the participatory approach, the legislative framework, the current condition and forecasts regarding the transport demand and supply, the use of a cost-benefit analysis to evaluate the effectiveness, efficiency and equity of each proposed action. Differently from other contexts, the plan has followed a process of evaluation of the single measures, which only subsequently are combined into two main scenarios. The first one is called "Reference Scenario" and simulates a standard development based on the current trends, while the other one is the plan scenario, which collects those measures that have been considered more appropriate. The analysis of the actions is performed by dividing them into four thematic clusters: actions for the development of the infrastructures and transport services; actions that aim to improve the efficiency of the PT (e.g., average speed and frequency); actions that develop the quality of the public space and reduce the negative externalities of transport; and actions that try to influence the demand side and the users' behavior. These clusters are evaluated according to different types of future assessments, including their contribution to the reduction of CO_2, CH_4 and NO_2 and in aggregate terms as GHG emissions. Methodologically, GHG estimation excludes beltway traffic, limiting it to the municipal borders. Vehicular distances are then divided in classes of vehicles in function of alimentation, Euro class, engine size, and presence of particulate filters. For each class, emission factors are calculated based on the COPERT4 11.0 model, in line with the process described by the EMEP/EEA Air Pollution Emission Inventory Guidebook (European Environmental Agency, 2016). Urban emissions are expected to decrease by 27% by 2024, while for the outskirts of the city the decrease is lower, −15%. The main lack of this scenario is that no quantitative data referred to the contribution of each measure is proposed. Furthermore, the technical approach brings out some doubts regarding its clarity and the way to address the numerous scientific and economic sources of uncertainty described in Section 2.

4.5 MST of London

The new mobility plan of London (MST) is currently under development (Mayor of London, 2017). A draft of this plan was published in the summer of 2017, followed by two complementary documents named "Mayor's

Transport Strategy: Supporting Evidence Outcomes and Appraisal" (Transport for London, 2017a) and "Mayor's Transport Strategy: Supporting Evidence Challenges & Opportunities" (Transport for London, 2017b) both provided by Transport for London, the authority responsible for the public transport management at metropolitan level. Differently for the UK plans described in Section 3, these documents propose past trends and future perspectives regarding carbon emissions. The plan is very ambitious, aiming at *being on track to be zero emissions by 2050* (Mayor of London, 2017). Accordingly, it fixes as primary objective an overall reduction by 72% of GHG emissions from transport (including road and rail traffic, and excluding aviation) by 2041, compared to the data of 2013. To reach this goal, many measures are first described, and then subsequently taken into account with their expected contribution. The conceptual visions are labeled under the concept of *healthy streets and healthy people*. Several actions are proposed, as ultra-low and zero-emission technologies, transformation of infrastructures and streets, zero-emission PT, zero-emission private and commercial vehicles, strong reductions in emissions of non-road transport sources and changes in citizens' behavior. Measures are then grouped into packages, which provide a specific contribution to the progressive reduction of carbon emissions by 2041 through the definition of specific steps. They match measures with quantitative estimates. More in detail, the first step represents the status quo at the reference year (2013), when an amount of 7 Mio tons produced by road, rail and shipping traffic is estimated. The second step, which considers the adoption of *investments in public transport*, shows a reduction of emissions to about 4.5 Mio tons, while the third phase, which proposes further investments in PT, and the inclusion of measures to shift the demand from car to PT, cycling and walking, reaches about 3.5 Mio tons. Finally, the last step includes the substitution of pollutant vehicles with ultra-low and zero-emission ones, reaching the desired initial goal of 2 Mio tons within 2041 (Table 5).

This result is considered consistent with a more ambitious program, which aims at reaching the carbon neutrality of transport by 2050. To this aim, scenarios previously described are merged with more long-term GHG forecasts developed in the MTS: Supporting Evidence Challenges & Opportunities (Transport for London, 2017b). The contribution of aviation to carbon emissions is expected to remain more or less constant (about 1 Mio tons per year), whereas the railway one will become nearly zero by 2050. Finally, road transport emissions will decrease form the about 6.8 Mio of tons in 2013 to the expected 3.5 Mio in 2050. In the current version, these quantifications are not supported by methodological details.

Table 5 Measures Proposed by the Plan of London to Reduce GHG Emissions by 72% by 2041

London—MST

	Types of Measure	CO_2 Emission Variation (Absolute)	CO_2 Emission Variation (Relative)
1	No measure. Status at the year 2013	0	—
2	Investments in PT (bus and train services in particular) to make them more affordable, accessible and less crowded	−2.5 Mio tons	−35.7%
3	Investments in PT (bus and train services in particular) to make them more affordable, accessible and less crowded	−3.5 Mio tons	−50.0%
	Measures to encourage mode shift from car to PT, walking, cycling		
4	Investments in PT (bus and train services in particular) to make them more affordable, accessible and less crowded	−5.0 Mio tons	−71.4%
	Measures to encourage mode shift from car to PT, walking, cycling		
	Measure to accelerate complete transition to ultra-low and zero-emission vehicles		

Currently, this represents a relevant lack, which can be overcome by the publication of the final version of the document. Despite these lacks, the overall effort of the plan to propose a stronger integration between measures and corresponding consequences in terms of GHG emissions is undoubtedly one of the qualities offered by this approach.

4.6 PUMS of Parma

The *Piano Urbano della Mobilità Sostenibile* (PUMS) of Parma (Comune di Pama, 2017a), approved by the City Council in March 2017, represents an interesting approach for two main reasons. First, it is the first Italian mobility plan combined with a Strategic Environmental Assessment (Comune di Pama, 2017b); second, it is the only example described in this section that refers to a small–medium city (Parma has less than 190,000 inhabitants), thus confirming the applicability of this type of analysis to different urban scales. This plan is based on the construction of three alternative scenarios, each one characterized by specific measures. The most appropriate one as result of a comprehensive evaluation that includes also GHG reduction is the basis for the concrete implementation of the measures. Among the objectives set to evaluate the scenarios, one concerns the environmental quality. Under this general objective, a specific aim (no. 3d) assesses the decrease in GHG emissions resulting from transport. This specific objective is analyzed quantitatively for each scenario (SP0, SP1 and SP2) and compared to the baseline one (SR). More in detail:

- SR is based on the natural evolution of the current situation in absence of the PUMS.
- SP0 is based on the measures proposed by the *Piano Aria Integrato Regionale 2020* (Integrated Regional Air Plan 2020), in order to clean up the air (Regione Emilia-Romagna, 2017).
- SP1 includes a substantial renewal of transport infrastructures, in order to solve the main mobility issues.
- SP2 drives its measures toward the aim of an increasing environmental, social and economic sustainability.

This last scenario has been selected for the plan, since it responds better to the objectives fixed by the local public administration. The concrete measures are then defined. They include the extension of the limited traffic zone, significant investments for renewing the public transport fleet, the development of the cycling routes and infrastructures, of the e-mobility and of alternative forms of transport (e.g. car-sharing and mobility services for schools and companies). The scenario is then evaluated in terms of quantitative decrease in GHG emissions, compared to the SR. Carbon dioxide (CO_2) is chosen as representative for GHGs and considered as one of the environmental indicators, together with PM, VOC, CO and NO_x. The first analysis regards the comparative trend of emissions. Compared to the current condition (year 2016, set at 100%), in 2025 SR shows an increase in emissions by 10%, whereas SP2 reveals a decrease by 2%. For the calculation, different types of vehicle, their average speed and their driving cycles are taken into account to estimate the overall carbon impact. Driving cycles have been developed starting from the European model *TRUST* (TRT, 2016). This methodological process is sided by forecasts about changes in vehicular fleet based on 2015 data provided by the municipality of Parma. Even if results of SP2 show only a limited reduction of GHG emissions, the valuable quality of this plan lies in its consistent approach adopted to include carbon issues. Differently from the experiences recalled in the previous section, the main role assigned to climate change during the definition of the objectives has been coherently extended also during the definition of future scenarios and the selection of the measures to be adopted. More detailed estimations regarding the consistency of each proposed measure, as well as the economic valuation of the emissions saved are still missing; nevertheless, this local plan represents a valid example of a change of paradigm in the way of addressing the carbon issue.

4.7 An Extra-EU overview

In extending the analysis to a broader scale, some preliminary aspects have to be considered. First, the extra-EU panorama is extremely heterogenic. In most of the developing countries, a primary attention to carbon reduction is not yet one of the priorities, since other economic and social targets are normally set (Füssel, 2010). Second, this section is only a selection of a wide and very dynamic framework. No claim for comprehensiveness is given to this analysis, but rather some evidences of a changing condition.

As regards the developing contexts, the metropolitan area of Lagos (Nigeria) is an example of a reality with a growing attention to environmental issues. It has an estimated population of about 22.5 Mio inhabitants in the entire State, and about 16 Mio in the city, and these numbers are expected to more than double by 2050 (Lagos State Government, 2013a). Strategic planning tools are crucial to shape this growth, such as the Lagos development Plan 2025 (Lagos State Government, 2013b) and the STMP Strategic Transport Masterplan 2032 (lagosstate.ng, 2018). This last one has been developed by the Lagos Metropolitan Area Transport Authority, a government agency responsible for transport planning. The main mobility challenges regard the current incapacity of formal PT to cover the growing demand (PT contributes with only 2.75% of daily mobility), and the consequent expansion of spontaneous transport modes. In this context, the main challenge lies in the structure of the mobility itself. Nevertheless, a growing attention to environmental issues is taking place, as well. Focusing on specific solutions, as early as 2009, a first reduction of GHG emissions by 13% (24.7 kt) per year in selected routes was reached thanks to the partial replacement of older busses with a new fleet (The World Bank, 2016). Focusing on planning, the Lagos CO_2 Emissions Assessment Handbook (2010) tries to estimate the GHG contribution. It compares two scenarios to highlight the expected environmental role of the STMP: the first is a no-action scenario ("Business as usual"), which forecasts 10 Mio tons of CO_2 emitted in 2032; the second one includes the actions proposed by the STMP, and foresees an annual amount of about 5 Mio tons. From these quantities, the expected role of the STMP in reducing by 50% the carbon emissions until 2032. Even if partial, the attention given to carbon issues shows the growing awareness on the problem, which seems rather strategic at the national level, since over 50% of the transport GHG emissions in Nigeria are produced by Lagos (Komolafe et al., 2014).

In North America, San Francisco represents a relevant positive example. The San Francisco Transportation Plan (SFTP) 2040 (San Francisco County, 2013) was adopted by the Transportation Authority Board in December 2013; in October 2017 a new update of the plan (2017 SFTP Update Final Report) was published (San Francisco County, 2017), in order to check and revise the direction held by the plan in the previous 4 years. Moreover, the complementary report named Transport Sector Climate Action Strategy—TSCAS (published in its latest version in 2017 by the San Francisco Municipal Transportation Agency) completes the framework of the main documents that deal in an active way with the carbon issue (SFMTA, 2017). San Francisco represents a virtuous example of transport planning, since in 2017 it achieved two main goals proposed by the SFTP in 2013: first, it has reduced its annual GHG emissions by 28% compared to 1990 levels; second, the share of walking, cycling and PT has increased up to 52% of total traffic share. A new goal has been set: to shift 80% of all trips to environmentally sustainable modes by 2030, and to reduce GHG emissions by 80% compared to 1990 levels, by 2050. For this ambitious target, a significant change in modal habits is considered a key point, as well as maximizing the vehicle occupancy rate, using low/zero-emission fuels and reducing total vehicle miles traveled. Also the approach followed by the TSCAS to propose carbon efficient measures is worthy to be mentioned, even if quite general. Firstly, eight main fields are proposed: transit, land use and transport, pricing and congestion management, transportation demand management, complete streets, zero-emission vehicles and infrastructure, and emerging mobility services and tech. Then, each field is further developed, by proposing three concrete measures. Finally, for each of the 24 measures, a synthetic table shows its carbon effectiveness and affordability, with a score from 1 to 3 for both the aspects.

In Asia, the Indian cities of Zivag, Rajkot and Udaipur are worthy to be mentioned. They are involved in a common project named Low Carbon Transport in India (unep.org, 2018), launched in 2010 by UNEP, the United Nations Environment Programme (unenvironment.org). The project aims at designing solutions to develop sustainable transport systems in

Indian cities, by taking into account climate change condition and the requirement of the National Action Plan on Climate Change (Government of India, 2008). The project tries to improve institutional capacities in urban areas, in order to enhance mobility services for local population and lower CO_2 emissions from transport. Focusing on Zivag (city located in the eastern coast of India, with about 1.73 Mio inhabitants), its Low-Carbon Comprehensive Mobility Plan (UNEP, 2014a) covers the period 2011–30. The planning process starts from a data collection that provides the modal share within the city: 52% by feet, 18% by bus, 17% by private vehicle. This results in the baseline scenario, which displays the starting condition at the year 2011 and it is used as basis for the preparation of future forecasts. The first scenario is the Business as Usual (BAU) that considers the development of the current trend until 2030. Other scenarios are based on the combination of four strategies about land use management (LU), public transport improvement (PT), non-motorized transport development (NMT), and new technologies application (TECH; Table 6).

The analysis, carried out using a vehicle kilometers prevision, shows that the BAU scenario increases GHG emissions from 0.94 Mio tons per year in 2011 (with an amount of 1.73 Mio inhabitants) to 4.34 Mio tons per year in 2030 (equal to about +360%) with a forecasted population of about 2.96 Mio. On the other hand, other scenarios achieve a maximum result of 1.5 Mio tons in 2030 (about +59%) with the same demographic trend. This is an interesting result, since, differently form EU plans, a constant increase of GHG emissions is expected in all scenarios, due to the demographic trend of the area. A similar structure, with an active analysis of carbon emissions is included also in the plans of Rajkot and Udaipur (UNEP, 2014a, b, 2015), respectively, developed for the years 2011–31 and 2013–41.

Similarly to the previous section, a final summary is proposed (Table 7), in order to provide an overview of these new trends regarding GHG evaluation.

4.8 Lesson Learnt

The third and fourth sections of this chapter allow a comparison between the traditional mobility plans and some innovative trends that are currently under development. At least at the European level, SUMP has been found as the most appropriate form of plan to deal with GHG emissions, also according to the theoretical framework elaborated by

Table 6 Actions Proposed by the Plan of Zivag and Corresponding GHG Emissions Results by 2030

Zivag—Mobility Plan

			Modal Share			
Scenarios	**Estimated Population (Absolute Value) Mio**	**Vehicles on Road (Absolute Value)**	**Walking, Cycling and PT (Relative Value Compared to 2011) %**	**Private Vehicles (Relative Value Compared to 2011) %**	**Emission (Absolute Value) CO_2 Mio tons**	**Emission (Relative Values Value Compared to 2011) %**
BAU	2.95	1,983,481	67%	33%	4.34	+360%
LU	2.95	1,511,377	75%	25%	2.76	+193%
LU + PT	2.95	957,723	85%	15%	2.39	+154%
LU + PT + NMT	2.95	859,966	87%	13%	2.28	+142%
LU + PT + NMT + TECH	2.95	859,966	87%	13%	1.50	+59%

Table 7 An Overview of New European and Extra-European Trends

Country	City or Region	Adoption	Expected Validity	GHG Analysis		
				Past Values	General Forecast	Contribution of Measures
Denmark	Copenhagen	2012	2012–25	✓✓	✓✓	✓
Germany	Dresden	2014	2014–25	✓	✓	✓✓
India	Zivag	2014	2011–30	✓	✓	✓✓
Italy	Milan	2015	—	✓✓	✓✓	✓
Italy	Parma	2017	—	✓	✓✓	✓✓
Nigeria	Lagos	2015	2015–32	✓	✓	~
Spain	Barcelona	2013	2013–18	✓	✓✓	✓
UK	London	2017	2017–41	✓	✓	✓✓
USA	San Francisco	2013	2013–40	✓✓	✓✓	✓

Legend: ✓✓: very complete info; ✓: complete or almost complete info; ~: partial info.

Wefering et al. (2014). The methodological inclusion of GHG emissions in these plans is a crucial topic, which involves a global scale that is not easily coverable by metropolitan planning (as confirmed by the example of Berlin). On the other hand, GHG quantification is necessary, in order to hold the quantitative objectives set at European level properly (EU, 2014; COM 2014; UN, 2015; EC, 2017). These European targets have caused a fundamental change in the theoretical way to address the carbon issue, even if absolute results may not seem particularly positive. The plan of Dresden is exemplificative in this sense, since the inclusion of GHG evaluation in the plan contributes to the selection of the best overall strategy (even if not the best in terms of GHG reduction). Furthermore, not only the planning aspect but also the monitoring activities are crucial and need to be performed on a regularly basis, since they check the correspondence between forecasts and concrete results.

This approach is even more important considering that the correspondence between the proper quantitative analysis of GHG emissions and the achievement of an actual decrease in emissions is not straightforward (as confirmed by Parma, where in the most virtuous approach emissions are expected to decrease only by 2%). Indeed, the precision of the method does not guarantee the quality of results; it rather aims at identifying more clearly the objectives and the way to reach them. This difficulty in establishing a condition of cause and effect is maybe linked to the elusive borders of the issue and the several sources of uncertainty. Despite this, the availability of active methods that take into account carbon emissions represents the occasion to establish a control (at least partial) on a challenging topic.

5. FUTURE PERSPECTIVES

The effects of GHG emissions, borne by the community primarily in relation to the global warming, determine non-negligible economic effects. However, if we refer to the definition of external costs more rigorously and consider hence the multitude of the effects caused by GHG emissions (Watkiss et al., 2005), the actual value of such emissions tends to be significantly higher. In the updated version of the EU guidelines (Ricard-AEA, 2014), the value of GHG emissions is more than double than in the previous reports (CE Delft et al., 2011; Maibach et al., 2008). This precautionary approach is due to the difficulty of both measuring the effects of carbon pollution on a local scale at an adequate degree of certainty, and of attributing a shared economic value for the tons emitted. The latter effect is also due to the difficulty of directly linking the cause of the carbon production to the effects in terms of directly and indirectly caused damages.

In order to measure and quantify carbon emissions, it can be dealt upon bottom-up and top-down approaches (Nocera et al., 2017; Nocera and Cavallaro, 2016). The former one allows considering each single part of the complex transport system that affect GHG emissions—whether transport activity, fuels, or vehicles. This approach allows linking carbon pollution to the single parts of the process and reveals how any specific change to it would affect carbon production. Particularly, especially during a programming process, it must be considered that reduction of specific emissions is expected through a number of improvements in technology and to the incremental use of intelligent transport systems that should improve traffic conditions—both sets of measures having been designed especially for reducing the effects of primary pollutants. Measuring such progress would require consistent information on which vehicle consumes which fuels and on the exact distance traveled. Such information would allow a good estimation of the carbon pollution for each vehicle, as in our previous literature (Ayyildiz et al., 2017). The margin of uncertainty of this kind of approach may however be significant.

On the one side, a top-down approach would derive overall fuel use from prices and incomes, in some cases also including information on vehicle stock and on its traction system. This may not provide a good understanding of the problems and may also not consider the connections among various important parameters—such as vehicle kilometer and driving style, if not integrated with a bottom-up methodology. On the other side, the potential tools available for the legislator to contest the global warming can be manifold—and not all of them based on the perception of potential damage through monetary instruments. The dissemination of an adequate culture, with preventive educational campaigns, accompanied by the certainty of sanctions at the governmental level, can have potentially greater effects than massive spending aimed at infrastructure improvement and produce concrete results in the low and medium terms.

The massive, recent attention on this topic has allowed the development of a good number of virtuous cases, some of which have been described in Section 4. To further analyze the issue, considerations are needed on the effectiveness of surveys conducted in a situation of high uncertainty. Referring to our previous literature for further considerations (Nocera et al., 2018), and also on the challenges that must be overcome for the successful application of strategies to climate change policy (Nocera et al., 2015a, 2015b), the focus for the creation of a shared future policy seems to be on the identity of the information to be collected and on the methods for analyzing results.[b]

Obtaining information about passenger and freight travel demand, from which to derive carbon pollution with enough degree of certainty, is one of the most intriguing challenges of current transport planning. At the moment, neither the impacts of policies designed to influence transport, nor the policies aimed directly at reducing GHG emissions, can be measured with a high degree of accuracy.

This represents however just a minimal consequence within the carbon issue in transport planning: what would be really needed is a global program of carbon awareness based on the capacity to increase the ability to collect and analyze consistent data on transport activities with carbon purposes. The general framework has been set; the practical methodologies are still under definition. To develop a significant carbon policy, administrations should be able to assess consistently what they do really know at present, what new

[b] The challenging issue of extracting data from social media has been analyzed in Grant-Muller et al. (2015) and Kuflik et al. (2017)

information needs to be gathered on a regular, accurate, reliable, and transparent basis, and eventually how this information can be obtained effectively. The carbon cost-benefit analysis presented in Section 2 may be a helpful tool to this aim.

In a screen of such uncertainty, insights gained from the process of working through shared methods may be primarily beneficial for the creation of a common carbon policy, and possibly a common set of information upon which to base future carbon consideration. This is in fact a global issue: it affects the world globally, and it is caused not only by transport but also by other fields. Such sentiment was echoed in this chapter: the use of multiple and multidisciplinary methods—supported by a careful analysis of the results, by the evaluations of the participants, and the discussion with stakeholders—seems a requirement to deal with, in order to analyze the carbon issue in the present and future times.

REFERENCES

Agencia de Ecología Urbana de Barcelona, 2012. Online at http://www.bcnecologia.net/en/projects/sustainable-urban-mobility-plan-barcelona-2013-2018. (11.02.2018).

Ajuntament de Barcelona, 2013. Sustainable Urban Mobility Plan of Barcelona (2013–2018). Online at http://www.bcnecologia.net/sites/default/files/proyectos/pmu_bcn_2013-2018_proposta.pdf. (11.02.2018).

Ajuntament de Barcelona, 2017. Dades bàsiques de mobilitat Informe 2016. Online at http://mobilitat.ajuntament.barcelona.cat/sites/default/files/DADES-BASIQUES-MOBILITAT16_13.pdf.

Ayyildiz, K., Cavallaro, F., Nocera, S., Willenbrock, R., 2017. Reducing fuel consumption and carbon emissions through eco-drive training. Transport. Res. F: Traffic Psychol. Behav. 46, 96–110. https://doi.org/10.1016/j.trf.2017.01.006.

Banister, D., 2004. Implementing the possible? Plan. Theor. Pract. 5 (4), 499–501. A commentary on the interface paper by Ken Livingstone.

BKK Centre for Budapest Transport, 2014. Balázs Mór Plan. In: Budapest Transport Development Strategy 2014–2030. Online at http://www.eltis.org/sites/default/files/case-studies/documents/bmt_en.pdf. (02.02.2018).

Cambridgeshire County Council, 2015. Cambridgeshire Local Transport Plan 2011–2031. Policies and Strategy. Online at https://ccc-live.storage.googleapis.com/upload/www.cambridgeshire.gov.uk/residents/travel-roads-and-parking/The_Local_Transport_Plan_3%20%281%29.pdf?inline=true. (09.02.2018).

Capital city of Warsaw, 2010. The Transportation System of Warsaw: Sustainable Development Strategy up to the Year 2015 and Successive Years. Online at http://strategiatransportowa.um.warszawa.pl/sites/default/files/pdfs/STRATEGIA_synteza%20ENG.pdf. (10.02.2018).

CE Delft, INFRAS, Fraunhofer-ISI, 2011. External Costs of Transport in Europe. Update Study for 2008. CE Delft, Delft. Available at www.cedelft.eu. (13.12.2016).

Città di Torino, Divisione Infrastrutture e Mobilità, 2010. Piano Urbano della Mobilità Sostenibile. Online at http://www.comune.torino.it/geoportale/pums/cms/images/files/introduzione/PUMS_sintesi_non_tecnica.pdf. (12.02.2018).

City of Helsinki, City Planning Department of Helsinki, 2013. Urban Plan—The New Helsinki City Plan—Vision 2050. Online at https://www.hel.fi/hel2/ksv/julkaisut/yos_2013-23_en.pdf.

City of Munich, Department of Urban Planning and Building Regulation, 2006. Transport Development Plan. Online at http://www.leipzig.de/fileadmin/mediendatenbank/leipzig-de/Stadt/02.6_Dez6_Stadtentwicklung_Bau/66_Verkehrs_und_Tiefbauamt/broschuere_step_analyse__2012.pdf?L=0. (07.02.2018).

City of Stockholm, Environmental and Health Administration, 2010. Stockholm Action Plan for Climate and Energy 2012–2020. Online at http://projects.centralbaltic.eu/images/files/result_pdf/COMBAT_result2_Stockholm.pdf.

City of Stockholm, The City of Stockholm Traffic Administration, 2012. Urban Mobility Strategy. Online at http://international.stockholm.se/globalassets/ovriga-bilder-och-filer/urban-mobility-strategy.pdf.

City of Toronto, ConsumersNext, 2017. Transportation Master Plan Report. Online at https://www.toronto.ca/legdocs/mmis/2017/pg/bgrd/backgroundfile-103947.pdf. (10.02.2018).

City of Vienna, 2010. KLiP II.n The City of Vienna's Climate Protection Programme 2010–2020. Online at https://www.wien.gv.at/english/environment/klip/pdf/klip-brochure.pdf. (14.02.2018).

Comune di Milano, 2015a. Settore Pianificazione, Programmazione e Mobilità. Piano Urbano della Mobilità Sostenibile PUMS di Milano. Online at http://download.comune.milano.it/24_03_2015/Documento%20di%20Piano%20febbraio%202015%20(1427206289866).pdf. (10.02.2018).

Comune di Milano, 2015b. Settore Pianificazione, Programmazione e Mobilità. Valutazione Ambientale Strategica. Rapporto Ambientale. Online at http://download.comune.milano.it/24_03_2015/VAS-Rapporto%20Ambientale%20febbraio%202015%20(1427206355842).pdf?pgpath=/SA_SiteContent/UTILIZZA_SERVIZI/MOBILITA/Pianificazione_mobilita/piano_urbano_mobilita. (10.02.2018).

Comune di Pama, 2017a.Piano Urbano della Mobilità Sostenibile 2015–2025 di Parma. Documento di Piano. Online at https://ssl.comune.parma.it/RicercaAtti/Handlers/VediDocumento.ashx?path=/DDD/1//2017/PD/0000870/201703151047363242112753051_2.PDF&name=2017_PD_0000870_Allegato_3_signed.pdf&logname=2017_PD_0000870_Allegato_3_signed.pdf. (12.02.2018).

Comune di Pama, 2017b. Piano Urbano della Mobilità Sostenibile 2015-2025 di Parma. V.A.S. VALUTAZIONE AMBIENTALE STRATEGICA. Online at https://ssl.comune.parma.it/RicercaAtti/Handlers/VediDocumento.ashx?path=/DDD/1//2017/PD/0000870/20170315104749016116697869_2.PDF&name=2017_PD_0000870_Allegato_5_signed.pdf&logname=2017_PD_0000870_Allegato_5_signed.pdf. (06.02.2018).

Comune di Pescara, 2017. PUMS Piano Urbano della Mobilità Sostenibile. Online at http://versopescara2027.comune.pescara.it/wp-content/uploads/2017/04/PUMS-definitivo.pdf. (07.02.2018).

Comune di Roma, 2009. Assessorato alle Politiche della Mobilità. In: Piano Strategico per la Mobilità Sostenibile. Linee di indirizzo Online at https://www.pumsroma.it/download/filebase/Piano-Strategico-per-la-Mobilita-Sostenibile.pdf.

CRI, Conseil Regional d'Île-de-France, 2012. Île-de-france. plan de déplacements urbains. Conseil Regional d'Île-de-France, Paris. Online at http://debatspublics.iledefrance.fr/sites/default/files/liste_de_fichier_article/pdu.pdf. (06.02.2018).

EC, European Commission, 2008. Joint Research Centre, Institute for Environment and Sustainability, Backcasting approach for sustainable mobility. Office for Official Publications of the European Communities, Luxembourg.

EC, European Commission, 2014. Communication From the Commission to the European Parliament, the Council, the European Economic and Social Committee and the Committee of the Regions. A Policy Framework for Climate and Energy in the Period From

2020 to 2030. Online at: https://eur-lex.europa.eu/legal-content/EN/TXT/PDF/?uri=CELEX:52014DC0015&from=EN. (10.08.2018).

EC, European Commission, 2017. White Paper on the Future of Europe, Reflections and Scenarios for the eu27 by 2025. Brussels, 2017, Online at: https://ec.europa.eu/commission/sites/beta-political/files/white_paper_on_the_future_of_europe_en.pdf. (10.08.2018).

EEA, European Environment Agency, 2016. Climate Change, Impacts and Vulnerability in Europe 2016. An Indicator-Based Report. https://doi.org/10.2800/534806 Luxembourg. Online at http://climate-adapt.eea.europa.eu/metadata/publications/climate-change-impacts-and-vulnerability-in-europe-2016/climate-change-impacts-and-vulnerabilities-2016-thal17001enn.pdf/view. (09.02.2018).

Emisia. (2018) Mission for Environment. Copert. Emisia.com. Online at http://emisia.com/products/copert. (09.02.2018).

EU, European Union, 2014. Analysis of Options to Move Beyond 20% Greenhouse Gas Emission Reductions and Assessing the Risk of Carbon Leakage. Online at http://eur-lex.europa.eu/LexUriServ/LexUriServ.do?uri=COM:2010:0265:FIN:EN:PDF. (03.02.2018).

EU, European Union, 2017. European Urban Mobility. Policy Context. Brussels, March 2017https://doi.org/10.2832/827766 Online at https://ec.europa.eu/transport/sites/transport/files/2017-sustainable-urban-mobility-policy-context.pdf. (08.02.2018).

European Environmental Agency, 2016. EMEP/EEA Air Pollutant Emission Inventory Guidebook 2016. Technical Guidance to Prepare National Emission Inventories. Online at https://www.eea.europa.eu/publications/emep-eea-guidebook-2016/at_download/file.

Freie Hansestadt Bremen, 2008. Sustainable Urban Mobility Plan Bremen 2025. Online at https://www.bauumwelt.bremen.de/sixcms/media.php/13/SUMP_Bremen2025_web.pdf. (13.02.2018).

Freie und Hansestadt Hamburg, 2012. Mobilitätsprogramm 2013. Grundlage für eine kontinuierliche Verkehrsentwicklungsplanung in Hamburg. Online at http://www.hamburg.de/contentblob/4119700/50fd34e0e06432b8ea113bf40cfc6ca7/data/mobilitaetsprogramm-2013.pdf;jsessionid=AD1D2AC5C9B9CF9066DA837E496DE40F.liveWorker2. (10.02.2018).

Füssel, H.M., 2010. How inequitable is the global distribution of responsibility, capability, and vulnerability to climate change: a comprehensive indicator-based assessment. Glob. Environ. Chang. 20 (4), 597–611. ISSN 0959-3780. https://doi.org/10.1016/j.gloenvcha.2010.07.009.

Glaeser, E.L., Kahn, M.E., 2010. The greenness of cities: carbon dioxide emissions and urban development. J. Urban Econ. 67 (3), 404–418.

Government of India, 2008. Prime Minister´s Council on Climate Change. National Action Plan for Climate Change. Online at http://www.cseindia.org/userfiles/National%20Action%20Plan%20on%20Climate%20Change.pdf. (07.02.2018).

Grant-Muller, S.M., Gal-Tzur, A., Minkov, E., Nocera, S., Kuflik, T., Shoor, I., 2015. Enhancing transport data collection through social media sources: methods, challenges and opportunities for textual data. IET Intell. Transp. Syst. 9 (4), 407–417.

Infras—Thinking for Tomorrow, 2017. HBEFA Handbook Emission Factors for Road Transport 3.1/3.2/3.3. Quick reference. Bern, 2017. Online at http://www.hbefa.net/e/help/HBEFA33_help_en.pdf.

Komolafe, A., Adegboyega, S.A., Anifowose, A.Y.B., Akinluyi, F.O., Awoniran, D.R., 2014. Air pollution and climate change in Lagos, Nigeria: need for proactive approaches to risk management and adaption. Am. J. Environ. Sci. 10 (4), 412–423. 2014.

Kuflik, T., Minkov, E., Nocera, S., Grant-Muller, S., Gal-Tzur, A., Shoor, I., 2017. Automating a framework to extract and analyse transport related social media content: the potential and the challenges. Transp. Res. C: Emerg. Technol. 77, 275–291.

Lagos State Government, 2013a. Ministry of Economic Planning & Budget. Online at http://mepb.lagosstate.gov.ng/wp-content/uploads/sites/29/2017/01/FURTHER-ANALYSIS-DEMOGRAPHIC-DATA-2011-TO-2013.pdf. (04.02.2018).

Lagos State Government, 2013b. Toward Reforming Lagos' Transport Sector. Online at https://lagosstate.gov.ng/blog/2017/03/28/towards-reforming-lagostransport-sector/. (06.02.2018).

Land Transport Authority of Singapore, 2013. Land Transport Masterplan 2013. Online at https://www.lta.gov.sg/content/dam/ltaweb/corp/PublicationsResearch/files/Report Newsletter/LTMP2013Report.pdf. (10.02.2018).

Landeshauptstadt Dresden, 2014. Verkehrsentwicklungsplan 2025plus. Online at https://www.dresden.de/de/stadtraum/verkehr/verkehrsplanung/verkehrsentwicklungsplanung/svep/VEP_RT__18_Beschluss_-_Text_Anlagen.pdf. (06.02.2018).

Landeshauptstadt Hannover, 2011. Hannover Masterplan Mobilität 2025. Der Verkehrsentwicklungsplan für die Stadt Hannover. Online at https://www.hannover.de/Leben-in-der-Region-Hannover/Mobilität/Verkehrsplanung-entwicklung/Masterplan-Mobilität-2025. (10.02.2018).

Lille Métropole Communauté urbaine, 2011. Le PDU 2010 > 2020 de Lille Métropole. Online at http://www.lillemetropole.fr/files/live/sites/lmcu/files/contributed/Rebecca/Doc/176651.pdf. (08.02.2018).

Maibach, M.C., Schreyer, D., Sutter, H.P., van Essen, B.H., Boon, R., Smokers, A., Schroten, C., Doll, B., Pawlowska, M., Bak, M., 2008. Handbook on Estimation of External Costs in the Transport Sector Internalisation. Measures and Policies for All external Cost of Transport (IMPACT). Version 1.1. Delft, CE.

Malmö stad, 2016. Sustainable Urban Mobility Plan, Creating More Accessible Malmö. Online at http://malmo.se/download/18.16ac037b154961d0287384d/1491301288704/Sustainable+urban+mobility+plan%252528TROMP%252529_ENG.pdf.

Mayor of London, 2017. Mayor's Transport Strategy. Draft for Public Consultation. Online at https://consultations.tfl.gov.uk/policy/mayors-transport-strategy/user_uploads/pub16_001_mts_online-2.pdf. (03.02.2018).

Nocera, S., Cavallaro, F., 2014. The ancillary role of CO2 reduction in urban transport plans. Transp. Res. Procedia 3, 760–769. ISSN 2352-1465. https://doi.org/10.1016/j.trpro.2014.10.055.

Nocera, S., Cavallaro, F., 2016. Economic valuation of well-to-wheel CO_2 emissions from freight transport along the main transalpine corridors. Transp. Res. Part D: Transp. Environ. 47, 222–236. https://doi.org/10.1016/j.trd.2016.06.004.

Nocera, S., Tonin, S., Cavallaro, F., 2015a. Carbon estimation and urban mobility plans: opportunities in a context of austerity. Res. Transp. Econ. 51, 71–82. https://doi.org/10.1016/j.retrec.2015.07.009.

Nocera, S., Tonin, S., Cavallaro, F., 2015b. The economic impact of greenhouse gas abatement through a meta-analysis: valuation, consequences and implications in terms of transport policy. Transp. Policy 37, 31–43. https://doi.org/10.1016/j.tranpol.2014.10.004.

Nocera, S., Basso, M., Cavallaro, F., 2017. Micro and macro modelling approaches for the evaluation of the carbon impacts from transportation. Transp. Res. Procedia 24C, 146–154. https://doi.org/10.1016/j.trpro.2017.05.080.

Nocera, S., Irranca Galati, O., Cavallaro, F., 2018. On the uncertainty in the economic valuation of carbon emissions from transport. JTEP 52 (Pt. 1), 68–94. January 2018.

Nottingham City Council, 2011. Nottingham Local Transport Plan Strategy (2011–2016). Online at http://www.nottinghamshire.gov.uk/media/123040/local-transport-plan-strategy.pdf. (10.02.2018).

Nottingham City Council, 2017. Delivery Report April 2016—March 2017: Year Six. Online at https://www.nottinghaminsight.org.uk/d/188433. (03.02.2018).

Nottinghamshire County Council, 2011. Nottingham Local Transport Plan. Online at http://www.nottinghamshire.gov.uk/transport/public-transport/plans-strategies-policies/local-transport-plan. (31.01.2018).
Oxfordshire County Council, 2015a. Connecting Oxfordshire: Local Transport Plan 2015–2031. Volume 1: Policy & Overall Strategy. Online at https://www.oxfordshire.gov.uk/cms/sites/default/files/folders/documents/roadsandtransport/transportpoliciesandplans/localtransportplan/ConnectingOxfordshirevol1policyandoverallstrategy.pdf. (09.02.2018).
Oxfordshire County Council, 2015b. Environmental Report. Connecting Oxfordshire: Local Transport Plan 4 (LTP4): Strategic Environmental Assessment. Online at https://consultations.oxfordshire.gov.uk/gf2.ti/f/545058/16035781.1/PDF/-/Final_SEA_July_2015.pdf. (10.02.2018).
Regione Emilia-Romagna, 2017. Piano Aria Integrato Regionale 2020. Online at http://ambiente.regione.emilia-romagna.it/aria-rumore-elettrosmog/temi/pair2020. (10.02.2018).
Ricard-AEA, 2014. Update of the Handbook on External Costs of Transport. Final Report. Online at https://ec.europa.eu/transport/sites/transport/files/handbook_on_external_costs_of_transport_2014_0.pdf. (09.02.2018).
Roma Capitale, 2018. PUMS. Piano Urbano della Mobilità Sostenibile. pumsroma.it. Online at https://www.pumsroma.it/chisiamo/. (09.02.2018).
Russian Federation, 2011. City of St. Petersburg: Transport Strategy for 2011–2025. Online at http://documents.worldbank.org/curated/en/232341468107660391/pdf/707690ESW0P1240ort0Strategy007MAR11.pdf. (05.02.2018).
San Francisco County, 2013. San Francisco Transportation Plan 2040. Final Report. Online at http://www.sfcta.org/sites/default/files/content/Planning/SFTP2/FinalReport/SFTP_final_report_low-res.pdf. (08.02.2018).
San Francisco County, 2017. San Francisco Transportation Plan 2040. 2017 SFTP Update Final Report. Online at http://www.sfcta.org/sites/default/files/content/Planning/SFTP2/2017_revision/SFTP_final_report_10.24.17.pdf. (10.02.2018).
San Francisco Municipal Transport Agency SFMTA, 2017. Transport Sector Climate Action Strategy. Online at https://www.sfmta.com/sites/default/files/reports-and-documents/2017/12/12-5-17_item_15_transportation_sector_climate_action_strategy.pdf. (10.02.2018).
Senatsverwaltung für Stadtentwicklung und Umwelt, 2014. Urban Transportation Development Plan 2025 Sustainable Mobility. Online at http://www.berlin.de/senuvk/verkehr/politik_planung/step_verkehr/download/Stadtentwicklungsplan_Verkehr_Berlin_gesamt.pdf. (04.02.2018).
Stadt Frankfurt am Main, 2012. Frankfurt Urban Development Report. Online at http://www.stadtplanungsamt-frankfurt.de/show.php?ID=13159&psid=0ed14953f57faf9b28c856c62b016654. (12.02.2018).
Stadt Leipzig, 2013. Mobilität 2020. Stadtentwicklungsplan Verkehr und öffentlicher Rau. Online at http://www.leipzig.de/fileadmin/mediendatenbank/leipzig-de/Stadt/02.6_Dez6_Stadtentwicklung_Bau/66_Verkehrs_und_Tiefbauamt/broschuere_step_analyse__2012.pdf?L=0. (07.02.2018).
Strasburg.eu & Communautè Urbaine, 2012. Plan de Déplacements Urbains (PDU) de la Communauté Urbaine de Strasbou. Online at http://media.strasbourg.eu/alfresco/d/d/workspace/SpacesStore/d0d2c522-1381-4314-a907-5ceea6b72aff/Projet_PDU.pdf. (08.02.2018).
TDA Cape Town, 2017. The City of Cape Town's Transport and Urban Development Authority. Comprehensive Integrated Transport Plan 2017–2020. Online at http://resource.capetown.gov.za/documentcentre/Documents/City%20strategies%2C%20plans%20and%20frameworks/HYS_Draft%20Comprehensive%20Integrated%20Transport%20Plan%202017%20-%202022.pdf. (13.02.2018).

The City of Copenhagen, Technical and Environmental Administration, 2009. The Copenhagen Climate Plan. Online at https://www.energycommunity.org/documents/copenhagen.pdf.

The City of Copenhagen, Technical and Environmental Administration, 2012a. CHP 2025 Climate Plan. A Green, Smart and Carbon Neutral City. Online at http://kk.sites.itera.dk/apps/kk_pub2/pdf/983_jkP0ekKMyD.pdf.

The City of Copenhagen, Technical and Environmental Administration, 2012b. Bicycle Strategy 2011–2025. Online at http://kk.sites.itera.dk/apps/kk_pub2/?mode=detalje&id=823.

The City of Copenhagen, Technical and Environmental Administration, 2013. City of Cyclist—Copenhagen Bicycle Life. Online at http://kk.sites.itera.dk/apps/kk_pub2/index.asp?mode=detalje&id=1135.

The City of Copenhagen, Technical and Environmental Administration, 2016. CHP 2025 Climate Plan. A Green, Smart and Carbon Neutral City. Roadmap 2017–2020. Online at http://kk.sites.itera.dk/apps/kk_pub2/pdf/1586_0kE7bzR28V.pdf.

The World Bank. International Bank for Reconstruction and Development, 2016. Report no. 103068. Project performance assessment report. Nigeria, Lagos urban transport project. Online at http://documents.worldbank.org/curated/en/410431469427889576/pdf/103068-ppa-P074963-PUBLIC-IEG-r-nigeria-0716.pdf. (10.02.2018).

Tol, R.S.J., 2013. Targets for global climate policy: an overview. J. Econ. Dyn. Control. 37 (5), 911–928. ISSN 0165-1889. https://doi.org/10.1016/j.jedc.2013.01.001.

Transport for London, 2017a. Mayor's Transport Strategy: Supporting Evidence Outcomes and Appraisal. Online at http://content.tfl.gov.uk/mts-outcomes-summary-report-2017.pdf. (04.02.2018).

Transport for London, 2017b. Mayor's Transport Strategy: Supporting Evidence Challenges & Opportunities. Online at http://content.tfl.gov.uk/mts-supporting-evidence-challenges-opportunities.pdf. (08.02.2018).

TRT TRASPORTI E TERRITORIO, 2016. TRUST (TRansport eUropean Simulation Tool). Www.trt.it. Online at http://www.trt.it/en/tools/trust/.

UN, United Nations, 2015. Adoption of the Paris agreement. Online at: http://unfccc.int/resource/docs/2015/cop21/eng/l09r01.pdf. (10.08.2018).

UNEP United Nations Environment Programme, 2014a. Low Carbon Transport in India. Low-Carbon Comprehensive Mobility Plan 2011–2030 Zivag. Online at https://wedocs.unep.org/bitstream/handle/20.500.11822/16985/LCMP_Vizag.pdf?sequence=1&isAllowed=y. ISBN: 978-87-93130-25-8. (12.02.2018).

UNEP United Nations Environment Programme, 2014b. Low Carbon Transport in India. Low-Carbon Comprehensive Mobility Plan 2011–2031 Rajkot. Online at https://wedocs.unep.org/bitstream/handle/20.500.11822/16983/LCMP_Rajkot.pdf?sequence=1&isAllowed=y. (10.02.2018).

UNEP United Nations Environment Programme, 2015. Low Carbon Transport in India. Low-Carbon Comprehensive Mobility Plan 2013–2041 Udaipur. Online at http://staging.unep.org/transport/lowcarbon/PDFs/LCMP_Udaipur.pdf. (10.02.2018).

Urban Development Vienna, 2014. STEP 20–25. Urban Mobility Plan Vienna. Online at https://www.wien.gv.at/stadtentwicklung/studien/pdf/b008443.pdf. (10.02.2018).

Vanston, J.H., Vanston, L.K., 2004. Testing the tea leaves: evaluating the validity of forecasts. Res. Technol. Manag. 47 (5), 33–39.

Watkiss, P., Anthoff, D., Downing, T., et al., 2005. The Social Costs of Carbon (SCC) Review: Methodological Approaches for Using SCC Estimates in Policy Assessment. Department for Environment, Food and Rural Affairs (Defra), London.

Wefering, F., Rupprecht, F., Bührmann, S., 2014. Guidelines. Developing and Implementing a Sustainable Urban Mobility Plan. Brussels. Online at http://www.mobilityplans.eu/docs/file/guidelines-developing-and-implementing-a-sump_final_web_jan2014b.pdf. (05.02.2018).

Winkel, A., 2006. In: Urban Development and Urban Planning Transport Planning and Regional Development Section (Ed.), Transport Master Plan Vienna 2003. Abridged version. Stadtentwicklung Wien.

FURTHER READING

Endurance Italy, 2018. Osservatorio PUMS. Ovvervatoriopums.it. With the Patronage of the Italian Environmental Ministry. Online at http://www.osservatoriopums.it/osservatorio/pums. (11.02.2018).

Lagos State Government, 2010. Lagos CO2 Emission Assessment Handbook. Integrated Transport Planning Ltd., Lagos, Nigeria

UNEP United Nations Environment Programme, 2018a. Low Carbon Transport in India. Online at http://web.unep.org/transport/lowcarbon/who-we-are/about-project. (07.02.2018).

UNEP United Nations Environment Programme, 2018b. unenvironment.org. online at https://www.unenvironment.org/?_ga=2.209492882.1614507275.1517987711-673763613.1517987711. (07.02.2018).